HOLT

LITERATURE AND LANGUAGE ARTS

Warriner's Handbook

Introductory Course

Grammar • Usage • Mechanics • Sentences

Mastering the CALIFORNIA STANDARDS in English-Language Conventions

Instructional Framework by

John E. Warriner

HOLT, RINEHART AND WINSTON

AUTHOR **JOHN E. WARRINER** taught for thirty-two years in junior and senior high schools and in college. He was a high school English teacher when he developed the original organizational structure for his classic *English Grammar and Composition* series. The approach pioneered by Mr. Warriner was distinctive, and the editorial staff of Holt, Rinehart and Winston have worked diligently to retain the unique qualities of his pedagogy in the *Holt Handbook.* John Warriner also co-authored the *English Workshop* series and edited *Short Stories: Characters in Conflict.*

Printed in the United States of America

ISBN 978-0-03-099237-7

ISBN 0-03-099237-0

2 3 4 5 6 043 11 10 09

CONTENTS IN BRIEF

PART 1 Grammar, Usage, and Mechanics

PART 2 Sentences

PART 3 Resources

CONTENTS

CHAPTER 1

The Parts of a Sentence

Standards Focus

Sentence Structure 1.1 Use effective coordination and subordination of ideas to express complete thoughts.

CHAPTER 2

Parts of Speech Overview

Standards Focus

Grammar 1.2 Identify and properly use indefinite pronouns.

Capitalization 1.4 Use correct capitalization.

CHAPTER

Parts of Speech Overview

Verb, Adverb, Preposition, Conjunction, Interjection 48

Standards Focus

Sentence Structure 1.1 Use effective coordination of ideas to express complete thoughts.

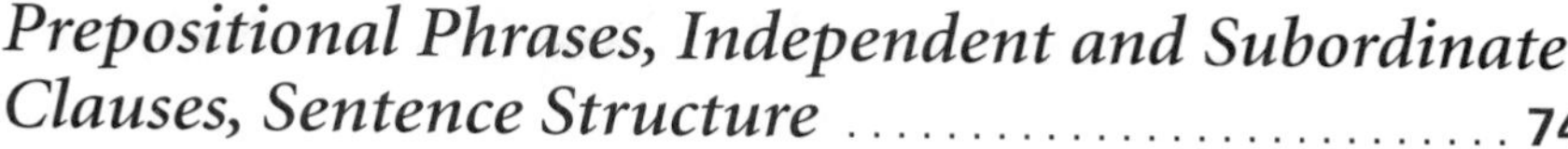

CHAPTER 4

The Phrase and the Clause

Prepositional Phrases, Independent and Subordinate Clauses, Sentence Structure 74

Standards Focus

Sentence Structure 1.1 Use simple, compound, and compound-complex sentences; use effective coordination and subordination of ideas to express complete thoughts.

Punctuation 1.3 Use semicolons to connect independent clauses and commas when linking two clauses with a conjunction in compound sentences.

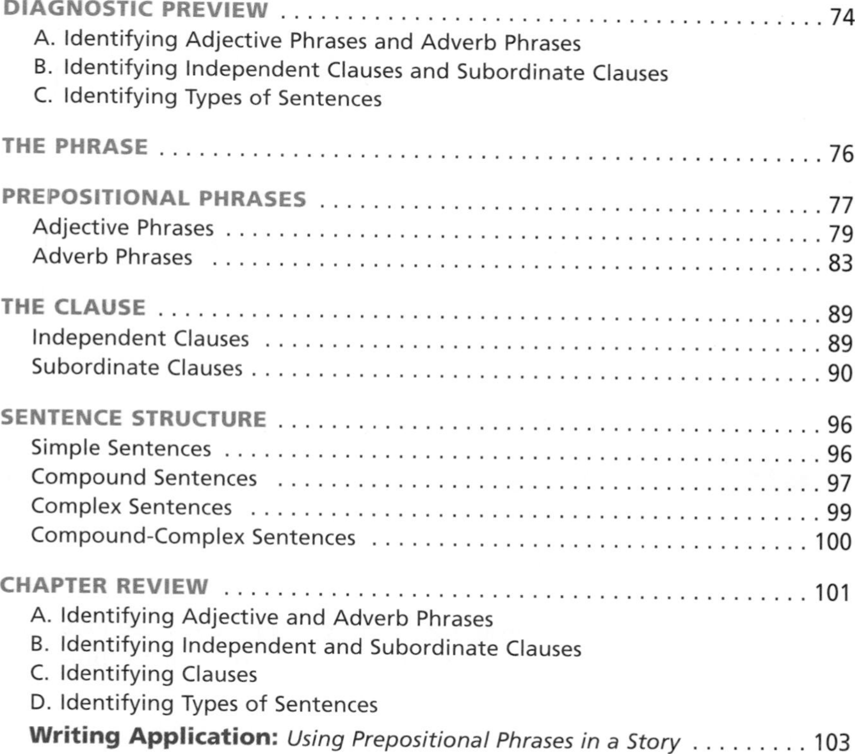

CHAPTER 5

Complements

Standards Focus

Language Convention 1.0 Students write and speak with a command of standard English conventions appropriate to this grade level.

CHAPTER 6

Agreement

Standards Focus

Grammar 1.2 Identify and properly use indefinite pronouns, and ensure that verbs agree with compound subjects.

Standards Focus

Grammar 1.2 Identify and properly use present perfect, past perfect, and future perfect verb tenses.

CHAPTER 8

Using Pronouns Correctly

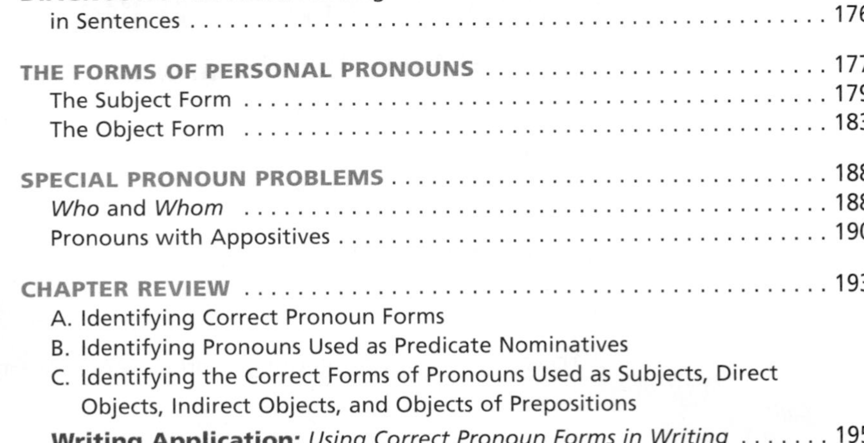

Standards Focus

Language Convention 1.0 Students write and speak with a command of standard English conventions appropriate to this grade level.

CHAPTER 9

Using Modifiers Correctly

Standards Focus

Language Convention 1.0 Students write and speak with a command of standard English conventions appropriate to this grade level.

CHAPTER 10

A Glossary of Usage

Standards Focus

Spelling 1.5 Spell frequently misspelled words correctly (e.g., *their, they're, there*).

CHAPTER 11

Capital Letters

Standards Focus

Capitalization 1.4 Use correct capitalization.

Punctuation

End Marks, Commas, Semicolons, Colons 262

Standards Focus

Punctuation 1.3 Use colons after the salutation in business letters, semicolons to connect independent clauses, and commas when linking two clauses with a conjunction in compound sentences.

Punctuation

Underlining (Italics), Quotation Marks, Apostrophes, Hyphens, Parentheses 288

Standards Focus

Language Convention 1.0 Students write and speak with a command of standard English conventions appropriate to this grade level.

CHAPTER 14

Spelling

Standards Focus

Spelling 1.5 Spell frequently misspelled words correctly (e.g., *their, they're, there*).

Correcting Common Errors

Key Language Skills Review **346**

Standards Focus

Language Convention 1.0 Students write and speak with a command of standard English conventions appropriate to this grade level.

Standards Focus

Sentence Structure 1.1 Use simple, compound, and compound-complex sentences; use effective coordination and subordination of ideas to express complete thoughts.

CHAPTER 17

Sentence Diagramming 412

Standards Focus

Sentence Structure 1.1 Use simple, compound, and compound-complex sentences.

TO OUR STUDENTS

Why should I study grammar, usage, and mechanics?

Many people would say that you should study grammar to learn to root out errors in your speech and writing. Certainly, *Warriner's Handbook* can help you learn to avoid making errors and to correct the errors you do make. More importantly, though, studying grammar, usage, and mechanics gives you the skills you need to take sentences and passages apart and to put them together, to learn which parts go together and which don't. Instead of writing sentences and passages that you hope sound good, you can craft your sentences to create just the meaning and style you want.

Knowing grammar, usage, and mechanics gives you the tools to understand and discuss your own language, to communicate clearly the things you want to communicate, and to develop your own communication style. Further, mastery of language skills can help you succeed in your other classes, in future classes, on standardized tests, and in the larger world, including, eventually, the workplace.

How do I use *Warriner's Handbook*?

Warriner's Handbook is part of the Holt Literature and Language Arts program. The skills taught in *Warriner's Handbook* are important to your success in the reading, writing, speaking, and listening components of this program.

Not only can you use this book as a complete grammar, usage, and mechanics textbook, but you can also use it as a reference guide when you work on any piece of writing. Whether you are writing a personal letter, a report for your social studies class, or some other piece of writing, you can use *Warriner's Handbook* to answer your questions about grammar, usage, capitalization, punctuation, and spelling.

How is *Warriner's Handbook* organized?

Warriner's Handbook is divided into three main parts:

PART 1 The **Grammar, Usage, and Mechanics** chapters provide instruction on and practice using the building blocks of language—words, phrases, clauses, capitalization, punctuation, and spelling. Use these chapters to discover how to take sentences apart and put them together. The last chapter, **Correcting Common Errors**, provides additional practice on key language skills as well as standardized test practice in grammar, usage, and mechanics.

PART 2 The **Sentences** chapters include Writing Effective Sentences and Sentence Diagramming. **Writing Effective Sentences** provides instruction on and practice with writing correct, clear, and interesting sentences. **Sentence Diagramming** teaches you to analyze and diagram sentences so you can see how the parts of a sentence relate to each other.

PART 3 The **Resources** section includes **History of English**, a concise history of the English language; **Test Smarts**, a handy guide to taking standardized tests in grammar, usage, and mechanics; and **Grammar at a Glance**, a glossary of grammatical terms.

How are the chapters organized?

Each chapter begins with a Diagnostic Preview, a short test that covers the whole chapter and alerts you to skills that need improvement, and ends with a Chapter Review, another short test that tells you how well you have mastered that chapter. In between, you'll see rules, which are basic statements of grammar, usage, and mechanics principles. The rules are illustrated with examples and followed by exercises and reviews that help you practice what you have learned.

What are some other features of this textbook?

- **Oral Practice**—spoken practice and reinforcement of rules and concepts
- **Writing Applications**—activities that let you apply grammar, usage, and mechanics concepts in your writing
- **Tips & Tricks**—easy-to-use hints about grammar, usage, and mechanics

- **Meeting the Challenge**—questions or short activities that ask you to approach a concept from a new angle
- **Style Tips**—information about formal and informal uses of language
- **Help**—pointers to help you understand either key rules and concepts or exercise directions

go.hrw.com

Warriner's Handbook on the Internet

As you move through *Warriner's Handbook*, you will find the best online resources at **go.hrw.com.**

What are the California standards?

The California State Board of Education has adopted a set of standards for achievement in Written and Oral English Language Conventions. You will be expected to master these standards during the school year. Each chapter of *Warriner's Handbook* begins with a box listing the California standards that you will cover in that chapter.

1.0 Written and Oral English Language Conventions

Students write and speak with a command of standard English conventions appropriate to this grade level.

Sentence Structure

1.1 Use simple, compound, and compound-complex sentences; use effective coordination and subordination of ideas to express complete thoughts.

Grammar

1.2 Identify and properly use indefinite pronouns and present perfect, past perfect, and future perfect verb tenses; ensure that verbs agree with compound subjects.

Punctuation

1.3 Use colons after the salutation in business letters, semicolons to connect independent clauses, and commas when linking two clauses with a conjunction in compound sentences.

Capitalization

1.4 Use correct capitalization.

Spelling

1.5 Spell frequently misspelled words correctly (e.g., *their, they're, there*).

PART 1

Grammar, Usage, and Mechanics

Grammar

1 The Parts of a Sentence

2 Parts of Speech Overview: Noun, Pronoun, Adjective

3 Parts of Speech Overview: Verb, Adverb, Preposition, Conjunction, Interjection

4 The Phrase and the Clause

5 Complements

Usage

6 Agreement

7 Using Verbs Correctly

8 Using Pronouns Correctly

9 Using Modifiers Correctly

10 A Glossary of Usage

Mechanics

11 Capital Letters

12 Punctuation: End Marks, Commas, Semicolons, Colons

13 Punctuation: Underlining (Italics), Quotation Marks, Apostrophes, Hyphens, Parentheses

14 Spelling

15 Correcting Common Errors

GO TO: go.hrw.com
KEYWORD: HLLA

CHAPTER

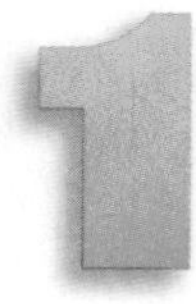

The Parts of a Sentence

Subject and Predicate, Kinds of Sentences

1.0 Written and Oral English Language Conventions
Students write and speak with a command of standard English conventions appropriate to this grade level.
1.1 Use effective coordination and subordination of ideas to express complete thoughts.

Diagnostic Preview

A. Identifying Sentences

If a word group is a sentence fragment, rewrite it to make it a complete sentence. If a word group is a sentence, write *sentence.*

EXAMPLES **1.** Followed the trail on the map.
1. I followed the trail on the map.

2. The López twins come from Nuevo Laredo, Mexico.
2. sentence

1. We read the postcards from our Asian pen pals.
2. Our school has a homework hot line.
3. definitely mailed the invitations yesterday.
4. Will you practice guitar before dinner?
5. going to the Washington Monument?

B. Identifying Simple Subjects and Simple Predicates

Identify the simple subject and the simple predicate in each of the following sentences.

EXAMPLES 1. Last year my family traveled to Mecca, Saudi Arabia.
1. family—simple subject; traveled—simple predicate

2. The crowded corner market is having a sale.
2. market—simple subject; is having—simple predicate

6. My grandmother plays mah-jongg with my friends and me every Saturday.
7. The farmers have plowed the fields and will plant potatoes.
8. At night you can rent roller skates for half price at the rink near my house.
9. On the sand lay a beautiful seashell.
10. On Saturday, Amy, Theo, and I walked through Chinatown and took pictures.
11. Many students in our class have volunteered for the charity softball game.
12. Where did you put Isabella's fuzzy, green wool sweater?
13. *Island of the Blue Dolphins* by Scott O'Dell is one of my favorite books.
14. Beyond the large rocks at the far end of the beach is a small cave.
15. During the last week of vacation, my brother, sister and I hiked through the rain forest.

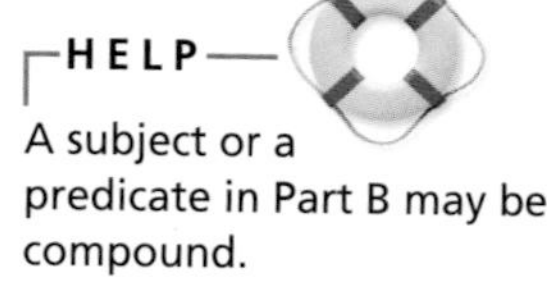

HELP

A subject or a predicate in Part B may be compound.

GRAMMAR

C. Punctuating and Classifying Sentences by Purpose

For each of the following sentences, add the appropriate end mark. Then, classify each sentence as *declarative, interrogative, imperative,* or *exclamatory.*

EXAMPLES 1. Have you read this poem by José Garcia Villa
1. Have you read this poem by José Garcia Villa?—interrogative

2. We sampled a Cuban dish at the international fair
2. We sampled a Cuban dish at the international fair.—declarative

16. Please answer the phone
17. What a good time we had
18. Has anyone seen the cat
19. They sat on a bench and played checkers
20. Whose book is this

21. Hang that jacket in the hall closet
22. How we laughed
23. Water is composed of oxygen and hydrogen
24. Call this number in case of an emergency
25. Did you say to turn left here

Sentence or Sentence Fragment?

1a. A *sentence* is a word group that contains a subject and a verb and that expresses a complete thought.

A sentence begins with a capital letter and ends with a period, a question mark, or an exclamation point.

EXAMPLES **O**ctavio Paz won a Nobel Prize in literature**.** [The subject is *Octavio Paz,* and the verb is *won.*]

Stop**.** [The understood subject is *you,* and the verb is *Stop.*]

Do you collect coins**?** [The subject is *you,* and the verb is *Do collect.*]

I actually rode on an elephant**!** [The subject is *I,* and the verb is *rode.*]

A ***sentence fragment*** is a word group that looks like a sentence but either does not contain both a subject and a verb or does not express a complete thought.

SENTENCE FRAGMENT Visited an old Spanish mission in San Diego. [The subject is missing. Who visited the mission?]

SENTENCE My family visited an old Spanish mission in San Diego.

SENTENCE FRAGMENT Alonzo's sisters and brothers. [The verb is missing. What did Alonzo's sisters and brothers do?]

SENTENCE Alonzo's sisters and brothers planned a surprise party for his birthday.

Reference Note

For information on the **understood subject,** see page 18.

HELP

To tell whether a group of words is a sentence or a sentence fragment, ask yourself these three questions:

1. What is the subject?
2. What is the verb?
3. What is the complete thought the word group expresses?

If you cannot answer any one of these questions, the word group may not be a sentence.

SENTENCE FRAGMENT	As I walked to school yesterday. [This thought is not complete. What happened as I walked to school yesterday?]
SENTENCE	As I walked to school yesterday, I saw Mr. Saunders walking his dog.

NOTE A word group that has a subject and a verb and that expresses a complete thought is called an ***independent clause.*** An independent clause can stand alone as a sentence. A word group that has a subject and a verb but does not express a complete thought (such as *As I walked to school yesterday*) is called a ***subordinate clause.***

Reference Note

For more about **independent and subordinate clauses,** see page 89.

Exercise 1 Identifying Sentences

Identify each of the following word groups as a *sentence* or a *sentence fragment.* If a word group is a sentence fragment, rewrite it to make it a complete sentence.

EXAMPLE **1.** My aunt and uncle raise shar-peis.
1. sentence

1. My aunt, my uncle, and my cousins at their house in the country last weekend.
2. After dinner, Aunt Marie told me about the history of the shar-pei breed.
3. Bred these dogs in China.
4. Just look at all that loose, wrinkled skin.
5. Protects them from injury during fights.
6. Gentle with children.
7. Playing catch with Queenie.
8. The little balls of fur were Queenie's new puppies.
9. Have you ever seen such a sight as these puppies?
10. What a good time we had!

STYLE  TIP

In speech, people often use sentence fragments. Such fragments usually are not confusing because the context and the speaker's tone of voice and expressions help to complete the meaning.

Professional writers, too, may use sentence fragments to create specific effects in their writing. However, in your writing at school, you should use complete sentences.

Reference Note

For more information on **revising sentence fragments,** see page 386.

Exercise 2 Identifying and Revising Sentences and Sentence Fragments

Some of the following word groups are sentences, and others are sentence fragments. If a word group is a sentence, write *sentence.* If a word group is not a sentence, add words to make the word group a sentence.

EXAMPLE **1.** A common custom worldwide.

1. Weddings are a common custom worldwide.

1. Having been introduced to the guest of honor.
2. Hold your horses there, young fellow.
3. Dancing in the air around the garden.
4. It will be on your right.
5. Just how does a fire extinguisher work?
6. One of the only examples of this type of Aztec art in this area.
7. Three pennies, a quarter, a bus token, and four acorns.
8. He called Sunday night.
9. An instrument popular in Africa, the kalimba.
10. How we laughed at that movie!

COMPUTER TIP

If sentence fragments are a problem in your writing, a computer may be able to help you. Some style-checking programs can find fragments for you. Such programs are useful, but they are not perfect. It is best to check each sentence yourself. Make sure each sentence has a subject and a verb and expresses a complete thought.

Review A Writing Complete Sentences

Some of the following word groups are sentences. If a word group is a sentence, rewrite it, adding a capital letter and end punctuation. If a word group is not a sentence, rewrite it, adding a subject or a verb, a capital letter, and end punctuation to make it a sentence.

EXAMPLE **1.** wrote a play

1. Our language arts class wrote a play.

1. sent us a postcard from the Philippines
2. it was cold at the skating rink
3. helped me with my science project
4. a surfer on a huge wave
5. was hungry at lunchtime
6. it is too late for a game of checkers
7. is that the American Falls or the Horseshoe Falls
8. the Cuban family next door
9. what time is your mom picking us up
10. the governor of my state

Subject and Predicate

Sentences consist of two basic parts: *subjects* and *predicates.*

The Subject

1b. The ***subject*** tells *whom* or *what* the sentence is about.

EXAMPLES **Lois Lenski** wrote *Strawberry Girl.*

The tooth with a point is called a canine.

To find the subject, ask yourself *who* or *what* is doing something or *about whom* or *what* something is being said.

EXAMPLES **My best friend** sits next to me in science class. [*Who* sits? My best friend sits.]

Science class is very interesting this year. [*What* is interesting? Science class is.]

The Position of the Subject

The subject may come at the beginning, in the middle, or even at the end of a sentence.

EXAMPLES After school, **Theresa** went to band practice.

Under our house was **a tiny kitten.**

Exercise 3 Identifying Subjects

Identify the subject in each of these sentences.

EXAMPLE **1.** The final score was tied.
1. The final score

1. Many games use rackets or paddles.
2. Tennis can be an exhausting sport.
3. Badminton rackets don't weigh very much.
4. Table-tennis paddles are covered with rubber.
5. Racquetball uses special rackets.
6. In Florida, citrus trees grow an important crop.
7. After three to five years, fruit grows on the new trees.
8. Does Florida grow all of the citrus fruit in the nation?
9. California also grows oranges and other citrus fruit.
10. From Texas comes the Star Ruby grapefruit.

Complete Subject and Simple Subject

The ***complete subject*** consists of all the words needed to tell *whom* or *what* the sentence is about. The ***simple subject*** is part of the complete subject.

1c. The *simple subject* is the main word or word group that tells *whom* or *what* the sentence is about.

EXAMPLES **The Korean market** is closed today.

complete subject The Korean market

simple subject market

A brightly colored blue jay sat on the windowsill.

complete subject A brightly colored blue jay

simple subject blue jay

Sometimes the same word or words make up both the simple subject and the complete subject.

EXAMPLES In the canyon, **we** saw hawks. [*We* is both the complete subject and the simple subject.]

Little Rascal is the story of a boy and his pet raccoon. [The title *Little Rascal* is both the complete subject and the simple subject.]

NOTE In this book, the term *subject* generally refers to the simple subject unless otherwise indicated.

TIPS & TRICKS

If you leave the simple subject out of a sentence, the sentence will not make sense.

EXAMPLES

The Korean . . . is closed today.

A brightly colored . . . sat on the windowsill.

Exercise 4 Identifying Complete Subjects and Simple Subjects

Identify the complete subject of each of the following sentences. Then, underline the simple subject.

EXAMPLE **1.** From the chimney came a thick cloud of smoke.

1. a thick cloud of smoke

1. Several tents were set up in the park.
2. Have you heard the new CD by Gloria Estefan?
3. News travels fast in our town.
4. Above the fort, the flag was still flying.
5. Beyond those distant mountains lies an ancient American Indian village.

6. Those newspaper reporters have been interviewing the mayor all morning.
7. On the shelf was a beautiful blue bowl.
8. According to folklore, Pecos Bill made the Grand Canyon.
9. The light in the lighthouse shone all night long.
10. In the drawer were some chopsticks.

The Predicate

1d. **The *predicate* of a sentence tells something about the subject.**

EXAMPLES Lois Lenski **wrote *Strawberry Girl.***

The tooth with a point **is called a canine.**

Exercise 5 Identifying Predicates

Identify the predicate in each of the following sentences.

EXAMPLE 1. Many people would like to have a robot.

1. would like to have a robot

1. Robots are machines with "brains."
2. The robot's brain is a computer.
3. Not all robots look like humans.
4. Some robots look like toy cars.
5. One robot explored some of the surface of Mars.
6. Many companies use robots.
7. Cars of the future may be guided by robots.
8. Some household jobs can be done by robots.
9. A robot could clean your room.
10. You might like to have a robot to help with your daily chores.

The Position of the Predicate

The predicate usually comes after the subject. Sometimes, however, part or all of the predicate comes before the subject.

EXAMPLES **Quickly** we **learned the layout of the small Hopi village.**

At the entrance to the science fair were maps of the exhibits.

Exercise 6 Identifying Predicates

Write each of the following sentences. Then, underline the predicate.

EXAMPLE **1.** At noon we went to a Mexican restaurant.

1. At noon we went to a Mexican restaurant.

1. Our family likes different kinds of food.
2. Last night Dad prepared spaghetti and a salad for supper.
3. Sometimes Mom makes chow mein.
4. With chow mein she serves egg rolls.
5. At the Greek bakery we buy fresh pita bread.
6. Tomorrow Erica will make German potato salad.
7. Lately, tacos have become my favorite food.
8. Carefully, I spoon grated lettuce and cheese into a tortilla.
9. After that come the other ingredients.
10. In the United States, people enjoy a wide variety of foods.

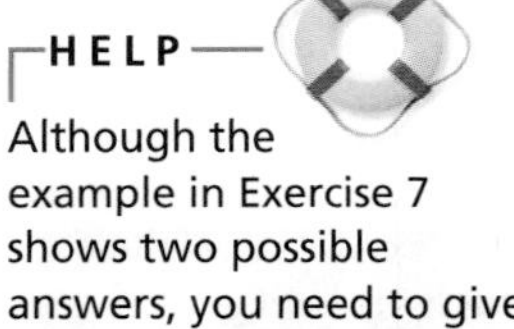

HELP

Although the example in Exercise 7 shows two possible answers, you need to give only one answer for each item.

Exercise 7 Writing Predicates

Make a sentence out of each of the following words or word groups by adding a predicate to fill the blank or blanks.

EXAMPLE **1.** ____ everyone ____

1. With a shout of joy, everyone took a paddle and began to row.

or

As the waves crashed against the raft, everyone grabbed for the sides.

1. Foamy white water ____.
2. The hot summer air ____.
3. A strong current ____.
4. ____ the eyes of every person on board ____.
5. The lightweight paddles ____.
6. ____ dangerous rocks and swirls ____.
7. Quick action by everyone ____.
8. A sleek, blue rubber raft ____.
9. The man in the white helmet and blue life jacket ____.
10. ____ the people in this photograph ____.

Complete Predicate and Simple Predicate

The ***complete predicate*** consists of a verb and all the words that describe the verb and complete its meaning.

1e. The *simple predicate,* or *verb,* is the main word or word group in the complete predicate.

EXAMPLES The nurse **lifted the patient carefully.**

complete predicate lifted the patient carefully
simple predicate (verb) lifted

I **saw a picture of a Siberian tiger.**

complete predicate saw a picture of a Siberian tiger
simple predicate (verb) saw

HELP — In this book, the simple predicate is generally called the *verb*.

Exercise 8 Identifying Complete Predicates and Verbs

Identify the complete predicate of each of the following sentences. Then, underline the verb.

EXAMPLE **1.** For several reasons, space travel fascinates me.
1. For several reasons fascinates me

1. My class traveled by train to Houston, Texas.
2. In Houston my classmates and I visited the Lyndon B. Johnson Space Center.
3. The center displays moon rocks.
4. At the center, astronauts train for their flights.
5. In one room we saw several unusual computers.
6. Some chambers reproduce conditions like those on the moon.
7. Do see the films about the space program in the visitors' center.
8. We also toured the San Jacinto Battleground State Historical Park.
9. There, in 1836, Texas won its independence from Mexico.
10. Actually, I had more fun at the space center.

The simple predicate may be a single verb or a ***verb phrase*** (a verb with one or more helping verbs).

EXAMPLES Yoshi **went** to Japan last summer. [single verb]

The park **is located** near a lake. [verb phrase]

We **should have planned** a picnic. [verb phrase]

Reference Note
For information on **helping verbs,** see page 49.

NOTE The words *not* and *never* and the contraction *–n't* are not verbs. They are never part of a verb or verb phrase.

EXAMPLE Kendra **should**n't **have added** another hot pepper to the sauce.

Exercise 9 Identifying Complete Predicates and Verbs

Identify the complete predicate in each of the following sentences. Then, underline the verb.

EXAMPLE 1. The Liberty Bell was made in England.
1. was made in England

1. I am writing a report on the Liberty Bell.
2. The Pennsylvania Assembly ordered the Liberty Bell.
3. Thomas Lester had made the bell in London.
4. In 1752, the bell was cracked by its own clapper.
5. American patriots hid the bell from the British army.
6. The bell was not brought back to Philadelphia until 1778.
7. The Liberty Bell cracked again in 1835.
8. This bell has been rung on many historic occasions.
9. The bell is exhibited in the Liberty Bell Pavilion.
10. We will be seeing it on our field trip to Philadelphia.

Finding the Subject

Sometimes it may be difficult to find the subject of a sentence. In such cases, find the verb first. Then, ask yourself *Who?* or *What?* before the verb.

EXAMPLES Next semester you may take art or music. [The verb is *may take. Who* may take? *You* may take. *You* is the subject of the sentence.]

Can your sister drive us to the park? [The verb is *Can drive. Who* can drive? *Sister* can drive. *Sister* is the subject of the sentence.]

Please read the first chapter. [The verb is *read. Who* should read? *You* should read. *You* is the understood subject of the sentence.]

Reference Note

For more information on **understood subjects,** see page 18.

Compound Subject and Compound Verb

Compound Subject

1f. A ***compound subject*** consists of two or more subjects that are joined by a conjunction and that have the same verb.

The parts of a compound subject are most often connected by *and* or *or.*

EXAMPLES **Minneapolis** and **St. Paul** are called the "Twin Cities." [The two parts of the compound subject have the same verb, *are called.*]

Will **Mrs. Jones** or **Ms. Lopez** chaperone our field trip? [The two parts of the compound subject have the same verb, *Will chaperone.*]

Flutes, clarinets, and **oboes** are all woodwind instruments. [The three parts of the compound subject have the same verb, *are.*]

Reference Note

Notice that **commas** are **used to separate three or more parts of a compound subject.** For more about this use of commas, see page 268.

Exercise 10 Identifying Compound Subjects

Identify the compound subjects in each of the following sentences.

EXAMPLE 1. October and June are my favorite months.
1. October, June

1. Wild ducks and geese migrate south each year.
2. Stars and planets form a galaxy.
3. Someday dolphins and people may be able to communicate with each other.
4. Baseball and soccer are the two most popular sports at my sister's school.
5. Eggs and flour are two ingredients in pancakes.
6. Every year bugs and rabbits raid our vegetable garden.
7. Pizza or ravioli will be served.
8. At a party, balloons or horns make the best noisemakers.
9. Dachshunds, Chihuahuas, Lhasa apsos, and Pekingese ran around in the yard.
10. In the Tower of London are famous jewels and crowns.

Compound Verb

1g. A ***compound verb*** consists of two or more verbs that are joined by a conjunction and that have the same subject.

A connecting word such as *and* or *but* is used to join the parts of a compound verb.

EXAMPLES Ben **overslept** but **caught** his bus anyway.

Conchita **hums, sings,** or **listens** to the radio all day.

My father **bought** a Chinese wok and **cooked** vegetables in it.

Exercise 11 Identifying Compound Verbs

HELP — Remember to include helping verbs when you are identifying verbs in Exercise 11.

Identify the compound verbs in the following sentences.

EXAMPLE **1.** I have proofread my paper and made a final copy.
1. have proofread, made

1. Mai and her parents left Vietnam and arrived in California in 1994.
2. Julie received good grades and made the honor roll.
3. Every week, our band practices together and writes songs.
4. Before supper I usually set the table or peel the vegetables.
5. Floyd asked for a watch but received a bike instead.
6. We gathered firewood and headed back to camp.
7. Last week everyone gave a speech or recited a poem.
8. The referee will call a rain delay or postpone the game.
9. I remembered the bread but forgot the milk.
10. The Greek restaurant has closed but will reopen soon.

Exercise 12 Writing Compound Subjects and Compound Verbs

Make sentences by adding compound subjects or compound verbs to fill in the blanks in the following word groups.

EXAMPLES **1.** _____ are coming to the party.
1. Fran and Terry are coming to the party.

2. At the mall, we _____.
2. At the mall, we ate lunch and went to a movie.

1. _____ are beginning a stamp collection.

2. ____ were my favorite teachers last year.
3. The creature from outer space ____.
4. At the end of the play, the cast ____.
5. Last week ____ were interviewed on a talk show.
6. In the garage are ____.
7. During the storm, we ____.
8. At the front door were ____.
9. After school, my friends ____.
10. He ____ before the birthday party.

HELP—
Some of the subjects and verbs in Review B are compound.

Review B Identifying Subjects and Verbs

Identify the subjects and verbs in each of the following sentences.

EXAMPLE 1. In the history of African American music are many unforgettable names.
1. *names—subject; are—verb*

1. You may recognize the man in the picture on this page.
2. Most people immediately think of his deep, raspy voice.
3. Ray Charles is called the father of soul music.
4. He lost his sight at the age of seven and became an orphan at fifteen.
5. However, misfortune and trouble did not stop Ray Charles.
6. His musical genius turned his troubles into songs.
7. Today, the songs of Ray Charles are heard all over the world.
8. Do his songs contain different musical styles?
9. Gospel, jazz, blues, and even pop are all part of his sound.
10. His special style and powerful performances have long drawn fans to Ray Charles's music.

A sentence may have both a compound subject and a compound verb.

EXAMPLES
S S V V
Zina and **I bought** corn and **fed** the ducks.

S S V V
Carrots and **celery are** crunchy and **satisfy** your appetite.

GRAMMAR

NOTE Sometimes a sentence will contain more than one subject and verb, but neither the subject nor verb will be compound.

EXAMPLES

S V / S V
I like apples, but my **sister prefers** oranges.
[compound sentence]

S V / S V
In San Antonio, **we toured** the Alamo, while our **friends visited** the Riverwalk.
[complex sentence]

S V / S V / S V
David wipes the table, and **Cindy dries** the dishes that **Dad has washed.**
[compound-complex sentence]

Reference Note

For more information about **compound, complex,** and **compound-complex sentences,** see page 97.

STYLE TIP

In your own writing, you can combine ideas by creating compound subjects and verbs. Combining sentences in this way will help make your writing smoother and easier to read. Compare the examples below.

CHOPPY
Susan went hiking in the mountains. Mark went hiking, too. Aunt Connie went with them.

REVISED
Susan, Mark, and Aunt Connie went hiking in the mountains.

Exercise 13 Identifying Compound Subjects and Compound Verbs

Identify the compound subject and the compound verb in each of the following sentences.

EXAMPLE 1. Tina and Julia washed the dog and dried it.
1. Tina, Julia—subject; washed, dried—verb

1. Alice and Reiko sang and played the piano.
2. Either Dwayne or I will find the coach and ask his advice.
3. Patrick and she read the same biography of Dr. Martin Luther King, Jr., and reported on it.
4. Roses and lilacs look pretty and smell good.
5. The dentist or her assistant cleans and polishes my teeth.
6. In many traditional Japanese homes, doors or partitions are framed in wood, left open in the middle, and then covered with rice paper.
7. Larry and she washed the dishes but did not dry them.
8. The lamb and its mother had leapt the fence but were still inside the yard.
9. Fish, rays, turtles, and dolphins live in the Gulf of Mexico and often swim near the shore.
10. Did Uncle Ted or his children call or visit you on their way through town?

Reference Note

For more information on **combining sentences,** see page 396.

Review C Identifying Subjects and Predicates

Identify the complete subject and the complete predicate in each of the following sentences. Then, underline the simple subject and the verb.

EXAMPLE 1. Reports and legends of huge apelike creatures fascinate many people.

1. subject—Reports and legends of huge apelike creatures; predicate—fascinate many people

1. These creatures are known as *Yeti* in the Himalayas and as *Rakshas* in Katmandu.
2. American Indians of the Northwest call them *Mammoth.*
3. *Sasquatch* and *Bigfoot* are other common names for these mysterious creatures.
4. Since 1818, they have been seen and described by people in the United States and Canada.
5. According to most accounts, Bigfoot adults are very strong and large and smell very bad.
6. Their huge footprints have been measured and cast in plaster by eager searchers.
7. However, these reports and bits of evidence generally do not convince scientists.
8. Not one live Bigfoot has ever been captured by either scientists or the general public.
9. As a result, the Bigfoot is simply a fantasy to most people.
10. Still, in pockets of deep wilderness across the country might live whole families of these shy creatures.

HELP Some of the subjects and verbs in Review C are compound.

GRAMMAR

Review D Writing Sentences

Tell whether each of the following sentence parts can be used as a *subject* or a *predicate.* Then, use each sentence part in a sentence. Begin each sentence with a capital letter, and end it with the correct mark of punctuation. Use a variety of subjects and verbs in your sentences.

EXAMPLE 1. will drive us home

1. predicate—Will your mother drive us home?

1. my favorite book
2. watched a good mystery

GRAMMAR

3. the flying saucer
4. the oldest house in town
5. prepares delicious Korean food
6. growled and bared its teeth
7. the shiny red car and the bicycle
8. caught a huge fish
9. can borrow your skates
10. the best tacos and enchiladas in town

Kinds of Sentences

Sentences may be classified according to purpose.

Reference Note

For information on **how sentences can be classified according to structure,** see page 96.

1h. A *declarative sentence* makes a statement and ends with a period.

EXAMPLES Our media center has several computers.

Patrick Henry lived in Virginia.

1i. An *imperative sentence* gives a command or makes a request. Most imperative sentences end with a period. A strong command ends with an exclamation point.

EXAMPLES Please pass the potatoes. [request]

Sit down. [command]

Stop shouting! [strong command]

The subject of a command or a request is always *you,* even if the word *you* never appears in the sentence. In such cases, *you* is called the ***understood subject.***

EXAMPLES [**You**] Please pass the potatoes.

[**You**] Stop shouting!

1j. An *interrogative sentence* asks a question and ends with a question mark.

EXAMPLES Did the Apollo 13 spacecraft reach the moon?

How old are you?

1k. An ***exclamatory sentence*** **shows excitement or expresses strong feeling and ends with an exclamation point.**

EXAMPLES What a difficult assignment that was**!**

I got her autograph**!**

Oral Practice **Classifying Sentences by Purpose**

Read each of the following sentences aloud, and say which end mark—a period, a question mark, or an exclamation point—should be added. Then, identify each sentence as *declarative, interrogative, imperative,* or *exclamatory.*

EXAMPLE **1.** What a funny show that was
1. What a funny show that was!—exclamatory

1. Please help me find my umbrella
2. How happy I am
3. Have you and your sister been to the new video store on Congress Avenue
4. Go east for three blocks, and look for a yellow mailbox next to a red door
5. My father and I are cleaning the attic together later this afternoon
6. What a delicious salad this is
7. During our last summer vacation, we toured the garment district in New York City
8. Do you like barbecued chicken
9. My surprise visit last month pleased both my grandmother and Aunt Gabriela
10. When is your next piano lesson

Review E **Classifying Sentences by Purpose**

For each of the sentences on the following page, add an appropriate end mark. Then, identify each sentence as *declarative, imperative, interrogative,* or *exclamatory.*

EXAMPLE **1.** Have you ever seen the Grand Canyon
1. Have you ever seen the Grand Canyon?
—interrogative

STYLE TIP

Be careful not to overuse exclamation points in your writing. Save them for sentences that really do show strong emotion. When used too much, exclamation points lose their effect.

OVERUSED
For her birthday, Katy's parents threw her a bowling party! About twenty friends and family members attended, and we all had a great time! I had two strikes in one game!

IMPROVED
For her birthday, Katy's parents threw her a bowling party. About twenty friends and family members attended, and we all had a great time. I had two strikes in one game!

MEETING THE CHALLENGE

In any kind of writing, correct end punctuation is important. However, it is especially important in written dialogue. The punctuation helps a reader know how a speaker says something. A sentence can mean very different things when its end punctuation is changed.

Write a short dialogue that includes the same sentence used three times—each time with different punctuation and different meaning.

1. We enjoyed our vacation in the Southwest
2. Dad took these photographs when our family visited the Grand Canyon
3. Our guide spoke both Spanish and English
4. How pretty the sunset is
5. Don't stand so close to the edge
6. Did you buy any turquoise-and-silver jewelry
7. It was quite chilly at night
8. What a great movie we saw about the canyon
9. Did you take the short hike or the long one
10. Look at us riding on mules in this canyon

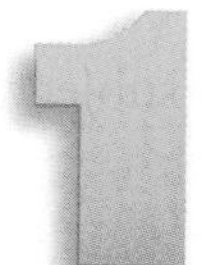

Chapter Review

A. Identifying Sentences

For each of the following word groups that is a sentence fragment, revise the word group to make it a complete sentence. If a group is a sentence, write *sentence.*

1. Burned brightly throughout the night.
2. He studies computer programming after school.
3. The band sounds so wonderful tonight!
4. Whenever the mountains are covered with fog.
5. Over the past two thousand years.
6. Be seated.
7. Behind us barked the dogs.
8. Just as I neared the castle's drawbridge.
9. Should we sand the wood now?
10. The artist carving the totem pole?

B. Identifying the Complete Subject and the Complete Predicate

Write each of the following sentences. Then, underline the complete subject once and the complete predicate twice.

11. *Black Beauty* is a story about a horse.
12. Sometimes bats fly into our chimney.
13. A wonderful smell of baking bread came from the kitchen and filled the house.
14. The chief will speak to you now.
15. Milk and cheese can help you develop strong bones.
16. Two eagles and a hawk live near our house.
17. Adele peeled and ate the orange.
18. Several knights guarded the castle and drove off the dragon.
19. Under the lettuce was my tomato.
20. Will Ahmad and Nadim set the table before lunch?

C. Identifying Simple Subjects and Simple Predicates

HELP — Sentences in Part C may contain compound subjects and compound verbs.

For each of the following sentences, write the simple subject and the simple predicate.

21. The winner is Mr. Otis Kwan!
22. Suddenly, the clock stopped.
23. Many cactuses have grown in the garden.
24. Have you ever eaten yakitori?
25. Yancy and Rollo will meet us at the shopping mall.
26. When did they reach the summit of Mount Fairweather?
27. Yellow, orange, and red have always been my favorite colors.
28. Prince and Princess jumped the fence and barked at my brother's friend.
29. The sports banquet will be held on April 4.
30. We bought milk and bread but forgot the eggs.

D. Punctuating and Classifying Sentences by Purpose

Write each sentence, adding an appropriate end mark. Then, classify each sentence as *declarative, imperative, interrogative,* or *exclamatory.*

31. Listen to them
32. What music they make
33. My name is Lucy
34. Tell me more about your trip to Romania
35. How long has Marlon played the zither
36. I will ask her to come over for dinner
37. Who is the star of the film
38. Stop it now
39. I'm so happy to see you
40. Which pair of shoes did you decide to buy

Writing Application

Using Sentence Variety

Sentences Classified by Purpose As a special project, your social studies class is creating a comic book. Each class member will contribute a comic strip about a particular historical event or historical person. In your comic strip, include at least one of each of the four kinds of sentences—declarative, imperative, interrogative, and exclamatory.

Prewriting First, jot down some ideas for the characters and story line of your comic strip. You may want to look through your social studies book for ideas. Then, plan the frames of your comic strip. Think about how you could include the four types of sentences in your characters' dialogue. For example, what request or command could a character make?

Writing Use your prewriting notes to help you make a draft of your comic strip. Use word balloons to add the dialogue to the pictures. As you write, you may decide to add details. Keep in mind that you will be able to add details in the pictures that go with the words.

Revising Ask a friend to read your cartoon. Are your characters' conversations clear? Can your friend follow the story line? If not, you may need to add, revise, or rearrange sentences.

Publishing Check your comic strip for errors in grammar, spelling, and punctuation. Make sure that you have used all four kinds of sentences and that you have used periods, question marks, and exclamation points correctly for each kind of sentence. You and your classmates may want to photocopy all the comic strips and gather them in a folder for each member of the class.

CHAPTER

Parts of Speech Overview

Noun, Pronoun, Adjective

1.0 Written and Oral English Language Conventions
Students write and speak with a command of standard English conventions appropriate to this grade level.
1.2 Identify and properly use indefinite pronouns.
1.4 Use correct capitalization.

Diagnostic Preview

Identifying Nouns, Pronouns, and Adjectives

Identify each of the italicized words in the following sentences as a *noun*, a *pronoun*, or an *adjective*.

EXAMPLE **1.** Her older *brother* has an *important* test today.
1. brother—noun; important—adjective

1. The *Romans* built a huge system of roads, *some* of which are still used.
2. Last summer we visited *Alaska,* which is our *largest* state.
3. *Which* of the projects does *that* illustrate?
4. The *Hawaiian* dancers wore *colorful* costumes.
5. *The* bubbling volcano, *inactive* for years, is now a popular tourist attraction.
6. The campers enjoyed *themselves* as they watched the sun set behind the *mountains.*
7. "*That* notebook is *mine,*" Angela said.
8. *They* made a touchdown just before the final *whistle.*
9. *Colombo* is the capital *city* of Sri Lanka.
10. The pen with the *blue* ink is *hers.*

The Noun

2a. A ***noun*** is a word or word group that is used to name a person, place, thing, or idea.

Persons	parents, Scott, teacher, Ms. Theresa Vargas, sister, linebackers, baby sitter
Places	White House, states, Nairobi, school
Things	rocket, desks, ocean, hamster, computer, Newbery Medal, Golden Gate Bridge
Ideas	danger, freedom, kindness, fears, dream

Notice that some nouns are made up of more than one word. A ***compound noun*** is a single noun made up of two or more words used together. The compound noun may be written as one word, as a hyphenated word, or as two or more words.

One Word	daydream, Iceland
Hyphenated Word	self-esteem, sister-in-law
Two Words	Rita Rodriguez, family room

Exercise 1 Identifying Nouns

Identify the nouns in the following sentences.

EXAMPLE **1.** Clara Barton was the founder of the American Red Cross.
1. Clara Barton, founder, American Red Cross

1. Clara Barton was born in Massachusetts.
2. She was educated in a rural school and grew up with a love of books.
3. She began her career as a teacher.
4. During the Civil War, however, she distributed medicine and other supplies.
5. Later she helped find soldiers who were missing in action.

6. She organized the American Red Cross and was its president for many years.
7. She raised money for the Red Cross and worked with victims of floods and other disasters.
8. Her kindness touched the lives of countless men, women and children.
9. Her life has been an inspiration to many people who have followed in her footsteps.
10. What a remarkable career and legacy she left the people of the world!

Proper Nouns and Common Nouns

Reference Note

For information about **capitalizing proper nouns,** see page 241.

A ***proper noun*** names a particular person, place, thing, or idea and begins with a capital letter. A ***common noun*** names any one of a group of persons, places, things, or ideas. It is usually not capitalized.

Common Nouns	Proper Nouns
woman	Aunt Josie
teacher	Jaime Escalante
city	Los Angeles
country	Germany
continent	Asia
monument	Lincoln Memorial
team	Karr Cougars
book	*Barrio Boy*
holiday	Chinese New Year
religion	Judaism
language	Swahili

Exercise 2 Identifying Common and Proper Nouns

Identify the nouns in the following sentences, and label them *common* or *proper.*

EXAMPLE 1. The people of Japan celebrate many holidays.
1. people—common; Japan—proper; holidays—common

1. The picture below is of the Snow Festival in Sapporo.
2. Many groups work together to build these giant sculptures of snow.
3. Do you recognize any of the statues or buildings?
4. Is that the Statue of Liberty made out of snow?

5. In the historic city of Kyoto each June, you can see a parade of spears.
6. A popular fair in Tokyo offers pickled radishes.
7. Many villages are colorfully decorated for the Feast of the Lanterns.
8. Toshiro said that his town enjoys the Star Festival every summer.
9. Several flowers, among them the iris and the lily, have their own special days.
10. The birthday of Buddha is observed in April.

Exercise 3 Substituting Proper Nouns for Common Nouns

In the sentences on the next page, substitute a proper noun for each italicized common noun. You will need to change or leave out some other words in each sentence. You may also make up proper names to use.

GRAMMAR

EXAMPLE 1. The *principal* awarded the *student* the prize for the best creative essay.

1. *Ms. Chen awarded Paula Perez the prize for the best creative essay.*

1. The *student* is from a *city.*
2. Usually, my *uncle* looks through the *newspaper* after we finish dinner.
3. The *child* watched a *movie.*
4. A *teacher* asked a *student* to talk about growing up in Mexico.
5. My *cousin* read that *book.*
6. Surrounded by newspaper reporters, the *mayor* stood outside the *building.*
7. Does the *girl* go to this *school*?
8. That *singer* wrote the *song.*
9. My *neighbor* bought her husband a new *car* for his birthday last Saturday.
10. When he was a college student, the *coach* played for that *team.*
11. The *painting* is in a *museum.*
12. The *officer* directed us to the *bridge.*
13. My relatives, who are originally from a *town,* now live in a *city.*
14. The librarian asked my *classmate* to return the *book* as soon as possible.
15. That *newspaper* is published daily; this *magazine* is published weekly.
16. Ted read a *poem* for the *teacher.*
17. That *state* borders the *ocean.*
18. The owner of that store visited a *country* during a *month.*
19. A *man* flew to a *city* one day.
20. Last week the *president* talked about the history of our *nation.*

Exercise 4 Using Proper Nouns

Developers are planning to build a new shopping mall in your neighborhood. They are trying to find out what kinds of stores and other attractions the community would like at the mall. The developers have prepared the following survey.

Answer each question with a complete sentence. Underline each proper noun that you use.

EXAMPLE 1. When would you be most likely to go to the mall?

1. I would be most likely to visit the mall on Saturdays, especially in August and November.

New Mall Questionnaire

1. What stores would you most like to see at the mall?
2. What would you be most likely to buy at the mall?
3. What types of movies would you prefer to see at the mall theater?
4. What restaurants would you like to have in the mall's food court?
5. Would you go to the mall arcade? If so, what games would you play?
6. What brands of clothes do you prefer?
7. Would you purchase books or magazines at the mall? If so, what books or magazines interest you?
8. To what clubs, organizations, or associations do you belong?
9. What special or seasonal events would attract you to the mall?
10. At what nearby malls do you sometimes shop?

Review A Identifying and Classifying Nouns

Identify the nouns in the following sentences, and label them *common* or *proper.*

EXAMPLE 1. In 2004, voters elected Barack Obama, Jr., to the United States Senate.

1. 2004—common; voters—common; Barack Obama, Jr.—proper; United States Senate—proper

GRAMMAR

GRAMMAR

1. Obama, a senator serving Illinois, has an interesting international background.
2. His father came to the United States from Kenya but eventually returned.
3. Thus, Obama was raised by his mother and maternal grandparents.
4. He grew up mostly in Hawaii but also lived in Indonesia as a child.
5. After he graduated from Columbia University in New York City, he moved to Chicago.
6. There he worked for three years with a nonprofit organization.
7. Obama then attended Harvard Law School.
8. Did you know he was the first African American to serve as editor of the *Harvard Law Review*?
9. The young lawyer moved back to Chicago and represented victims of discrimination.
10. As a politician, Obama has become known for his inspiring speeches.

The Pronoun

2b. A *pronoun* is a word that is used in place of one or more nouns or pronouns.

In each of the following examples, an arrow is drawn from a pronoun to the noun or nouns it stands for in the sentence.

EXAMPLES When Cindy Davis came to the bus stop, **she** was wearing a cast.

The trees and bushes are dry; **they** should be watered.

This stable is large. **It** has stalls for thirty horses.

The word or word group that a pronoun stands for is called its ***antecedent.***

EXAMPLES My **aunt** sold her car. [*Aunt* is the antecedent of *her*.]

Anthony, call your mother. [*Anthony* is the antecedent of *your*.]

Reference Note

For information about choosing **pronouns that agree with their antecedents,** see page 137.

Sometimes the antecedent is not stated because the reader can understand the meaning of the sentence without it.

EXAMPLES Call **your** mother. [The antecedent of *your* is clearly the person to whom the sentence is directed.]

They beat **us** fair and square. [The antecedent of *They* is clearly the team that the speaker played against. The antecedent of *us* is clearly the team of which the speaker is a member.]

Oral Practice **Substituting Pronouns for Nouns**

Read each of the following sentences aloud, replacing the repeated nouns with pronouns.

EXAMPLE 1. Viviana set up Viviana's game on the table.

1. Viviana set up her game on the table.

1. The passengers on the departing ocean liner waved to the passengers' friends on shore.
2. The test was so long that I almost didn't finish the test.
3. Rachel's neighbors asked Rachel to baby-sit.
4. Carlos said that Carlos had already cleaned Carlos's room.
5. The directions were long, but the directions were clear.
6. Mom was born in Nigeria, and Mom speaks French, English, Spanish, and Italian.
7. Ask those police officers if the police officers know the way to Alhambra Avenue.
8. The twins saved the twins' money; now, that new bicycle built for two is the twins'.
9. Did Warren's aunt fix some tacos for Warren?
10. Our whole family spent the weekend at home, but our whole family had the best time ever.

Personal Pronouns

A ***personal pronoun*** refers to the one speaking (***first person***), the one spoken to (***second person***), or the one spoken about (***third person***). Personal pronouns have both singular and plural forms.

EXAMPLE **I** am sure **he** told **you** about **their** plans.

HELP

When you use a pronoun, always be sure that its antecedent is clear to the reader. If the pronoun could possibly refer to one of two or more antecedents, revise the sentence to make the meaning more clear.

UNCLEAR

My aunt called my sister after she won the talent contest. [Who won the talent contest, my aunt or my sister?]

CLEAR

After my sister won the talent contest, my aunt called her.

Personal Pronouns		
	Singular	**Plural**
First person	I, me, my, mine	we, us, our, ours
Second person	you, your, yours	you, your, yours
Third person	he, him, his, she, her, hers, it, its	they, them, their, theirs

The ***possessive pronouns***—*my, mine, our, ours, your, yours, her, hers, his, its, their,* and *theirs*—are personal pronouns that are used to show ownership or possession.

EXAMPLES Nina stored **her** suitcase under **her** bed.

Is that paper **yours** or **mine**?

NOTE Some teachers prefer to call some possessive forms of pronouns (such as *my, your,* and *our*) adjectives. Follow your teacher's instructions regarding possessive forms.

Reflexive and Intensive Pronouns

A ***reflexive pronoun*** refers to the subject and is necessary to the basic meaning of the sentence. An ***intensive pronoun*** emphasizes its antecedent and is unnecessary to the basic meaning of the sentence.

Reflexive and Intensive Pronouns	
First person	myself, ourselves
Second person	yourself, yourselves
Third person	himself, herself, itself, themselves

REFLEXIVE They chose new books for **themselves.**

She gave **herself** the day off from practicing.

INTENSIVE David **himself** bought a sandwich.

The award will be presented by the principal **herself.**

HELP — Do not confuse the possessive pronoun *its* with the contraction *it's*. The pronoun *its* means "belonging to it." The contraction *it's* means "it is" or "it has." The apostrophe shows that letters have been left out.

Some other possessive pronouns that are often confused with contractions are *their*, meaning "belonging to them," (confused with *they're*, meaning "they are") and *your*, meaning "belonging to you" (confused with *you're*, meaning "you are").

Reference Note

For more information about **words that are often confused,** see page 329.

Exercise 5 Identifying Pronouns

Identify all of the pronouns in each of the following sentences.

EXAMPLE 1. I lent her my camera.
1. *I, her, my*

1. The dentist asked me several questions before examining my teeth.
2. Dad asked the mechanics working on his car to call him about his bill.
3. Our cousins have decided they will visit Peru.
4. She asked herself where she could have put her book.
5. He washed the mats thoroughly and put them out in the sun to dry.
6. Here is a postcard from Egypt for you and me.
7. We helped ourselves to tacos and beans.
8. You gave us your support when we needed it.
9. He had to do his social studies homework before playing soccer with us.
10. I found the weak battery and replaced it myself.

Exercise 6 Identifying Types of Pronouns

In each of the following sentences, identify the italicized pronoun as *personal, reflexive,* or *intensive.*

EXAMPLE 1. Eric gave *her* a flower.
1. *personal*

1. Darren *himself* did not know where the gifts were hidden.
2. Did Teri offer *them* directions to the community center?
3. Elena is a very good actress, and *she* always learns her lines very quickly.
4. Kara treated *herself* to a short nap after a long day.
5. Although *it* fell from the top branches of the elm tree, the chipmunk was not injured.
6. Have *you* told Dennis about the new sports complex?
7. Tracy and Ed carried the aquarium to the car *themselves.*
8. Brian and Erin just arrived home, so *they* have not started their homework assignment yet.
9. Rosalia congratulated *herself* on meeting her goal.
10. The dog made *itself* dizzy by chasing its own tail.

MEETING THE CHALLENGE

If you are not sure whether a pronoun is reflexive or intensive, use this test: Read the sentence aloud, omitting the pronoun. If the meaning of the sentence stays the same, the pronoun is intensive. If the meaning changes, the pronoun is reflexive.

Identify the boldface pronoun in each of the following sentences as *reflexive* or *intensive*. Use the test described above to explain how you made your choice.

1. The children enjoyed **themselves** at the park.
2. Jeremy repaired the tire **himself.**

GRAMMAR

Demonstrative Pronouns

A ***demonstrative pronoun*** points out a specific person, place, thing, or idea.

Demonstrative Pronouns			
this	that	these	those

EXAMPLES What is **that**?

This is the uniform once worn by Satchel Paige.

These are the shoes he used to wear.

Are **those** really his autographs?

Reference Note

For information on **adjectives,** see page 38.

NOTE *This*, *that*, *these*, and *those* can also be used as adjectives. When these words are used to modify a noun or pronoun, they are called ***demonstrative adjectives.***

PRONOUN **This** is a delicious papaya. [*This* refers to *papaya.*]

ADJECTIVE **This** papaya is delicious. [*This* modifies *papaya.*]

PRONOUN **That** is the stamp my cousin sent from Sweden. [*That* refers to *stamp.*]

ADJECTIVE **That** stamp was the first in my collection. [*That* modifies *stamp.*]

Indefinite Pronouns

Reference Note

For more information on **indefinite pronouns,** see page 129.

An ***indefinite pronoun*** refers to a person, a place, a thing, or an idea that may or may not be specifically named.

Common Indefinite Pronouns			
all	each	more	one
any	either	much	other
anybody	everybody	neither	several
anyone	everyone	nobody	some
anything	few	none	somebody
both	many	no one	something

EXAMPLES **Everyone** in the class was invited to the party.

None of the boys knew **much** about camping.

NOTE Most words that can be used as indefinite pronouns can also be used as adjectives.

PRONOUN **Some** are bored by this movie.

ADJECTIVE **Some** people are bored by this movie.

GRAMMAR

Exercise 7 Identifying Pronouns

Identify the italicized pronoun in each of the following sentences as *indefinite* or *demonstrative.*

EXAMPLE **1.** *Someone* has been sitting in my chair.

1. indefinite

1. Are you asking *anyone* to the dance this weekend?
2. *This* is my jacket; that one must be yours.
3. *Something* is different about your hair.
4. *That* was the funniest thing I have ever seen a kitten do!
5. *This* is good, but Chrissy's report is better.
6. The armadillo paused at the puddle and drank *some* of the water.
7. Are *those* the socks you are wearing with those shoes?
8. We have to choose between *these* and the ones we looked at yesterday.
9. Linda did more sit-ups than *several* who tried before her.
10. *Nobody* knows the answer to that.

Review B Identifying Pronouns

Identify the pronoun or pronouns in each of the following sentences.

EXAMPLE **1.** Everyone in my class likes going on field trips.

1. Everyone; my

1. Last week, we really enjoyed ourselves at the National Museum of African Art.
2. It has been part of the Smithsonian Institution in Washington, D.C., since 1979.

3. In 1987, the museum's collection was moved to its present underground facility.
4. Our teacher, Ms. Martinez, told us about the museum before we went there.
5. She said the entrance is made of pink granite.
6. I was surprised by the six domes on top.
7. Everyone had at least one question to ask our museum guide.
8. We enjoyed hearing her lively explanations of the artwork.
9. This is a photograph of one of my favorite objects at the museum.
10. Do you like it?

Mask, Bassa Peoples, Liberia. Wood, pigment, bone or ivory, iron (9 $\frac{1}{2}$" X 5 $\frac{3}{4}$" X 4 $\frac{1}{2}$"). National Museum of African Art, Eliot Elisofon Archives, Smithsonian Institution, #88-5-1. Photo Credit: Franko Khoury.

Interrogative Pronouns

An ***interrogative pronoun*** introduces a question.

Interrogative Pronouns				
what	which	who	whom	whose

EXAMPLES **What** is the first event in the contest?

Who is going to represent our team?

To **whom** is the e-mail addressed?

Which of the books are you reading?

Whose is the car in the driveway?

Relative Pronouns

A ***relative pronoun*** introduces an adjective clause.

Common Relative Pronouns				
that	which	who	whom	whose

EXAMPLES Harry S. Truman, **who** became president when Franklin D. Roosevelt died, surprised many people with his victory over Thomas Dewey in 1948.

Robins are among the birds **that** migrate south for the winter.

Reference Note

For information on **adjective clauses,** see page 91.

GRAMMAR

Exercise 8 Identifying Relative and Interrogative Pronouns

Identify the italicized pronouns in each of the following sentences as *relative* or *interrogative.*

EXAMPLE **1.** *Which* of those snow sculptures do you think will win the prize?

1. interrogative

1. The only student *that* could complete the obstacle course was Sophia.

2. *What* was the name of the volcano that erupted in Washington?

3. *What* was causing that sound outside your room at night?

4. "*Who* left all of those markers on the floor yesterday?" asked Ms. Jackson.

5. Lilacs, *which* are known throughout the world for their fragrant flowers, grow best in northern climates.

6. The new teacher, *whom* we have not yet met, will start Monday.

7. *Which* of you remembers the name of the author of "The Celebrated Jumping Frog of Calaveras County"?

8. *Whose* turn is it to take out the trash?

9. The light bulb, *which* had been flickering for a few days, finally burned out.

10. To *whom* did you lend your textbook?

GRAMMAR

STYLE TIP

Some adjectives are more specific and vivid than others. You can make your writing more interesting by replacing dull adjectives with more vivid ones.

ORIGINAL
Mr. Sato is a **nice** man. [The adjective *nice* is dull and doesn't really say much about Mr. Sato.]

REVISED
Mr. Sato is a **generous** man. [The adjective *generous* is more specific about Mr. Sato.]

Reference Note

For information on using ***predicate adjectives,*** see page 114.

Reference Note

For information on using ***a*** and ***an,*** see page 222.

The Adjective

2c. An *adjective* is a word that is used to modify a noun or a pronoun.

To ***modify*** a word means to describe the word or to make its meaning more definite. An adjective modifies a noun or pronoun by telling *what kind, which one, how many,* or *how much.*

What Kind?	Which One or Ones?	How Many or How Much?
gentle dog	**sixth** grade	**two** tickets
Irish town	**these** books	**full** pitcher
scary movie	**other** people	**most** players
purple shoes	**any** CD	**no** work

Adjectives usually come before the words they modify. Sometimes, however, an adjective comes after the word it modifies.

EXAMPLES The dog is **gentle.** [The predicate adjective *gentle* modifies *dog.*]

The sea, **blue** and **sparkling,** stretched out before us invitingly. [The adjectives *blue* and *sparkling* modify the noun *sea.*]

NOTE The adjectives *a, an,* and *the* are called ***articles.***

Exercise 9 Identifying Adjectives

Identify each adjective in the following sentences. Do not include *a, an,* or *the.*

EXAMPLE **1.** The sky was clear, and the night was cold.
1. clear, cold

1. A silvery moon rode down the western sky.
2. It shed a pale light on the quiet countryside.
3. Long meadows spread out between two hills.
4. The smell of the wild onion was strong.
5. The only sound we heard was the sharp crackle of the fire.

6. Suddenly, several stars came out.
7. I watched until the entire sky glowed with bright stars.
8. I was lonely and happy at the same time.
9. I finally became sleepy and longed for my warm bed.
10. Soon I went indoors and fell into a deep sleep.

Exercise 10 Identifying Adjectives and the Words They Modify

Identify the adjectives and the words they modify in the following sentences. Do not include *a, an,* or *the.*

EXAMPLE **1.** It costs five dollars to go to that movie.
1. five—dollars; that—movie

1. I have a free ticket for the last game.
2. We ate spicy crawfish, and they were delicious.
3. The new neighbor is helpful and nice.
4. The bear, angry and hungry, surprised the campers.
5. Many students compete in the regional events.
6. Will country musicians play at the county fair?
7. Despite the long delay, we remained cheerful.
8. A shiny coin stared up at me from the the icy sidewalk.
9. Take one booklet and pass the rest to the next row.
10. A few colorful birds perched in the tall, green trees on the bank of the river.

COMPUTER TIP 

Some software includes a thesaurus feature. You can use the computer thesaurus to find synonyms to replace dull or overused adjectives in your writing. Always check the meaning of an unfamiliar adjective in a dictionary, though, to make sure it is just the right word.

Exercise 11 Writing Adjectives for a Story

The following story is about a cave exploration. Copy the sentences, adding an appropriate adjective for each blank. Underline the adjectives you add.

EXAMPLE **1.** Exploring caves is ____ on ____ days.
1. Exploring caves is fun on hot days.

1. Have you ever been in a ____ cave like the one shown at right?
2. Would you say it looks ____ and ____?
3. My father and I explored this ____ cave once.
4. It was ____ but ____, too.
5. We found some ____ rock formations.
6. We also heard ____ sounds.

GRAMMAR

7. My father took some ____ photographs.
8. We looked up and saw ____ bats flying above our heads.
9. After exploring for about ____ hours, we were ready to see the sky again.
10. Spelunking, as cave exploring is called, can be a very ____ experience, if you have a ____ guide.

Proper Adjectives

A ***proper adjective*** is formed from a proper noun and begins with a capital letter.

Reference Note

For information on **capitalizing proper adjectives,** see page 250.

Proper Nouns	Proper Adjectives
Japan	**Japanese** islands
Easter	**Easter** Sunday
Queen Victoria	**Victorian** drama
Sioux	**Sioux** customs

HELP

Some proper nouns, such as *Easter* and *Sioux*, do not change spelling when they are used as proper adjectives.

Exercise 12 Identifying Adjectives

Identify all of the adjectives in the following sentences. Then, underline each proper adjective. Do not include the articles *a*, *an*, or *the*.

EXAMPLE 1. The Navajo weaver made a blanket on a wooden loom.

1. *Navajo, wooden*

1. Music can express sad or happy feelings.
2. The quartet sang several Irish songs.
3. The gold watch with the fancy chain was made by a famous Swiss watchmaker.
4. She is a Balinese dancer.
5. On vacation, Mom enjoys long, quiet breakfasts.
6. Many Australian people are of British origin.
7. The Egyptian mummies are on display on the first floor.
8. We are proud of Joshua.
9. The movie is based on a popular Russian novel.
10. In Canadian football, a team has twelve players on the field at one time.

Exercise 13 **Writing Proper Adjectives**

Change the following proper nouns into proper adjectives. Then, use each proper adjective in a sentence.

EXAMPLE **1.** France

1. French—We bought French bread at the bakery.

1. England
2. Inca
3. Hinduism
4. Celt
5. Alaska
6. Thanksgiving
7. Shakespeare
8. Korea
9. Navajo
10. Boston

HELP

You may want to use a dictionary to help you spell the adjectives in Exercise 13.

Demonstrative Adjectives

This, that, these, and *those* can be used both as adjectives and as pronouns. When they modify nouns or pronouns, they are called ***demonstrative adjectives.*** When they are used alone, they are called ***demonstrative pronouns.***

ADJECTIVE What are **these** skates doing in the living room?

PRONOUN What are **these** doing in the living room?

ADJECTIVE I prefer **that** brand of frozen yogurt.

PRONOUN I prefer **that.**

Reference Note

For more information on **demonstrative pronouns,** see page 34.

Exercise 14 **Identifying Demonstrative Pronouns and Demonstrative Adjectives**

In each of the following sentences, identify the italicized word as a *demonstrative pronoun* or a *demonstrative adjective.*

EXAMPLE **1.** Who gave you *those* beautiful flowers?

1. demonstrative adjective

1. *That* is the strangest hot-air balloon I have ever seen!
2. Will *those* squirrels find enough to eat during the winter?
3. My dog, Manda, has been chewing on *this* piece of rawhide for three weeks.
4. *These* are the only shoes I can find that will fit you.
5. According to the guidebook, *those* are the largest trees in North America.

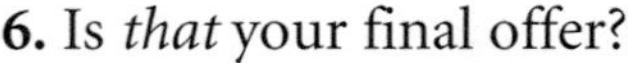

6. Is *that* your final offer?
7. The geese always return to *these* same lakes.
8. What do you plan to do with *that* lump of clay?
9. I'm afraid she's gone too far *this* time.
10. Can *this* be the same person I knew back in third grade?

Review C **Identifying Adjectives**

Identify the adjectives in the following sentences. Do not include *a, an,* or *the.*

EXAMPLE 1. I enjoy visiting the large railroad museum in our city.

1. *large, railroad*

1. Museums can be interesting.
2. Large cities have different kinds of museums.
3. Some museums display sculpture and paintings.
4. These museums may focus on one special kind of art.
5. For example, they might specialize in Chinese art or Mexican art.
6. Other museums feature birds, sea creatures, dinosaurs, and other animals.
7. A curator holds an important job in a museum.
8. A curator needs to know many facts about a particular display.
9. Some valuable objects must be displayed in a stable environment.
10. Some people prefer displays of modern art, while others enjoy exhibits of folk art.

Review D **Identifying Nouns, Pronouns, and Adjectives**

Identify all of the nouns, pronouns, and adjectives in each of the following sentences. Do not include *a, an,* or *the.*

EXAMPLE 1. I think models make a great hobby.

1. *I—pronoun; models—noun; great—adjective; hobby—noun*

1. Do you have a favorite hobby?
2. Models are enjoyable and educational.

3. They require little space.
4. I keep mine on a bookshelf my dad and I built ourselves.
5. Models are packaged in kits.
6. My favorite models are historic ships and antique planes.
7. On my last birthday, my parents gave me two model kits of biplanes.
8. They came with directions in several languages.
9. Many of the tiny parts are designed for an exact fit.
10. Do you think the bright decals add a realistic look?

GRAMMAR

Review E Identifying Nouns, Pronouns, and Adjectives

Identify all of the nouns, pronouns, and adjectives in each of the following sentences. Do not include *a, an,* or *the.*

EXAMPLE 1. Pueblos are practical housing for people in hot, dry regions.

1. Pueblos—noun; practical—adjective; housing—noun; people—noun; hot—adjective; dry—adjective; regions—noun

1. The brown building in the photograph contains several individual homes.
2. *Pueblo* is a Spanish word for a structure like this and for a town.
3. This building is located at the Taos Pueblo in New Mexico.

4. Can you tell how pueblos are made?
5. They are built of adobe.
6. People make adobe by mixing mud with grass or straw.
7. They shape the mixture into bricks and let them bake in the sun.
8. Buildings made with this material stay cool during the summer months.
9. Anyone on a visit to the Southwest can find other pueblos like this one.
10. Old pueblos built by the Hopi and the Zuni fascinate me.

Review F Writing Sentences Using Nouns, Pronouns, and Adjectives

Write ten original sentences using the parts of speech given below. In each sentence, underline the word that is the listed part of speech.

EXAMPLE 1. an adjective that comes after the word it describes
1. Our guide was very helpful.

1. a proper noun
2. a possessive pronoun
3. an adjective that tells *how many*
4. a reflexive pronoun
5. a proper adjective
6. an article
7. a third-person pronoun
8. a demonstrative adjective
9. an indefinite pronoun
10. a noun that names an idea

Chapter Review

A. Identifying Nouns, Pronouns, and Adjectives

Identify each italicized word or word group in the following sentences as a *noun*, a *pronoun*, or an *adjective*.

1. My *best* friend plays *soccer.*
2. *We* went to *Boston* last summer.
3. Help *yourself* to some *Chinese* food.
4. What a *beautiful* garden *Mrs. Murakami* has!
5. *These* directions were *accurate.*
6. *That* is a fast *merry-go-round.*
7. Juana invited *us* to *her* fiesta.
8. *Sharp* tools are *necessary* for making a wood carving.
9. Almost *everyone* in the band takes private music *lessons.*
10. *This* story is my *favorite* one.

B. Identifying Common and Proper Nouns

Identify the nouns in the following sentences, and label each *common* or *proper.*

11. The religion our family practices is Islam.
12. Was Spanish the first language your mother spoke?
13. The musicians in the band play guitars, keyboards, and drums.
14. My favorite movie is *Willy Wonka and the Chocolate Factory.*
15. Many American tourists visit London in the summer.

C. Identifying Pronouns

Identify all of the pronouns in each of the following sentences.

16. My cat ate all of its food this morning.
17. Each of the girls said someone had already told her about the band concert.
18. I brought a casserole to the potluck dinner and put it in the oven.

19. The doctor herself removed his bandages.
20. Did anyone notice the person who delivered the package?
21. "I think this winter is going to be long and cold," he said to himself.
22. Didn't you ask him not to do that?
23. That book is not the one that I wanted to read.
24. We asked ourselves if he really intended to come to our party.
25. Which of the sweaters is yours?

D. Identifying Proper and Demonstrative Adjectives

Identify the adjectives in the following sentences. Do not include the articles *a, an,* or *the.* Then, label each *proper adjective* and each *demonstrative adjective.*

26. The Easter holiday lasted for one short week.
27. The apple, glossy and red, rolled out of the bag and across the smooth table.
28. The rain was steady throughout that gloomy afternoon.
29. Would you like these French posters, or would you rather have those?
30. The Siamese cat is playful, but that old tabby is aloof.

E. Identifying Nouns, Pronouns, and Adjectives

Identify each *noun, pronoun,* and *adjective* in the following sentences. Do not include the articles *a, an,* and *the.*

31. Someone told me about the movie.
32. We are moving to Belgium, a European country.
33. J. S. Bach, a German composer, wrote many pieces for the harpsichord.
34. "Is this the tape you wanted?" asked Mr. Imagi.
35. Ted talked himself into the purchase of a new computer.
36. Some of the old songs are lovely.
37. These colors are brighter than those.

38. Professor Auerbach herself will present the award to us.
39. The Swedish car in the driveway is ours.
40. Does anybody know when the city of San Antonio was founded?

Writing Application

Using Pronouns in a Plot Summary

Pronouns and Antecedents You are in a filmmaking class at the community center and need ideas for a project. The theme of the project is science fiction movie spoofs. Write a plot summary for a short movie. Explain the plot of the movie, and describe the characters. Be sure that the pronouns you use refer clearly to their antecedents.

Prewriting In a spoof, a writer imitates and makes fun of another work. Imagine several science fiction movie spoofs—for example, *There's an Alien in My Soup* or *Nerds from Neptune.* Choose the idea that you like the best. Then, brainstorm some ideas for a simple plot. Jot down brief descriptions of the setting and the characters in the movie.

Writing Use your notes to help you write your first draft. Summarize what happens in the movie from beginning to end. Describe each character as you introduce him or her. Keep the props and costumes simple—you are working on a low budget.

Revising Ask a friend to read your movie idea. Is the plot interesting? Is it funny? Can your friend tell which character is performing each action? If not, you may need to revise some details. Check to make sure each pronoun refers clearly to its antecedent.

Publishing Read your summary one more time to catch other errors in spelling, grammar, and punctuation. You may want to develop one scene from your plot summary. With the help of several classmates, dramatize this scene in front of the class. Use simple masks and props to create the effect of science fiction.

CHAPTER

Parts of Speech Overview

Verb, Adverb, Preposition, Conjunction, Interjection

1.0 Written and Oral English Language Conventions

Students write and speak with a command of standard English conventions appropriate to this grade level.

1.1 Use effective coordination of ideas to express complete thoughts.

Diagnostic Preview

Identifying Verbs, Adverbs, Prepositions, Conjunctions, and Interjections

Identify each of the italicized words or word groups in the following sentences as a *verb,* an *adverb,* a *preposition,* a *conjunction,* or an *interjection.*

EXAMPLE **1.** A tornado *is* a terrible *and* violent storm.
1. is—verb; and—conjunction

1. The tornado *struck* our neighborhood *without* warning.
2. We do *not* have a basement in our house.
3. I grabbed my dog Muffin *and* ran *into* the bathroom, the safest room in the house.
4. Muffin and I were *tightly* wedged *between* the sink and the bathtub.
5. *Either* the house was shaking *or* I was, and the air *became* very cold.
6. *Suddenly,* a siren went *off.*

7. A tornado *had been sighted* right *in* the area.
8. Then everything suddenly *grew* calm—it seemed almost *too* calm.
9. I *was* ready for the worst, *but* the tornado did not touch my house *or* any other home in the area.
10. *Well,* I was frightened, *but* I was not hurt.

The Verb

3a. A *verb* is a word that expresses action or a state of being.

EXAMPLES We **went** to Boston last April.

Is a firefly a kind of beetle?

Every complete sentence has a verb. The verb says something about the subject.

In this book, verbs are classified in three ways — (1) as *main* or *helping* verbs, (2) as *action* or *linking* verbs, and (3) as *transitive* or *intransitive* verbs.

Reference Note

For more information about **verbs,** see page 146.

Main Verbs and Helping Verbs

In many sentences, a single word is all that is needed to express the action or the state of being.

EXAMPLES The dog **barked** all night.

Brett **throws** the ball a long way.

Mr. Rivera **is** the new English teacher.

In other sentences, the verb consists of a main verb and one or more helping verbs.

A ***helping verb*** (also called an *auxiliary* verb) helps the ***main verb*** to express action or a state of being.

EXAMPLES **can** speak

will learn

should have been fed

HELP

Remember, a verb cannot be a helping verb unless there is another verb for it to help. If a verb such as *was* or *had* is the only verb in a sentence, it is not a helping verb.

EXAMPLES

I **had** called my grandmother already. [*Had* is helping the main verb, *called*.]

They **had** a good time at the nature center. [*Had* is the only verb; there is no other verb for it to help.]

Together, the main verb and its helping verb or verbs are called a ***verb phrase.***

EXAMPLES Many students **can speak** Spanish.

I **will be learning** all the state capitals tonight.

The dog **should have been fed** by now.

Commonly Used Helping Verbs					
am	being	do	have	must	were
are	can	does	is	shall	will
be	could	had	may	should	would
been	did	has	might	was	

NOTE Some words can be used as both helping verbs and main verbs.

HELPING VERB I **do** wash the dishes.

MAIN VERB I will **do** the dishes.

Sometimes a verb phrase is interrupted by another part of speech.

EXAMPLES Suzanne **should** not **call** so late at night. [The verb phrase *should call* is interrupted by the adverb *not.*]

The scientists **did**n't **think** the asteroid would hit the earth. [The verb phrase *did think* is interrupted by *–n't,* the contraction for *not.*]

Did you **watch** the new video? [The verb phrase *Did watch* is interrupted by the subject *you.*]

HELP—The word *not* and its contraction, *–n't,* are adverbs telling *to what extent;* neither is part of a verb phrase.

Exercise 1 Identifying Verb Phrases and Helping Verbs

Identify the verb phrase in each of the following sentences. Then, underline the helping verb or verbs.

EXAMPLE **1.** We are going to Arizona this summer.

1. are going

1. The Petrified Forest has long attracted many tourists.

2. Its spectacular beauty has captured their imaginations.
3. Visitors can see the Painted Desert at the same time.
4. The colors of the desert do not remain the same for long.
5. Specimens of petrified wood are exhibited at the tourist information center.
6. Have you ever seen a piece of petrified wood?
7. A guide will gladly explain the process of petrification.
8. Visitors can purchase the fossilized wood as a souvenir.
9. Tours of the Petrified Forest are not recommended for amateur hikers.
10. Hikes must be arranged with park rangers.

Exercise 2 **Using Verb Phrases in Original Sentences**

Use each of the following word groups as the subject of a sentence with a verb phrase. Make some of your sentences questions. Underline each helping verb and the main verb in each sentence.

EXAMPLE 1. your neighbor's dog
1. Can your neighbor's dog do tricks?

1. my bicycle
2. the astronauts
3. a tiny kitten
4. the hard assignment
5. a famous singer
6. some strange footprints
7. my grandmother
8. the subway
9. a funny costume
10. the refreshments
11. our softball team
12. his favorite movie
13. the bird watchers' club
14. the new computer chip
15. Queen Elizabeth
16. her school picture
17. today's newspaper
18. a slice of bread
19. the pencil sharpener
20. my calendar

Review A **Identifying Verbs**

Identify the verbs in each of the following sentences. Be sure to include helping verbs.

EXAMPLE 1. Fairy tales are sometimes called folk tales.
1. are called

1. Long ago, many people could not read.

GRAMMAR

2. Instead, they would memorize stories.
3. Then they would tell the stories to their family members and friends.
4. In this way, the people, or folk, passed the tales on from generation to generation.
5. Finally, some people wrote the collected stories.
6. Two German brothers, Jakob and Wilhelm Grimm, published a famous collection of German folk tales.
7. The brothers had heard many of the tales from their older relatives.
8. Their collection of stories became extremely popular all over the world.
9. "Sleeping Beauty," "Cinderella," and "Rumpelstiltskin" were all preserved by the brothers Grimm.
10. In your library, you can probably find these tales and many others, too.

Action Verbs

An ***action verb*** expresses either physical or mental activity.

PHYSICAL ACTIVITY	I **have used** a computer in math class.
	Please **cook** dinner, Jerome.
MENTAL ACTIVITY	Fran **understands** the science assignment better than anyone else does.
	The magician **is thinking** of a number.

Exercise 3 Identifying Action Verbs

Identify the action verb in each of the following sentences.

EXAMPLE 1. The Maricopa people live in Arizona.
1. live

1. The Maricopa make unusual pottery.
2. For this pottery they use two kinds of clay.
3. One kind of clay forms the bowl or platter itself.
4. The other kind of clay colors the pottery.
5. First, the potters mold the clay by hand.
6. Then, they shape it into beautiful bowls and vases.
7. With the second type of clay, the potters create designs.

8. They often etch designs on the pottery with a toothpick.
9. Each family of potters has its own special designs.
10. These designs preserve Maricopa traditions from generation to generation.

GRAMMAR

Linking Verbs

A ***linking verb*** connects, or links, the subject to a word or word group that identifies or describes the subject.

EXAMPLES Sandra Cisneros **is** a writer. [The verb *is* connects *writer* with the subject *Sandra Cisneros.*]

The firefighters **had appeared** victorious. [The verb phrase *had appeared* connects *victorious* with the subject *firefighters.*]

The new superintendent **was** she. [The verb *was* connects *she* with the subject *superintendent.*]

Some Linking Verbs Formed from the Verb *Be*		
am	has been	may be
is	have been	might be
are	had been	can be
was	will be	should be
were	shall be	would have been

Other Linking Verbs			
appear	grow	seem	stay
become	look	smell	taste
feel	remain	sound	turn

Some verbs may be either action verbs or linking verbs, depending on how they are used.

ACTION They **sounded** the bell for a fire drill.

LINKING Mom **sounded** happy about her new job. [The verb *sounded* links *happy* with the subject *Mom.*]

STYLE  TIP

In the sentence *The new superintendent was she,* the pronoun *she* after the linking verb may sound strange. Many people would use *her* in informal speech. However, in formal, standard English, *she* is the correct form in this sentence.

Reference Note

For more about **pronouns following linking verbs,** see page 113. For information on **formal and informal language,** see page 221.

ACTION	The judge **will look** at my science project.
LINKING	Ann **will look** funny in her gorilla costume. [The verb phrase *will look* links *funny* with the subject *Ann.*]

Exercise 4 Identifying Linking Verbs

Identify the linking verbs or verb phrases in the following sentences.

EXAMPLE
1. Peanut soup made from fresh roasted peanuts tastes good.
1. *tastes*

1. Peanuts remain an important crop around the world.
2. The peanut, which is high in protein, is native to South America.
3. Peanuts grow ripe underground.
4. The seeds are the edible part of the plant.
5. The peanut has become an important ingredient in more than three hundred common products, such as wood stains, shampoo, printer's ink, and soap.
6. Of course, roasting peanuts smell wonderful.
7. Peanut butter was the invention of a St. Louis doctor in 1890.
8. Before then, thanks to George Washington Carver, the peanut had become one of the major crops of the South.
9. Carver, a scientist who experimented with peanuts and other plants, had been a slave.
10. It may seem strange, but Carver once prepared an entire dinner out of peanuts.

Exercise 5 Identifying Action Verbs and Linking Verbs

Identify the verb in each of the following sentences as an *action verb* or a *linking verb.*

EXAMPLES
1. Russell Simmons is one of the most influential people in the music and fashion industries.
1. *is—linking verb*
2. Simmons began his career as a promoter of hip hop concerts in New York City.
2. *began—action verb*

GRAMMAR

TIPS & TRICKS

If you are not sure whether a verb is being used as a linking verb or an action verb, try substituting *is* or *are* for the verb. If the sentence still makes sense, the verb is probably a linking verb. If the sentence does not make sense, the verb is probably an action verb.

EXAMPLES

James **looks** taller. [*James is taller* makes sense; here, *looks* is a linking verb.]

James **looks** out the window. [*James is out the window* does not make sense; here, *looks* is an action verb.]

HELP

Remember to include helping verbs in your answers to Exercise 5.

1. To most record companies, hip hop seemed like a fad.
2. However, Simmons saw potential in this new type of music.
3. With partner Rick Rubin, he formed Def Jam Recordings in 1984.
4. Many of the label's artists became famous as pioneers of a new music scene.
5. In 1990, Simmons founded a larger business group, Rush Communications.
6. This company's core businesses are popular clothing brands.
7. Eventually, Simmons sold his hugely successful record label.
8. Hip hop music and its fans still inspire his other ventures.
9. He is more than just a good businessperson, though.
10. Simmons also contributes time, money, and ideas to important community organizations.

Transitive and Intransitive Verbs

A ***transitive verb*** is a verb that expresses an action directed toward a person, place, thing, or idea. With transitive verbs, the action passes from the doer—the subject—to the receiver of the action. Words that receive the action of a transitive verb are called ***objects.***

EXAMPLES Tamisha **entertained** the child. [The object *child* receives the action of the verb *entertained*.]

Felipe **visited** San Juan. [The object *San Juan* receives the action of the verb *visited*.]

Reference Note

For more about **objects in sentences,** see page 107.

An ***intransitive verb*** tells something about the subject or expresses action without the action passing to a receiver, or object.

EXAMPLES The children **smiled.**

The horses **galloped** across the prairie.

I **am** here.

GRAMMAR

NOTE Not everything that follows a verb is an object. Many words or word groups that come after the verb give more information without receiving the action of the verb.

EXAMPLES Tameka writes **poetry.** [The object *poetry* receives the action of the transitive verb *writes.*]

Tameka writes **daily.** [The word *daily* tells when she performs the action of the intransitive verb *writes,* but *daily* does not receive the action and is not an object.]

Tameka writes **in the morning.** [The word group *in the morning* tells when she performs the action of the verb *writes,* but *in the morning* does not receive the action and is not an object.]

Some action verbs may be either transitive or intransitive, depending on how they are used in a sentence.

EXAMPLES My cousin Julio **plays** baseball on a Caribbean League team. [transitive]

My cousin Julio **plays** every week. [intransitive]

Kanani **studies** Chinese each day after school. [transitive]

Kanani **studies** hard. [intransitive]

NOTE Linking verbs are intransitive.

EXAMPLES This soup **tastes** too salty. [The linking verb *tastes* does not express any action for an object to receive. When used as a linking verb, *tastes* is intransitive.]

Does the box **seem** heavier than it should be? [The linking verb *Does seem* does not express any action for an object to receive. *Does seem* is intransitive.]

Exercise 6 Identifying Transitive and Intransitive Verbs

For each of the following sentences, identify the italicized verb as *transitive* or *intransitive.*

EXAMPLE 1. Computers *affect* our lives every day.

1. *transitive*

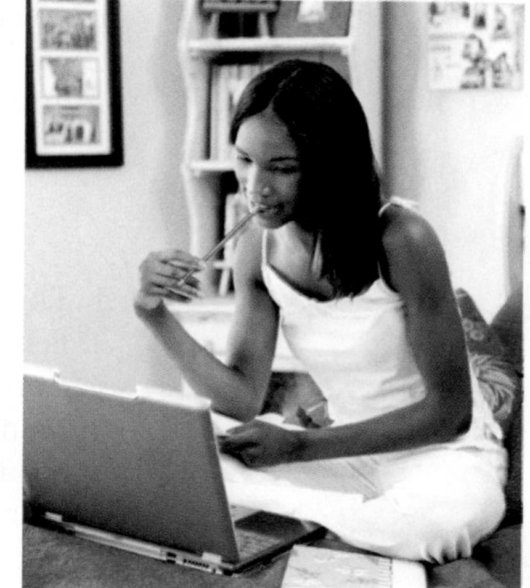

1. Computers *make* calculations incredibly quickly.
2. They *perform* many tasks that people often find boring and difficult.
3. Many businesses *benefit* from these machines.
4. Some people *work* at home using computers.
5. Computers *do* word processing, a very useful operation for writers.
6. They also *run* programs that allow you to make your own music and movies.
7. Hand-held computers *fit* easily into a purse, bag, or backpack.
8. My mother *bought* a laptop that weighs only two and a half pounds.
9. Because of high-speed Internet, Web sites *appear* almost instantly.
10. A computer's ability to store mass amounts of information *helps* my mother organize her work.

GRAMMAR

Oral Practice Using Transitive and Intransitive Verbs

Think of an appropriate verb for each of the following sentences, and read the completed sentence aloud. Then, identify each verb as *transitive* or *intransitive.*

EXAMPLE 1. He ____ my older brother's best friend.

1. *is—intransitive*

or

knows—transitive

1. Aunt Teresa ____ us about some Cherokee traditions.
2. Our experiment with plants and photosynthesis ____.
3. Billy and I ____ green beans and carrots.
4. By noon, the hot sun ____ the ice.
5. Everything ____ fine to me.
6. In the twilight, a shrimp boat ____ into the bay.
7. ____ these hurdles, Jason.
8. ____ Bogotá the capital of Colombia?
9. Wow! What a crazy tie that ____!
10. Several African nations ____ elections this year.

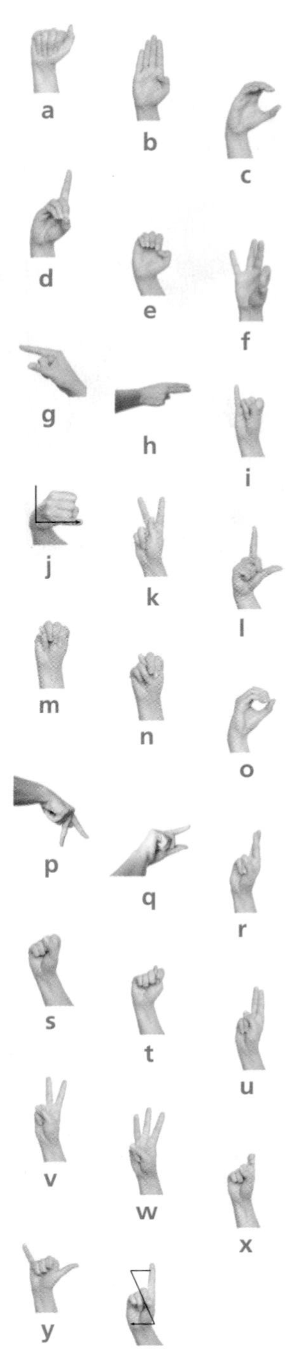

Review B Identifying Verbs

Identify the verb in each of the following sentences. Be sure to include helping verbs. Then, tell whether the verb is used as an *action* or *linking verb.* Then, tell whether it is *transitive* or *intransitive.*

EXAMPLE **1.** Can you form the letters of the sign language alphabet?

1. Can form—action, transitive

1. The alphabet chart at left is helpful.
2. Perhaps you and a friend could practice together.
3. At first, it may be a challenge.
4. Many people communicate with these letters as well as thousands of other signs.
5. Many people use forms of sign language.
6. For example, referees, coaches, and football players sometimes give signals in sign language.
7. Some stroke victims must learn sign language during their recovery period.
8. Scientists have taught hundreds of signs to gorillas and chimpanzees.
9. These animals have been talking to people and to each other in sign language.
10. In the picture below, the gorilla on the left and the woman are having a conversation in sign language.

The Adverb

3b. An *adverb* is a word that modifies a verb, an adjective, or another adverb.

Just as an adjective makes the meaning of a noun or a pronoun more definite, an adverb makes the meaning of a verb, an adjective, or another adverb more definite.

EXAMPLES Reporters **quickly** gather the news. [The adverb *quickly* modifies the verb *gather.*]

The route is **too** long. [The adverb *too* modifies the adjective *long.*]

Our newspaper carrier delivers the paper **very early.** [The adverb *very* modifies another adverb, *early.* The adverb *early* modifies the verb *delivers.*]

Adverbs answer the following questions:

Where?	How often?	To what extent?
When?	*or*	*or*
How?	How long?	How much?

EXAMPLES Please put the package **there.** [*There* modifies the verb *put* and tells *where.*]

I will call you **later.** [*Later* modifies the verb phrase *will call* and tells *when.*]

Softly, I shut my door. [*Softly* modifies the verb *shut* and tells *how.*]

Alannah **always** reads science fiction novels. [*Always* modifies the verb *reads* and tells *how often.*]

Would you please **briefly** explain what you mean? [*Briefly* modifies the verb phrase *Would explain* and tells *how long.*]

An owl hooted **very** late last night. [The adverb *very* modifies the adverb *late* and tells *to what extent.*]

The lemonade was **too** sour. [*Too* modifies the adjective *sour* and tells *how much.*]

HELP

Often, adverbs can be recognized by the suffix *–ly.* Remember, however, that not all adverbs end in *–ly* and not all words that end in *–ly* are adverbs.

ADVERBS

swam **quickly**

left **later**

ADJECTIVES

only friend

early flight

STYLE TIP

In your own writing, try not to overuse the adverb *very.* Replace it with a less common adverb, or revise the sentence so that other words carry more of the descriptive meaning.

EXAMPLE
The runt of the litter is still very small.

REVISED
The runt of the litter is still **quite** small.
or
The runt of the litter **weighs just one pound and is only six inches long.**

HELP
The word *not* and its contraction, *–n't,* are adverbs.

Words Often Used as Adverbs	
Where?	here, there, away, up, outside
When?	now, then, later, soon, ago
How?	clearly, easily, quietly, slowly
How often? *or* How long?	never, always, often, seldom frequently, usually, forever
To what extent? *or* How much?	very, hardly, almost, so, really most, nearly, quite, less, only

The Position of Adverbs

Adverbs may come before, after, or between the words they modify.

EXAMPLES **Quietly,** she will tiptoe from the stage. [*Quietly* comes before *will tiptoe,* the verb phrase it modifies.]

She will **quietly** tiptoe from the stage. [*Quietly* comes between *will* and *tiptoe,* the verb phrase it modifies.]

She will tiptoe **quietly** from the stage. [*Quietly* comes after *will tiptoe,* the verb phrase it modifies.]

Exercise 7 Identifying Adverbs

Identify the adverb in each of the following sentences. Then, give the word or words each adverb modifies.

EXAMPLE **1.** Williamsburg is a very interesting place.
1. very—interesting

1. Visitors to Williamsburg can truly imagine what life must have been like in the 1700s.
2. As you can see in the photo on the opposite page, Williamsburg was carefully built to resemble a small town of the past.
3. On one street a wigmaker slowly makes old-fashioned powdered wigs.
4. Nearby, a silversmith designs beautiful candlesticks, platters, and jewelry.

5. Down the block the bookbinder skillfully crafts book covers out of leather.
6. His neighbor, the blacksmith, is certainly important because he makes shoes for horses.
7. In colonial times people could seldom afford new shoes for themselves.
8. Nowadays, many curious tourists visit the bootmaker's shop.
9. Another very popular craftsman makes lovely musical instruments.
10. Williamsburg definitely gives tourists the feeling that they have visited the past.

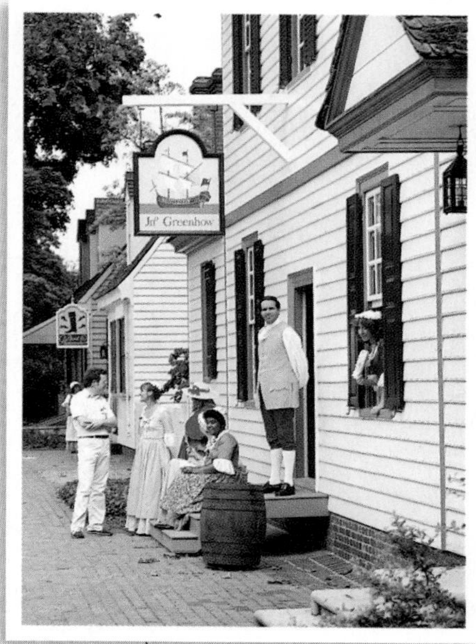

GRAMMAR

Exercise 8 **Identifying Adverbs and the Words They Modify**

Each of the following sentences contains at least one adverb. Identify each adverb. Then, give the word each adverb modifies. Be prepared to tell whether the word modified is a verb, an adjective, or an adverb.

EXAMPLE 1. If you look closely at a world map, you can quite easily find Brazil.

1. *closely—look; quite—easily; easily—can find*

HELP—
In the example sentence in Exercise 8, *look* is a verb, *easily* is an adverb, and *can find* is a verb.

1. The nation of Brazil actually covers almost half of the continent of South America.
2. A large portion of the Amazon rain forest grows there.
3. Many people have become more active in the preservation of the rain forest.
4. The loss of the rain forest may seriously affect the planet's climate.
5. Very early in the sixteenth century, Brazil was colonized by the Portuguese.
6. The country later became an independent republic.
7. Brazilians often say *Bom día*, which means "good day" in Portuguese.
8. In Brazil, sports fans can almost always find a soccer game in progress.
9. Brasília, the capital of Brazil, is an extremely modern city.
10. My aunt travels frequently, but she hasn't been to Brasília.

GRAMMAR

Exercise 9 **Writing Appropriate Adverbs**

Write the following sentences. Then, fill in each blank with an appropriate adverb. Use a different adverb in each sentence.

EXAMPLE **1.** ____ I learned some Spanish words.
1. Quickly, I learned some Spanish words.

1. I ____ watch TV after school.
2. You will ____ bait a hook yourself.
3. My little sister crept down the stairs ____.
4. Do you think that you can ____ find the answer to the math problem?
5. She is ____ eager for lunch.
6. In the evening, the African drums beat ____.
7. People in the highest balcony could ____ hear the speakers onstage.
8. Does thunder ____ follow lightning?
9. Would you dim the light ____ for me?
10. The sky over Honolulu was ____ clear that I could see for miles.

The Preposition

3c. A *preposition* is a word that shows the relationship between a noun or a pronoun and another word in the sentence.

EXAMPLES Your math book is **underneath** your coat, Allen. [The preposition *underneath* shows the relationship of *coat* to *book.*]

The one **behind** us honked his horn. [The preposition *behind* shows the relationship of *us* to *one.*]

Notice how changing the preposition in the following sentences changes the relationship between *hit* and *net.*

I hit the ball **over** the net.
I hit the ball **into** the net.
I hit the ball **under** the net.
I hit the ball **against** the net.
I hit the ball **across** the net.

TIPS & TRICKS

Many prepositions can be remembered as "anywhere a cat can go."

EXAMPLES
up the tree
behind the sofa
under the bed
through the door

Commonly Used Prepositions		
aboard	between	past
about	beyond	since
above	by	through
across	down	throughout
after	during	till
against	except	to
along	for	toward
among	from	under
around	in	underneath
at	into	until
before	like	up
behind	of	upon
below	off	with
beneath	on	within
beside	over	without

Some prepositions are made up of more than one word. These are called ***compound prepositions.***

Some Compound Prepositions		
according to	in addition to	next to
aside from	in place of	on account of
because of	in spite of	out of

The Prepositional Phrase

A preposition always has at least one noun or pronoun as an object. This noun or pronoun is called the ***object of the preposition.*** The preposition, its object, and any modifiers of the object make up a ***prepositional phrase.*** Generally, the object of the preposition follows the preposition.

EXAMPLES The pile **of dry leaves** had grown much larger. [The preposition *of* relates its object, *leaves,* to *pile.* The adjective *dry* modifies *leaves.*]

Reference Note

For more information about **prepositional phrases,** see Chapter 4.

He poured sauce **over the pizza.** [The preposition *over* relates its object, *pizza,* to *poured.* The article *the* modifies *pizza.*]

A preposition may have more than one object.

EXAMPLES This flea collar is **for cats** and **dogs.** [The preposition *for* has the two objects *cats* and *dogs.*]

My big sister had to decide **between the University of Wisconsin** and **Carroll College.** [The preposition *between* has the two objects *the University of Wisconsin* and *Carroll College.*]

GRAMMAR

TIPS & TRICKS

When you are looking for the object of a preposition, be careful. Sometimes the object comes before, not after, the preposition.

EXAMPLES
This is the movie that I told you about on Tuesday. [*That* is the object of the preposition *about.*]

STYLE TIP

Ending a sentence with a preposition is becoming more accepted in casual speech and informal writing. However, in formal writing it is generally best to avoid doing so.

Exercise 10 Identifying Prepositions and Their Objects

Identify the prepositional phrase in each of the following sentences. Underline the preposition, and circle its object.

EXAMPLE **1.** Otters are related to weasels and minks.
1. to (weasels) and (minks)

1. Yesterday afternoon, we planted a sapling behind the garage.
2. I bought a pattern for a sari.
3. They live near the airport.
4. For his birthday, my brother wants a guitar.
5. The pictures won't be developed until Friday or Monday.
6. I received a letter from my aunt and uncle.
7. The largest of all falcons is the arctic falcon.
8. What are the answers to the third and fourth questions?
9. There are many uses for peanuts.
10. I think that you might need a graphing calculator for that problem.

Exercise 11 Using Prepositions

Using the treasure map on the next page, give an appropriate preposition for each of the following sentences. Be sure to use a variety of prepositions.

EXAMPLE **1.** Can you find the *X* ____ this map?
1. on

1. Our rowboat rests ____ Mournful Beach.
2. Follow the path ____ the treasure.

3. Notice that Skull Rock lies ____ the cliff.
4. A sandy path leads ____ the stone ruins.
5. Did you jump ____ the fallen tree along the cliff?
6. Don't slip ____ the path up Lookout Hill!
7. Walk ____ the river.
8. Go ____ the waterfall!
9. You need not walk ____ the woods.
10. The treasure is ____ the open field and the gnarled oak tree.

Preposition or Adverb?

Some words may be used as both prepositions and adverbs. Remember that a preposition always has at least one noun or pronoun as an object. An adverb never does. If you can't tell whether a word is used as an adverb or a preposition, look for an object.

PREPOSITION Clouds gathered **above** us. [*Us* is the object of the preposition *above*.]

ADVERB Clouds gathered **above.** [no object]

GRAMMAR

PREPOSITION	Meet me **outside** the gym tomorrow morning. [*Gym* is the object of the preposition *outside.*]
ADVERB	Meet me **outside** tomorrow morning. [no object]

Exercise 12 Identifying Adverbs and Prepositions

Identify the italicized word in each of the following sentences as either an *adverb* or a *preposition.*

EXAMPLE **1.** *Above* us, wispy clouds filled the sky.
1. preposition

1. Before it rains, bring your bike *in.*
2. Had you ever seen an authentic Chinese New Year Parade *before*?
3. Bright red and green lights sparkled *down* the street.
4. Smoke from the campfire quickly disappeared *in* the heavy fog.
5. Andy turned the log *over* and found fat, squirming worms.
6. A submarine surfaced *next to* an aircraft carrier.
7. Will we read a poem by Nikki Giovanni *next*?
8. Turn that stereo *down* right now!
9. Millicent, did you remember to send a thank-you note *to* Mr. Bernstein?
10. What kind *of* dog is that?

You can remember the coordinating conjunctions as FANBOYS:

For
And
Nor
But
Or
Yet
So

The Conjunction

3d. A *conjunction* is a word that joins words or groups of words.

A ***coordinating conjunction*** joins words or word groups that are used in the same way.

Coordinating Conjunctions						
and	but	for	nor	or	so	yet

CONJUNCTIONS	beans **and** rice	movies **or** television
JOINING WORDS	sad **but** true	Egypt, Italy, **and** Spain

CONJUNCTIONS JOINING PHRASES	could write **or** could telephone
	after breakfast **but** before lunch
	cooking dinner **and** fixing breakfast

CONJUNCTIONS JOINING CLAUSES	I wanted to call, **but** it was late.
	The deer ran, **for** they smelled smoke.
	We knocked on the door, **and** they answered.

NOTE The word *for* can be used either as a conjunction or as a preposition.

CONJUNCTION The zebra turned toward the watering hole, **for** it was getting thirsty. [*For* joins the two sentences.]

PREPOSITION The zebra lay down in the shade **for** a nap. [*For* shows the relationship between the object *nap* and the verb *lay.*]

Correlative conjunctions are pairs of conjunctions that join words or word groups that are used in the same way.

Correlative Conjunctions	
both . . . . and	not only . . . but also
either . . . . or	whether . . . or
neither . . . . nor	

EXAMPLES **Both** Michael Jordan **and** David Robinson planned to play in the charity softball game. [two nouns]

Chris turned **neither** to the west **nor** to the east. [two prepositional phrases]

Not only did Babe Didrikson Zaharias set world records in track and field, **but** she **also** won more than fifty golf tournaments. [two independent clauses]

Exercise 13 Identifying Conjunctions

Identify the conjunction in each of the following sentences.

EXAMPLE **1.** Lena or I will pitch at batting practice.

1. or

Reference Note

For information on using **commas to join words, phrases, or clauses,** see page 268.

Reference Note

For more information on using **prepositions,** see page 62.

GRAMMAR

STYLE TIP

The conjunction *so* is often overused. Whenever you can, reword a sentence to avoid using *so*.

EXAMPLE
The scarves were on sale, so Hector bought two.

REVISED
Because the scarves were on sale, Hector bought two.

1. Julio and Roger joined the soccer team.
2. Whether it rains or not, we will be there.
3. Many Chinese plays include dancing and acrobatics.
4. The squirrels are burying nuts, for the long, cold winter will be here soon.
5. Did Nancy finish her final book report, or is she still working on it?
6. Not only strong but also graceful, the eagle is a beautiful bird.
7. He is not here, nor has he called.
8. The Boys Choir of Harlem will be singing tonight, so we bought tickets.
9. I already addressed the envelope but have not taken it to the post office yet.
10. I have enough money for either popcorn or juice.

MEETING THE CHALLENGE

Write a three-stanza poem in which each stanza consists of only a verb, an adverb, a prepositional phrase, a conjunction, and an interjection. (You can put the parts of speech in any order you choose.)

The Interjection

3e. An *interjection* is a word that expresses emotion.

An interjection has no grammatical relation to the rest of the sentence.

Often, an interjection is followed by an exclamation point.

EXAMPLES **Aha!** I knew you were hiding there.

Oops! I punched in the wrong numbers.

Is that a wasp? **Ouch!**

Sometimes an interjection is set off by a comma or a pair of commas.

EXAMPLES **Well,** what do you think?

The fish weighed**, oh,** about three pounds.

It's time to go**, alas.**

Common Interjections			
aha	hey	ouch	whew
alas	hooray	ow	wow
aw	oh	ugh	yikes
goodness	oops	well	yippee

Exercise 14 Writing Interjections

Have you ever heard the expression "an accident waiting to happen"? How many accidents are waiting to happen in the picture below? Write appropriate interjections to complete the following sentences that the people in the picture might say.

EXAMPLE **1.** ____, Vince, have you seen my other roller skate anywhere?

1. Oh, Vince, have you seen my other roller skate anywhere?

1. ____! I almost sat on the cat.
2. ____! Watch out for that book!
3. ____! Something on the stove is burning.
4. ____, Lila! Be careful with that milk!
5. ____, we will have to get a new cord for our lamp.
6. That smells so bad. ____!
7. Down the stairs comes Dad with, ____, the biggest present I've ever seen!
8. At last the party is over. ____! What a relief!
9. ____! Look out for the roller skate.
10. The party was, ____, interesting to say the least.

HELP

In Exercise 14, use a variety of interjections from the list on the previous page.

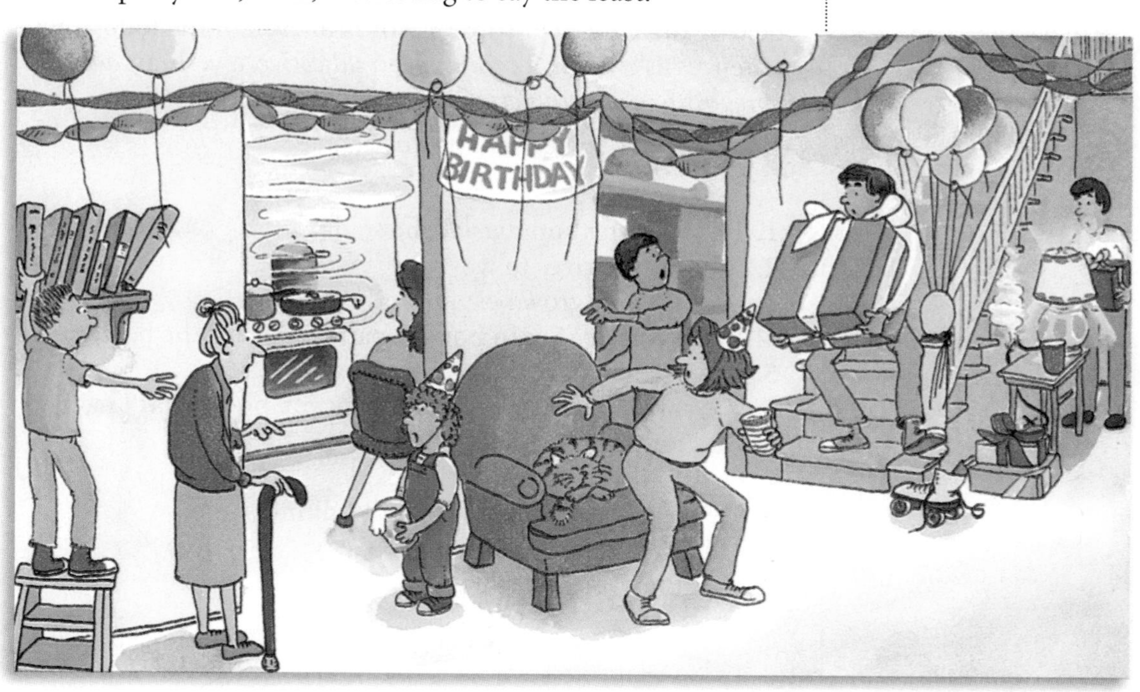

GRAMMAR

Determining Parts of Speech

3f. **The way a word is used in a sentence determines what part of speech the word is.**

Remember that you cannot tell what part of speech a word is until you know how it is used in a particular sentence. The same word may be used as different parts of speech.

VERB	Do you **like** guacamole?
PREPOSITION	That looks **like** guacamole.
ADVERB	The cat climbed **up.**
PREPOSITION	The cat climbed **up** the tree.
NOUN	We threw pennies into the wishing **well.**
ADJECTIVE	Janice isn't feeling **well.**
ADVERB	Did you do **well** on the test?
INTERJECTION	**Well,** what did he say?

HELP — You may want to review Chapter 2 before completing Review C.

Review C **Identifying Parts of Speech**

Identify the italicized word or words in each of the following sentences as a *noun*, a *pronoun*, an *adjective*, a *verb*, an *adverb*, a *preposition*, a *conjunction*, or an *interjection*.

EXAMPLE **1.** Some scientists *study* bones.
1. study—verb

1. The fans lined up *outside* the stadium.
2. *She* always drives to work.
3. Those *plants* grow best in sandy soil.
4. *Either* Rhea *or* Susan bought paper cups for the party.
5. Their parents *own* a card store.
6. N. Scott Momaday has written several books, *but* I have read only one of them.
7. *Oops*! I dropped my backpack.
8. We play *outdoors* every day until dinner time.
9. This videotape looks *new.*
10. You don't sound *too* happy.

Chapter Review

A. Identifying Verb Phrases and Helping Verbs

Identify the verb phrase in each of the following sentences. Then, underline each helping verb.

1. Tolbert could not see his brother in the fog.
2. Does Nguyen know the words to the song?
3. Dana might come to the party after all.
4. You should have brought your friend home for our special Chinese dinner last night.
5. Will you join the dance?

B. Identifying Action and Linking Verbs

Identify the verb in each of the following sentences as an *action verb* or a *linking verb.*

6. Ivan will be a superb guitar player someday.
7. Our dog Tadger brought an old bone home yesterday.
8. The whole-wheat bread smelled delicious.
9. Jacqui smelled the exhaust of the huge truck in the next lane of the freeway.
10. Will you look for me in the parade tomorrow?

C. Identifying Transitive and Intransitive Verbs

For each of the following sentences, identify the italicized verb as *transitive* or *intransitive.*

11. Francisco *opened* the door to the cellar.
12. Even the judge *seemed* uncertain about the answer.
13. The piano player *performs* twice each night.
14. We *performed* the play three times that weekend.
15. We *dine* every night at seven.

D. Identifying Adverbs and the Words They Modify

Identify the adverb or adverbs in each of the following sentences. Then, give the word each adverb modifies.

16. Mr. Chavez never watches television, but he listens to the radio often.
17. Carefully open the dryer, and check to see whether the clothes are too wet.
18. Did you awake very early?
19. Our old cat creeps gingerly from room to room.
20. Recently, I received an extremely interesting letter from my pen pal in Italy.

E. Identifying Prepositions and Their Objects

Identify the prepositional phrase in each of the following sentences. Underline the preposition and circle its object.

21. Tanya's pet hamster likes sleeping behind the computer.
22. Has your house ever lost power during a thunderstorm?
23. Some animals hunt only between dusk and dawn.
24. Bring me the largest head of lettuce, please.
25. According to my father, my uncle was a carpenter.

F. Identifying Verbs, Adverbs, Prepositions, Conjunctions, and Interjections

Identify each italicized word or word group in the following sentences as a *verb,* an *adverb,* a *preposition,* a *conjunction,* or an *interjection.*

26. I always have fun *at* a water park.
27. You *can slide* as fast as a sled down the huge water slide.
28. *Wow*! What a truly exciting ride that is!
29. Some parks *rent* inner tubes *inexpensively.*
30. You *may become* tired, *but* you won't be bored.

G. Determining Parts of Speech

Identify the italicized word in each of the following sentences as a *verb,* an *adjective,* an *adverb,* a *preposition,* or an *interjection.*

31. *Well,* I suppose you know what you are doing.
32. Ms. Jefferson will not be back in school until she is *well.*
33. When I sat down on the couch, my sister moved *over.*
34. The bowls are in the cupboard *over* the sink.
35. Did you *test* the batteries before you installed them?

Writing Application

Using Verbs in a List

Helping Verbs and Linking Verbs You and your classmates have decided to list some goals for the coming year. The theme for your lists is "How I Can Make the World a Better Place." Write a list of ten or more goals or resolutions for yourself. Make each of your resolutions a complete sentence. In your list, use the verb form *be* at least two times as a helping verb and three times as a linking verb.

Prewriting First, think of some realistic goals you can set for yourself. List as many goals as you can.

Writing From your list, choose the resolutions that seem the most important and the most manageable. Write each of them as a complete sentence.

Revising Read through your list. Are your resolutions clear and specific? Will you really be able to keep them? If not, revise or replace some of the resolutions.

Publishing Be sure that you've used a form of the verb *be* as a helping verb twice and as a linking verb three times. Make sure that all of your sentences are complete. Identify each helping verb and linking verb. Do a final check for errors in grammar, spelling, and punctuation. You and your classmates may want to have everyone in the class submit one or two of their favorite resolutions and compile a list of resolutions for the entire class. Post the list on the bulletin board.

Reference Note

For information on **complete sentences,** see page 386.

The Phrase and the Clause

Prepositional Phrases, Independent and Subordinate Clauses, Sentence Structure

1.0 Written and Oral English Language Conventions
Students write and speak with a command of standard English conventions appropriate to this grade level.
1.1 Use simple, compound, and compound-complex sentences; use effective coordination and subordination of ideas to express complete thoughts.
1.3 Use semicolons to connect independent clauses and commas when linking two clauses with a conjunction in compound sentences.

Diagnostic Preview

A. Identifying Adjective Phrases and Adverb Phrases

Identify the prepositional phrase in each of the following sentences, and tell whether the phrase is used as an *adjective phrase* or an *adverb phrase.* Then, give the word or words that the phrase modifies.

EXAMPLE **1.** This newspaper article on weather patterns is interesting.
1. on weather patterns; adjective phrase—article

1. The hikers are ready for a break.
2. Yesterday we rode our bikes through the park.
3. That store has something for everyone.
4. The Reverend Jesse Jackson spoke at the convention.
5. Most children like books with colorful pictures.
6. Students from both South America and North America attended the meet.

7. I wear heavy wool socks under my hiking boots.
8. Joel and Tina are participating in the Special Olympics.
9. The door to the secret room is locked.
10. According to the map, Tony's farm is just ahead.

B. Identifying Independent Clauses and Subordinate Clauses

For each of the following items, identify the italicized word group as either an *independent clause* or a *subordinate clause.*

EXAMPLE **1.** Marco got the tables ready *while Nestor set up the chairs.*
1. subordinate clause

11. *When school is out,* these halls seem quite lonely.
12. As far as I can tell, the red piece goes right here, and *the green piece goes under there.*
13. *If you exercise regularly,* your endurance will increase.
14. Just before the train sped across the road, *the bell rang,* and the gate went down.
15. *Geronimo,* who was a leader of the Apache, *died in the early part of the twentieth century.*

C. Identifying Types of Sentences

Identify each of the following sentences as *simple, compound, complex,* or *compound-complex.*

EXAMPLE **1.** Mom is late, but she will be here soon.
1. compound

16. Jaleel learned several African folk tales and recited them.
17. Raccoons and opossums steal our garbage as the dogs bark at them from inside the house.
18. The school bus stopped suddenly, but no one was hurt.
19. The dance committee has chosen a Hawaiian theme, so the volunteers will decorate the gym with flowers and greenery while Todd finds the right music.
20. Luis Gonzalez stepped up to the plate, and the crowd roared enthusiastically.

GRAMMAR

The Phrase

4a. **A *phrase* is a group of related words that is used as a single part of speech and that does not contain both a verb and its subject.**

EXAMPLES could have been looking [no subject]

in the backyard [no subject or verb]

to reach the highest shelf [no subject or verb]

Reference Note

For more about **clauses,** see page 89.

NOTE If a word group has both a subject and a verb, it is called a ***clause.***

EXAMPLES The coyote howled. [*Coyote* is the subject of the verb *howled.*]

when Al left [*Al* is the subject of the verb *left.*]

Phrases cannot stand alone as sentences. They must be used with other words to make a complete sentence.

PHRASE **in the box**
SENTENCE We put the CD's **in the box.**

Exercise 1 **Identifying Phrases**

Identify each of the following word groups as *a phrase* or *not a phrase.*

EXAMPLE **1.** some people enjoy skiing
1. not a phrase

1. ski lifts are used for Alpine skiing
2. down the snowy hills
3. slalom skiers race through gates
4. during the race
5. before the other skiers
6. skiers love the Colorado slopes
7. with tiny snowflakes on my face
8. for a hot cup of soup
9. we sat beside the cozy fire
10. maybe I can go again next year

Prepositional Phrases

4b. A ***prepositional phrase*** **includes a preposition, the object of the preposition, and any modifiers of that object.**

The prepositional phrase is one kind of phrase. Prepositions show the relationship of a noun or pronoun to another word in the sentence. The noun or pronoun that follows a preposition is called the ***object of the preposition.*** A preposition, its object, and any modifiers of the object are all part of the prepositional phrase.

EXAMPLES The man **from Singapore** was giving a speech. [The preposition *from* shows the relationship between the object *Singapore* and the noun *man.*]

The tree **in front of the window** blocks our view. [The compound preposition *in front of* shows the relationship between the object *window* and the noun *tree. The* modifies *window.*]

Please hand me the book **on the long, green table.** [The preposition *on* shows the relationship between the object *table* and the noun *book.* The adjectives *the, long,* and *green* modify *table.*]

A preposition may have more than one object.

EXAMPLES Aaron showed his arrowhead collection to **Tranh** and **her.** [The preposition *to* has two objects.]

The dinner of **baked chicken, salad,** and **two vegetables** also came with dessert. [The preposition *of* has three objects.]

Reference Note

For more about **objects of prepositions,** see page 63.

GRAMMAR

Exercise 2 Identifying Prepositional Phrases and Their Objects

For each of the following sentences, identify the prepositional phrase and circle the object or objects of the preposition.

EXAMPLE **1.** Dinosaurs and other giant reptiles roamed across the earth sixty-five million years ago.

1. across the (earth)

1. Although some of the dinosaurs were enormous, others were quite small.

GRAMMAR

HELP

Like some prepositional phrases, an *infinitive* is a word group beginning with the word *to.* However, a prepositional phrase has a noun or pronoun as its object, while an infinitive contains *to* and a verb form.

2. The drawing on this page includes a stegosaurus, twenty feet long, and a saltopus, about two feet long.
3. Many dinosaurs fed on plants and vegetables.
4. Dinosaurs with sharp teeth ate flesh.
5. Can you imagine seeing this flying reptile, the pterodactyl, above you?
6. It once lived in Europe and Africa.
7. Until a few years ago, scientists believed that all dinosaurs were coldblooded.
8. According to recent studies, however, some dinosaurs may have been warmblooded.
9. Many scientists say that birds and crocodiles may be related to dinosaurs.
10. Some people in science even claim that birds are living dinosaurs.

Exercise 3 Identifying Prepositional Phrases and Their Objects

Identify the prepositional phrase in each of the following sentences. Underline each preposition, and circle its object or objects.

EXAMPLE 1. The package was for my brother and me.
1. for my (brother) and (me)

1. The Sahara is a huge desert that lies south of the Mediterranean.

2. We waited until lunchtime.
3. The house across the street has green shutters.
4. Do not make repairs on the brakes yourself.
5. Maura said that the word *lasso* comes from a Spanish word that means "snare."
6. May I sit between you and him?
7. The woman in the blue uniform is my aunt.
8. The *Cherokee Phoenix* was the first newspaper printed in an American Indian language.
9. He is saving money for a stereo and a guitar.
10. The messenger slipped the note under the door.

Oral Practice **Using Appropriate Prepositional Phrases**

Read the following sentences aloud, filling in each blank with an appropriate prepositional phrase.

EXAMPLE **1.** We saw Jason ____.

1. We saw Jason at the mall.

1. My favorite comedian will appear ____.
2. That bus always arrives ____.
3. The fans ____ cheered every score.
4. The children tumbled ____.
5. The light ____ is broken.
6. Our car waited ____.
7. ____ sat a bald eagle.
8. A rich vein of gold ran ____.
9. ____ dashed a frightened squirrel.
10. His grandmother told us a story ____.

Adjective Phrases

4c. **A prepositional phrase that modifies a noun or pronoun is called an *adjective phrase.***

In other words, an adjective phrase is a prepositional phrase that is used as an adjective.

ADJECTIVE **Icy** chunks fell from the skyscraper.

ADJECTIVE PHRASE Chunks **of ice** fell from the skyscraper.

Reference Note

For more information about **adjectives,** see page 38.

STYLE  TIP

You can use adjective phrases to add details to your writing or to combine ideas into one sentence.

ORIGINAL
His favorite pastime is reading books.

REVISED
His favorite pastime is reading books **about space exploration.**

ORIGINAL
The squirrel was in the top of the tree. The squirrel chattered at me.

REVISED
The squirrel **in the top of the tree** chattered at me.

Adjective phrases answer the same questions that single-word adjectives answer.

What kind?	Which one?
How many?	How much?

EXAMPLES Mr. Arnaud ordered a dinner **of boiled crawfish.** [The adjective phrase modifies the noun *dinner.* The phrase answers the question *What kind?*]

The one **with the big pockets** costs a little more. [The adjective phrase modifies the pronoun *one.* The phrase answers the question *Which one?*]

There was enough room **for only three people.** [The adjective phrase modifies the noun *room.* The phrase answers the question *How much?*]

Notice in these examples that an adjective phrase generally follows the word it modifies.

Exercise 4 Identifying Adjective Phrases

Identify the adjective phrase in each of the following sentences. Then, give the word that the phrase modifies.

EXAMPLE 1. Diego Rivera was a famous painter from Mexico.
1. from Mexico—painter

1. People throughout the world enjoy Rivera's art.
2. One photograph on the next page shows an indoor mural that he painted.
3. Rivera often painted the walls of buildings.
4. His murals are beautiful examples of popular twentieth-century art.
5. Rivera's artworks often include symbols of Mexican culture.
6. His work with other Mexican artists was also very important.
7. Rivera was a major influence on the mural artist Juan O'Gorman.

8. O'Gorman's mural on the left beautifies a university library.
9. O'Gorman does not paint his murals; instead, he uses tiny pieces of colored tile.
10. The complicated pattern upon the library walls fascinates everyone who sees it.

Tile mural by Juan O'Gorman on the outside wall of a university library. SEF/Art Resource, New York

The Making of a Fresco Showing the Building of a City by Diego Rivera, 1931. True Fresco, 22'7" x 29'9", San Francisco Art Institute. Photo Credit: David Wakely

More than one adjective phrase may modify the same noun or pronoun.

EXAMPLE That painting **of sunflowers by van Gogh** is famous. [The two adjective phrases, *of sunflowers* and *by van Gogh,* both answer the question *Which painting?*]

An adjective phrase may also modify the object of another adjective phrase.

EXAMPLE A number **of the paintings by that artist** are landscapes. [The adjective phrase *of the paintings* answers the question *What kind of number?* The adjective phrase *by that artist* answers the question *Which paintings?*]

GRAMMAR

HELP—Some sentences in Exercise 5 contain more than one adjective phrase.

Exercise 5 Identifying Adjective Phrases

Identify each adjective phrase in the following sentences. Then, give the noun or pronoun the phrase modifies.

EXAMPLE 1. This book about birds of North America has won many awards for photography.

1. *about birds—book; of North America—birds; for photography—awards*

1. It explains the importance of flight in the survival of the bird population.
2. The key to successful flight is the structure of the feather.
3. As you can see, the shaft and the vane are the two main parts of a feather.
4. The area inside the quill of a feather is hollow.
5. Barbs on the shaft form a feather's vane.
6. The curves in the vane and the notches of the feather permit easy, quick movement.
7. The wings of airplanes resemble birds' wings.
8. Feathers on the wings and tails of birds often are quite showy.
9. Fast-flying birds like swifts usually have pointed wings.
10. Have you ever seen any of the birds that have these kinds of feathers?

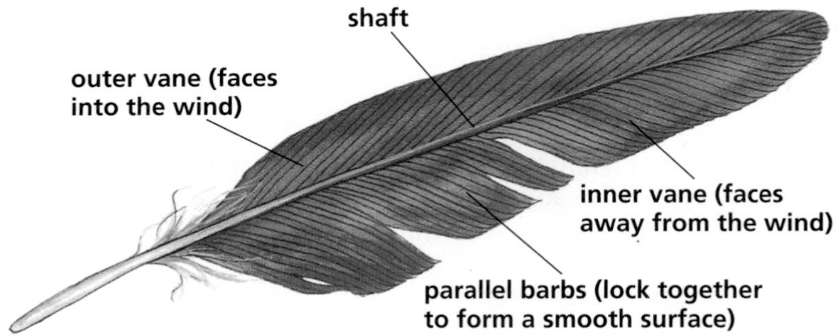

Exercise 6 Writing Adjective Phrases

Fill in the blank in each of the following sentences with an appropriate adjective phrase.

EXAMPLE 1. That storm _____ might be dangerous.

1. *That storm from the east might be dangerous.*

1. The shelf ____ is too high to reach.
2. I certainly hope that my gorilla costume wins a prize ____.
3. The girl ____ is one of my best friends.
4. The argument ____ really wasn't very important.
5. My favorite birthday present was the one ____.
6. Give your ticket to the man ____.
7. Did you see a bear on your trip ____?
8. Put the groceries ____ away, please.
9. My sister is the girl ____.
10. As I looked around the house, I noticed that an African design decorated the wall ____.

Adverb Phrases

4d. A prepositional phrase that is used to modify a verb, an adjective, or an adverb is called an ***adverb phrase.***

Reference Note

For more about **adverbs,** see page 59.

In other words, an adverb phrase is a prepositional phrase that is used as an adverb.

ADVERB We walk **there** every Saturday.

ADVERB PHRASE We walk **along the lake** every Saturday.

Adverb phrases answer the same questions that single-word adverbs answer.

When?	Where?	Why?
How?	How often?	How long?

EXAMPLES The statue stands **next to a large oak tree.** [The adverb phrase modifies the verb *stands* and answers the question *Where?*]

Ready **by dawn,** the travelers set out early to reach the capital. [The adverb phrase modifies the adjective *Ready* and answers the question *When?*]

Are these jeans long enough **for you**? [The adverb phrase modifies the adverb *enough* and answers the question *How?*]

HELP Be sure to ask yourself what question the phrase answers. Often, a phrase that comes right after a noun looks as though it is modifying that noun, but it is actually answering the question *When*?, *Where*?, or *How long*? about the verb. In the last example to the right, *over the bridge* does not tell us *which* bikes, but *where* we rode them.

HELP Remember, an adverb phrase modifies a verb, an adjective, or an adverb.

GRAMMAR

NOTE Adverb phrases may appear anywhere in a sentence. They may come before or after the words they modify. Also, other words may come between an adverb phrase and the word or words it modifies.

EXAMPLES **After swimming lessons,** Aunt Helen drove us home.

Dad has been afraid **of snakes** since he was a boy.

We rode our bikes **over the bridge.**

Exercise 7 Identifying Adverb Phrases

Identify the adverb phrase used in each of the following sentences. Then, write the word or words the phrase modifies.

EXAMPLE **1.** My hamster disappeared for three days.
1. for three days—disappeared

1. That mirror hung in the front hall.
2. The cat is afraid of thunderstorms.
3. The normally graceful acrobat plunged into the net but did not hurt herself.
4. Jimmy Smits will speak at our school.
5. Mom discovered several field mice in the cellar.
6. With great courage, Rosa Parks disobeyed the bus driver.
7. She jogs around the reservoir every morning.
8. In the evenings, they played word games.
9. Soon, my shoes were full of sand.
10. We have planted several new varieties of day lilies along the fence.

As with adjective phrases, more than one adverb phrase can modify the same word.

EXAMPLE Cesar Chavez worked **with the United Farm Workers for many years.** [Both adverb phrases, *with the United Farm Workers* and *for many years,* modify the verb *worked.*]

An adverb phrase may be followed by an adjective phrase that modifies the object of the preposition in the adverb phrase.

EXAMPLE Yesterday we went **to an exhibit of rare coins.** [The adverb phrase *to an exhibit* modifies the verb *went.* The adjective phrase *of rare coins* modifies *exhibit,* the object of the preposition in the adverb phrase.]

GRAMMAR

Exercise 8 Identifying Adverb Phrases

Identify the adverb phrase used in each of the following sentences. After each phrase, give the word or words the phrase modifies.

EXAMPLES

1. On Passover evening, we prepare a Seder, which is a Jewish holiday meal and ceremony.
   1. *On Passover evening—prepare*
2. Passover celebrates a time long ago when Jewish slaves freed themselves from their masters.
   2. *from their masters—freed*

1. On Passover, many of our relatives visit our home.
2. We always invite them for the Seder.
3. Our whole family helps with the preparations.
4. Soon, everything is ready for this special meal.
5. In this photograph you can see how beautiful our holiday table is.
6. Holding all the special Passover foods, the Seder plate is displayed in the center of the table.
7. On the plate is a roasted egg representing new life.
8. Horseradish, which represents slavery's bitterness, is placed near the egg.
9. The other carefully arranged foods are also used during the Passover feast.
10. Throughout the entire meal, everyone enjoys a variety of delicious foods.

GRAMMAR

Exercise 9 Writing Sentences with Adverb Phrases

Write ten sentences using the following word groups as adverb phrases. Underline each phrase. Then, draw an arrow from the phrase to the word or words it modifies.

EXAMPLE **1.** for the airport
1. My grandparents left for the airport.

1. down the hall
2. by them
3. in the mall
4. under the car
5. onto the diving board
6. over our heads
7. by a Navajo woman
8. through the sky
9. at five o'clock sharp
10. from Egypt

HELP

To determine if a prepositional phrase is an adjective or an adverb phrase, ask yourself what question the phrase answers. Adjective phrases modify a noun or a pronoun and answer the questions *What kind? How many? Which one?* and *How much?* Adverb phrases modify verbs, adjectives, or adverbs and answer the questions *When? Where? Why? How? How often?* and *How long?*

EXAMPLES
Please hand me the book **on the table**. [The phrase answers the question *Which book?*, so *on the table* is an adjective phrase.]
They bicycled **through the park.** [The phrase answers the question *Where?*, so *through the park* is an adverb phrase.]

Review A Identifying Adjective and Adverb Phrases

Each of the following sentences contains a prepositional phrase. Identify each phrase, and label it *adjective phrase* or *adverb phrase.*

EXAMPLES **1.** Wilma Rudolph won three gold medals in the 1960 Olympic games.
1. in the 1960 Olympic games—adverb phrase
2. Rudolph overcame many obstacles in her life.
2. in her life—adjective phrase

1. Wilma Rudolph did not have the childhood you might expect of a future Olympic athlete.
2. She and her twenty-one sisters and brothers were raised in a needy family.
3. Rudolph suffered from polio and scarlet fever when she was four years old.
4. Illnesses like these were often deadly.
5. For many years afterward, Rudolph used a leg brace when she walked.
6. Still, she never lost sight of her dreams.
7. She battled the odds against her.
8. With her family's help, she exercised hard every day.
9. All of her hard work made her strong.
10. Years later, she gained fame as a world-class athlete.

Review B Identifying Adjective and Adverb Phrases

Each of the following sentences contains at least one prepositional phrase. Identify each prepositional phrase, and label each one *adjective phrase* or *adverb phrase.*

EXAMPLES

1. In China, farmers are considered the backbone of the country.

   1. In China—adverb phrase; of the country—adjective phrase

2. With over one billion people to feed, China asks much from its farmers.

   2. With over one billion people to feed—adjective phrase; from its farmers—adverb phrase

1. Many of the Chinese people are farmers.
2. They generally work their farms by hand.
3. Chinese farmers usually use hand tools instead of large machines.
4. Farmland throughout China is carefully prepared, planted, and weeded.
5. Farmers also harvest their crops with great care.
6. In the hills, the Chinese make flat terraces.
7. As you can see, water from high terraces can flow to lower terraces.
8. Farmers build ridges around the terraces so that the terraces can be flooded during the growing season.
9. In flat areas, water is pumped out of the ground.
10. Another Chinese method of irrigation is shown in the lower picture.

GRAMMAR

GRAMMAR

HELP

Although two possible answers are shown in the example, you need to write only one sentence for each item in Review C.

Review C Using Prepositional Phrases in Sentences

Use each of the following prepositional phrases in a sentence. Then, underline the word or word group that the prepositional phrase modifies.

EXAMPLE **1.** across the street

1. They live across the street.

or

The store across the street is open.

1. among the papers
2. over the fence
3. for your sister
4. toward him
5. about the schedule
6. before class
7. along the wall
8. through the door
9. under the table
10. in the evening
11. across the narrow bridge
12. near you and Anna Maria
13. aboard the sailboat
14. to the Grand Canyon
15. beneath the handmade quilt
16. according to the scientist
17. beyond the farthest planet
18. next to the blue helmet
19. upon the highest tree branch
20. from my brother and me

Review D Writing Sentences with Adjective Phrases and Adverb Phrases

Use each of the following phrases in two separate sentences. In the first sentence, use the phrase as an adjective. In the second sentence, use the phrase as an adverb.

EXAMPLE **1.** in Indiana

1. The people in Indiana are called "Hoosiers."

We once lived in Indiana.

1. from California
2. in my class
3. along the path
4. under the bridge
5. behind you
6. throughout the summer
7. at the beginning
8. around the corner
9. during dinner
10. on the patio

The Clause

4e. **A *clause* is a word group that contains a verb and its subject and that is used as a sentence or as part of a sentence.**

Every clause contains a subject and a verb. However, not all clauses express complete thoughts. Clauses that express complete thoughts are called ***independent clauses.*** Clauses that do not express complete thoughts are called ***subordinate clauses.***

Independent Clauses

4f. **An *independent* (or *main*) *clause* expresses a complete thought and can stand by itself as a sentence.**

EXAMPLES Gertie [S] practices [V] soccer every day.

She [S] has improved [V] a great deal.

Her team [S] won [V] yesterday's game.

When an independent clause stands alone, it is called a sentence. Usually, the term *independent clause* is used only when such a clause is joined with another clause.

SENTENCE **He worked on the jigsaw puzzle.**

INDEPENDENT CLAUSE After Kevin had fed the cats, **he worked on the jigsaw puzzle.**

GRAMMAR

HELP

A subordinate clause that is capitalized and punctuated as if it were a sentence is a **sentence fragment.** Avoid using sentence fragments in your writing.

Reference Note

For more on **correcting sentence fragments,** see page 386.

Subordinate Clauses

4g. A *subordinate* (or *dependent*) *clause* does not express a complete thought and cannot stand by itself as a complete sentence.

EXAMPLES if you finish on time (S: you, V: finish)

which we found on the sidewalk (S: we, V: found)

Subordinate means "lesser in rank or importance." A subordinate clause must be joined with at least one independent clause to make a sentence and express a complete thought.

SUBORDINATE CLAUSES
that Dad cooked for us
if you set realistic goals
before the sun sets

SENTENCES
We all enjoyed the dinner **that Dad cooked for us.**

If you set realistic goals, you are more likely to succeed.

Before the sun sets, I need to mow the lawn.

Notice the words that begin the subordinate clauses: *that, if,* and *before.* The chart below lists some other words that can signal the beginning of a subordinate clause.

Words Often Used to Begin Subordinate Clauses			
after	how	unless	which
although	if	until	while
as	since	when	who
as if	so that	whenever	whom
as though	than	where	whose
because	that	wherever	
before	though	whether	

Exercise 10 Identifying Independent and Subordinate Clauses

For each of the following items, identify the italicized word group as either an *independent clause* or a *subordinate clause.*

EXAMPLES 1. I'll do the experiment *if you will record the results.*
1. *subordinate clause*

2. *Ignacio,* who is an artist, *painted the banner.*
2. *independent clause*

1. *While Dad was sleeping,* we decorated the house for his birthday party.
2. Just as Terri came in the door, *the phone rang.*
3. Somalis, *who traditionally raise and export livestock,* are nomadic.
4. Before you accept the invitation, *ask your mother.*
5. Do you know *when the train should arrive*?
6. *Although he was better at social studies,* he loved art.
7. Two uniformed soldiers guarded the entrance *where an iron gate stood.*
8. When the snows melt, *these streams will fill and rush down to the valley.*
9. That art paper *that you are using* really soaks up ink.
10. *Toni Morrison,* whose parents were once sharecroppers, *won the Pulitzer Prize.*

Adjective Clauses

4h. An *adjective clause* is a subordinate clause that modifies a noun or pronoun.

Like an adjective or an adjective phrase, an adjective clause may modify a noun or a pronoun. Unlike an adjective phrase, an adjective clause contains both a subject and verb.

ADJECTIVE a **white** cat

ADJECTIVE PHRASE a cat **with white fur** [*With white fur* does not have a subject and verb.]

ADJECTIVE CLAUSE a cat **that has white fur** [*That has white fur* has a subject, *that,* and a verb, *has.*]

Reference Note

For information about **nouns,** see page 25. For information about **pronouns,** see page 30.

An adjective clause usually follows the noun or pronoun it modifies and tells *Which one?* or *What kind?*

EXAMPLES The runner **who came in second** was Tina. [The adjective clause modifies the noun *runner* and answers the question *Which one?*]

I would like a dog **that I could take for long walks.** [The adjective clause modifies the noun *dog* and answers the question *What kind?*]

Exercise 11 Identifying Adjective Clauses

Identify each adjective clause in the following sentences.

EXAMPLE **1.** Her coat was lined with fleece that kept her warm.
1. that kept her warm

1. Jordan, whose aunt once rode on the space shuttle, is visiting her this summer.
2. Grandfather gave me that arrowhead, which has been in our family for generations.
3. The doctor looked at the notes that the nurse had written.
4. What was the name of the man who helped us?
5. Panama hats, which are prized far and wide, are woven of jipijapa leaves.
6. We could not have done it without Harry, whose skill saved the day.
7. Have you heard of Sister Juana Ines de la Cruz, the Mexican nun who championed women's rights in 1691?
8. Argentina's pampas, where fine herds of cattle graze, offer ranchers rich and vast grasslands.
9. Since ancient times, Asian ginger has been prized for the tang that it gives many dishes.
10. Ric, whom Doris calls "The Prince," is always a good sport.

Exercise 12 Using Adjective Clauses in Sentences

Write ten sentences using the following word groups as adjective clauses.

EXAMPLE **1.** where I grew up
1. This is the street where I grew up.

1. which had been imported from Japan
2. who is always on time
3. that live in this ecosystem
4. where the roses grow
5. whose short stories appear in your text
6. whom you talked about yesterday
7. that was having a sale
8. which may or may not be true
9. for whom our school is named
10. whose hard work made this event possible

Adverb Clauses

4i. An *adverb clause* is a subordinate clause that modifies a verb, an adjective, or an adverb.

Like an adverb or an adverb phrase, an adverb clause may modify a verb, an adjective, or another adverb. Unlike an adverb phrase, an adverb clause contains a subject and verb.

ADVERB **Shyly,** the toddler hid behind her mother.

ADVERB PHRASE **With a shy smile,** the toddler hid behind her mother. [*With a shy smile* does not have a subject and verb.]

ADVERB CLAUSE **Since the toddler was shy,** she hid behind her mother. [*Since the toddler was shy* has a subject, *toddler,* and a verb, *was.*]

An adverb clause answers the following questions: *How? When? Where? Why? To what extent? How much? How long?* or *Under what conditions?*

EXAMPLES **After he had moved the books,** Marvin dusted the shelves. [The adverb clause tells *when* Marvin dusted the shelves.]

Then he put the books back **where they belonged.** [The adverb clause tells *where* he put the books.]

He cleaned his room **because it was very messy.** [The adverb clause tells *why* he cleaned his room.]

HELP—Introductory adverb clauses are usually set off by commas.

EXAMPLES
After we built the campfire, we roasted hot dogs.
Although the song is good, it is not one of their best.

Reference Note

For more information on **using commas to set off introductory elements,** see page 274.

GRAMMAR

Exercise 13 Identifying Adverb Clauses

Identify each adverb clause in the following sentences.

EXAMPLE **1.** Call when you can.
1. when you can

1. Tiny wildflowers sprang up wherever they could.
2. Unless you want to sink, do not pull that large plug at the bottom of the boat.
3. Wind blew softly across the sand dunes while the caravan made its way home.
4. As soon as the cows come in, they must be fed.
5. To our surprise, when we entered the woods, a dozen armadillos were foraging right in front of us.
6. Although the piano had not been used for some time, it was still in tune.
7. Unless the shipment arrives today, the order will not be ready on time.
8. Because the airplane had been painted yellow, it was easily seen from the ground.
9. I'm not going if you're not going.
10. I had never heard anyone sing as he did.

STYLE TIP

In most cases, deciding where to place an adverb clause is a matter of style, not correctness.

As he leapt across the gorge, Rex glanced back at his alien pursuers.

Rex glanced back at his alien pursuers as he leapt across the gorge.

Which sentence might you use in a science fiction story? The sentence to choose would be the one that looks and sounds better in the context—the rest of the paragraph to which the sentence belongs.

Exercise 14 Writing Sentences with Adverb Clauses

Write twenty sentences using the following word groups as adverb clauses.

EXAMPLE **1.** as soon as he can
1. He will be here as soon as he can.

1. when I save enough money
2. if things go according to the schedule
3. since we have lived here
4. after the assembly was over
5. before school starts
6. although we couldn't speak Japanese
7. than she is
8. because they were going to the rink
9. until the sun set
10. while the lions are drinking from the river

11. as long as the band plays
12. whenever the train arrives at the station
13. unless the dog is on a leash
14. wherever you see grasshoppers
15. although the trail was steep
16. when Alexa won the marathon
17. so that we could use the computer
18. while the storm was raging
19. than you are
20. as though they had run ten miles

GRAMMAR

Review E Identifying Clauses

For each of the following sentences, identify the italicized clause as an *independent clause* or a *subordinate clause.* Then, identify each subordinate clause as an *adjective clause* or an *adverb clause.*

EXAMPLE **1.** Those Japanese sandals *that you are wearing* are zoris.

1. subordinate clause—adjective clause

1. *Camels stamped and bellowed in annoyance* when packs were put on them.
2. Aloe plants, *which originated in Africa,* are now widely available in the United States.
3. As far as scientists can tell, *there is no connection between these two events.*
4. *If you adjust the blinds,* you won't have that glare on your monitor.
5. *The castanets,* which were quite old, *had been Melanie's grandmother's.*
6. *You were always singing* when you were little.
7. Three Indian elephants patiently towed the logs *that had just been cut.*
8. Stay with us *as long as you want.*
9. *Southeast Asia depends heavily on the seasonal rain* that the monsoons bring.
10. The Forbidden City, *where China's emperors lived,* is enclosed by walls.

GRAMMAR

HELP
Although two possible answers are shown in the example, you need to write only one sentence for each item in Review F.

Review F **Writing Sentences with Clauses and Prepositional Phrases**

Use each of the following phrases and clauses in a sentence. Then, underline the word that the phrase or clause modifies.

EXAMPLE **1.** under the flat rock

1. Under the flat rock lived many odd insects.

or

The insects under the flat rock wriggled.

1. with a cowboy hat
2. who told us about computers
3. under the surface
4. since the club meets in the afternoon
5. for yourself
6. through the puddles
7. over the treetops
8. before we ate dinner
9. that grow along the fence
10. toward us

Sentence Structure

Simple Sentences

4j. A *simple sentence* has one independent clause and no subordinate clauses.

Reference Note
For information about **independent clauses** and **subordinate clauses,** see page 89.

A simple sentence may have a compound subject, a compound verb, or both. Although a compound subject has two or more parts, it is still considered a single subject. In the same way, a compound verb or verb phrase is considered one verb.

EXAMPLES My **mother belongs** to the Friends of the Library. [single subject and single verb]
(S: mother; V: belongs)

Argentina and **Chile are** in South America. [compound subject]
(S: Argentina; S: Chile; V: are)

S V V
Jeannette read *Stuart Little* and **reported** on it. [compound verb]

S S V
The **acrobats** and **jugglers did** amazing tricks and
V
were rewarded with a standing ovation. [compound subject and compound verb]

Compound Sentences

4k. A *compound sentence* consists of two or more independent clauses, usually joined by a comma and a connecting word.

In a compound sentence, a coordinating conjunction (*and, but, for, nor, or, so,* or *yet*) generally connects the simple sentences. A comma usually comes before the conjunction in a compound sentence.

EXAMPLES I forgot my lunch**,** **but** Dad ran to the bus with it.

She likes sweets**,** **yet** she seldom eats them.

Notice in the second example above that, usually, a sentence is compound if the subject is repeated.

Sometimes the independent clauses in a compound sentence are joined by a semicolon.

EXAMPLES The blue one is mine**;** it has my initials on it.

The spider is not an insect**;** it is an arachnid.

Reference Note

For more information about **using commas with conjunctions,** see page 270. For more about using **semicolons,** see page 279.

STYLE  TIP

Sometimes you can combine two simple sentences to make one compound sentence. Just connect the two simple sentences by using a comma and *and, but, for, nor, or, so,* or *yet.*

ORIGINAL
The rain has stopped. The sky is still dreary and gray.

COMBINED
The rain has stopped**,** **but** the sky is still dreary and gray.

Combining sentences this way can help make your writing smoother and more interesting.

Exercise 15 Identifying Simple Sentences and Compound Sentences

Identify each of the following sentences as *simple* or *compound.*

EXAMPLE 1. That story by Lensey Namioka is good, and you should read it.
1. compound

1. My dad and I like tacos, and we're making them for dinner.
2. Some trees and shrubs live thousands of years.
3. It rained, but we marched in the parade anyway.
4. Mr. Edwards will lead the singing, for Ms. Cruz is ill.

5. My aunts, uncles, and cousins from Costa Rica visited us last summer.
6. I had worked hard all morning, yet I had not finished the job by lunchtime.
7. Abe peeled and chopped all of the onions and dumped them into a huge pot.
8. All ravens are crows, but not all crows are ravens.
9. Chippewa and Ojibwa are two names for the same American Indian people.
10. I liked this movie best; it was more exciting than the others.

Review G Identifying Simple Sentences and Compound Sentences

Identify each of the following sentences as *simple* or *compound.*

EXAMPLE 1. Have you or Sandy ever seen the movie *The Bridge on the River Kwai*?
1. simple

1. My stepbrother is only eight years old, and he is fascinated by bridges.
2. We buy postcards with pictures of bridges, for he likes to collect them.
3. He has several cards of stone bridges.

4. Stone bridges are strong but are costly to build.
5. Many bridges are quite beautiful.
6. The Central American rope bridge shown here is one kind of suspension bridge.
7. The modern bridge on the previous page is another kind of suspension bridge.
8. Suspension bridges may look dangerous, yet most are safe.
9. Bridges must be inspected regularly.
10. My stepbrother collects postcards of bridges, and I collect postcards of towers.

Complex Sentences

4l. A *complex sentence* contains one independent clause and at least one subordinate clause.

Subordinate clauses usually begin with a word such as *who, whose, which, that, after, as, if, since,* and *when.* A subordinate clause can appear at the beginning, in the middle, or at the end of a complex sentence.

EXAMPLES Before Chen planted his garden, he made a sketch of the layout.

independent clause he made a sketch of the layout (S: he; V: made)

subordinate clause Before Chen planted his garden (S: Chen; V: planted)

When bees collect pollen, they pollinate the plants that they visit.

independent clause they pollinate the plants (S: they; V: pollinate)

subordinate clause When bees collect pollen (S: bees; V: collect)

subordinate clause that they visit (S: they; V: visit)

GRAMMAR

MEETING THE CHALLENGE

Write directions telling someone exactly how to get to your favorite place. Use at least five prepositional phrases, three adverb clauses, and two adjective clauses to add details that help your reader follow your directions. When you are finished, underline the prepositional phrases, adverb clauses, and adjective clauses in your directions.

Compound-Complex Sentences

4m. A sentence with two or more independent clauses and at least one subordinate clause is a ***compound-complex sentence.***

EXAMPLE I picked up the branches that had fallen during the storm, and Rosa mowed the grass.

	S V
independent clause	I picked up the branches
	S V
independent clause	Rosa mowed the grass
	S V
subordinate clause	that had fallen during the storm

Exercise 16 **Classifying Sentences by Structure**

Identify each of the following sentences as *simple, compound, complex,* or *compound-complex.*

EXAMPLE **1.** It was raining, but the sun was shining when we looked out the window.

1. compound-complex

1. Cuba's capital is Havana, and this beautiful city has been the center of Cuban culture since 1552.
2. The heavy branches of an oak tree hung over our table and shaded us from the sun.
3. When you are looking at a work by Monet, stand back at least fifteen or twenty feet.
4. As it happens, you're right and I'm wrong.
5. Seashells filled Liz's suitcase and spilled onto the floor.
6. According to our records, your next appointment isn't until next month, but we do thank you for your call.
7. The Internet and other forms of electronic communication are shaping the world's future.
8. Because opinions are still divided, further discussion will be necessary.
9. The clock's minute hand is moving, but the second hand has stopped.
10. Between Asia and Africa lies a land bridge that is known as the Sinai Peninsula.

Chapter Review

A. Identifying Adjective and Adverb Phrases

Identify the prepositional phrase in each of the following sentences, and tell whether the phrase is used as an *adjective phrase* or an *adverb phrase.* Then, give the word or words that the phrase modifies.

1. The crowd waved banners during the game.
2. That book about the Underground Railroad is interesting.
3. Have you seen the pictures of the Wongs' new house?
4. The water in my glass was cold.
5. Uncle Eduardo carefully knocked the snow off his boots.
6. You should travel to Utah if you have never seen a beautiful desert.
7. Do you have the new CD by the Three Tenors?
8. The swings in the park are a bit rusty.
9. A clown handed balloons to the children.
10. The mail carrier left a package on the front porch.

B. Identifying Independent and Subordinate Clauses

For each of the following items, identify the italicized word group as either an *independent clause* or a *subordinate clause.*

11. Yamile and her family enjoyed their vacation in Indonesia, *which is a country made up of thousands of islands.*
12. *Whenever he pressed the button,* another buzzer sounded.
13. After Luis worked out on the weight machines and swam ten laps in the pool, *he took a shower.*
14. Bring an extra sweatshirt with you *if you have one.*
15. *Martin enjoys speaking Japanese* when he visits the Nakamuras.
16. Before you leave for school, *do you always remember to brush your teeth*?
17. Is Rena the one *who went to New Zealand*?
18. *Did our grandmother ever tell you* how she came to this country from Latvia?

19. *Unless you don't like getting wet and working outside all day,* we could use your help at the Spanish club car wash on Saturday.
20. *Mr. Boylan,* whom we met several times at school events, *is the author of a novel.*

C. Identifying Clauses

For each of the following sentences, identify each italicized clause as an *adjective clause* or an *adverb clause.*

21. *When you have a chance,* send me an e-mail.
22. Anyone *who knows Vita* can tell you how smart she is.
23. *When the Castillo family arrived at the ski lodge that evening,* they went right to bed.
24. The theater company, *which had come to town only that afternoon,* put on a spectacular show.
25. Sherlock Holmes, *whose creator was Sir Arthur Conan Doyle,* is probably the most famous fictional detective in literature.

D. Identifying Types of Sentences

Identify each of the following sentences as *simple, compound, complex,* or *compound-complex.*

26. Sir Ernest Shackleton was an Antarctic explorer.
27. He wanted to be the first man to reach the South Pole, and in 1908, he led a party that came within ninety-seven miles of the pole.
28. In 1914, he led the British Imperial Trans-Antarctic Expedition to Antarctica.
29. Shackleton intended to cross Antarctica, which no one else had ever crossed before.
30. Before the expedition could land, Shackleton's ship, the *Endurance,* was trapped in the ice of the Weddell Sea for ten months.
31. Finally, the ice crushed the ship, and Shackleton and his men were stranded on the ice for five more months.
32. The men escaped the ice in small boats, and they landed on Elephant Island, where they lived in a makeshift camp.

33. Shackleton and five other men sailed to South Georgia Island, where they sought help from Norwegian whalers.

34. Shackleton's first attempts to return to Elephant Island did not succeed, but he finally rescued his crew on August 30, 1916.

35. Shackleton's expedition failed to cross Antarctica, but he brought all of his men home safely.

Writing Application

Using Prepositional Phrases in a Story

Using Prepositional Phrases to Add Detail The Friends of Animals Society is having a contest for the best true-life pet story. The winner of the contest will have his or her story published in the local newspaper. Write a brief story to enter in the contest. In your story, tell about an unusual pet that you have heard about or known. Use at least five adjective phrases and five adverb phrases in your story.

Prewriting First, you will need to choose a pet about which to write. Then, jot down details about how the animal looks and how it acts. In your notes, focus on a specific time when the animal did something funny or amazing.

Writing Begin your draft with an attention-grabbing paragraph. Introduce and describe your main character. Be sure that you have included any human characters that play a part in the story. Also, describe the story's setting—for example, your kitchen, your neighbor's backyard, or the woods.

Revising Ask a friend to read your draft. Depending on what your friend tells you, you may need to add, cut, or rearrange details. Make sure you have used at least five adjective phrases and five adverb phrases.

Publishing Check your story carefully for errors in grammar, spelling, and punctuation. You and your classmates may want to collect your stories into a booklet. Along with your stories, you might include pictures or drawings of the pets you have written about.

Complements

Direct and Indirect Objects, Subject Complements

1.0 Written and Oral English Language Conventions
Students write and speak with a command of standard English conventions appropriate to this grade level.

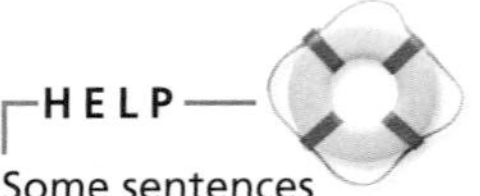

HELP
Some sentences in the Diagnostic Preview have more than one complement.

Diagnostic Preview

Identifying Complements

Identify each complement in the following sentences as a *direct object,* an *indirect object,* a *predicate nominative,* or a *predicate adjective.*

EXAMPLE **1.** Many forests are cold and snowy.
1. cold—predicate adjective; snowy—predicate adjective

1. We made our parents a family tree for their anniversary.
2. The sun disappeared, and the wind suddenly grew cold.
3. The home of the former president is now a library and museum.
4. The newspaper published an article and an editorial about ex-Mayor Sharon Pratt Dixon.
5. My uncle gave my sister and brother ice skates.
6. After the long hike, all of the Scouts felt sore and sleepy.
7. Leaders of the Ojibwa people held a meeting last summer.
8. I wrote my name and address in my book.
9. Your dog certainly appears healthy to me.
10. They always send us grapefruit and oranges from Florida.
11. Most stars in our galaxy are invisible to the human eye.

12. Did the workers capture an alligator in the sewer system?
13. Our trip on the Staten Island ferry became an adventure.
14. The air show featured balloons and parachutes.
15. The maples are becoming gold and red early this year.
16. My parents bought themselves several Celia Cruz CDs.
17. Aunt Kathleen gave Ricardo and me tickets for the show.
18. The two most popular sports at my school are football and volleyball.
19. The water in the pool looked clean and fresh.
20. My mother's homemade Sabbath bread tastes delicious.

Recognizing Complements

5a. A *complement* is a word or word group that completes the meaning of a verb.

Every sentence has a subject and a verb. Sometimes the subject and the verb can express a complete thought all by themselves.

EXAMPLES
S **V**
Adriana swam.

S **V**
The puppy was sleeping.

Often, however, a verb needs a complement to complete its meaning.

INCOMPLETE
S **V**
My aunt found [*what?*]

COMPLETE
S **V** **C**
My aunt found a **wallet.** [The noun *wallet* completes the meaning of the verb *found.*]

INCOMPLETE
S **V**
Sarah bought [*what?*]

COMPLETE
S **V** **C** **C**
Sarah bought **herself** a new **jacket.** [The pronoun *herself* and the noun *jacket* complete the meaning of the verb *bought.*]

TIPS & TRICKS

You can remember the difference in spelling between *complement* (the grammar term) and *compliment* (an expression of affection or respect) by remembering that a compl**e**ment compl**e**tes a sentence.

GRAMMAR

TIPS & TRICKS

To find the complement in a sentence, try this trick. Cross out all the prepositional phrases first. Then, look for the subject, verb, and any complements that are in the rest of the sentence.

EXAMPLE

James threw the ball ~~over the defender~~ and ~~into the receiver's arms~~. [The subject is *James.* The verb is *threw. Defender* and *arms* cannot be complements because they are both in prepositional phrases. The complement is *ball.*]

Reference Note

For more about **adverbs,** see page 59. For more about **prepositions** and **prepositional phrases,** see page 62.

INCOMPLETE — The longcase clock (S) was (V) [*what?*]

COMPLETE — The longcase clock (S) was (V) an **antique.** (C) [The noun *antique* completes the meaning of the verb *was.*]

INCOMPLETE — The elephant (S) seemed (V) [*what?*]

COMPLETE — The elephant (S) seemed (V) **tired.** (C) [The adjective *tired* completes the meaning of the verb *seemed.*]

An adverb is never a complement.

ADVERB — The koala chews slowly. [The adverb *slowly* modifies the verb by telling *how* the koala chews.]

COMPLEMENT — The koala chews eucalyptus **leaves.** [The noun *leaves* completes the meaning of the verb *chews* by telling *what* the koala chews.]

A complement is never a part of a prepositional phrase.

OBJECT OF PREPOSITION — Hannah is riding to her friend's house. [The noun *house* is the object of the preposition *to.*]

COMPLEMENT — Hannah is riding her **bicycle.** [The noun *bicycle* completes the meaning of the verb phrase *is riding* by telling *what* Hannah is riding.]

Exercise 1 Writing Complements

Write an appropriate complement to complete each of the following sentences.

EXAMPLE **1.** The class seemed ____ to go on the field trip.

1. happy

1. Yesterday, Uncle Joe sent me a ____ in the mail.
2. Did you lend ____ your calculator?
3. After college, she became a ____ in Chicago.
4. This puppy looks ____ to me, Doctor.
5. Is your brother still a ____ in Montana?
6. The sky was ____ and ____ that winter night.
7. Give ____ a hand, please.

8. Was that ____ in the dinosaur costume?
9. My little brother ran into the house and showed us a ____.
10. Next on the program for the recital, the middle school chorus will sing ____.

Objects of Verbs

Direct objects and *indirect objects* complete the meaning of transitive verbs.

Direct Objects

The direct object is one type of complement. It completes the meaning of a transitive verb.

Reference Note

For more information about **transitive verbs,** see page 55.

5b. A *direct object* is a noun, pronoun, or word group that tells *who* or *what* receives the action of the verb.

A direct object answers the question *Whom?* or *What?* after a transitive verb.

EXAMPLES My brother bought a **model.** [My brother bought *what*? Bought a *model.* The noun *model* receives the action of the verb *bought.*]

Jan called **somebody** for the assignment. [Jan called *whom*? Called *somebody.* The pronoun *somebody* receives the action of the verb *called.*]

Corey studied **Mother Teresa** in his history class. [Corey studied *whom*? Studied *Mother Teresa*. The compound noun *Mother Teresa* receives the action of the verb *studied.*]

A direct object may be a compound of two or more objects.

EXAMPLES Did the car have spoked **wheels** and a **spoiler**? [The compound direct object of the verb *Did have* is *wheels* and *spoiler.*]

She needed **glue, paint,** and **decals** for her model. [The compound direct object of the verb *needed* is *glue, paint,* and *decals.*]

Reference Note

For more about **linking verbs,** see page 53.

GRAMMAR

A direct object can never follow a linking verb because a linking verb does not express action.

LINKING VERB Julia Morgan **was** an architect. [The verb *was* does not express action; therefore, *architect* is not a direct object.]

Exercise 2 Identifying Direct Objects

Identify each direct object in the following sentences. Remember that a direct object may be compound.

EXAMPLE **1.** Do you enjoy books and movies about horses?

1. books, movies

1. If so, then you probably know some stories by Marguerite Henry.
2. Her books about horses have thrilled readers for more than sixty years.
3. Henry wrote many popular books, such as *Misty of Chincoteague* and *King of the Wind.*
4. Her book *King of the Wind* won the Newbery Medal in 1949.

5. The book tells the adventures of the boy Agba and his beautiful Arabian horse.
6. Agba fed milk and honey to the newborn colt.
7. Sometimes the playful colt bit Agba's fingers.
8. The head of the stables often mistreated Agba and the young colt.
9. Later, the boy and the horse left their home and traveled to England.
10. Read *King of the Wind*, and learn more about the adventures of Agba and his horse.

Wesley Dennis, illustration from *King of the Wind* by Marguerite Henry. Illustration © 1947; copyright renewed 1976 by Morgan and Charles Reid Dennis.

Indirect Objects

The indirect object is another type of complement. Like the direct object, the indirect object helps complete the meaning of a transitive verb. If a sentence has an indirect object, it must also have a direct object.

5c. An *indirect object* is a noun, pronoun, or word group that usually comes between the verb and the direct object. An indirect object tells *to whom* or *to what* or *for whom* or *for what* the action of the verb is done.

EXAMPLES I gave that **problem** some thought. [The noun *problem* is the indirect object of the verb *gave* and answers the question "*To what* did I give some thought?"]

Dad bought **himself** some peanuts. [The pronoun *himself* is the indirect object of the verb *bought* and answers the question "*For whom* did Dad buy peanuts?"]

Luke sent **David Robinson** a fan letter. [The compound noun *David Robinson* is the indirect object of the verb *sent* and answers the question "*To whom* did Luke send a fan letter?"]

TIPS & TRICKS

Here is a trick you can use to see whether a word is an indirect object. Move the word from before the direct object to after it, and add either *to* or *for*. If the sentence still makes sense, you know the word is an indirect object in the original sentence.

EXAMPLE
Carol sold Steve her old television.

Carol sold her old television **to** Steve. [The sentence means the same thing either way.]

GRAMMAR

Reference Note

For more information about **prepositional phrases** and **objects of prepositions,** see page 77.

If the word *to* or *for* is used, the noun, pronoun, or word group following it is part of a prepositional phrase and cannot be an indirect object.

OBJECTS OF PREPOSITIONS	The ship's captain gave orders to the **crew.**
	Vinnie made some lasagna for **us.**
INDIRECT OBJECTS	The ship's captain gave the **crew** orders.
	Vinnie made **us** some lasagna.

Like a direct object, an indirect object can be compound.

EXAMPLES She gave **Ed** and **me** the list of summer activities. [*Ed* and *me* are indirect objects of the verb *gave.* They answer the question "*To whom* did she give the list?"]

Did the peacock show **you** and your **sister** its tail feathers? [*You* and *sister* are indirect objects of the verb *Did show.* They answer the question "*To whom* did the peacock show its tail feathers?"]

HELP

Some sentences in Exercise 3 do not have indirect objects.

Exercise 3 Identifying Direct and Indirect Objects

Identify the direct objects and indirect objects in the following sentences. Remember not to confuse objects of prepositions with direct objects and indirect objects.

EXAMPLE **1.** Gabriel sent me a postcard from Ecuador.

1. me—indirect object; postcard—direct object

1. In Ecuador, Gabriel visited many of his relatives.
2. His aunt Luz and uncle Rodrigo showed him the railroad in San Lorenzo.
3. They also visited the port in Esmeraldas.
4. Ecuador exports bananas and coffee.
5. Gabriel's cousin showed him some other sights.
6. She told Gabriel stories about Ecuadoran heroes.
7. Gabriel and his relatives rode a train high into the Andes Mountains.
8. They took photos from the train.
9. Gabriel enjoyed his visit to Ecuador.
10. He brought us some unusual souvenirs.

Exercise 4 Writing Direct and Indirect Objects

Write an appropriate direct or indirect object to complete each of the following sentences.

EXAMPLE
1. This weekend we are painting the ____.
1. *kitchen*

1. The President made a ____ on television last night.
2. Did your dad teach ____ those magic tricks?
3. Wow! The governor wrote ____ a letter!
4. Then Marianne asked ____ the question in all our minds.
5. A mechanic replaced the truck's ____.
6. Save ____ a place at your table.
7. Are you still studying ____?
8. Okay, I'll owe ____ two hours' use of my skateboard.
9. Have you taken ____ for a walk?
10. Sam made ____ a table in shop class.

Review A Identifying Direct and Indirect Objects

Identify the direct objects and indirect objects in the following sentences.

EXAMPLE
1. Have you ever given board games much thought?
1. *board games—indirect object; thought—direct object*

1. For centuries, people have enjoyed games of strategy.
2. Interest in strategy games has given us chess and checkers.
3. My brother showed me a book about different kinds of board games.
4. Board games reflect many different interests and appeal to all kinds of people.
5. Some games teach players lessons useful in careers and sports.
6. Of course, word games can give people hours of fun.
7. During the more difficult word games, Mrs. Hampton sometimes helps Chen and me.
8. Do you like trivia games?
9. Sharon's uncle bought Ronnie and her one of the new quiz games.
10. A popular television show inspired the game.

GRAMMAR

HELP—
Some sentences in Review A do not have indirect objects.

Subject Complements

5d. A *subject complement* is a word or word group that is in the predicate and that identifies or describes the subject.

A linking verb connects a subject complement to the subject.

EXAMPLES Mrs. Suarez is a helpful **neighbor.** [The subject complement *neighbor* identifies the subject *Mrs. Suarez.* The linking verb *is* connects *Mrs. Suarez* and *neighbor.*]

The airport appears very **busy.** [The subject complement *busy* describes the subject *airport.* The linking verb *appears* connects *airport* and *busy.*]

What smells so **good**? [The subject complement *good* describes the subject *What.* The linking verb *smells* connects *What* and *good.*]

He was the **one** in the middle of the line, in fact. [The subject complement *one* identifies the subject *He.* The linking verb *was* connects *He* and *one.*]

The author of that story is **Anne McCaffrey.** [The subject complement *Anne McCaffrey* identifies the subject *author.* The linking verb *is* connects *author* and *Anne McCaffrey.*]

Subject complements always complete the meaning of linking verbs, not action verbs.

Common Linking Verbs					
appear	become	grow	remain	smell	stay
be	feel	look	seem	sound	taste

The two kinds of subject complements are the *predicate nominative* and the *predicate adjective.*

Predicate Nominatives

5e. A *predicate nominative* is a word or word group that is in the predicate and that identifies the subject or refers to it.

HELP

To find the subject complement in a question, rearrange the sentence to make a statement.

EXAMPLE
Is Crystal the pitcher for the softball team?
Crystal is the **pitcher** for the softball team.

Reference Note

For more about **linking verbs,** see page 53.

TIPS & TRICKS

Remember that some linking verbs (such as *appear, feel, grow, smell,* and *taste*) can also be used as action verbs.

LINKING VERB
The yogurt **smells** sour.

ACTION VERB
I **smell** fresh bagels.

In sentences with verbs like these, first decide whether the verb is used as a linking verb or an action verb. Then, determine what kind of complement, if any, the sentence contains.

A predicate nominative may be a noun, a pronoun, or a word group that functions as a noun. A predicate nominative is connected to the subject by a linking verb.

EXAMPLES Seaweed is **algae,** as I remember. [The noun *algae* is a predicate nominative following the linking verb *is. Algae* identifies the subject *Seaweed.*]

Was the first runner-up really **he**? [The pronoun *he* is a predicate nominative completing the meaning of the linking verb *Was. He* identifies the subject *runner-up.*]

NOTE Expressions such as *It's I* and *That was she* may sound awkward even though they are correct. In informal situations, many people use *It's me* and *That was her.* Such expressions may one day become acceptable in formal situations as well. For now, however, it is best to follow the rules of standard, formal English in all formal speaking and writing.

Reference Note

For more about **formal and informal English,** see page 221.

Be careful not to mistake a direct object for a predicate nominative. A predicate nominative always completes the meaning of a linking verb.

DIRECT OBJECT My brother admired the **gymnast.** [*Gymnast* is the direct object of the action verb *admired.*]

PREDICATE NOMINATIVE My brother became a **gymnast.** [*Gymnast* is the predicate nominative completing the meaning of the linking verb *became.*]

A predicate nominative may be compound.

EXAMPLES Maya Angelou is a great **poet** and **storyteller.** [*Poet* and *storyteller* are predicate nominatives. They identify the subject *Maya Angelou* and complete the meaning of the linking verb *is.*]

Is the shark a **fish** or a **mammal**? [*Fish* and *mammal* are predicate nominatives. They refer to the subject *shark* and complete the meaning of the linking verb *Is.*]

Yesterday was my **birthday, Labor Day,** and the first **day** of the week! [*Birthday, Labor Day,* and *day* are predicate nominatives. They identify the subject *Yesterday* and complete the meaning of the linking verb *was.*]

MEETING THE CHALLENGE

Metaphors A metaphor is a kind of figurative language that says that one thing *is* another (for instance, *My little brother is such a monkey!*). Many metaphors use predicate nominatives. In the example in parentheses, *monkey* is a predicate nominative for *brother*. Look in a collection of poems or stories to find an example of a metaphor that uses a predicate nominative. Write down the metaphor, and underline the predicate nominative. Make sure to also write down the title of the poem or story in which you found the metaphor.

GRAMMAR

HELP—
Some sentences in Exercise 5 have a compound predicate nominative.

STYLE TIP

Be careful not to overuse the linking verb *be* in your writing. Read your writing. Do you get the feeling that nothing is happening, that nobody is doing anything? If so, you may have used too many *be* verbs. When possible, replace a dull *be* verb with a verb that expresses action.

BE VERB
My father **is** a cabinet maker.

ACTION VERB
My father **makes** cabinets.

Exercise 5 **Identifying Predicate Nominatives**

Identify the predicate nominative in each of the following sentences.

EXAMPLES **1.** Mount Rushmore is a national memorial.
1. memorial

2. Is that bird a finch or a sparrow?
2. finch, sparrow

1. San Juan is the capital of Puerto Rico.
2. Her mother will remain president of the P.T.A.
3. Athens, Greece, has long been a center of art and drama.
4. The platypus and the spiny anteater are mammals.
5. The object of Juan Ponce de León's quest was the Fountain of Youth.
6. The peace pipe, or calumet, is a symbol of honor and power among American Indians.
7. Quebec is the largest province in Canada.
8. In 1959, Hawaii became our fiftieth state.
9. That bird must be an eagle.
10. The fourth planet from the sun is Mars.
11. Didn't she eventually become a senator?
12. He remained an umpire for over thirty years.
13. You are not the only one in the room.
14. Hiawatha was a real person.
15. Aren't you the oldest daughter in your family?
16. Could the problem with the engine be an empty gas tank?
17. Lucy Craft Laney was the founder of the Haines Normal and Industrial Institute.
18. For more information about Sadaharu Oh, Japan's great baseball star, a good source is "Move Over for Oh-San" in *Sports Illustrated.*
19. Was the author Chaim Potok or Amy Tan?
20. Be an example for others.

Predicate Adjectives

5f. A *predicate adjective* is an adjective that is in the predicate and that describes the subject.

A predicate adjective is connected to the subject by a linking verb.

EXAMPLES By 9:30 P.M., I was very **tired.** [The adjective *tired* describes the subject *I*.]

I believe that Jacob is **Nigerian.** [The adjective *Nigerian* describes the subject *Jacob*.]

Like a predicate nominative, a predicate adjective may be compound.

EXAMPLES The blanket felt **soft** and **fuzzy.** [Both *soft* and *fuzzy* describe the subject *blanket*.]

The cave looked **cold, damp,** and **uncomfortable.** [*Cold, damp,* and *uncomfortable* all describe the subject *cave*.]

COMPUTER TIP

If you do overuse *be* verbs in your writing, a computer can help you fix the problem. Use the computer's search function to find each occurrence of *am, are, is, was, were, be, been,* and *being* in a piece of your writing. For each case, decide whether you need to use the *be* verb. If possible, replace it with an action verb, or revise the sentence some other way to add variety.

GRAMMAR

Exercise 6 Identifying Predicate Adjectives

Identify the predicate adjective in each of the following sentences.

EXAMPLES
1. The porpoise seemed friendly.
   1. *friendly*
2. Does that alligator look hungry?
   2. *hungry*

HELP

Some sentences in Exercise 6 have a compound predicate adjective.

1. Everyone felt ready for the test.
2. Those fresh strawberries smell delicious.
3. The front tire looks flat to me.
4. Everyone appeared interested in the debate.
5. That scratch may become worse.
6. She is talented in music.
7. During the movie, I became restless and bored.
8. Van looks upset about his grades.
9. Queen Liliuokalani was quite popular with the Hawaiian people.
10. The computer program does not seem difficult to Dana.
11. After a two-hour nap, the baby was still sleepy.
12. These ants are quick and industrious.
13. Even in winter, pine trees stay green.
14. Remain calm in an emergency, and do not panic.
15. This machine has always been inexpensive but efficient.

16. A giraffe's legs are very skinny.
17. The hikers were hot and thirsty after the long trek.
18. Isn't that statue African?
19. Don't be jealous of Tiger, the new kitten.
20. Is that myth Greek or Roman?

GRAMMAR

HELP — A sentence in Review B may have a compound subject complement.

Review B Identifying Subject Complements

Identify each subject complement in the following sentences, and label it a *predicate nominative* or a *predicate adjective.*

EXAMPLE 1. The character Jahdu is a trickster.
1. *trickster—predicate nominative*

1. A trickster is a character who plays tricks on others.
2. Tricksters have been popular in many folk tales throughout the world.
3. Jahdu, however, is the creation of Virginia Hamilton.
4. Her collections of folk tales, such as *The Time-Ago Tales of Jahdu* and *In the Beginning,* are very enjoyable.
5. Jahdu may be her most unusual hero.
6. He certainly seems clever and playful.
7. Even Jahdu's home, a forest on the Mountain of Paths, sounds mysterious.
8. Jahdu can stay invisible, a very useful skill.
9. He can become any object, from a boy to a taxicab.
10. Why are tricksters like Jahdu always such entertaining characters?

HELP — Some sentences in Review C have more than one complement or a compound complement.

Review C Identifying Complements

Identify each complement in the following sentences, and label it a *direct object,* an *indirect object,* a *predicate nominative,* or a *predicate adjective.*

EXAMPLE 1. One pet of President Theodore Roosevelt's family was Algonquin, a pony.
1. *Algonquin—predicate nominative*

1. Some presidents' pets have become famous.
2. Someone may have shown you the book by President George H. W. Bush's pet, Millie.
3. Millie, a spaniel, became an author.

4. With the help of Mrs. Bush, Millie told a great deal about her days at the White House.
5. President Richard Nixon's best-known pet was Checkers, a cocker spaniel.
6. President Bill Clinton had both a cat named Socks and a dog named Buddy.
7. President William Howard Taft kept a pet cow.
8. Some presidential pets looked quite strange at the White House.
9. A pet mockingbird was a favorite companion of Thomas Jefferson.
10. Calvin Coolidge's raccoon, Rebecca, appeared comfortable at the White House.

GRAMMAR

Review D Identifying Complements

Identify each complement in the following sentences as a *direct object,* an *indirect object,* a *predicate nominative,* or a *predicate adjective.*

EXAMPLE 1. Have you ever seen a sari or a bindi?
1. sari—direct object; bindi—direct object

1. Many women from India wear these items.
2. A sari is a traditional Indian garment of cotton or silk.
3. Women wrap the sari's long, brightly printed cloth around their bodies.
4. As you can see, the softly draped sari is both graceful and charming.
5. Some women buy themselves cloth woven with golden threads for an elegant look.
6. As you might imagine, sari wearers can become quite chilled in the winter.
7. In cold climates, Indian women wear their beautiful, lightweight garments under sturdy winter coats.
8. Another traditional ornament for many Indian women is the colored dot in the middle of their foreheads.
9. The word for the dot is *bindi.*
10. The bindi gives the wearer a look of beauty and refinement.

HELP Some sentences in Review D have more than one complement or a compound complement.

GRAMMAR

Oral Practice Creating Sentences with Complements

Think of an example of each of the following kinds of complements. Then, create a sentence aloud, using your example. Use a variety of subjects and verbs in your sentences.

EXAMPLES **1.** a compound predicate nominative

1. My aunt is a swimmer and a jogger.

2. a direct object

2. Lindsey tossed Sabra the softball.

3. a pronoun used as a predicate nominative

3. The winner of the science fair is she.

1. a predicate adjective
2. an indirect object
3. a direct object
4. a predicate nominative
5. a compound predicate adjective
6. a compound predicate nominative
7. a compound direct object
8. a compound indirect object
9. a pronoun used as an indirect object
10. a pronoun used as a direct object

Chapter Review

A. Identifying Direct and Indirect Objects

Identify the *direct objects* and *indirect objects* in the following sentences.

HELP — Not all sentences in Part A have indirect objects.

1. James Baldwin wrote stories, novels, and essays.
2. Vita made her mother a scarf for her birthday.
3. He handed Amy and me an ad for the concert.
4. A park ranger told Mike the story of Forest Park.
5. Tropical forests give us many helpful plants.
6. Did she tell you about the bear?
7. The senator read the crowd a rousing speech.
8. The tourist gave the pigeons in Trafalgar Square some of his sandwich.
9. On the ferry to Ireland, Mr. McCourt told us the history of Dublin.
10. Bring me the wrench from the workbench, please.

B. Identifying Subject Complements

Identify the subject complements in the following sentences, and label each a *predicate nominative* or a *predicate adjective.*

11. Tuesday is the last day for soccer tryouts.
12. These peaches taste sweet and juicy.
13. Two common desert creatures are the lizard and the snake.
14. My cousin Tena has become an excellent weaver of Navajo blankets.
15. The soil in that pot feels dry to me.
16. The hero of the movie was a songwriter and a singer.
17. Why is Bill Gates so famous and so successful?
18. The three Brontë sisters were Charlotte, Emily, and Anne.
19. *The Adventures of Huckleberry Finn* is probably Mark Twain's best-known book.
20. The movie is shallow, silly, and boring.

GRAMMAR

C. Identifying Complements

Identify the complements in the following sentences, and label each a *direct object,* an *indirect object,* a *predicate nominative,* or a *predicate adjective.*

21. Madrid is the capital of Spain.
22. Did you give me your new address?
23. These sketches of yours are wonderful!
24. Dr. Jonas Salk developed a vaccine to prevent polio.
25. Pam Adams is my best friend.
26. My father sent his mother and father two tickets to Mexico.
27. Your handwriting is neat and readable.
28. The longest play by Shakespeare is *Hamlet.*
29. Hugo handed his teacher the papers.
30. My father tossed the dog an old bone.
31. That new country performer is my favorite singer.
32. Thunder sometimes gives me a headache.
33. Are these toys safe for children?
34. My dad is buying my mother a bicycle.
35. Light reflectors for a bike are a good idea.
36. The king granted them three wishes.
37. Our trip to Villahermosa was short but exciting.
38. Angelo painted a beautiful picture of his mother.
39. Have you eaten lunch yet?
40. Miki is one of the best spellers in the class.

Writing Application

Using Complements in a Paragraph

Direct Objects and Indirect Objects For National Hobby Month, students in your class are making posters about their hobbies. Each poster will include drawings or pictures and a written description of the hobby. Write a paragraph about your hobby to go on your poster. Use at least three direct objects and two indirect objects in your paragraph.

Prewriting Choose a topic for your poster project. You could write about any collection, sport, craft, or activity that you enjoy in your free time. You could also write about a hobby that you are interested in starting. Freewrite about the hobby. Be sure to tell why you enjoy it or why you think you would enjoy it. If the hobby is new to you, find out more about it from another hobbyist or from the library.

Writing Begin your paragraph with a main-idea sentence that clearly identifies the hobby or special interest. Check your prewriting notes often to find details you can use in describing the hobby.

Revising Read your paragraph aloud. Does it give enough information about your hobby? Would someone unfamiliar with the hobby find it interesting? Add, cut, or rearrange details to make your paragraph easier to understand. Identify the transitive verbs in your paragraph. Have you used at least three direct objects and two indirect objects? You may need to revise some sentences.

Publishing Read over your paragraph for spelling, grammar, and punctuation errors, and correct any you find. You and your classmates may want to make posters using your paragraphs and some pictures. Cut pictures out of magazines and brochures, or draw your own. Then, attach your writing and art to pieces of poster board and display the posters in the classroom.

CHAPTER

Agreement

Subject and Verb, Pronoun and Antecedent

1.0 Written and Oral English Language Conventions

Students write and speak with a command of standard English conventions appropriate to this grade level.

1.2 Identify and properly use indefinite pronouns and ensure that verbs agree with compound subjects.

Diagnostic Preview

A. Choosing Verbs That Agree in Number with Their Subjects

Find the subject of each of the following sentences. Then, choose the form of the verb in parentheses that agrees with the subject.

EXAMPLE **1.** Janelle and Brad (*are, is*) in the drama club.
1. Janelle, Brad—are

1. Neither the passengers nor the pilot (*was, were*) injured.
2. There (*are, is*) two exciting new rides at the amusement park.
3. That book of Spanish folk tales (*is, are*) selling out.
4. (*Here are, Here's*) some books about Hawaii.
5. Shel Silverstein and Ogden Nash (*appeal, appeals*) to both children and grown-ups.
6. Velma and her little sister (*was, were*) reading a story by Gyo Fujikawa.
7. (*Was, Were*) your parents happy with the results?
8. Why (*doesn't, don't*) she and Megan bring the lemonade with them to the picnic?
9. The dishes on that shelf (*look, looks*) clean.

10. Either the cats or the dog (*has, have*) upset the plants.
11. There (*go, goes*) two more deer!
12. I (*am, is*) crocheting an afghan.
13. Why (*wasn't, weren't*) you at the scout meeting yesterday?
14. Several paintings by that artist (*are, is*) now on exhibit at the mall.
15. They (*doesn't, don't*) know how to find their way to the family reunion.

B. Choosing Pronouns That Agree with Their Antecedents

For each of the following sentences, identify the pronoun that agrees with its antecedent.

EXAMPLES
1. Either Eileen or Barbara will bring (*her, their*) notes.
   1. her
2. When Dennis and Aaron were younger, (*he, they*) rode the same bus to school.
   2. they

16. A student should proofread (*his or her, their*) work carefully before turning in the final copy.
17. Carlos and Andrew finally watched the videos (*he, they*) had borrowed.
18. Everyone on the girls' volleyball team has picked up (*her, their*) equipment.
19. The cat had batted its toy under the sofa and couldn't reach (*it, them*).
20. Jennifer or Sharon will leave early so that (*she, they*) can prepare the display.
21. Most of the trees in the park had lost (*its, their*) leaves.
22. If you aren't going to finish those crossword puzzles, may I do (*it, them*)?
23. Each of the drawings was hung on the wall in (*its, their*) frame.
24. When Martin and Stephanie were not rehearsing onstage, (*he or she, they*) studied their lines in the hall.
25. Did one of the chickens lose (*its, their*) feathers?

Number

Number is the form a word takes to show whether the word is singular or plural.

6a. Words that refer to one person, place, thing, or idea are generally *singular* in number. Words that refer to more than one person, place, thing, or idea are generally *plural* in number.

Singular	tepee	I	baby	mouse
Plural	tepees	we	babies	mice

HELP

Most nouns that end in *–s* are plural (*igloos, sisters*). Most verbs that end in *–s* are singular (*sings, tries*).

EXAMPLES
My sister**s** sing.
My sister sing**s**.

However, verbs used with the singular pronouns *I* and *you* do not end in *–s*.

EXAMPLES
I sing.
You sing.

USAGE

Exercise 1 Identifying Singular and Plural Words

Identify each of the following words as *singular* or *plural*.

EXAMPLE **1.** activities
1. plural

1. peach
2. libraries
3. highway
4. knife
5. shelves
6. children
7. they
8. enchiladas
9. women
10. America
11. dirt
12. dress
13. someone
14. feet
15. fantasy
16. society
17. potatoes
18. people
19. several
20. fathers-in-law

Reference Note

The plurals of some nouns do not end in *–s* (*mice, Chinese, aircraft*). For more about **spelling the plural forms of nouns,** see page 325.

Agreement of Subject and Verb

6b. A verb should agree in number with its subject.

A subject and verb *agree* when they have the same number.

(1) Singular subjects take singular verbs.

EXAMPLES The **ocean roars** in the distance. [The singular verb *roars* agrees with the singular subject *ocean.*]

She plays the violin well. [The singular verb *plays* agrees with the singular subject *She.*]

(2) Plural subjects take plural verbs.

EXAMPLES **Squirrels eat** the seeds from the bird feeder. [The plural verb *eat* agrees with the plural subject *Squirrels.*]

They practice after school. [The plural verb *practice* agrees with the plural subject *They.*]

When a sentence contains a verb phrase, the first helping verb in the phrase agrees with the subject.

EXAMPLES **Latrice has** been studying Arabic.

They have been studying Arabic.

Reference Note

For information on **verb phrases,** see page 50.

Exercise 2 Identifying the Number of Subjects and Verbs

Identify each of the following subjects and verbs as either *singular* or *plural.*

EXAMPLE 1. flag waves
1. singular

HELP

All verbs in Exercise 2 agree with their subjects.

1. socks match
2. lightning crackles
3. leaves rustle
4. mosquitoes buzz
5. Lyle baby-sits
6. bands march
7. Richelle knits
8. they listen
9. singer practices
10. horses whinny
11. crows fly
12. Shannon chooses
13. boat floats
14. we learn
15. leg aches
16. Roger guesses
17. poets write
18. cells divide
19. he knows
20. ice cube melts

Exercise 3 Changing the Number of Subjects and Verbs

All of the subjects and verbs in the following sentences agree in number. Rewrite each sentence, changing the subject and verb from singular to plural or from plural to singular.

EXAMPLE 1. Lions roar on the plains of Kenya.
1. A lion roars on the plains of Kenya.

1. Maps show the shape of a country.

2. What countries are highlighted on the map below?
3. Does an ocean form Kenya's eastern border?
4. Visitors enjoy Kenya's beautiful scenery.
5. Mount Kenya's peaks are covered with snow.
6. Wildlife parks have been created in Kenya.
7. In the picture below, rangers patrol a park to protect the animals.
8. They certainly have unusual transportation.
9. Many industries are located in Kenya's capital, Nairobi.
10. Kenyan farmers grow such crops as wheat, corn, and rice.

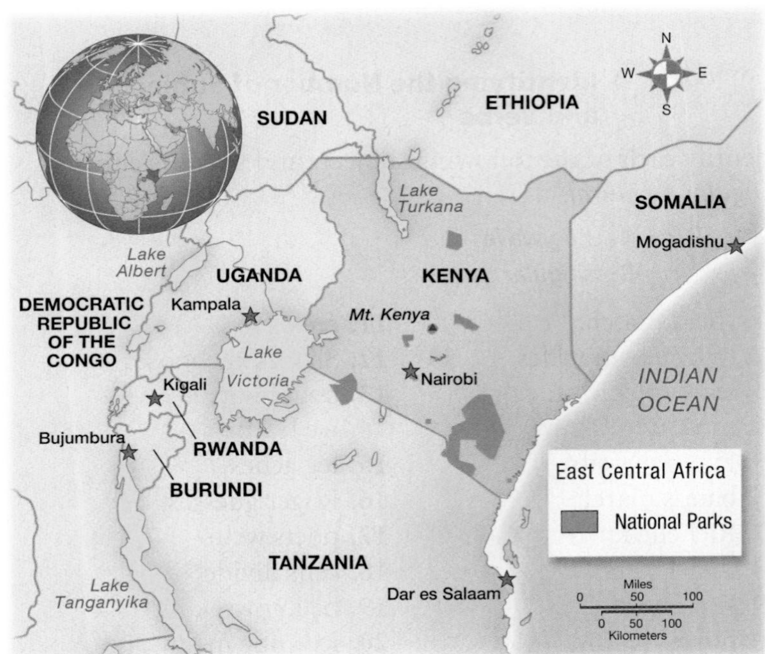

USAGE

Exercise 4 Choosing Verbs That Agree in Number with Their Subjects

For each of the following sentences, choose the form of the verb in parentheses that agrees with the subject.

EXAMPLE 1. The kitten (*pounces, pounce*) on the ball.
1. pounces

1. Firefighters (*risks, risk*) their lives to save others.
2. The snowplow (*clears, clear*) the road quickly.
3. Some dancers (*like, likes*) reggae music best.
4. St. Augustine, Florida, (*has, have*) many old buildings.
5. Some students (*chooses, choose*) to play volleyball.
6. At the science fair, the winner always (*receives, receive*) a savings bond.
7. Strong winds (*whistles, whistle*) through the old house.
8. Each Saturday, club members (*picks, pick*) up the litter in the park.
9. The principal (*makes, make*) announcements over the loudspeaker each day.
10. Doctors (*says, say*) that listening to loud music can harm people's hearing.

Problems in Agreement

Phrases Between Subject and Verb

6c. The number of a subject is not changed by a phrase following the subject.

EXAMPLES These **shades** of blue **are** my favorite colors.

The **ballerina** with long black braids **has** been my sister's ballet teacher for two years.

However, if the subject is the indefinite pronoun *all, any, more, most, none,* or *some,* its number may be determined by the object of a prepositional phrase that follows it.

EXAMPLES **Some** of the oranges **are** gone. [*Some* refers to the plural noun *oranges.*]

Some of the fruit **is** gone. [*Some* refers to the singular noun *fruit.*]

Reference Note

For information on **phrases,** see Chapter 4.

HELP

The subject of a sentence is never in a prepositional phrase.

EXAMPLE
The **apples** in the refrigerator are not cold yet. [*Apples* is the subject. *Refrigerator* cannot be the subject because it is part of the prepositional phrase *in the refrigerator.*]

NOTE *As well as, along with, together with,* and *in addition to* are compound prepositions. Phrases beginning with compound prepositions do not affect the number of a subject or verb.

EXAMPLE **Myra,** along with her brothers, **helps** with household chores each evening. [The prepositional phrase *along with her brothers* does not affect the number of the subject *Myra. Myra* is singular and takes a singular verb, *helps.*]

USAGE

Exercise 5 Choosing Verbs That Agree in Number with Their Subjects

In each of the following sentences, choose the form of the verb in parentheses that agrees with the subject.

EXAMPLE 1. Islands off the coast (*has, have*) a life of their own.
1. *have*

1. The second-largest island of the United States (*is, are*) located in the Gulf of Alaska.
2. The thirteen thousand people on Kodiak Island (*is, are*) mostly of Scandinavian, Russian, or Native Arctic descent.

3. The citizens of Kodiak (*calls, call*) Alaska the mainland.
4. Sacks of mail (*is, are*) flown there from the mainland.
5. Industries in the community, originally known as Kikhtak, (*includes, include*) farming, fishing, and mining.
6. One cannery on the island (*cans, can*) salmon eggs, or roe.
7. Many residents on the mainland (*considers, consider*) roe a delicacy.
8. Bears like this one (*catch, catches*) fresh salmon.
9. However, their search for leftovers often (*create, creates*) problems for Kodiak.
10. The officials of one town (*has, have*) had to put a special bear-proof fence around the garbage dump.

Indefinite Pronouns

Personal pronouns refer to specific people, places, things, or ideas. A pronoun that does not refer to a definite person, place, thing, or idea is called an ***indefinite pronoun.***

Personal Pronouns	she	you	we	them
Indefinite Pronouns	each	many	anyone	all

6d. The following indefinite pronouns are singular: *anybody, anyone, anything, each, either, everybody, everyone, everything, neither, nobody, no one, nothing, one, somebody, someone,* and *something.*

EXAMPLES **One** of the supergiant stars **is** Antares.

Each of the tourists **was** given a souvenir.

Does everybody in the restaurant like pita bread?

Exercise 6 **Choosing Verbs That Agree in Number with Their Subjects**

In the following sentences, choose the form of the verb in parentheses that agrees with the subject.

EXAMPLE 1. Neither of the teams (*is, are*) on the field.

1. is

1. Nearly everybody in Ruby Lee's family (*enjoy, enjoys*) tomato soup.
2. Neither of them (*was, were*) wearing a hat.
3. Somebody in the class (*speaks, speak*) French.
4. Nobody in the first two rows (*want, wants*) to volunteer to be the magician's assistant.
5. Each of these songs (*is, are*) by the Beatles.
6. Someone in the crowd (*is, are*) waving a pennant, but I can't tell whether it's Nick.
7. Everyone in those exercise classes (*has, have*) lost weight.
8. One of the band members (*play, plays*) lead guitar and sings backup vocals.
9. No one (*was, were*) listening to the music.
10. (*Do, Does*) either of them know how?

HELP—

The words *one, thing,* and *body* are singular. The indefinite pronouns that contain these words are singular, too.

EXAMPLES

Was every**one** there?

Some**body has** answered.

No**thing works** better.

HELP—

Remember that the subject is never part of a prepositional phrase.

USAGE

COMPUTER TIP

Using indefinite pronouns correctly can be tricky. To help yourself, you may want to create an indefinite pronoun guide. First, summarize the information in Rules 6d–6f. Then, choose several example sentences to illustrate the rules.

If you use a computer, you can create a help file with these rules and examples. Call up your help file whenever you have trouble with indefinite pronouns in your writing. If you don't use a computer, you can keep your guide in a writing notebook.

HELP

The pronouns listed in Rule 6f aren't always followed by prepositional phrases.

EXAMPLES
All are here.

Some has spilled.

In such cases you should look at the ***context***—the sentences before and after the pronoun—to see if the pronoun refers to a singular or a plural word.

6e. The following indefinite pronouns are plural: *both, few, many, several.*

EXAMPLES **Both overflow** occasionally.

Few of the guests **are** wearing formal clothes.

Many of the newer houses **have** built-in smoke detectors.

Several in the group **say** yes.

6f. The indefinite pronouns *all, any, more, most, none,* and *some* may be singular or plural, depending on their meaning in a sentence.

Often, the object of a preposition that follows the pronoun indicates whether the pronoun is singular or plural. If the object of the preposition is singular, the pronoun usually is singular. If the object is plural, the pronoun usually is plural.

EXAMPLES **All** of the snow **has** melted. [*All* is singular because *snow* is singular. The helping verb *has* is singular to agree with *All.*]

All of the snowflakes **have** melted. [*All* is plural because *snowflakes* is plural. The helping verb *have* is plural to agree with *All.*]

Some of the birdseed **is** left in the feeder. [*Some* is singular because *birdseed* is singular. The helping verb *is* is singular to agree with *Some.*]

Some of the sunflower seeds **are** left in the feeder. [*Some* is plural because *seeds* is plural. The helping verb *are* is plural to agree with *Some.*]

Exercise 7 Choosing Verbs That Agree in Number with Their Subjects

Choose the correct form of the verb in parentheses in each of the following sentences.

EXAMPLE **1.** Many of these puppies (*needs, need*) a good home.
1. need

1. Most of the balloons (*has, have*) long strings.
2. All of the girls wearing purple uniforms (*plays, play*) on the softball team.

3. Both of the sneakers (*gives, give*) me blisters.
4. Most of these recipes (*requires, require*) ricotta cheese.
5. Some of the artists (*paint, paints*) landscapes.
6. Few of those songs (*was, were*) composed by Duke Ellington.
7. None of the apartments (*has, have*) been painted.
8. All of the jewels (*is, are*) in the safe.
9. Many in the crowd (*waves, wave*) signs.
10. All of the writing (*is, are*) upside down.

HELP

Some indefinite pronouns, such as *both, each,* and *some,* can also be used as adjectives. When an indefinite adjective comes before the subject of a sentence, the verb agrees with the subject as it normally would.

EXAMPLES

Children love playing in the park.

Both children love playing in the park.

The **child loves** playing in the park.

Each child loves playing in the park.

Compound Subjects

A compound subject is made up of two or more subjects that are connected by the conjunction *and, or,* or *nor.* These connected subjects share the same verb.

6g. Subjects joined by *and* generally take a plural verb.

EXAMPLES **Red** and **blue are** the school's colors.

New **uniforms** and **instruments were ordered** for the marching band.

Mr. Lewis, Mrs. Kirk, and **Ms. Jefferson have applied** for new jobs.

Reference Note

For information on **conjunctions,** see page 66.

Exercise 8 Choosing Verbs That Agree in Number with Their Subjects

Identify the compound subject in each of the following sentences. Then, choose the form of the verb in parentheses that agrees with the compound subject.

EXAMPLE 1. Volcanoes and earthquakes (*is, are*) common in that area.

1. *Volcanoes, earthquakes—are*

1. The blanket and the robe (*has, have*) Navajo designs.
2. Wind, hail, and freezing rain (*is, are*) predicted for Thursday.
3. A desk and a bookcase (*were, was*) moved into Ella's room.
4. Savannas and velds (*is, are*) two kinds of grasslands found in Africa.

5. A delivery truck and a car with a trailer (*were, was*) stalled on the highway.
6. A raccoon and a possum (*raid, raids*) our vegetable garden every night.
7. Mandy and her aunt (*goes, go*) to the Chinese market every Saturday.
8. Eric and Jarvis (*were, was*) asked to introduce the speaker.
9. Mosquitoes and earwigs (*has, have*) invaded our backyard.
10. Ketchup, onions, and mustard (*goes, go*) well on many sandwiches.

USAGE

6h. Singular subjects that are joined by *or* or *nor* take a singular verb.

EXAMPLES A new marble **statue** or a **fountain has been planned** for the park.

On Mondays, either **Manuel** or **Stephie baby-sits** the children.

6i. Plural subjects joined by *or* or *nor* take a plural verb.

EXAMPLES Either **potatoes** or **beans are served** with the baked chicken.

Tulips or **pansies make** a lovely border for a sidewalk.

6j. When a singular subject and a plural subject are joined by *or* or *nor,* the verb agrees with the subject nearer the verb.

EXAMPLES Either the **engineers** or their **boss has made** this mistake. [The singular helping verb *has* agrees with the nearer subject, *boss.*]

Either the **boss** or the **engineers have made** this mistake. [The plural helping verb *have* agrees with the nearer subject, *engineers.*]

A soft **blanket** or some warm **booties make** a baby comfortable. [The plural helping verb *make* agrees with the nearer subject, *booties.*]

Some warm **booties** or a soft **blanket makes** a baby comfortable. [The singular verb *makes* agrees with the nearer subject, *blanket.*]

Oral Practice 1 Using Correct Verbs with Compound Subjects Joined by *Or* or *Nor*

Read each of the following sentences aloud, stressing the words in italics.

1. A *desert* or a *jungle is* the setting for the play.
2. The *table* or the *bookshelves need* dusting first.
3. Neither the *bus* nor the *train stops* in our town.
4. Neither *jokes* nor funny *stories make* Gordon laugh.
5. *Flowers* or a colorful *picture makes* a room brighter and more cheerful.
6. Either the *story* or the *poems are* by Langston Hughes.
7. At this restaurant, *rice* or *potatoes come* with the tandoori chicken dinner.
8. Neither the *Carolinas* nor *Illinois borders* Texas.

Review A Choosing Verbs That Agree in Number with Their Subjects

For each of the following sentences, choose the form of the verb in parentheses that agrees with the subject.

EXAMPLE 1. Tara and Chen (*are, is*) reading the same book.
1. are

1. Many vegetables (*grow, grows*) quite large during Alaska's long summer days.
2. His mother (*teach, teaches*) math.
3. All of the boats in the harbor (*belong, belongs*) to the village.
4. You and your cousins (*are, is*) invited to the party.
5. Either the wall clock or our wristwatches (*tell, tells*) the correct time.
6. The new magazines on the kitchen table (*are, is*) for the hospital waiting room.
7. My list of favorite foods (*include, includes*) vegetable lasagna and wonton soup.
8. Both my big brother and my sister (*deliver, delivers*) the morning newspaper.
9. Neither pencils nor an eraser (*are, is*) permitted.
10. The clowns and jugglers (*has, have*) always been my favorite circus performers.

STYLE TIP

Compound subjects that have both singular and plural parts can sound awkward even though they are correct. Try to avoid such constructions by revising the sentence.

AWKWARD
Jewelry or flowers make a nice Mother's Day gift.

REVISED
Jewelry makes a nice Mother's Day gift, and **flowers do,** too.

USAGE

Review B Proofreading a Paragraph for Errors in Subject-Verb Agreement

Most sentences in the following paragraph contain a verb that does not agree in number with its subject. If a sentence is incorrect, give the correct verb form. If a sentence is already correct, write *C.*

EXAMPLE **[1]** Holiday customs throughout the world is fun to study.
1. are

[**1**] In Sweden, adults and children celebrates St. Lucia's Day. [**2**] Everyone there know St. Lucia as the Queen of Light. [**3**] Many people eagerly look forward to the December 13 holiday. [**4**] Girls especially enjoys the day. [**5**] By tradition, the oldest girl in the family dress as St. Lucia. [**6**] The girl in the picture above is ready to play her part. [**7**] You surely has noticed the girl's headdress. [**8**] A crown of lighted candles are hard to miss! [**9**] Each of the young Lucias also wear a white robe. [**10**] Early in the morning, the costumed girls bring breakfast to the adults of the household.

TIPS & TRICKS

When the subject of a sentence comes after the verb, the word order is said to be ***inverted.*** To find the subject of a sentence with inverted order, restate the sentence in normal subject-verb word order.

INVERTED
How much time **has he spent** at the lake?

NORMAL
He has spent how much time at the lake?

INVERTED
Here **are** the **toys.**

NORMAL
The **toys are** here.

Subject After the Verb

6k. When the subject follows the verb, find the subject and make sure that the verb agrees with it.

The subject usually follows the verb in questions and in sentences that begin with *there* and *here.*

EXAMPLES **Are** the **birds** in the nest?
Is the **nest** on a high branch?

There **go** the **dragons.**
There **goes** the **dragon.**

NOTE The contractions *there's* and *here's* contain the verb *is.* These contractions are singular and should be used only with singular subjects.

EXAMPLES There**'s Uncle Max.**

Here**'s** your **allowance.**

Exercise 9 **Choosing Verbs That Agree in Number with Their Subjects**

Identify the subject of each sentence. Then, choose the form of the verb in parentheses that agrees with the subject.

EXAMPLE **1.** There (*was, were*) a baby rabbit hiding in the grass.
1. rabbit—was

1. There (*are, is*) a new foreign-exchange student at my brother's high school.
2. (*Was, Were*) the fans cheering for the other team?
3. (*Has, Have*) the Washingtons moved into their new home?
4. Here (*stand, stands*) one brave, young woman and her only son, Dale.
5. (*Has, Have*) the bees left the hive?
6. (*There's, There are*) several correct answers to that tough question.
7. How long (*has, have*) the Huang family owned this tai chi studio?
8. (*Here are, Here's*) the shells that we collected from Driftwood Beach.
9. (*There's, There are*) a pint of fresh strawberries on the kitchen table.
10. There (*were, was*) Amy and Wanda in the doorway.

MEETING THE CHALLENGE

Your little brother or sister will be attending a movie with your family for the first time Saturday afternoon. To ensure that the outing is a pleasant experience for everyone, you have offered to make a list of good theater manners. Write a list of five rules about how to behave in the theater. Use *don't* or *doesn't* correctly as needed, and be sure your rules use correct subject-verb and pronoun-antecedent agreement.

USAGE

The Contractions *Don't* and *Doesn't*

6l. **The word *don't* is the contraction of *do not.* Use *don't* with all plural subjects and with the pronouns *I* and *you.***

EXAMPLES	**I don't** have my keys.	**Dogs don't** meow.
	You don't care.	**Don't they** know?
	We don't agree.	The **boots don't** fit.

Reference Note

For more information on **contractions,** see page 304.

6m. **The word *doesn't* is the contraction of *does not.* Use *doesn't* with all singular subjects except the pronouns *I* and *you.***

EXAMPLES	**He doesn't** know you.	**Don doesn't** like thunder.
	She doesn't see it.	**Doesn't** the **car** run?
	It doesn't work.	A **penguin doesn't** fly.

USAGE

Oral Practice 2 Using *Don't* and *Doesn't* Correctly

Read each of the following sentences aloud, stressing the words in italics.

1. *He doesn't* want us to give him a party.
2. *Margo* and *Jim don't* have any juice left.
3. *Lynna doesn't* remember the punchline.
4. The *bus doesn't* stop here.
5. *They don't* believe that old story.
6. *It doesn't* snow here in October.
7. *You don't* sing the blues anymore.
8. That Zuni *vase doesn't* look very old.

Exercise 10 Writing *Don't* and *Doesn't* with Subjects

Identify the subject in each of the following sentences. Then, choose the contraction, either *don't* or *doesn't,* that agrees with the subject.

EXAMPLE **1.** Our cats ____ like catnip.
1. cats—don't

1. My parents ____ listen to rap music.
2. I ____ have much homework tonight.
3. Jerome ____ play the guitar as well as Angela does.
4. The pizza ____ have enough onions, mushrooms, green peppers, or cheese.
5. They ____ permit diving into the pool.
6. This bedroom ____ look very neat.
7. My ski boots ____ fit me this year.
8. Matthew enjoys playing lacrosse, but he ____ like to play soccer.
9. You ____ live on this street anymore.
10. It ____ seem possible that Leon grew an inch in one month.

Review C Proofreading for Errors in Subject-Verb Agreement

Most of the following sentences contain a verb that does not agree in number with its subject. Correct each incorrect verb. If a sentence is already correct, write *C.*

EXAMPLE 1. Is the people in the picture worried?

1. *Are*

1. There is sharks swimming all around them.
2. However, the people doesn't seem to care.
3. Has they lost their senses?
4. No, there aren't anything for them to worry about in this shark exhibit.
5. There's a transparent tunnel right through the shark pool.
6. Everyone who visits the exhibit ride a moving walkway through the tunnel.
7. The sharks don't seem to mind the people.
8. Actually, sharks in the wild doesn't attack people very often.
9. Of course, sharks does eat almost anything.
10. Caution and respect, therefore, is necessary in shark-inhabited waters.

Agreement of Pronoun and Antecedent

A pronoun usually refers to a noun or another pronoun called its ***antecedent.*** When you use a pronoun, make sure that it agrees with its antecedent.

Reference Note

For more information on **antecedents,** see page 30.

6n. A pronoun should agree in gender with its antecedent.

Some singular personal pronouns have forms that indicate gender. Feminine pronouns refer to females. Masculine pronouns refer to males. Neuter pronouns refer to things (neither male nor female) and sometimes to animals.

Feminine	she	her	hers
Masculine	he	him	his
Neuter	it	it	its

EXAMPLES **Rosa** said **she** lost **her** glasses.

Hank took **his** journal to the beach with **him.**

Manny chose that **bike** because of **its** color and styling.

The antecedent of a personal pronoun can be another kind of pronoun. In such cases, you can often look in a phrase that follows the antecedent to tell which personal pronoun to use.

EXAMPLE **One** of those **ladies** left **her** scarf in the car.

Each of the **boys** brought **his** own softball mitt.

Some singular antecedents may be either masculine or feminine. In such cases, use both the masculine and feminine forms of the pronoun.

EXAMPLE **Nobody** in the class finished **his or her** paper early.

NOTE In informal speech and writing, people often use a plural pronoun to refer to a singular antecedent that may be either feminine or masculine.

INFORMAL Every actor in the play had already memorized their lines.

Such usage is grammatically incorrect and should be avoided, especially in formal situations.

USAGE

STYLE TIP

To avoid the awkward use of *his or her,* try to rephrase the sentence.

AWKWARD
Each of the actors had memorized **his or her** lines.

REVISED
All of the actors had memorized **their** lines.

6o. A pronoun should agree in number with its antecedent.

A pronoun that refers to a singular antecedent is singular in number. A pronoun that refers to a plural antecedent is plural in number.

EXAMPLES Please put the lawn **mower** away after you have finished using **it.**

These **tools** will last longer if you take good care of **them.**

(1) Use a singular pronoun to refer to the indefinite pronouns *anybody, anyone, anything, each, either, everybody, everyone, everything, neither, nobody, no one, nothing, one, somebody, someone,* and *something.*

Reference Note

For more information about **indefinite pronouns,** see page 34.

EXAMPLES Has **one** of the hamsters hurt **its** leg?

Someone left **his or her** jacket on the bus.

Everyone on the girls' team has **her** own locker.

(2) Use a plural pronoun to refer to the indefinite pronouns *both, few, many,* and *several.*

EXAMPLES **Both** of the birds had hidden **their** nests well.

Several of the spiders continue to live under that log; it is where **they** hatched.

On a night like this, **few** of the travelers will reach **their** destinations on schedule.

(3) The indefinite pronouns *all, any, more, most, none,* and *some* may be singular or plural, depending on their meaning in a sentence.

EXAMPLES **None** of the cereal has lost **its** crunch. [*None* is singular because it refers to the singular noun *cereal*.]

None of the cereal flakes have lost **their** crunch. [*None* is plural because it refers to the plural noun *flakes*.]

(4) Use a singular pronoun to refer to two or more singular antecedents joined by *or* or *nor.*

EXAMPLES Either **Miguel or Randall** has **his** paintings on display.

Neither **Karli nor Marta** will lend you **her** book.

Using a pronoun to refer to antecedents of different numbers may create an unclear or awkward sentence.

UNCLEAR Neither the kittens nor their mother liked her new food. [*Her* agrees with the nearest antecedent, *mother.* However, it is unclear if the kittens disliked their own new food or if they disliked their mother's new food.]

UNCLEAR Neither the kittens' mother nor the kittens liked their new food. [*Their* agrees with the nearest antecedent, *kittens.* However, it is unclear if the mother disliked her own new food or if she disliked her kittens' new food.]

AWKWARD Neither the kittens nor their mother liked their or her new food.

STYLE TIP

Sentences with singular antecedents joined by *or* can sound awkward if the antecedents are of different genders. If a sentence sounds awkward, revise it to avoid the problem.

AWKWARD
Mark or Sherrie will bring his or her flashlight.

REVISED
Either **Mark** will bring **his** flashlight, or **Sherrie** will bring **hers.**

It is best to revise sentences to avoid unclear and awkward constructions like the ones on the previous page.

REVISED Neither the kittens nor their mother liked **the** new food.

None of the cats liked **their** new food.

HELP—

Remember that a pronoun should refer clearly to its antecedent. If a pronoun could possibly refer to one of two or more antecedents, revise the sentence to make the pronoun's meaning obvious.

UNCLEAR
Marcia wrote Sharon while she was on vacation. [Who was on vacation—Marcia or Sharon?]

CLEAR
When Marcia was on vacation, she wrote Sharon.

USAGE

(5) Use a plural pronoun to refer to two or more antecedents joined by *and*.

EXAMPLES When **Tyrell and Davis** get home, **they** will be surprised.

Have **Chelsea and Susan** tried on **their** new outfits?

Exercise 11 Proofreading for Pronoun-Antecedent Agreement

Most of the following sentences contain errors in pronoun-antecedent agreement. Identify the incorrect pronoun, and write the correct pronoun. If a sentence is already correct, write *C.*

EXAMPLE **1.** Colby and everybody else brought his or her calculators.

1. his or her—their

1. Neither Chile nor Argentina has given their consent to the project.
2. These tools are sharp; be careful with it!
3. Of course, Mrs. Chin and her daughters will give us her assistance.
4. Everyone needs to take their project home by Friday.
5. Many of the houses were decorated with ribbons on its doors for the holidays.
6. Neither Frank nor Paul has had their hair cut recently.
7. Every one of the dogs is required to have a numbered tag attached to their collar.
8. That song on the radio sounds familiar, but I can't remember its title.
9. Roseanne and Kimberly, I believe, recently lost her glasses.
10. Have any of the horses escaped its corral?

Exercise 12 Proofreading for Pronoun-Antecedent Agreement

Most of the following sentences contain pronouns that do not agree with their antecedents. Identify each incorrect pronoun, and write the correct pronoun. If a sentence is already correct, write *C.*

EXAMPLE 1. On the first day, no one knew their partner.
1. their—his or her

1. Somebody in the back row left their umbrella behind.
2. At last, all of the kittens were having their nap.
3. Several of the students had large scholarships given to him or her by local businesses.
4. Anybody in the sixth grade should know their mother's maiden name.
5. Neither of the antique cars had their original paint job.
6. Did many of the apprentices later change his or her trade?
7. Yes, anyone can enter their pet in the contest.
8. Few of the boys know the procedure, but he will learn it quickly.
9. None of the girls brought their books.
10. Both of the packages had been opened, and it sat forgotten on the floor.

Exercise 13 Proofreading for Pronoun-Antecedent Agreement

Most of the following sentences contain a pronoun that does not agree in number or gender with its antecedent or antecedents. Identify each incorrect pronoun, and write the correct pronoun. If a sentence is already correct, write *C.*

EXAMPLE 1. Either Abe or Brian will give their speech first.
1. their—his

1. Gold and silver gain worth from its rarity.
2. Ask Mr. Reed or Mr. Steinhauer if they will lend you a pen or a pencil.
3. The house at the corner and the house next door have flowers growing in front of it.

USAGE

4. The birds and the butterflies have flown south to their winter homes.
5. Can even a princess or a queen have their every wish?
6. Pepper tastes good in a recipe, but not all by themselves.
7. A single red rose or a lily does not cost much, and it will look nice on the table.
8. Each of the grocery stores advertises their sales in the Sunday paper.
9. Neither Dan nor Bob likes onions on his sandwich.
10. More of the oranges have stickers on it than I thought.

Exercise 14 Proofreading for Pronoun-Antecedent Agreement

Most of the following sentences contain a pronoun that does not agree in number or gender with its antecedent or antecedents. Identify and correct each incorrect pronoun. If a sentence is already correct, write *C.*

EXAMPLE 1. Delia and Dawn told me about her idea for a neighborhood show.
1. *her—their*

1. Both of my parents gave us his or her permission, so we used my front yard.
2. The name of our play, which was actually a rock opera, was *Strange Night,* and I wrote it.
3. Two trees lent us its trunks for a stage.
4. Somebody bought popcorn with their allowance and sold it to the audience.
5. Everyone in the neighborhood brought his or her own chair to the show.
6. Either Matt or Freddy practiced his dance routine.
7. Lisa and Tanya play guitar, so we asked her to be in our band.
8. Joan wore a costume with pink flowers and bluebirds on it.
9. Of course, a few dogs and one unhappy cat made its entrance at an improper moment.
10. Tickets were only fifty cents, and we sold all of it before the show began.

Chapter Review

A. Choosing Verbs That Agree in Number with Their Subjects

For each of the following sentences, identify the subject. Then, choose the form of the verb in parentheses that agrees with the subject.

1. The flowers in that garden (*need, needs*) water.
2. She and her cousin (*play, plays*) tennis every weekend except in the winter.
3. Either Paulette or Lily (*attend, attends*) all the local performances of the Alvin Ailey dancers.
4. There (*was, were*) several teachers at the game.
5. All of the corn (*has, have*) dried up.
6. (*Was, Were*) Liang and his sister born in Taiwan?
7. None of the trucks (*has, have*) arrived yet.
8. My best friend at school (*doesn't, don't*) live in our neighborhood.
9. (*Was, Were*) you heating some bean and cheese burritos in the microwave?
10. Here (*come, comes*) Elena and James.
11. Only one of my three dogs, my beagle Neptune, really (*enjoy, enjoys*) the beach.
12. Either the students or their teacher (*has, have*) decided on the color of the new bulletin board.
13. (*Doesn't, Don't*) that sweater belong to Ralph?
14. Neither the clerk nor the shoppers (*was, were*) aware of the fire down the street.
15. Where (*was, were*) you last night around supper time?
16. Several houses in our neighborhood (*is, are*) for sale.
17. My brother and I often (*play, plays*) checkers together.
18. Either he or she (*is, are*) next in line.
19. Marilu (*don't, doesn't*) know the name of the author.
20. There (*was, were*) no other people there besides us.

B. Changing the Number of Subjects and Verbs

All the subjects and verbs in the following sentences agree in number. Rewrite each sentence, changing the subject and verb from singular to plural or from plural to singular. You may have to add or delete *a, an,* or *the.*

21. Dogs bark in the middle of the night.
22. A bird sings in the distance.
23. Books have fallen off the shelf.
24. A camel passes.
25. Cars move down the highway.
26. Do elephants eat grass?
27. The man has eaten lunch.
28. Many people are at the river today.
29. She has an unusual hobby.
30. Police officers protect the people.

C. Proofreading for Errors in Pronoun-Antecedent Agreement

Most of the following sentences contain a pronoun that does not agree in number or gender with its antecedent or antecedents. Write each incorrect pronoun. Then, write the pronoun that agrees with the antecedent. If a sentence is already correct, write *C.*

31. We had to call the parking lot attendant because two cars and one truck had its lights on.
32. Each of the ducks was tagged with an electronic device around their left leg.
33. Tim and Donny promised he would bring some snacks to the party.
34. Frances or Donna will sing her favorite number.
35. I can't remember which one of my grandfathers spent their eighteenth and nineteenth years fighting in World War II.
36. Both my brother and my sister might lend me his or her favorite videos.

37. Somebody left the engine running in their car.

38. Did one of the applicants forget to sign his or her forms?

39. Most of the customers complained that his or her food was cold.

40. Neither of the robins had their winter plumage.

Writing Application

Using Agreement in Instructions

Subject-Verb Agreement Your family is going on a weekend trip. A neighbor has agreed to look after your pets. Write a note giving your neighbor complete instructions for tending the animals. To avoid confusing your reader, make sure the subjects and verbs in your sentences agree.

Prewriting Think about pets that you have had or that someone you know has had. If you have never cared for a pet, talk to someone who has. Take notes on caring for each pet.

Writing Write a draft of your note. Explain the daily care of the pets step by step. The more specific your instructions are, the better. With your teacher's permission, you may use informal, standard English if you are writing to someone you know well.

Reference Note

For more about **informal English,** see page 221.

Revising Read your note aloud. Can you follow each step of the instructions? Are all the steps in order? Have you included all the necessary information? If not, revise your note to make it clear and complete.

Publishing After you have revised your note, check each sentence for subject-verb and pronoun-antecedent agreement. Take special care with any verb that is part of a contraction. Check your note for any other errors in grammar, punctuation, and spelling. Find or make pictures that illustrate each of your steps. With your teacher's permission, mount the pictures on a storyboard and display the storyboard in your classroom.

Using Verbs Correctly

Principal Parts, Regular and Irregular Verbs, Tense

1.0 Written and Oral English Language Conventions
Students write and speak with a command of standard English conventions appropriate to this grade level.
1.2 Identify and properly use present perfect, past perfect, and future perfect verb tenses.

Diagnostic Preview

Revising Incorrect Verb Forms in Sentences

Most of the following sentences contain an error in the use of verbs. If a verb form is incorrect, write the correct form. If the sentence is already correct, write *C.*

EXAMPLE 1. The last movie I seen was terrible.
1. saw

1. My friends and I recently have set through several bad movies.
2. Has anyone ever wrote a letter to complain about how many bad movies there are?
3. Last Saturday our local theater run two bad movies!
4. My friends J. D. and Carolyn had went with me to the movie theater.
5. We had hoped that we would enjoy *Out of the Swamp.*
6. In the beginning of the movie, a huge swamp creature raised out of the muddy water.
7. It begun to crawl slowly toward a cow in a field.
8. The cow had been laying under a tree.

9. She never even seen the swamp monster.
10. I had sank back in my seat, expecting the monster to pounce.
11. Then the lights come back on.
12. What a disappointment—the film had broke!
13. It taked a long time before the machine came back on.
14. Some people throwed their hands up in disgust.
15. Children drunk noisily through their straws.
16. I had sat my popcorn on the floor by my seat, and someone accidentally kicked it over.
17. Finally, the theater manager choosed another movie, but it was only a silly cartoon about a penguin and a polar bear.
18. The penguin wore a coat it had stole from a sleeping polar bear.
19. The bear awoke, becomes angry, and chased the penguin all over the place.
20. Finally, the penguin gave back the coat and swum to Miami Beach to get warm.

Principal Parts of Verbs

The four basic forms of a verb are called the ***principal parts*** of the verb.

7a. The four principal parts of a verb are the *base form,* the *present participle,* the *past,* and the *past participle.*

Base Form	Present Participle	Past	Past Participle
start	[is] starting	started	[have] started
wear	[is] wearing	wore	[have] worn

NOTE The words *is* and *have* are included in this chart because present participle and past participle verb forms require helping verbs (forms of *be* and *have*) to form tenses.

HELP—
Some people refer to the base form as the *infinitive.* Follow your teacher's directions when labeling this form.

Reference Note

For more information about **helping verbs,** see page 49.

As you can see from their names, the principal parts of a verb are used to express time.

PRESENT TIME She **wears** a blue uniform.

Ray **has been wearing** his baseball cap.

PAST TIME Yesterday, we **wore** sweaters.

I **had worn** braces for three months.

FUTURE TIME Jessica **will wear** her new dress at the party.

By next spring, Joey **will have worn** holes in those shoes.

A verb that forms its past and past participle by adding *–d* or *–ed* is called a ***regular verb.*** A verb that forms its past and past participle differently is called an ***irregular verb.***

USAGE

Regular Verbs

7b. A *regular verb* forms its past and past participle by adding *–d* or *–ed* to the base form.

Base Form	Present Participle	Past	Past Participle
wash	[is] washing	washed	[have] washed
hop	[is] hopping	hopped	[have] hopped
use	[is] using	used	[have] used

Reference Note

For more about **spelling rules,** see Chapter 14.

NOTE Most regular verbs that end in *–e* drop the *–e* before adding *–ing.* Some regular verbs double the final consonant before adding *–ing* or *–ed.*

EXAMPLES cause **caus**ing **caus**ed
drop **dropp**ing **dropp**ed

Reference Note

For more about **standard** and **nonstandard English,** see page 221.

One common error in forming the past or past participle of a regular verb is to leave off the *–d* or *–ed* ending.

NONSTANDARD Josh was suppose to meet us here.

STANDARD Josh was **supposed** to meet us here.

Oral Practice 1 Using Regular Verbs

Read the following sentences aloud, stressing each italicized verb.

1. We *are supposed* to practice sit-ups this morning.
2. With the help of his guide dog, the man *crossed* the street.
3. Carlos and Rita *have ordered* soup and salad.
4. Her family *had moved* from Trinidad to Brooklyn.
5. Some American Indians *used* to use shells for money.
6. Many *called* shell money "wampum."
7. Larry *has saved* most of his allowance for the past two months.
8. My grandmother *worked* at the computer store.

Exercise 1 Forming the Principal Parts of Regular Verbs

Write the four principal parts for each of the following verbs.

EXAMPLE 1. hope
1. *hope; [is] hoping; hoped; [have] hoped*

1. skate
2. pick
3. live
4. move
5. talk
6. stun
7. enjoy
8. rob
9. laugh
10. love
11. hop
12. snow
13. cook
14. examine
15. imagine
16. question
17. ask
18. worry
19. turn
20. experiment

HELP— Remember that the spelling of some verbs changes when *–ing* or *–ed* is added.

Exercise 2 Using the Principal Parts of Regular Verbs

Complete each of the following sentences with the correct form of the given italicized verb.

EXAMPLE 1. *paint* Henry Ossawa Tanner ____ many kinds of subjects.
1. *painted*

1. *create* Tanner ____ images showing people, nature, history, and religion.

The Banjo Lesson by Henry Ossawa Tanner, 1893. Oil on canvas. Hampton University Museum, Hampton, Virginia.

USAGE

2. *learn* What is the boy in this painting ____ to do?
3. *title* Not surprisingly, Tanner ____ this painting *The Banjo Lesson.*
4. *live* The artist, a native of Pittsburgh, ____ from 1859 to 1937.
5. *move* At the age of thirty-two, Tanner ____ to Paris to study and work.
6. *visit* Other African American artists ____ Tanner in France.
7. *admire* For years, people have ____ Tanner's paintings.
8. *plan* Our teacher is ____ to show us more of Tanner's work.
9. *want* I have ____ to see Tanner's famous portrait of Booker T. Washington.
10. *praise* In his book *Up from Slavery,* Washington ____ Tanner's talent.

Irregular Verbs

7c. An *irregular verb* forms its past and past participle in some other way than by adding *–d* or *–ed* to the base form.

An irregular verb forms its past and past participle in one of the following ways:

- changing vowels

Base Form	Past	Past Participle
win	won	[have] won
sing	sang	[have] sung
hold	held	[have] held

- changing consonants

Base Form	Past	Past Participle
make	made	[have] made
lend	lent	[have] lent
hear	heard	[have] heard

- changing vowels *and* consonants

Base Form	Past	Past Participle
catch	caught	[have] caught
draw	drew	[have] drawn
tear	tore	[have] torn

- making no change

Base Form	Past	Past Participle
burst	burst	[have] burst
cut	cut	[have] cut
hurt	hurt	[have] hurt

NOTE If you are not sure about the principal parts of a verb, look up the verb in a current dictionary. Entries for irregular verbs list the principal parts of the verb.

Common Irregular Verbs

Base Form	Present Participle	Past	Past Participle
become	[is] becoming	became	[have] become
begin	[is] beginning	began	[have] begun
blow	[is] blowing	blew	[have] blown
break	[is] breaking	broke	[have] broken

(continued)

USAGE

(continued)

Common Irregular Verbs			
Base Form	**Present Participle**	**Past**	**Past Participle**
bring	[is] bringing	brought	[have] brought
buy	[is] buying	bought	[have] bought
choose	[is] choosing	chose	[have] chosen
come	[is] coming	came	[have] come
do	[is] doing	did	[have] done
drink	[is] drinking	drank	[have] drunk
drive	[is] driving	drove	[have] driven
eat	[is] eating	ate	[have] eaten
fall	[is] falling	fell	[have] fallen
feel	[is] feeling	felt	[have] felt
find	[is] finding	found	[have] found
freeze	[is] freezing	froze	[have] frozen
get	[is] getting	got	[have] gotten *or* got
give	[is] giving	gave	[have] given
go	[is] going	went	[have] gone
grow	[is] growing	grew	[have] grown
have	[is] having	had	[have] had
hear	[is] hearing	heard	[have] heard
hit	[is] hitting	hit	[have] hit
hold	[is] holding	held	[have] held
keep	[is] keeping	kept	[have] kept
know	[is] knowing	knew	[have] known

Oral Practice 2 Using Irregular Verbs

Read the following sentences aloud, stressing each italicized verb.

1. I *have begun* to learn karate.
2. We *chose* to stay indoors.
3. Earline never *had drunk* buttermilk before.
4. We *did* our homework after dinner.
5. Anna and Dee *have* almost *broken* the school record for the fifty-yard dash.

6. The wind *has blown* fiercely for three days.
7. Last Saturday, Isaac *brought* me a tape of reggae music.
8. The water pipes in the laundry room *have frozen* again.

Exercise 3 Identifying the Correct Forms of Irregular Verbs

Choose the correct verb form in parentheses in each of the following sentences.

EXAMPLE 1. The children have finally (*broke, broken*) the piñata.
1. *broken*

1. We had just (*began, begun*) our project when I got sick.
2. The Ruiz family (*drove, driven*) across the country.
3. Has anyone (*brung, brought*) extra batteries for the radio?
4. I have finally (*chose, chosen*) a book to borrow.
5. Last week the lake (*froze, frozen*) hard enough for skating.
6. My brother and I have (*gave, given*) away all our comic books to the children's hospital.
7. My sister, who is learning to ride, has (*fell, fallen*) off her bicycle several times.
8. Everyone (*went, gone*) back to the classroom to watch the videotape of the spelling bee.
9. David's aunt (*came, come*) here to attend his bar mitzvah.
10. Have you (*ate, eaten*) at the new Philippine restaurant?
11. They should not have (*drank, drunk*) so much ice water after playing tennis.
12. After our guests had (*ate, eaten*), we all toured the city.
13. We have (*came, come*) to expect great things from you.
14. By the time Jason arrived, Gina had already (*went, gone*).
15. When they left, Uncle Enrique (*gave, given*) them some Cuban bread.
16. Their team (*chose, chosen*) another topic for the debate.
17. Oh, yes, Chris and I have (*knew, known*) each other since kindergarten.
18. He (*did, done*) the experiment that very afternoon.
19. Lenny had never (*drove, driven*) a tractor before that day.
20. We must have (*blew, blown*) up a hundred balloons for my little brother's birthday party.

USAGE

Exercise 4 Identifying the Correct Forms of Irregular Verbs

Choose the correct verb form in parentheses in each of the following sentences.

EXAMPLE **1.** Jameel has already (*drank, drunk*) a large glass of orange juice, but he is still thirsty.

1. drunk

1. The wool sweater (*felt, feeled*) scratchy, so I did not buy it.
2. Ramón (*got, gotten*) a part in the school play.
3. The new houseplant has already (*grew, grown*) several inches since we bought it.
4. Leslie (*become, became*) my best friend back in first grade.
5. I (*holded, held*) on to the dog's leash tightly.
6. Our neighbors have (*buyed, bought*) a new doghouse for their German shepherd.
7. Kani has (*kept, keeped*) a log of his study time.
8. Yesterday we finally (*finded, found*) a copy of Pat Mora's latest book.
9. In last night's ballgame, Heather (*hit, hitted*) another home run.
10. Have you ever (*hear, heard*) traditional Japanese music?

More Common Irregular Verbs

Base Form	Present Participle	Past	Past Participle
lead	[is] leading	led	[have] led
leave	[is] leaving	left	[have] left
lose	[is] losing	lost	[have] lost
pay	[is] paying	paid	[have] paid
put	[is] putting	put	[have] put
read	[is] reading	read	[have] read
ride	[is] riding	rode	[have] ridden
ring	[is] ringing	rang	[have] rung
run	[is] running	ran	[have] run
say	[is] saying	said	[have] said

More Common Irregular Verbs			
Base Form	**Present Participle**	**Past**	**Past Participle**
see	[is] seeing	saw	[have] seen
send	[is] sending	sent	[have] sent
shrink	[is] shrinking	shrank *or* shrunk	[have] shrunk
sing	[is] singing	sang	[have] sung
sink	[is] sinking	sank *or* sunk	[have] sunk
speak	[is] speaking	spoke	[have] spoken
stand	[is] standing	stood	[have] stood
steal	[is] stealing	stole	[have] stolen
swim	[is] swimming	swam	[have] swum
take	[is] taking	took	[have] taken
teach	[is] teaching	taught	[have] taught
tell	[is] telling	told	[have] told
throw	[is] throwing	threw	[have] thrown
wear	[is] wearing	wore	[have] worn
write	[is] writing	wrote	[have] written

Oral Practice 3 Using Irregular Verbs

Read the following sentences aloud, stressing the italicized verbs.

1. Despite the blinding snowstorm, the Saint Bernard *had led* the rescue party to the stranded hikers.
2. The school bell *rang* five minutes late every afternoon this week.
3. When she visited New York City, Julia *saw* the Ellis Island Immigration Museum.
4. How many sixth-graders would you guess *have ridden* on this school bus?
5. What is the longest distance you *have swum*?
6. George *ran* to the corner to see the antique fire engine.
7. Gloria and Rose *sang* at the talent show.
8. *Have* you ever *written* haiku?

"You don't say 'He taked my chair'...it's 'My chair was tooken'."

Exercise 5 **Identifying the Correct Forms of Irregular Verbs**

Choose the correct verb form in parentheses in each of the following sentences.

EXAMPLE 1. Ms. Toyama (*took, taken*) her new kitten to the veterinarian.

1. took

1. Who (*ran, run*) faster, Jesse or Cindy?
2. That cute little puppy has (*stole, stolen*) a dog biscuit.
3. The Boys Choir of Harlem has never (*sang, sung*) more beautifully.
4. Jimmy's toy sailboat had (*sank, sunk*) to the bottom of the lake.
5. Have you (*thrown, throwed*) yesterday's paper into the recycling bin?
6. Maria had (*wore, worn*) her new spring outfit to the party.
7. Until yesterday, no one had ever (*swam, swum*) across Crystal Lake.
8. Before she followed the white rabbit through the tiny door, Alice had (*shrank, shrunk*) to a very small size!
9. The students have (*written, wrote*) a letter to the mayor.
10. I have never (*spoke, spoken*) to a large audience before.
11. An open convertible (*lead, led*) the ticker tape parade.
12. Vulcan's hammer (*rang, rung*) as he worked metal for the Roman gods.
13. Why had the dog (*took, taken*) the portable phone outside?
14. We (*saw, seen*) a whole stack of petri dishes in the back of the lab closet.
15. Not only have I never (*rode, ridden*) a roller coaster, but I probably never will.
16. Have you (*spoke, spoken*) to your parents about taking those tuba lessons?
17. The children simply (*sang, sung*) "The Bear Went over the Mountain" until the baby sitter read them another story.
18. Why have all those people (*swam, swum*) across the English Channel?
19. The detective always (*wore, worn*) a porkpie hat.
20. The clever fox (*threw, throw*) the dog off the trail.

Exercise 6 Identifying the Correct Forms of Irregular Verbs

Choose the correct verb form in parentheses in each of the following sentences.

EXAMPLE 1. Uncle Alberto (*leaded, led*) the parade.
1. led

1. Justin (*putted, put*) the soy sauce on the table.
2. Have Grandma and Grandpa (*left, leaved*) already?
3. The family (*said, sayed*) grace and then ate dinner.
4. The senator (*stood, standed*) up and waved to the crowd.
5. Has Leta (*readed, read*) the story "Miss Awful" yet?
6. After school Angela (*taught, teached*) me the new dance.
7. Each Christmas, Aunt Arlene has (*sended, sent*) me a classic children's book.
8. Mom (*paid, payed*) for the groceries, and we went home.
9. Ms. Cata (*telled, told*) the children a Hopi myth.
10. Lucas has (*losed, lost*) his favorite CD.

USAGE

Review A Proofreading for Errors in Irregular Verbs

Most of the following sentences contain an incorrect verb form. Identify each error, and write the correct form of the verb. If a sentence is already correct, write *C.*

EXAMPLE 1. Many stories have been wrote about the American athlete Jesse Owens.
1. wrote—written

1. Owens breaked several sports records during his career.
2. At the Olympic games of 1936, he winned four gold medals.
3. A photographer took this picture of one of Owens's victories.
4. Owens's career begun in an unusual way.
5. As a little boy, Owens had been very sick, and later he run to strengthen his lungs.
6. In high school, the other boys on the track team done their practicing after school, but Owens had to work.

7. Owens's coach encouraged him to practice an hour before school and brung him breakfast every morning.
8. The coach knowed Owens's parents couldn't afford to send their son to college.
9. The coach seen that something had to be done, and he helped Owens's father find a job.
10. Later, Owens went to Ohio State University, where he became a track star.

USAGE

Review B Writing the Past and Past Participle Forms of Irregular Verbs

For each of the following sentences, write the correct past or past participle form of the italicized verb.

EXAMPLE 1. *take* Gloria has ____ the last envelope.
1. *taken*

1. *read* Has everyone ____ the assignment for today?
2. *burst* Suddenly, the door ____ open.
3. *drive* We have ____ on Oklahoma's Indian Nation Turnpike.
4. *find* Have you ____ your socks yet?
5. *speak* Who ____ at this year's Hispanic Heritage awards ceremony?
6. *grow* Patricia has ____ two inches in one year.
7. *hear* One of the hikers had ____ the distant growl of thunder.
8. *give* Mrs. Matsuo ____ me a copy of the book *Origami: Japanese Paper-Folding.*
9. *freeze* The water in the birdbath has ____ again.
10. *choose* Which play have they ____ to perform?
11. *wear* The Highland School Band has always ____ Scottish kilts.
12. *know* Noriko ____ the way to Lynn's house.
13. *teach* Ms. Brook has ____ all of us how to work together.
14. *send* My sweater was too small, so I ____ it to my cousin.
15. *ring* Who ____ the doorbell a moment ago?
16. *hold* The puppy ____ up its injured paw.

17. *hit* David ____ a ball past third base in the ninth inning.
18. *leave* Have you ____ your towel at the pool?
19. *see* We had never ____ a koala before.
20. *buy* Jerome ____ the decorations for the party.

Review C **Proofreading for Incorrect Verb Forms**

Read each of the following sentences. If the form of a verb is wrong, write the correct past or past participle form. If the sentence is already correct, write *C.*

EXAMPLE 1. Dr. Seuss knowed how to please readers of all ages.
1. *knew*

1. Have you ever saw the wacky characters shown here?
2. The imagination of Dr. Seuss brought both of them to life.
3. You may have bursted out laughing at the Cat in the Hat, Horton the elephant, or the Grinch.
4. In one story, the mean Grinch stoled Christmas.
5. In another, a bird gived Horton an egg to hatch.
6. The Lorax spoke out in support of the trees and the environment.
7. The Cat in the Hat has always wore his striped hat.
8. During his lifetime, Dr. Seuss must have wrote about fifty books with unusual characters.
9. Many children have began reading with his books.
10. Dr. Seuss choosed *The Lorax* as his own favorite book.

USAGE

USAGE

Tense

7d. The *tense* of a verb indicates the time of the action or of the state of being that is expressed by the verb.

The six tenses are *present, past, future, present perfect, past perfect,* and *future perfect.* These tenses are formed from the principal parts of verbs. Each of these six tenses has its own uses. The following time line shows the relationships between tenses.

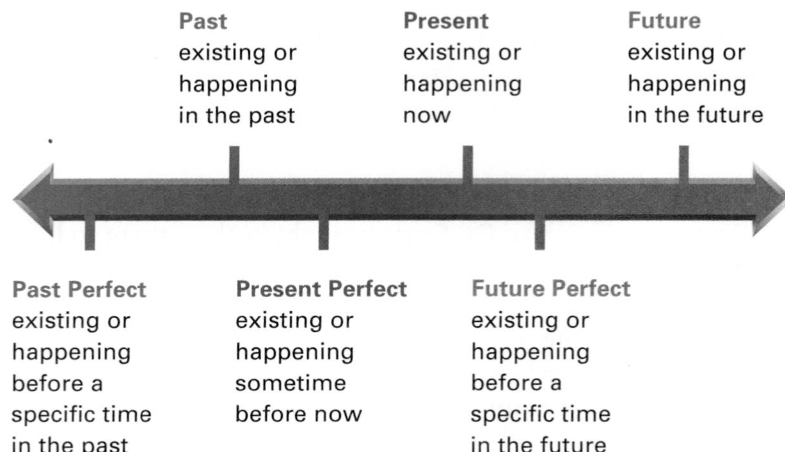

Listing all the forms of a verb is called ***conjugating*** the verb.

Conjugation of the Verb *Wear*	
Present Tense	
Singular	**Plural**
I wear	we wear
you wear	you wear
he, she, *or* it wears	they wear
Past Tense	
Singular	**Plural**
I wore	we wore
you wore	you wore
he, she, *or* it wore	they wore

Conjugation of the Verb *Wear*

Future Tense	
Singular	**Plural**
I will (shall) wear	we will (shall) wear
you will (shall) wear	you will (shall) wear
he, she, *or* it will (shall) wear	they will (shall) wear
Present Perfect Tense	
Singular	**Plural**
I have worn	we have worn
you have worn	you have worn
he, she, *or* it has worn	they have worn
Past Perfect Tense	
Singular	**Plural**
I had worn	we had worn
you had worn	you had worn
he, she, *or* it had worn	they had worn
Future Perfect Tense	
Singular	**Plural**
I will (shall) have worn	we will (shall) have worn
you will (shall) have worn	you will (shall) have worn
he, she, *or* it will (shall) have worn	they will (shall) have worn

Progressive Forms

Each of the six tenses also has a form called the ***progressive form.*** The progressive form expresses continuing action or state of being. It is made up of the appropriate tense of the verb *be* plus the present participle of a verb. The progressive is not a separate tense. It is just a different form that each tense can take.

STYLE TIP

Traditionally, the helping verb *shall* was used only in certain situations. Now, however, *shall* can be used almost any time that you would use *will.*

Present Progressive	am, are, is wearing
Past Progressive	was, were wearing
Future Progressive	will (shall) be wearing
Present Perfect Progressive	has, have been wearing
Past Perfect Progressive	had been wearing
Future Perfect Progressive	will (shall) have been wearing

The Verb *Be*

The verb *be* is the most irregular of all the irregular verbs in English. Note the many different forms of *be* in the following conjugation.

Conjugation of the Verb *Be*	
Present Tense	
Singular	**Plural**
I am	we are
you are	you are
he, she, *or* it is	they are
Present Progressive: am, are, is being	
Past Tense	
Singular	**Plural**
I was	we were
you were	you were
he, she, *or* it was	they were
Past Progressive: was, were being	
Future Tense	
Singular	**Plural**
I will (shall) be	we will (shall) be
you will (shall) be	you will (shall) be
he, she, *or* it will (shall) be	they will (shall) be

HELP

The present and past progressive forms of *be* are the most common. The other progressive forms of *be* are hardly ever used.

EXAMPLES

will (shall) be being [future progressive]

has, have been being [present perfect progressive]

USAGE

Conjugation of the Verb *Be*	
Present Perfect Tense	
Singular	**Plural**
I have been	we have been
you have been	you have been
he, she, *or* it has been	they have been
Past Perfect Tense	
Singular	**Plural**
I had been	we had been
you had been	you had been
he, she, *or* it had been	they had been
Future Perfect Tense	
Singular	**Plural**
I will (shall) have been	we will (shall) have been
you will (shall) have been	you will (shall) have been
he, she, *or* it will (shall) have been	they will (shall) have been

USAGE

Exercise 7 Identifying Tenses

Identify the verb's tense in each of the following sentences.

EXAMPLE **1.** A trolley noisily rolled down the track.

1. past

1. Oh, no! Who fed this to the paper shredder?
2. Yes, Mom actually drinks that green stuff from the juicer.
3. Benjamin has left Des Moines.
4. Had you heard Andrés Segovia's music before then?
5. A mosaic of colorful tiles will decorate the entryway.
6. By my twenty-first birthday, I will have qualified for my pilot's license.
7. The committee will notify you of its decision.
8. Will you have saved enough money by then?
9. Evidently, I had thought of every possibility but one.
10. They are using the new modem now.

Consistency of Tense

7e. Do not change needlessly from one tense to another.

To write about events that take place at about the same time, use verbs in the same tense. To write about events that occur at different times, use verbs in different tenses.

INCONSISTENT The cat jumped onto the counter and steals the sandwich. [The events happen at about the same time, but *jumped* is in the past tense, and *steals* is in the present tense.]

CONSISTENT The cat **jumped** onto the counter and **stole** the sandwich. [Both verbs are in the past tense.]

CONSISTENT The cat **jumps** onto the counter and **steals** the sandwich. [Both verbs are in the present tense.]

COMPUTER TIP

Most word processors can help you check your writing to be sure that you have used verbs correctly. For example, a spell-checker will highlight misspelled verb forms such as *telled* and *growed*. Some style-checking software can point out inconsistent verb tense.

Remember, though, that the computer is just a tool to help you improve your writing. As a writer, you must make all the style and content choices that affect your writing.

USAGE

Exercise 8 Revising a Paragraph for Consistency of Tense

Read the following paragraph, and decide whether to rewrite it in the present or the past tense. Then, rewrite all of the sentences, changing the verb forms to correct any needless shifts in tense.

EXAMPLE **[1]** Since our school has a computer network, we "chatted" with students from other schools.

1. *Since our school has a computer network, we "chat" with students from other schools.*

or

Since our school had a computer network, we "chatted" with students from other schools.

HELP

Although the example in Exercise 8 gives two possible revisions, you need to give only one for each sentence.

[**1**] We trade essays with other English classes. [**2**] They read and commented on our essays, and we read and comment on theirs. [**3**] We also share reports with other classes in the school. [**4**] In Spanish I, we are writing letters to students in Argentina. [**5**] We practiced our Spanish. [**6**] They wrote back to us in English. [**7**] The computer classes sent a newsletter to all the other classes every week. [**8**] Every student has e-mail. [**9**] Students send messages to each other and to teachers. [**10**] E-mail made it easy to ask questions about assignments.

Six Confusing Verbs

Sit and *Set*

The verb *sit* means "to be seated" or "to rest." *Sit* seldom takes a direct object. The verb *set* means "to put (something) in a place." *Set* usually takes a direct object. Notice that *set* has the same form for the base form, past, and past participle.

Base Form	Present Participle	Past	Past Participle
sit	[is] sitting	sat	[have] sat
set	[is] setting	set	[have] set

EXAMPLES I **will sit** in the easy chair. [no direct object]

I **will set** the cushion in the easy chair. [I will set what? *Cushion* is the direct object.]

The worker **has sat** there. [no direct object]

The workers **have set** their equipment there. [The workers have set what? *Equipment* is the direct object.]

Oral Practice 4 Using the Forms of *Sit* and *Set* Correctly

Read the following sentences aloud, stressing each italicized verb.

1. Before she left, Josie *had set* two loaves of French bread on the table.
2. The clown *sat* on the broken chair.
3. They *are sitting* down to rest awhile.
4. *Has* she *set* her bracelet on the night stand?
5. The Clarks' car *has sat* in the driveway for a week.
6. My little brother *sits* still for only a few seconds at a time.
7. The teacher *is setting* the best projects in the display case in the hall.
8. The librarian *set* the book about Michael Jordan on the large table.

Reference Note

For more about **direct objects,** see page 107.

TIPS & TRICKS

If you do not know whether to use *sit* or *set* in a sentence, try substituting *put.* If the sentence makes sense with *put,* use *set.* If not, use *sit.*

EXAMPLE
Jill (*set, sat*) the CDs on the shelf.

TEST
Jill put the CDs on the shelf. [The sentence makes sense with *put.*]

ANSWER
Jill **set** the CDs on the shelf.

HELP

You may know that the word *set* has meanings that are not given at the top of this page. Check in a dictionary to see if the meaning you intend requires a direct object.

EXAMPLE
The sun **sets** in the west. [Here, *sets* does not take a direct object.]

HELP

Use the following short poem to help choose the correct form of *sit* and *set*.

Grandpa Jones **sits** in his chair
And watches the sun **set** in the cool, crisp air.
He **sets** his cup on the nearby table
And looks at the bird that **sits** on the gable.
"**Sit**, Rover," he says to the dog on the floor,
"**Sit** down, neighbor," to the man at the door.
And there they **sat,** two men and a dog,
Sitting together until the fog
Rolled in and made this whole poem—
A **set**up!

HELP

The verb *raise* has definitions other than the ones given here. Another common definition is "to grow" or "to bring to maturity."

EXAMPLES
They **raise** wheat.
She **raises** sheep.

Notice that both of these uses also take a direct object.

USAGE

Exercise 9 Writing the Forms of *Sit* and *Set*

Write the correct form of *sit* or *set* to complete each of the following sentences.

EXAMPLE 1. The girls ____ on the porch swing yesterday.
1. sat

1. At the party yesterday, we ____ the birthday presents on the coffee table.
2. Then we ____ on the floor to play a game.
3. Alana had been ____ next to Rosa.
4. The Jiménez twins never ____ together, even though it was their birthday.
5. Mrs. Jiménez ____ a large cake on the table.
6. Mr. Jiménez had already ____ party hats and favors around the table.
7. He also ____ out the plates.
8. One of the twins ____ on a hat by mistake.
9. At every party we always ____ quietly while the birthday person makes a wish.
10. Yesterday, we ____ still twice as long for the Jiménez twins!

Rise and *Raise*

The verb *rise* means "to go up" or "to get up." *Rise* does not take a direct object. The verb *raise* means "to lift (something) up" or "to cause (something) to rise." *Raise* usually takes a direct object.

Base Form	Present Participle	Past	Past Participle
rise	[is] rising	rose	[have] risen
raise	[is] raising	raised	[have] raised

EXAMPLES The winner **is rising** to receive his medal. [no direct object]

The winner **is raising** her arms in triumph. [The winner is raising what? *Arms* is the direct object.]

Taxes **rose** quickly. [no direct object]

Congress **raised** taxes. [Congress raised what? *Taxes* is the direct object.]

Oral Practice 5 Using the Forms of *Rise* and *Raise* Correctly

Read the following sentences aloud, stressing each italicized verb.

1. The audience *had risen* from their seats to applaud the singer.
2. They *raised* the curtains for the play to start.
3. Dark smoke *rose* from the fire.
4. They always *rise* early on Saturday mornings.
5. The wind *had raised* the Chinese dragon kite high above the trees.
6. They *are raising* the banners.
7. The huge crane *can raise* the steel beams off the ground.
8. The temperature *was rising* quickly.

MEETING THE CHALLENGE

Think up a new computer game or other game that you would enjoy playing. Then, write an advertisement that would encourage your friends to buy that item. Use as many of the six confusing verbs in your ad as you can—at least four. You may want to include graphics or artwork.

USAGE

Exercise 10 Writing the Forms of *Rise* and *Raise*

To complete each of the following sentences, supply the correct form of *rise* or *raise*.

EXAMPLE 1. We will _____ a banner.
1. raise

1. Before the game the color guards _____ the flag.
2. The fans were _____ for the national anthem.
3. The pitcher _____ his arm to throw the ball.
4. The baseball seemed to _____ above the batter's head.
5. Someone in front of me was _____ a sign that blocked my view.
6. I have _____ my voice to cheer a hundred times during one game.
7. When the sun had _____ too high, the players couldn't see the high fly balls.
8. Whenever someone hits a home run, the fans _____ their mitts to catch the baseball.
9. Yesterday, everyone _____ when the designated hitter hit a home run.
10. As soon as the ninth inning was over, we _____ to leave.

USAGE

HELP

The verb *lie* has definitions other than the ones given here. Another common definition is "to tell an untruth."

EXAMPLE
Little Terry did not **lie** about spilling the milk.

When used this way, *lie* usually does not take a direct object. Its past and past participle forms are *lied* and [*have*] *lied.*

Lie and *Lay*

The verb *lie* generally means "to recline," "to be in a place," or "to remain lying down." *Lie* does not take a direct object. The verb *lay* generally means "to put (something) down" or "to place (something)." *Lay* usually takes a direct object.

Base Form	Present Participle	Past	Past Participle
lie	[is] lying	lay	[have] lain
lay	[is] laying	laid	[have] laid

EXAMPLES The beam **is lying** near the edge. [no direct object]

The workers **are laying** the beams near the edge. [The workers are laying what? *Beams* is the direct object.]

The newspaper **lay** on the kitchen table. [no direct object]

Sara **laid** the newspaper on the kitchen table. [Sara laid what? *Newspaper* is the direct object.]

The beach blanket **has lain** under the umbrella. [no direct object]

They **have laid** the beach blanket under the umbrella. [They have laid what? *Blanket* is the direct object.]

COMPUTER TIP

If you have trouble using *sit, set, rise, raise, lie,* and *lay* correctly, a computer may be helpful. Use the search function to find and highlight all the uses of these confusing verbs in your writing. Then, look at each case carefully to determine whether you have used the correct form, and revise if necessary.

Oral Practice 6 Using the Forms of *Lie* and *Lay* Correctly

Read the following sentences aloud, stressing each italicized verb.

1. The corrected test paper *lay* on the desk.
2. My teddy bear *lies* on my bed all day.
3. Before the sale, the clerk *laid* samples on the counter.
4. *Have* those toys *lain* outside too long?
5. The Inuit hunter *was laying* his harpoon on the ice.
6. Last night, I *was lying* on the sofa reading a book when the phone rang.
7. I think the hero *has laid* a trap for the villain.
8. *Lay* the baby gently in the crib.

Exercise 11 Writing the Forms of *Lie* and *Lay*

To complete each of the following sentences, write the correct form of *lie* or *lay*.

EXAMPLE 1. Children often ____ toys in the wrong places.
1. lay

1. The remote control for the television is ____ under the rocking chair.
2. How long has it ____ there?
3. My brother Ramón probably ____ it there last night.
4. He was ____ on the floor, watching television.
5. Julia, my younger sister, is always ____ her toys in front of the television set.
6. She has ____ little parts from her board games all over the house.
7. Whenever Mom and Dad find one of these parts, they usually ____ it on the bookcase.
8. Yesterday, Dad ____ down on some hard plastic pieces on the sofa.
9. Now those broken bits of plastic ____ at the bottom of the wastebasket.
10. Today, Julia has ____ every single toy safely in the toy chest in her room.

Review D Identifying the Correct Forms of *Sit* and *Set*, *Rise* and *Raise*, and *Lie* and *Lay*

Choose the correct verb from the pair in parentheses in each of the following sentences.

EXAMPLE 1. Dad (*sat, set*) the scrapbook from our visit to the Hopi reservation on the table and opened it to the picture shown on the next page.
1. set

1. The Hopi villages (*lie, lay*) on and around three mesas in the Arizona desert.
2. Waalpi, a village that (*sits, sets*) atop one mesa, was established in 1150.
3. Many Hopi houses and fields have (*laid, lain*) in their present locations for hundreds of years.

4. At the reservation, everyone (*sat, set*) quietly during the Hopi Snake Dance.

5. One dancer had (*risen, raised*) a snake above his head for the crowd to see.

6. The growing corn (*rises, raises*) high in the Hopi country of Arizona.

7. Hot and very tired, I (*lay, laid*) on a bench at the Hopi trading post.

8. In a moment, Dad had (*rose, raised*) his hat to shade my face.

9. When we entered the pueblo, a Hopi woman (*rose, raised*) from her chair to greet us.

10. Smiling, the woman (*sat, set*) a beautiful coiled basket on the counter.

Review E Proofreading for Correct Verb Forms

Identify the incorrect verb form in each of the following sentences. Then, write the correct form.

EXAMPLE **1.** Lately, everyone in our neighborhood has did more to keep physically fit.

1. did—done

USAGE

1. No one is setting down anymore—except on stationary bicycles.
2. My mom has rode 150 miles so far.
3. In addition, I have never knew so many aerobic dancers.
4. Yesterday afternoon, I swum twelve laps in the pool.
5. Last month, a famous exercise instructor choosed our neighborhood for her new fitness center.
6. Many people seen her interviews on local talk shows.
7. All of a sudden, adults and children have began going to the center.
8. Each person is suppose to use different kinds of equipment.
9. Last night, I rose a fifty-pound weight.
10. So far, no one has broke a leg on the cross-country ski machine.
11. Mom had went to several gyms over the years.
12. After my workout, I just laid on the floor, out of breath.
13. She and I have took several classes at that gym.
14. I must have ran a thousand miles on that treadmill.
15. We never worn fancy outfits, only sweat pants and T-shirts.
16. I had chose an hour soaking in the whirlpool as my first exercise plan.
17. However, I seen the dancers and heard the music.
18. Now I have knowed many of the dancers for a long time.
19. My energy level has raised, and I'm happier.
20. Don't sit those free weights down; keep at it!

USAGE

Review F **Using the Correct Forms of Verbs**

Write the correct past or past participle form of the verb in parentheses in each of the following sentences.

EXAMPLE **1.** I have (*grow*) tired of this TV program.
1. grown

1. Grant (*feel*) proud and happy after winning the chess tournament.
2. Over the years, I have (*keep*) all the postcards from my grandparents.
3. Mother has (*lose*) the sash for her kimono.

4. The room quickly (*become*) crowded with curious fans.
5. Mr. Shaw (*tell*) us to read about the life of Harriet Jacobs.
6. Have you (*make*) the hat for your costume yet?
7. All night the faithful Irish setter (*stand*) watch over the homestead.
8. Has Yoshi ever (*ride*) a horse before?
9. Have you ever (*hear*) the story of Pocahontas?
10. Juanita (*say*) the biscuits would be ready soon.
11. As the sun set, the temperature (*begin*) to drop.
12. A squirrel had (*eat*) all the seed we put out for the birds.
13. Has Darius (*run*) ten laps yet?
14. All the band members (*wear*) the same color socks on Friday.
15. At halftime, our team (*lead*) by two goals.
16. The secret agent had easily (*break*) the code and deciphered the message.
17. A whippoorwill (*sing*), crickets chirped, and a breeze rustled the leaves.
18. While I washed the dishes, Diane (*take*) the trash out.
19. A baby raccoon had (*fall*) from the tree into the soft pile of pine needles.
20. Have you (*give*) Dad his Father's Day present?

FRANK & ERNEST reprinted by permission of Newspaper Enterprise Association, Inc.

Chapter Review

A. Using Correct Forms of Irregular Verbs

For each of the following sentences, write the correct past or past participle form of the verb in parentheses.

1. We had (*ride*) in the car for several hours.
2. Six inches of snow had (*fall*) the night before.
3. I never (*know*) snow was so beautiful.
4. The wind had (*blow*) some of it into high drifts.
5. As we (*go*) past them, they looked like white hills.
6. My brother Ernest had (*bring*) some comics to read.
7. I (*lie*) back and looked at the scenery.
8. Unfortunately, the car heater had (*break*).
9. We all (*wear*) our heavy coats and mittens.
10. However, my ears almost (*freeze*).
11. My favorite wool cap had (*shrink*) to a tiny size in the dryer.
12. During the long ride home, we (*sing*) some songs.
13. At noon, we (*eat*) lunch at a roadside cafeteria.
14. The clerk (*rise*) and asked if we would like some hot chocolate.
15. I (*drink*) two cups of hot cocoa.
16. Mom and I (*run*) around the parking lot to wake up.
17. After lunch, Ernie (*begin*) to feel sleepy.
18. I had never (*sit*) so long in a car before.
19. All warmed up, Ernie (*take*) a long nap.
20. We had (*come*) a long way.

B. Writing the Past and Past Participle Forms of Irregular Verbs

For each of the following sentences, write the correct past or past participle form of the verb in parentheses.

21. Have you (*hear*) the good news about Barbara?
22. The lower branches of the tree (*break*) in the storm.

23. Our current mayor has (*lead*) three successful administrations.
24. The train was crowded, so we stood in the aisle and (*hold*) on to the luggage rack.
25. The tired dog (*lie*) down as soon as it arrived home.
26. As far as I know, they haven't (*see*) that movie.
27. She has always (*set*) the table herself, but tonight she has no time.
28. "So far, children," said Ms. Espinosa, "that robin has (*fly*) all the way from Minnesota on its way to the Gulf Coast for the winter."
29. She (*wear*) her blue parka to the parade.
30. "Time to get up, everyone!" said Mom from the base of the stairs. "The sun has already (*rise*)."

USAGE

C. Proofreading for Correct Verb Forms

For each of the following sentences, identify the incorrect verb form. Then, write the correct form.

31. When Dad was a boy in Iowa, he keeped bees.
32. Before I laid down to sleep, I had packed everything I would need for today's trip.
33. Has Everett sit out the food for the picnic?
34. Nobody in our family had ever went to college before Mom did.
35. I have never rode on a camel, but I'd like to someday.
36. Yesterday's class begun with a speed drill.
37. She felt triumphant because she had never hitted a fly ball before.
38. The unit stood at attention as Corporal Martinez rose the flag.
39. The builder lay the plans on the table.
40. Both Leyla and Hussain brung some delicious falafel to the anniversary party.

Writing Application
Using Verbs in a Description

Forms and Tenses of Verbs Many scientists and writers make predictions about the future. They base their predictions on past and present trends. Write a paragraph or two describing how one everyday item such as a car, a house, a home appliance, or a school might be different one hundred years from now. In your description, be sure to use the correct forms and tenses of verbs.

Prewriting Choose a topic that interests you, such as video games or skyscrapers. Based on what you already know about the topic, make some predictions about the future. Write down as many details as you can.

Writing Begin your draft by telling what time period your predictions concern. Then, use your notes to write a clear, vivid description of something in that future time.

Revising Have a classmate read your composition. How does it sound? Do your predictions sound possible? Add, cut, or revise details to make your description clear and believable.

Publishing Read your paragraph carefully to check for errors in grammar, spelling, and punctuation. Take special care with the forms of verbs. Use a dictionary to check the forms of any irregular verbs you are not sure about. You may want to present your final draft to the class as a multimedia computer presentation, an illustrated bulletin board, or a three-dimensional mobile.

CHAPTER

Using Pronouns Correctly

Subject and Object Forms

1.0 Written and Oral English Language Conventions

Students write and speak with a command of standard English conventions appropriate to this grade level.

Diagnostic Preview

Revising Incorrect Pronoun Forms in Sentences

Most of the following sentences contain an incorrect pronoun form. If a pronoun is used incorrectly, write the incorrect form of the pronoun and give the correct form. If a sentence is already correct, write *C.*

EXAMPLE **1.** The police officer complimented us and they on knowing the rules of bicycle safety.

1. they—them

1. The members of our bicycle club are Everett, Coral, Jackie, and me.
2. Us four call our club the Ramblers, named after a bicycle that was popular in the early 1900s.
3. Mrs. Wheeler gave an old three-speed bike to we four.
4. Whom explained the special bicycle safety course?
5. Our cousins gave Coral and I their old ten-speed bikes.
6. Each of we Ramblers rides after school.
7. Sometimes we ride with the members of the Derailers, a racing club.
8. On Saturday mornings, we and them meet at the school.
9. Who told us about the bike trail along the river?

10. Everett warned we three about being careful because reckless riders can get hurt.
11. Reckless riders can cause you and they problems.
12. A car almost hit two of them!
13. When the Ramblers ride with the Derailers, it is us who obey all the safety rules.
14. Everett, Coral, Jackie, and I entered a safety contest.
15. Other clubs and us competed for a tandem bike.
16. Everett and her taught Jackie how to ride it and shift gears.
17. One by one, us contestants went through the course.
18. Of all of we riders, the least experienced were the Ramblers.
19. Jackie and me were nervous as the judges were deciding.
20. Finally, the judges announced that the winners of the contest were us Ramblers.

USAGE

The Forms of Personal Pronouns

The form of a personal pronoun shows how it can be used in a sentence. Pronouns used as subjects and predicate nominatives are in the ***subject form.***

EXAMPLES **He** and **I** went to the post office. [subject]

The winner of the marathon is **she.** [predicate nominative]

Pronouns used as direct objects and indirect objects of verbs and as objects of prepositions are in the ***object form.***

EXAMPLES Mr. García helped **him** and **me** with yesterday's homework. [direct objects]

The clerk gave **us** the package. [indirect object]

When is Theo going to give the flowers to **her**? [object of a preposition]

Possessive forms (*my, mine, your, yours, his, her, hers, its, their, theirs, our, ours*) are used to show ownership or possession.

EXAMPLES **My** sister had to turn the box on **its** end to get it through the door.

A mother bear is very protective of **her** cubs.

HELP 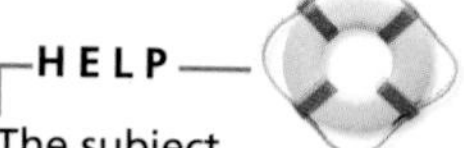

The subject form of pronouns is also sometimes known as the ***nominative case.*** The object form of pronouns is sometimes known as the ***objective case.***

Reference Note

For more information about **possessive pronouns,** see pages 32 and 303.

USAGE

Personal Pronouns		
	Singular	**Plural**
Subject Form	I you he, she, it	we you they
Object Form	me you him, her, it	us you them
Possessive Form	my, mine your, yours his, her, hers, its	our, ours your, yours their, theirs

Notice that the pronouns *you* and *it* are the same in the subject form and object form.

NOTE Some authorities prefer to call possessive forms such as *our, your,* and *their* possessive adjectives. Follow your teacher's instructions regarding possessive forms.

Exercise 1 Identifying Pronouns

Identify each of the following pronouns as a *subject form,* an *object form,* or a *possessive form.* If the pronoun can be used as either the subject form or the object form, write *subject or object.*

EXAMPLE **1.** they
1. subject form

1. him **3.** it **5.** our **7.** you **9.** he
2. me **4.** we **6.** them **8.** their **10.** your

Exercise 2 Identifying Pronouns in Sentences

For each of the following sentences, identify the pronoun in italics as a *subject form,* an *object form,* or a *possessive form.*

EXAMPLE **1.** Ever since *he* could remember, Edward Bannister had wanted to be an artist.
1. subject form

1. He had to work hard to reach *his* goal.
2. Although Bannister was born in Canada, many consider *him* an American artist.
3. Bannister's parents died when *he* was young.
4. The little money they had was left to *their* son.
5. The young Bannister couldn't afford paper, so *he* drew on barn doors and fences.
6. Later, Bannister met Christiana Carteaux and married *her*.
7. She was from Rhode Island, where *her* people, the Narragansett, lived.
8. In 1876, a Philadelphia artistic society recognized Bannister by awarding *him* a gold medal for the painting shown here.
9. Bannister treasured his prize and regarded *it* as a great honor.
10. What do *you* think of the painting?

Edward Bannister, *Under the Oaks* (1876). Oil on canvas. National Museum of American Art, Washington DC/Art Resource, New York.

The Subject Form

Pronoun as Subject

The ***subject*** tells whom or what the sentence is about.

8a. **Use the subject form for a pronoun that is the subject of a verb.**

TIPS & TRICKS

To test whether a pronoun is used correctly in a compound subject, try each form of the pronoun separately.

EXAMPLE
(*She, Her*) and (*I, me*) practiced hard. [*She practiced* or *Her practiced*? *I practiced* or *me practiced*?]

ANSWER
She and **I** practiced hard.

USAGE

EXAMPLES **I** walked to school. [*I* is the subject of the verb *walked.*]

Did **they** get to the theater on time? [*They* is the subject of the verb *Did get.*]

Dan said that **he** and **she** live on the Tigua reservation near El Paso, Texas. [*He* and *she* are the compound subject of the verb *live.*]

Oral Practice 1 Using Pronouns as Subjects

Read the following sentences aloud, stressing the italicized pronouns.

1. *She* and Ahmed solve crossword puzzles.
2. Are *they* very hard puzzles to solve?
3. Dad and *I* finished putting together a jigsaw puzzle last night.
4. *We* worked for three hours!
5. Finally, *you* and *he* found the missing pieces.
6. *He* and *I* liked the completed picture of flamenco dancers.
7. *They* are from Spain.
8. *We* agreed that *we* would like to see them dance.

Exercise 3 Identifying Correct Pronoun Forms

Choose the correct form of the pronoun in parentheses in each of the following sentences.

EXAMPLE 1. Brad and (*me, I*) wrote a skit based on the myth about Pygmalion.
1. I

1. (*Him, He*) and I thought the myth was funny.
2. (*We, Us*) asked Angela to play a part in the skit.
3. Neither (*she, her*) nor Doreen wanted to play a statue that came to life.
4. Finally Brad and (*me, I*) convinced Doreen that it would be a funny version of the myth.
5. (*Him, He*) and I flipped a coin to see who would play the part of Pygmalion.
6. The next day (*we, us*) were ready to perform.
7. Doreen and (*me, I*) began giggling when Brad pretended to be the beautiful statue.

8. In the skit, when Pygmalion returned from the festival of Venus, (*him, he*) and the statue were supposed to hug.
9. Instead of hugging, (*they, them*) laughed too hard to say the lines correctly.
10. Doreen, Brad, and (*I, me*) finally took a bow, and the class applauded.

Pronoun as Predicate Nominative

A ***predicate nominative*** completes the meaning of a linking verb and identifies or refers to the subject of the sentence.

8b. Use the subject form for a pronoun that is a predicate nominative.

A pronoun used as a predicate nominative usually follows a form of the verb *be* (such as *am, are, is, was, were, be, been,* or *being*).

EXAMPLES The next singer is **she.** [*She* completes the meaning of the linking verb *is* and identifies the subject *singer.*]

The first two speakers might be **he** and **I.** [*He* and *I* complete the meaning of the linking verb *might be* and identify the subject *speakers.*]

Was the winner really **she**? [*She* completes the meaning of the linking verb *Was* and identifies the subject *winner.*]

Reference Note

For more information on **predicate nominatives,** see page 112.

HELP—To choose the correct form of a pronoun used as a predicate nominative, try reversing the order of the sentence.

EXAMPLE
The best gymnast is (*she, her*).

REVERSED
(*She, Her*) is the best gymnast.

ANSWER
The best gymnast is **she.**

Oral Practice 2 Using Pronouns as Predicate Nominatives

Read the following sentences aloud, stressing the italicized pronouns.

1. The stars of that movie were *he* and *she.*
2. The actors from Australia must be *they.*
3. Of course, the mountain man is *he.*
4. Was the actress really *she*, Jeremy?
5. The director could have been *he.*
6. The villains are *he* and *they.*
7. The movie's biggest fans may be *you* and *I.*
8. The next ones to rent the film will be *we*, I think.

STYLE TIP

Expressions such as *It's me* and *That's him* are common in everyday speech. However, these expressions contain the object forms *me* and *him* used incorrectly as predicate nominatives.

Such expressions should be avoided in formal writing and speaking. If the subject form of the pronoun sounds awkward as the predicate nominative, revise the sentence.

AWKWARD
The next speakers will be **he** and **I.**

REVISED
He and **I** will be the next speakers.

USAGE

HELP

Although most of the sentences in Exercise 5 have more than one possible correct answer, you need to give only one for each sentence.

Exercise 4 Identifying Pronouns Used as Predicate Nominatives

Choose the correct form of the pronoun in parentheses in each of the following sentences.

EXAMPLE **1.** The man behind the curtain is *(him, he)*.
1. he

1. The winners are you and (*me, I*).
2. It might have been (*he, him*).
3. The cooks for the traditional Vietnamese meal were (*them, they*).
4. Could it have been (*we, us*)?
5. Every year the speaker has been (*her, she*).
6. That was Carl and (*they, them*) in the swimming pool.
7. The volleyball fans in our family are Dad and (*she, her*).
8. First on the Black History Month program will be (*us, we*).
9. Was that (*he, him*) at the door?
10. Last year, the class treasurer was (*he, him*).

Exercise 5 Writing Sentences with Pronouns Used as Predicate Nominatives

Supply pronouns to complete the following sentences correctly. Use a variety of pronouns, but do not use *you* or *it*.

EXAMPLE **1.** The man in the silliest costume was ____.
1. he

1. The person in the gorilla suit must be ____.
2. The next contestants will be ____ and ____.
3. The winners should have been ____.
4. Can that singer be ____, Samuel?
5. The one sitting in the back row was ____.
6. The first ones in line were my friends and ____.
7. "Excellent interpreters of Shakespeare's characters were ____ and ____," said Mr. Simmons.
8. Are the next entrants on stage ____?
9. The leader of that dragon team is probably ____.
10. Finalists in the contest will be Ted, Lisa, or ____.

Review A Identifying Correct Pronoun Forms

Choose the correct form of the pronoun in parentheses in each of the following sentences.

EXAMPLE 1. Last summer Carl, Felicia, and (*us, we*) went to San Antonio, Texas.

1. we

1. Carl and (*she, her*) took these photographs.
2. Early one morning (*him, he*) and (*she, her*) visited the Alamo.
3. That could be (*him, he*) in the crowd outside the Alamo.
4. Felicia and (*I, me*) listened to a mariachi band on the Riverwalk.
5. Of course, the musicians in the picture at right are (*they, them*).
6. Don't (*they, them*) look as though they're having a good time?
7. Carl and (*I, me*) enjoyed visiting the Spanish Governor's Palace in the afternoon.
8. Felicia, Carl, and (*us, we*) particularly liked the palace.
9. In fact, the first guests there that morning were (*us, we*).
10. Maybe you and (*they, them*) will get a chance to visit San Antonio someday.

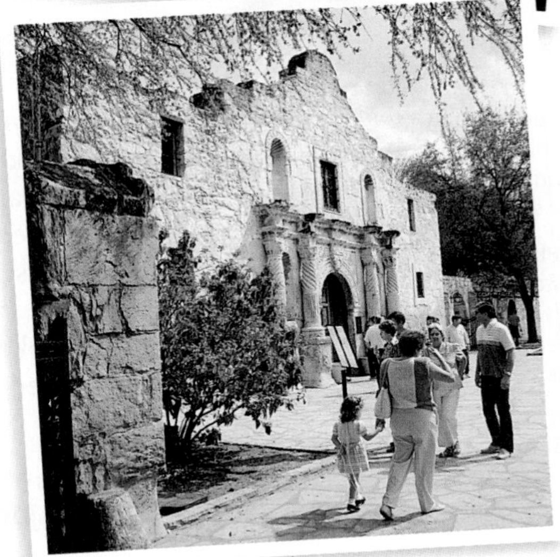

USAGE

The Object Form

Pronoun as Direct Object

A ***direct object*** completes the meaning of an action verb and tells *who* or *what* receives the action of the verb.

Reference Note

For more about **direct objects,** see page 107.

STYLE  **TIP**

Just as there are good manners in behavior, there are also good manners in language. In English, it is polite to put first-person pronouns (*I, me, mine, we, us, ours*) last in compound constructions.

EXAMPLES

Veronica showed **Roberto and me** how to use the software program.

She and I arrived early for softball practice.

USAGE

TIPS & TRICKS

To help you choose the correct pronoun in a compound object, try each pronoun separately in the sentence.

EXAMPLE

Ms. Stone praised Alonzo and (*we, us*). [*Ms. Stone praised we* or *Ms. Stone praised us*?]

ANSWER

Ms. Stone praised Alonzo and **us.**

8c. Use the object form for a pronoun that is the direct object of a verb.

EXAMPLES The teacher thanked **me** for cleaning the chalkboard. [*Teacher* is the subject of the verb *thanked.* The teacher thanked whom? The direct object is *me.*]

The answer surprised **us.** [*Answer* is the subject of the verb *surprised.* The answer surprised whom? The direct object is *us.*]

Have you told **him** about the change in plans? [*You* is the subject of the verb *Have told.* You have told whom? The direct object is *him.*]

Fred saw **them** and **me** last night. [*Fred* is the subject of the verb *saw.* Fred saw whom? The compound direct object is *them* and *me.*]

Oral Practice 3 Using Pronouns as Direct Objects

Read the following sentences aloud, stressing the italicized pronouns.

1. Kathy found *them* and *me* by the fountain.
2. Mr. Winters took *us* to the concert.
3. Did you see *her* and *him* at the Cajun restaurant?
4. Tyrone frightened *us* with his rubber spider.
5. Ellis invited Luis, Jared, and *me* to his party.
6. The mayor met *them* at Howard University.
7. Uncle Ken thanked *her* for the gift.
8. The fans cheered Anthony and *her.*

Exercise 6 Identifying Pronouns Used as Direct Objects

Choose the correct form of the pronoun in parentheses in each of the following sentences.

EXAMPLE 1. Marcus met Howard and (*I, me*) at the game.
1. *me*

1. Mrs. Freeman invited Leroy and (*I, me*) to a Kwanzaa party.
2. The spectators watched (*we, us*) and (*they, them*).
3. The shoes don't fit (*her, she*) or (*I, me*).

4. Sean called Marco and (*he, him*) on the telephone.
5. Our new neighbors asked (*we, us*) for directions to the synagogue.
6. They hired Tía and (*us, we*) to rake their yard.
7. The puppy followed Louis and (*he, him*) all the way home.
8. Last week, friends from Panama visited (*us, we*).
9. Odessa thanked (*her, she*) and (*me, I*) for helping.
10. The usher showed Greg and (*them, they*) to their seats.

Pronoun as Indirect Object

An ***indirect object*** may come between an action verb and a direct object. An indirect object tells *to whom* or *to what* or *for whom* or *for what* something is done.

Reference Note

For more about **indirect objects,** see page 109.

8d. Use the object form for a pronoun that is the indirect object of a verb.

EXAMPLES Scott handed **me** a note. [Scott handed what? *Note* is the direct object. To whom did he hand a note? The indirect object is *me.*]

Coretta baked **them** some muffins. [Coretta baked what? *Muffins* is the direct object. For whom did Coretta bake muffins? The indirect object is *them.*]

Elizabeth sent **him** and **me** some oranges from Florida. [Elizabeth sent what? *Oranges* is the direct object. To whom did Elizabeth send oranges? The compound indirect object is *him* and *me.*]

HELP

Indirect objects do not follow prepositions. If *to* or *for* precedes a pronoun, the pronoun is the object of a preposition, not an indirect object.

Reference Note

For more information about **prepositions and their objects,** see page 63.

Oral Practice 4 Using Pronouns as Indirect Objects

Read the following sentences aloud, stressing the italicized pronouns.

1. Mr. Krebs showed Bill and *them* the rock collection.
2. Paco told *me* the answer to the riddle.
3. Mr. Thibaut gives *us* lacrosse lessons.
4. We bought *her* and *him* a present.
5. The artists drew *us* and *them* some pictures.
6. The server brought *me* a bagel with cream cheese.
7. A pen pal in Hawaii sent *her* some shells.
8. My uncle Shannon told *us* a funny story about leprechauns.

USAGE

Exercise 7 Identifying Pronouns Used as Indirect Objects

Choose the correct form of the pronoun in parentheses in each of the following sentences.

EXAMPLE **1.** At the start of class, Mr. Chou assigned (*we, us*) new seats.

1. us

1. The store clerk gave (*they, them*) a discount.
2. For lunch, Anthony fixed (*he, him*) and (*she, her*) bean burritos with salsa.
3. Would you please show (*her, she*) and (*me, I*) that Navajo dream catcher?
4. Those green apples made both Christopher and (*he, him*) happy.
5. The waiter brought (*us, we*) some ice water.
6. Why don't you sing (*she, her*) a lullaby?
7. Have they made (*we, us*) the costumes for the play?
8. An usher handed (*me, I*) a program of the recital.
9. The Red Cross volunteers showed (*we, us*) and (*they, them*) a video about first aid.
10. Please send (*me, I*) your new address.

Review B Revising Incorrect Pronoun Forms in Paragraphs

In most of the sentences in the following paragraphs, at least one pronoun has been used incorrectly. Identify each incorrect pronoun, and give the correct form. If all of the pronouns in a sentence are already correct, write *C.*

EXAMPLE **[1]** Ms. Fisher took several of my friends and I to the museum.

1. I—me

[**1**] At the Museum of Natural History, Luisa and me wanted to see the American Indian exhibit. [**2**] The museum guide showed she and I the displays of Hopi pottery and baskets. [**3**] Both she and I were especially interested in the baskets. [**4**] After half an hour, Ms. Fisher found us.

[5] Then Luisa, her, and I joined the rest of the group. [6] Another guide had been giving Ms. Fisher and they information about the Masai people in Africa. [7] Them and us decided to see the exhibit about ancient Egypt next.

[8] A group of little children passed Ms. Fisher and we on the stairway as we were going to the exhibit. [9] The ones who reached the exhibit first were them. [10] Jeff, the jokester, said that they wanted to find their "mummies." [11] Ms. Fisher and us laughed at the terrible pun. [12] She gave him a pat on the back. [13] We asked her not to encourage him. [14] The museum guide led the children and we to the back of the room. [15] There, he showed us and they a model of a pyramid. [16] Then Ms. Fisher and him explained how the Egyptians prepared mummies. [17] Was it her who asked about King Tutankhamen? [18] Of course, Luisa and me recognized this golden mask right away. [19] As we were leaving, the guide gave the children and we some booklets about King Tut and other famous ancient Egyptians. [20] He handed Luisa and I booklets about the builders of the pyramids.

The golden funerary mask of Egyptian King Tutankhamen. Egyptian National Museum, Cairo, Egypt/SuperStock.

Pronoun as Object of a Preposition

The ***object of a preposition*** is a noun or a pronoun that follows a preposition. Together, the preposition, its object, and any modifiers of that object make a ***prepositional phrase.***

Reference Note

For more information about **prepositions,** see page 62.

8e. Use the object form for a pronoun that is the object of a preposition.

EXAMPLES	above **me**	beside **us**	with **them**
	for **him**	toward **you**	next to **her**

Oral Practice 5 Using Pronouns as Objects of Prepositions

Read the sentences on the following page aloud, stressing the italicized pronouns.

TIPS & TRICKS

When a preposition is followed by two or more pronouns, try each pronoun alone to be sure that you have used the correct forms.

EXAMPLE

Carrie divided the chores between (*they, them*) and (*we, us*). [*Carrie divided the chores between they or Carrie divided the chores between them? Carrie divided the chores between we or Carrie divided the chores between us?*]

ANSWER

Carrie divided the chores between **them** and **us.**

USAGE

1. The lemonade stand was built by Chuck and *me.*
2. The younger children rode in front of *us.*
3. Just between *you* and *me,* that game wasn't much fun.
4. Everyone has gone except the Taylors and *them.*
5. Give the message to *him* or *her.*
6. Why don't you sit here beside *me,* Ben?
7. Were those pictures of Amish families taken by *him*?
8. Donna went to the Cinco de Mayo parade with *them.*

Exercise 8 **Identifying Pronouns Used as Objects of Prepositions**

Choose the correct form of the pronoun in parentheses in each of the following sentences.

EXAMPLE 1. Someone else should have sent an invitation to (*they, them*).
1. them

1. In the first round, Michael Chang played against (*he, him*).
2. Did you sit with Martha or (*her, she*) at the game?
3. Peggy sent homemade birthday cards to Josh, you, and (*them, they*).
4. There is a bee flying around (*he, him*) and you.
5. If you have a complaint, tell it to Mr. Ramis or (*she, her*).
6. Ms. Young divided the projects among (*us, we*).
7. This secret is strictly between you and (*me, I*).
8. Can you believe the weather balloon dropped right in front of (*we, us*)?
9. Please don't ride the Alaskan ferry without Jim and (*me, I*).
10. One of the clowns threw confetti at us and (*they, them*).

Special Pronoun Problems

Who and *Whom*

The pronoun *who* has two different forms. *Who* is the subject form. *Whom* is the object form.

When you are choosing between *who* and *whom* in a question, follow these steps:

STEP 1 Rephrase the question as a statement.

STEP 2 Identify how the pronoun is used in the statement—as a subject, a predicate nominative, a direct object, an indirect object, or an object of a preposition.

STEP 3 Determine whether the subject form or the object form is correct according to the rules of standard English.

STEP 4 Select the correct form—*who* or *whom.*

EXAMPLE (*Who, Whom*) rang the bell?

STEP 1 The statement is (*Who, Whom*) *rang the bell.*

STEP 2 The pronoun is the subject of the verb *rang.*

STEP 3 As the subject, the pronoun should be in the subject form.

STEP 4 The subject form is *who.*

ANSWER **Who** rang the bell?

EXAMPLE (*Who, Whom*) does Lindsay see?

STEP 1 The statement is *Lindsay does see (who, whom).*

STEP 2 The pronoun is the direct object of the verb *does see.*

STEP 3 A direct object should be in the object form.

STEP 4 The object form is *whom.*

ANSWER **Whom** does Lindsay see?

EXAMPLE To (*who, whom*) did Jo give the gift?

STEP 1 The statement is *Jo did give the gift to (who, whom).*

STEP 2 The pronoun is the object of the preposition *to.*

STEP 3 The object of a preposition should be in the object form.

STEP 4 The object form is *whom.*

ANSWER To **whom** did Jo give the gift?

Oral Practice 6 Using Pronouns Correctly in Sentences

Read the following sentences aloud, stressing the italicized pronouns.

1. *Who* owns the sailboat over there?
2. To *whom* did you throw the ball?
3. *Whom* did Miguel marry?

STYLE TIP

The use of *whom* is becoming less common in informal English. Informally, you may begin any question with *who.* In formal written and spoken English, however, you should distinguish between *who* and *whom. Who* is used as a subject or a predicate nominative, and *whom* is used as an object.

MEETING THE CHALLENGE

Members of the marching band in your middle school are planning a garage sale to raise money for new uniforms.

Write two spoken announcements: a formal one to be given to a meeting of parents and teachers, and an informal one to be given during a school spirit rally. Describe when and where the garage sale will take place and what types of items are needed. Also, ask for volunteers to help with the sorting, pricing, and selling of items. Use *who* or *whom* twice in each announcement.

4. *Who* was the stranger with the ten-gallon hat?
5. For *whom* did you knit that sweater?
6. *Who* is the author of that book about Jackie Robinson?
7. *Whom* did Josh choose as his subject?
8. By *whom* was this work painted?

Reference Note

For more information about **appositives,** see page 272.

Pronouns with Appositives

Sometimes a pronoun is followed directly by a noun that identifies the pronoun. Such a noun is called an ***appositive.*** To help you choose which pronoun to use before an appositive, omit the appositive and try each form of the pronoun separately.

EXAMPLE (*We, Us*) Girl Scouts swam laps. [*Girl Scouts* is the appositive identifying the pronoun. *We swam laps* or *Us swam laps*?]

ANSWER **We** Girl Scouts swam laps.

EXAMPLE The director gave an award to (*we, us*) actors. [*Actors* is the appositive identifying the pronoun. *The director gave an award to we* or *The director gave an award to us*?]

ANSWER The director gave an award to **us** actors.

Exercise 9 Identifying the Correct Forms of Pronouns in Sentences

Choose the correct form of the pronoun in parentheses in each of the following sentences.

EXAMPLE 1. (*Who, Whom*) can do the most jumping jacks?
1. Who

1. (*We, Us*) baseball players always warm up before practice.
2. (*Who, Whom*) knows how to stretch properly?
3. Coach Anderson has special exercises for (*we, us*) pitchers.
4. To (*who, whom*) did the coach assign thirty sit-ups?
5. (*Who, Whom*) do you favor for tomorrow's game?
6. Would you teach (*we, us*) girls that new batting stance?
7. Please take (*we, us*) fans with you to the next game.

8. The ones with the new gloves and jerseys should have been (*we, us*) fielders.
9. (*Who, Whom*) should start the lineup?
10. With (*who, whom*) do you practice after school?

Review C **Revising Incorrect Pronoun Forms in Sentences**

Identify each incorrect pronoun in the following sentences. Then, write the correct pronoun. If a sentence is already correct, write *C*.

EXAMPLE 1. At first Karen and me thought that Lucy was imagining things.
1. *me—I*

1. Lucy told Karen and I that creatures from outer space had just landed.
2. She was certain it was them at the park.
3. Whom would believe such a ridiculous story?
4. Us girls laughed and laughed.
5. Lucy looked at we two with tears in her eyes.
6. Karen and I agreed to go to the park to look around.
7. Lucy walked between Karen and me, showing the way.
8. In the park she and us hid behind some tall bushes.
9. Suddenly a strong wind almost blew we three down.
10. A green light shone on Karen and I, and a red one shone on Lucy.
11. Whom could it be?
12. One of the creatures spoke to us girls.
13. Very slowly, Karen, Lucy, and me stepped out from behind the bushes.
14. "You almost scared they and me silly!" shouted a creature, pointing at the others.
15. Neither Karen nor her could speak, and I could make only a squeaking noise.
16. Then the man inside the costume explained to we three girls that a movie company was filming in the park.
17. They and we could be in the movie together.
18. The equipment hidden in the bushes might have been bumped by one of we girls.

USAGE

19. Lucy told the director and he about being afraid of the space creatures in the park.
20. If you see the movie, the short purple creatures under the spaceship are us three girls.

Review D Replacing Nouns with Pronouns

Revise each of the following sentences, substituting pronouns for the words in italics.

EXAMPLE 1. The bird hopped lightly into the *bird's* nest.
1. *The bird hopped lightly into its nest.*

1. David, I have already asked *David* several times to clean your room.
2. The raccoon reached into the water, caught a fish, and ate *the fish.*
3. *Anne and Paula* should be here in a few minutes.
4. *Sandra* will be reading my report to the class tomorrow.
5. Don't forget to return Reginald's book to *Reginald.*
6. As soon as Willis finishes dinner, *Willis* must leave for play practice.
7. Diane, did you turn in *Diane's* permission slip yet?
8. Mario and I have decided to do *Mario's and my* project as a musical skit.
9. In his locker, Felipe has a photograph of the presidential candidate with *Felipe.*
10. The dogs came running in as soon as they knew *the dogs'* food dish was filled.

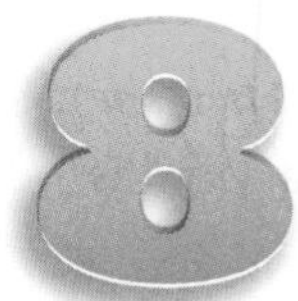

Chapter Review

A. Identifying Correct Pronoun Forms

For each of the following sentences, write the correct form of the pronoun in parentheses.

1. Could that be (*she, her*) at the bus stop?
2. The guest speakers were Dr. Lucia Sanchez and (*he, him*).
3. Are you and (*they, them*) going to the basketball game?
4. You and (*I, me*) have been friends for a long time.
5. Sometimes, even our parents cannot tell (*we, us*) apart.
6. (*We, Us*) players surprised the coach with a victory party.
7. (*Who, Whom*) is bringing the holiday turkey?
8. Laura lent my sister and (*I, me*) a new CD.
9. Mr. Lee will divide the money between you and (*I, me*).
10. To (*who, whom*) is the envelope addressed?
11. Please keep this information between you and (*she, her*).
12. Did Maria or (*she, her*) call Grandmother Lopez?
13. Mom and (*they, them*) have gone shopping.
14. Can you show Charlie and (*she, her*) how to fish?
15. Danny and (*I, me*) are practicing woodcraft for camp.
16. Why didn't you tell me about (*he, him*)?
17. Eldon and (*we, us*) were tired of playing checkers.
18. Mom and Dad promised Keith and (*they, them*) a puppy.
19. Was (*he, him*) the only one in the theater?
20. Would you lend your notes to (*we, us*)?

B. Identifying Pronouns Used as Predicate Nominatives

For each of the following sentences, write the correct form of the pronoun in parentheses.

21. The bus driver was (*he, him*).
22. That was Mr. San Miguel and (*they, them*) at the stadium last night.

23. The most devoted animal-lovers I know are Melanie and (*her, she*).
24. The junior racquetball champion last year was (*her, she*).
25. Once or twice a month the lifeguard at the local pool is (*he, him*).
26. Was that (*they, them*) in the parking lot?
27. Second on the program at the concert was (*he, him*).
28. It could have been (*her, she*), but I doubt it.
29. The devoted baseball fans in our class are Gregorio and (*he, him*).
30. The visitors from Taiwan must be (*they, them*).

USAGE

C. Identifying the Correct Forms of Pronouns Used as Subjects, Direct Objects, Indirect Objects, and Objects of Prepositions

For each of the following sentences, choose the correct form of the pronoun in parentheses and tell whether it is used as a *subject*, a *direct object*, an *indirect object*, or an *object of a preposition*.

31. The one who cheered loudest was the girl behind (*I, me*).
32. Did Isabel travel to Santa Fe with John and (*her, she*)?
33. (*We, Us*) baseball fans welcomed the decision not to move the team.
34. Peter called (*her, she*) and (*I, me*) last night.
35. (*We, Us*) cousins had a yard sale.
36. Tomas and José gave (*we, us*) their addresses in Mexico.
37. Her grandmother in Oregon sent (*her, she*) some apples.
38. On the hike, Christie and Maggie walked ahead of (*I, me*).
39. The teacher scolded us and (*he, him*) for being late.
40. I bought (*they, them*) an anniversary present.

Writing Application

Using Correct Pronoun Forms in Writing

Using Pronouns Health Awareness Week is coming up soon. Your class has been chosen to perform a skit on a health-related topic for the rest of the school. Your teacher has asked each class member to write down an idea for an entertaining, informative skit. Write a paragraph or two describing a skit that your class could perform. Be sure to use correct pronoun forms in your description.

Prewriting First, you will need to decide on a topic for the skit. Think about the health concerns of people your age. For example, you might plan a skit about the dangers of smoking or the importance of regular dental check-ups. After you choose a topic, brainstorm some ideas for a simple, entertaining skit. Be sure to list any props or costumes your class will need.

Writing Use your notes to help you write your draft. First, tell what the skit is about and why it is appropriate for Health Awareness Week. Then, explain what happens in the skit from beginning to end. Be sure to tell in a general way what each character does and says. Describe the props and costumes that your class can make or bring from home.

Revising Ask a classmate to read your paragraph. Is the information given in the skit correct? Does the skit sound entertaining? Is it clear which character does and says what? If not, revise your paragraph. Add details that will make the skit more fun and interesting.

Publishing Check your sentences to be sure you have used pronouns correctly and clearly. Read through your description carefully to check for errors in grammar, spelling, and punctuation. Use this chapter to help you check for errors in pronoun forms.

Your class may want to hold a contest for the best skit idea. Using the best idea, work together to develop the skit in more detail. Then, with your teacher's permission, give a performance of the skit for other classes.

Using Modifiers Correctly

Comparison and Placement

1.0 Written and Oral English Language Conventions
Students write and speak with a command of standard English conventions appropriate to this grade level.

Diagnostic Preview

Correcting Errors in the Form, Use, and Placement of Modifiers

Most of the following sentences contain an error in the use of modifiers or negative words. If a sentence has an error, rewrite the sentence correctly. If a sentence is already correct, write *C*.

EXAMPLE **1.** The weather looks more worse today.
1. The weather looks worse today.

1. Of the students in class, Odelle writes better.
2. Can you type fastest on a computer or on a typewriter?
3. Juan seemed very happy that we had visited him.
4. No one knew nothing about the tornado.
5. The vegetables were eaten by rabbits that we had planted.
6. Throughout history, many people have written regular in their diaries.
7. The people who moved in next door are the most friendliest neighbors who have ever lived there.
8. The bread smelled wonderfully.
9. Did that armadillo make it across the road with a limp?

10. Wynton Marsalis plays the trumpet good.
11. If you don't feel well today, you shouldn't go out.
12. We read a story written by Mark Twain yesterday.
13. Mai is one of the most persistent people I know.
14. I felt sadly at the end of *Old Yeller.*
15. The boy ordered a sandwich that was hungry.
16. The team usually wins the game that has the better defense.
17. Tanya is the youngest of my brothers and sisters.
18. It doesn't make no difference to Brian.
19. I'm not sure which I like best, the book or the movie.
20. Arthur's piano playing sounds very nicely to me.
21. The storm came up so sudden that it surprised us.
22. The house looks differently to me.
23. Lena and Ivan are twins, and Lena is the oldest one.
24. We couldn't hardly believe the news!
25. Miyoko looks well in her new school uniform.

What Is a Modifier?

A ***modifier*** is a word, a phrase, or a clause that makes the meaning of a word or word group more specific. The two kinds of modifiers are *adjectives* and *adverbs.*

Reference Note

For more about **adjectives,** see page 38. For more about **adverbs,** see page 59.

One-Word Modifiers

Adjectives

9a. ***Adjectives*** **make the meanings of nouns and pronouns more specific.**

EXAMPLES **That** one is my favorite. [The adjective *That* tells which one.]

Does Stephen know the **secret** combination? [The adjective *secret* tells what kind of combination.]

Estéban has saved **more** money than I have. [The adjective *more* tells how much money.]

Four horses grazed peacefully at the foot of the hill. [The adjective *Four* tells how many horses.]

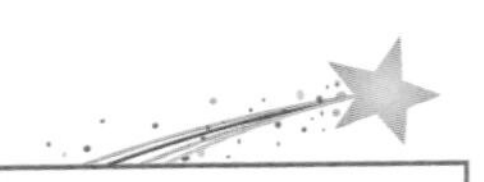

MEETING THE CHALLENGE

Many adverbs end in *–ly,* but others do not. Also, not all words with the *–ly* ending are adverbs. Some adjectives end in *–ly.* To decide whether a word is an adjective or an adverb, look at how the word is used in the sentence.

In each of the following sentences, identify the highlighted words as an *adjective* or an *adverb*.

1. The **elderly** man **calmly** crossed the street.
2. At first, she did **not** notice that the **holy** relic was missing.

USAGE

Reference Note

For more about **phrases,** see page 76.

Reference Note

For more about **clauses,** see page 89.

Adverbs

9b. *Adverbs* make the meanings of verbs, adjectives, and other adverbs more specific.

EXAMPLES The car backfired **loudly.** [The adverb *loudly* makes the meaning of the verb *backfired* more specific.]

The painting is **quite** old. [The adverb *quite* makes the meaning of the adjective *old* more specific.]

The bear traveled **surprisingly** quickly. [The adverb *surprisingly* makes the meaning of the adverb *quickly* more specific.]

Phrases Used as Modifiers

Like one-word modifiers, phrases can also be used as adjectives and adverbs.

EXAMPLES The cat **with the short tail** is my favorite. [The prepositional phrase *with the short tail* acts as an adjective that modifies the noun *cat.*]

Mr. Rodriguez planted the new bushes **along the fence.** [The prepositional phrase *along the fence* acts as an adverb that modifies the verb *planted.*]

Clauses Used as Modifiers

Like words and phrases, clauses can also be used as modifiers.

EXAMPLES Spaghetti is the food **that I like best.** [The adjective clause *that I like best* modifies the noun *food.*]

Before Mario went downstairs, he washed his face and hands. [The adverb clause *Before Mario went downstairs* modifies the verb *washed.*]

Exercise 1 Identifying Modifiers as Adjectives or Adverbs

Tell whether the italicized word or word group in each of the following sentences is used as an *adjective* or an *adverb.* Then, identify the word that it modifies.

EXAMPLE **1.** Ms. Olivarez is the woman *on the left.*

1. adjective—woman

1. The squirrel darted *quickly* up the tree trunk and hid among the leaves.
2. Wang Wei was a talented painter *of landscapes.*
3. Gabriela can ski faster *than I can.*
4. Is *this* poem the one that you wrote?
5. The man *who has curly hair* is my Uncle Thaddeus.
6. *Soon* you will need to put the bread in the oven.
7. *Before the performance* the actors practiced their lines and gestures.
8. Mountain biking is the sport *that I enjoy most.*
9. Tasmania is an island *off the coast of Australia.*
10. *Because the weather was hot,* we sat with our feet in the stream.

Comparison of Adjectives and Adverbs

When adjectives and adverbs are used in comparisons, they take different forms. The specific form they take depends upon how many things are being compared. The different forms of comparison are called ***degrees of comparison.***

9c. The three degrees of comparison of modifiers are the *positive,* the *comparative,* and the *superlative.*

(1) The ***positive degree*** is used when only one thing is being modified and no comparison is being made.

EXAMPLES *Felita* is a **good** book.

Shawn runs **quickly.**

The horse jumped **gracefully.**

(2) The ***comparative degree*** is used when two things are being compared.

EXAMPLES In my opinion, *Nilda* is a **better** book than *Felita.*

Juanita runs **more quickly** than Shawn.

Which of the two horses jumped **more gracefully**?

HELP

Here is a way to remember which form of a modifier to use. When comparing two things, use *–er* (the two-letter ending). When comparing three or more things, use *–est* (the three-letter ending).

STYLE TIP

In conversation you may hear such expressions as *Put your best foot forward.* Such uses of the superlative (to compare only two things) are acceptable in informal English. In formal speaking and writing, however, you should follow the rules in this chapter.

USAGE

STYLE TIP

Many two-syllable modifiers can form their comparative and their superlative forms either way. If adding *–er* or *–est* makes a word sound awkward, use *more* or *most* instead.

AWKWARD carefuller
BETTER **more careful**
AWKWARD commonest
BETTER **most common**

(3) The *superlative degree* is used when three or more things are being compared.

EXAMPLES *Nilda* is one of the **best** books I've read.

Which member of the team runs **most quickly**?

Regular Comparison

Most one-syllable modifiers form the comparative degree by adding *–er* and the superlative degree by adding *–est.*

Positive	Comparative	Superlative
near	near**er**	near**est**
sad	sadd**er**	sadd**est**
cute	cut**er**	cut**est**
bright	bright**er**	bright**est**

Two-syllable modifiers can form the comparative degree by adding *–er* or by using *more.* They can form the superlative degree by adding *–est* or by using *most.*

Positive	Comparative	Superlative
fancy	fanci**er**	fanci**est**
lonely	loneli**er**	loneli**est**
cheerful	**more** cheerful	**most** cheerful
quickly	**more** quickly	**most** quickly

NOTE When you add *–er* or *–est* to some modifiers, you may also need to change the spelling of the base word.

EXAMPLES sad **sadd**er **sadd**est
[The final *d* is doubled.]

cute **cut**er **cut**est
[The final *e* is dropped.]

fancy **fanci**er **fanci**est
[The final *y* is changed to *i.*]

Modifiers that have three or more syllables form the comparative degree by using *more* and the superlative degree by using *most.*

Positive	Comparative	Superlative
difficult	**more** difficult	**most** difficult
interesting	**more** interesting	**most** interesting
skillfully	**more** skillfully	**most** skillfully

Decreasing Comparison

To show a decrease in the qualities they express, modifiers form the comparative degree by using *less* and the superlative degree by using *least.*

Positive	Comparative	Superlative
clean	**less** clean	**least** clean
humorous	**less** humorous	**least** humorous
carefully	**less** carefully	**least** carefully

Exercise 2 Writing Comparative and Superlative Forms

Give the comparative forms and the superlative forms for each of the following modifiers.

EXAMPLES **1.** calm
1. calmer, calmest; less calm, least calm
2. happy
2. happier, happiest; less happy, least happy

1. nervous
2. great
3. hot
4. funny
5. noisy
6. easily
7. poor
8. young
9. swiftly
10. intelligent
11. politely
12. efficient
13. old
14. thoughtfully
15. sweet
16. angrily
17. ancient
18. neatly
19. lovely
20. long

HELP

A dictionary will tell you when a word forms its comparative or superlative form in some way other than just by adding *–er* or *–est* or *more* or *most.*

Be sure to look in a dictionary if you are not sure whether a word has irregular comparative or superlative forms.

A dictionary will also tell you if you need to double a final consonant (or otherwise change the spelling of a word) before adding *–er* or *–est.*

Reference Note

For more about **how to spell words when adding *–er* or *–est,*** see page 321.

HELP

Some words in Exercise 2 may have more than one acceptable comparative and superlative form. You need to give only one comparative and one superlative form for each item.

USAGE

HELP
In Exercise 3, do not use decreasing comparisons.

USAGE

Exercise 3 Using Comparative and Superlative Forms Correctly in Sentences

Give the correct form of the italicized modifier for each blank in the following sentences.

EXAMPLE 1. *large* As the illustration below shows, the moon appears ____ during the full-moon phase.

1. *largest*

1. *near* The moon is the earth's ____ neighbor in space.
2. *close* At its ____ point to the earth, the moon is 221,456 miles away.
3. *bright* Seen from the earth, the full moon is ____ than the new moon.
4. *small* The moon appears ____ during the crescent phase than at other times.
5. *difficult* It is ____ to see the new moon than the crescent moon.
6. *common* The word *crescent* is ____ than the word *gibbous*, which means "partly rounded."
7. *frequently* We notice the moon ____ when it is full than when it is new.
8. *big* Do you know why the moon appears ____ on some nights than on others?
9. *quickly* The changes in the moon's appearance take place because the moon travels ____ around the earth than the earth travels around the sun.
10. *slowly* The moons of some other planets move ____ than our moon.

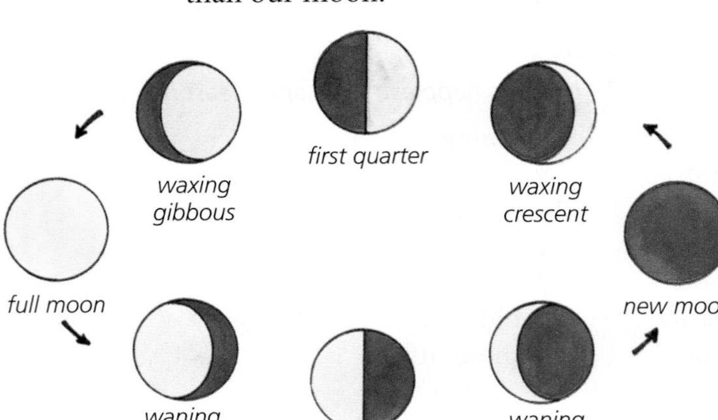

Irregular Comparison

Some modifiers do not form their comparative and superlative degrees by using the regular methods.

Positive	Comparative	Superlative
good	better	best
well	better	best
bad	worse	worst
many	more	most
much	more	most

NOTE You do not need to add *–er/–est, more/most,* or *less/least* to an irregular comparison. For example, *worse,* all by itself, is the comparative form of *bad. Worser* and *more worse* are nonstandard forms.

COMPUTER TIP

A computer can help you find and correct problems with modifiers. A spell-checker will highlight nonstandard forms such as *worser, bestest,* and *gracefuller.*

However, the computer cannot tell you that you have used the superlative form where you should have used the comparative. You will have to look carefully for such errors when you proofread your writing.

USAGE

Exercise 4 Using Irregular Comparative and Superlative Forms

Give the correct form of the italicized modifier for each blank in the following sentences.

EXAMPLE **1.** *many* Let's see which of the two teams can wash ____ cars.

1. more

1. *bad* This is the ____ cold I have ever had.
2. *much* We have ____ homework now than we had last year.
3. *well* Derrick feels ____ today than he did last night.
4. *good* This peach has a ____ flavor than that one.
5. *well* Of all the instruments he can play, Shen Li plays the banjo ____.
6. *much* Catherine ate ____ enchilada casserole on Monday than she had eaten on Sunday.
7. *many* Of all the volunteers, Doreen has collected the ____ donations for the animal shelter.
8. *bad* Our team played the ____ game in history.
9. *good* The judges will now award the prize for the ____ essay.

10. *many* I have ____ baseball cards than John does.
11. *good* Who is the ____ Japanese chef in town?
12. *much* Of all the ranchers, she knows the ____ about lambs and sheep.
13. *bad* Wow! That was the ____ storm I have ever seen.
14. *well* I think that another variety of blackberry might grow ____ than these do.
15. *many* Who got the ____ signatures for the petition?
16. *well* In my opinion, out of all the artists in the world, these Chinese masters paint landscapes ____.
17. *bad* Traffic is always ____ at this time of day than at any other time.
18. *many* This year, ____ people attended the ceremony at the reservation than last year.
19. *good* Of the book, the movie, and the play, which was ____?
20. *much* Of these two containers, which holds ____ juice?

Special Problems in Using Modifiers

9d. The modifiers *good* and *well* have different uses.

(1) Use *good* to modify a noun or a pronoun.

EXAMPLES The farmers had a **good** crop this year. [The adjective *good* modifies the noun *crop.*]

The book was **better** than the movie. [The adjective *better* modifies the noun *book.*]

Of all the players, she is the **best** one. [The adjective *best* modifies the pronoun *one.*]

Reference Note

For more about **standard usage,** see page 221.

Good should not be used to modify a verb.

NONSTANDARD N. Scott Momaday writes good.
STANDARD N. Scott Momaday writes **well.**

(2) Use *well* to modify a verb.

EXAMPLES The day started **well.** [The adverb *well* modifies the verb *started.*]

The team played **better** in the second half. [The adverb *better* modifies the verb *played.*]

Tina Thompson played **best** in the final game. [The adverb *best* modifies the verb *played.*]

Well can also mean "in good health." When *well* has this meaning, it acts as an adjective.

EXAMPLE Does Sherry feel **well** today? [The adjective *well* modifies the noun *Sherry.*]

9e. Use adjectives, not adverbs, after linking verbs.

Linking verbs, such as *look, feel, seem,* and *become,* are often followed by predicate adjectives. These adjectives describe, or modify, the subject.

EXAMPLES Mayor Rodríguez should feel **confident** [not *confidently*] about this election. [The predicate adjective *confident* modifies the subject *Mayor Rodríguez.*]

Did Chris seem **sad** [not *sadly*] to you? [The predicate adjective *sad* modifies the subject *Chris.*]

HELP

Some linking verbs can also be used as action verbs. As action verbs, they may be modified by adverbs.

LINKING VERB

Jeanette looked **alert** [not *alertly*] during the game. [*Alert* modifies the subject *Jeanette.*]

ACTION VERB

Jeanette looked **alertly** around the gym. [*Alertly* modifies the verb *looked.*]

Reference Note

For more about **linking verbs,** see page 53.

Exercise 5 Choosing Correct Modifiers After Linking Verbs and Action Verbs

Choose the correct modifier of the two in parentheses in each of the following sentences.

EXAMPLE 1. Ellen said that Murray's matzo ball soup tasted (*delicious, deliciously*).

1. *delicious*

1. The band became (*nervous, nervously*) before the show.
2. You may get a higher score if you remain (*calm, calmly*) while taking the test.
3. We (*eager, eagerly*) tasted the potato pancakes.
4. Cheryl sews (*good, well*), so she made all the puppets for the show.
5. The mariachi band appeared (*sudden, suddenly*) at our table.
6. Ooh, these wild strawberries taste (*good, well*).
7. The plums tasted (*sour, sourly*).
8. Mr. Duncan was looking (*close, closely*) at my essay.

USAGE

9. Those trophies certainly look (*good, well*) up there, Piper.
10. The bicyclist looked (*cautious, cautiously*) both ways before crossing the street.
11. Adobe, dried mud brick, stands up (*good, well*) under the hot Southwestern sun.
12. Peg looked at her broken skate (*anxious, anxiously*).
13. Don't you think vanilla smells as (*good, well*) as or better than those expensive perfumes?
14. Akira Kurosawa was (*good, well*) at making Shakespeare's plays into movies.
15. Sylvia certainly looked (*pretty, prettily*) in her new outfit.
16. Even for beginners, green beans grow (*good, well*), and quickly, too.
17. We didn't know that you could vault so (*good, well*).
18. Erica was (*happy, happily*) to help us.
19. Oh, you are too (*good, well*) at chess for me.
20. Some tropical fish don't get along very (*good, well*) with each other.

9f. Avoid using double comparisons.

A ***double comparison*** is the use of both *–er* and *more* (or *less*) or both *–est* and *most* (or *least*) to form a single comparison. When you make a comparison, use only one of these forms, not both.

NONSTANDARD That was Lon Chaney's most scariest role.
STANDARD That was Lon Chaney's **scariest** role.

NONSTANDARD The kitten is less livelier than the puppy.
STANDARD The kitten is **less lively** than the puppy.

NOTE Remember that irregular comparisons do not use *–er/–est, more/most* or *less/least*. Adding these to an irregular modifier is a double comparison.

NONSTANDARD more better
STANDARD **better**

NONSTANDARD worstest
STANDARD **worst**

Oral Practice Revising Double Comparisons

Each of the following sentences contains a double comparison. Read each sentence aloud, and identify the double comparison. Then, say the sentence again, using a correct comparison.

EXAMPLE **1.** Are you feeling more better now?
1. more better—better

1. That must be the bestest song you've written yet!
2. Hit the ball less harder next time.
3. Dates are one of the most popularest foods in Africa and Asia.
4. Nicki, this was the most liveliest party ever.
5. The ancient Chinese made paper more earlier than any other people.
6. Yikes, this computer game is the most hardest one I've played.
7. The least boringest of the characters was Jo.
8. Sure, I think Spanish is more easier to learn than English.
9. Please do visit us more oftener.
10. Maybe Friday will arrive more sooner this week.

Review A Writing Comparative and Superlative Forms in Sentences

For each blank in the following sentences, give the correct form of comparison of the italicized word.

EXAMPLE **1.** *noisy* This is the ____ class in school.
1. noisiest

1. *bad* Yesterday was the ____ day of my entire life.
2. *good* Tomorrow should be ____ than today was.
3. *old* The ____ American Indian tepee in the world can be seen at the Smithsonian Institution.
4. *soon* Your party ended ____ than I had hoped.
5. *funny* That is the ____ joke I've ever heard.
6. *rapidly* Which can run ____, the cheetah or the lion?
7. *beautifully* This piñata is ____ decorated than the other one.
8. *well* I did well on the first half of the test, but I did ____ on the second half.

USAGE

9. *joyfully* Of all the songbirds in our yard, the mockingbirds sing ____.

10. *strange* This is the ____ book I have ever read!

Review B Proofreading a Paragraph for Correct Forms of Modifiers

Most of the sentences in the following paragraph have errors in English usage. If a sentence contains an error, identify the error and then write the correct usage. If a sentence is already correct, write *C*.

EXAMPLE **[1]** You may not recognize the man in the picture on the left, but you probably know his more famous characters.

1. more famous—most famous

[**1**] This man, Alexandre Dumas, wrote two of the most popularest books in history—*The Three Musketeers* and *The Count of Monte Cristo.* [**2**] Born in France, Dumas was poor but had a good education. [**3**] As a young playwright, he rose quick to fame. [**4**] In person, Dumas always seemed cheerfully. [**5**] Like their author, his historical novels are colorful and full of adventure. [**6**] Their fame grew rapid, and the public demanded more of them. [**7**] In response to this demand, Dumas hired many assistants, who probably wrote most of his

USAGE

later books than he did. [**8**] Dumas's son, who was also named Alexandre, was a writer, too, and he became famously with the publication of *Camille.* [**9**] At that time, the younger Dumas was often thought of as a more better writer than his father. [**10**] Today, however, the friendship of the three musketeers remains aliver than ever in film, print, and even comic books.

Double Negatives

Negative words are a common part of everyday speaking and writing. These words include the modifiers *no, not, never,* and *hardly.* Notice how negative words change the meaning of the following sentences.

POSITIVE We can count in Spanish.
NEGATIVE We can**not** count in Spanish.

POSITIVE They ride their bikes on the highway.
NEGATIVE They **never** ride their bikes on the highway.

Common Negative Words			
barely	never	none	nothing
hardly	no	no one	nowhere
neither	nobody	not (–n't)	scarcely

9g. Avoid using double negatives.

A ***double negative*** is the use of two or more negative words to express one negative idea.

NONSTANDARD Sheila did not tell no one her idea. [The negative words are *not* and *no one.*]
STANDARD Sheila did **not** tell anyone her idea.
STANDARD Sheila told **no one** her idea.

NONSTANDARD Rodney hardly said nothing. [The negative words are *hardly* and *nothing.*]
STANDARD Rodney **hardly** said anything.
STANDARD Rodney said almost **nothing.**

STYLE TIP

Some fiction writers use double negatives in dialogue. This technique can help make certain characters sound more realistic. However, in your formal speaking and writing, you should avoid using double negatives.

Exercise 6 **Revising Sentences to Correct Double Negatives**

Revise each of the following sentences to eliminate the double negative.

EXAMPLE **1.** Those books don't have no pictures.

1. Those books don't have any pictures.

or

Those books have no pictures.

1. The Plains Indians did not waste no part of a bear, deer, or buffalo.
2. Ms. Wooster never tries nothing new to eat.
3. Movie and TV stars from Hollywood never visit nowhere near our town.
4. Until last summer, I didn't know nothing about Braille music notation.
5. By Thanksgiving, the store didn't have none of the silver jewelry left.
6. I'm so excited that I can't hardly sit still.
7. No one brought nothing to eat on the hike.
8. Strangely enough, Frieda hasn't never tasted our delicious Cuban bread.
9. There isn't no more salad in the bowl.
10. Our dog never fights with neither one of our cats.

HELP

Some double negatives in Exercise 6 may be corrected in more than one way. You need to give just one revision for each sentence.

USAGE

Review C **Proofreading Sentences for Correct Use of Modifiers**

Most of the following sentences contain errors in the use of modifiers. If a sentence is incorrect, write it correctly. If a sentence is already correct, write *C*.

EXAMPLE **1.** Haven't you never made a paper airplane or a paper hat?

1. Haven't you ever made a paper airplane or a paper hat?

or

Have you never made a paper airplane or a paper hat?

HELP

Some double negatives in Review C may be corrected in more than one way. You need to give just one revision for each sentence.

1. Making Japanese origami figures is much more easier than I thought it would be.
2. Origami, the ancient Japanese art of paper folding, wasn't hardly known in the United States before the 1960s.
3. Now, many people know how to fold the most cleverest traditional origami animals.
4. In true origami, artists do not never cut or paste the paper.
5. A beginner doesn't need nothing but a sheet of paper to create an origami figure.
6. With a bit of patience, anyone can make a folded-paper figure rather quick.
7. Even kindergartners can do a good job making the simple sailboat shown in the diagram.
8. Other origami figures require more greater time and patience than this sailboat.
9. Today, there probably isn't no one better at origami than Akira Yoshizawa.
10. Even the most difficult figure is not too hard for him, and he has invented many beautiful new figures.

Placement of Modifiers

9h. **Place modifying words, phrases, and clauses as close as possible to the words they modify.**

Notice how the meaning of the following sentences changes when the position of the phrase *from Brazil* changes.

The singer **from Brazil** gave a radio interview for her fans. [The phrase modifies *singer.*]

The singer gave a radio interview for her fans **from Brazil.** [The phrase modifies *fans.*]

From Brazil, the singer gave a radio interview for her fans. [The phrase modifies *gave.*]

A modifer that seems to modify the wrong word in a sentence is called a ***misplaced modifier.***

USAGE

Adjectives and Adverbs

The placement of an adjective or adverb may affect the meaning of a sentence. Avoid placing an adjective or adverb so that it appears to modify a word that you don't mean it to modify.

EXAMPLES Jackie borrowed some camping equipment **only** for the weekend. [She borrowed the equipment for the weekend, not for any other time.]

Only Jackie borrowed some camping equipment for the weekend. [Jackie—and no one else—borrowed some equipment.]

Jackie borrowed **only** some camping equipment for the weekend. [She borrowed some camping equipment but nothing else.]

Nearly all of the skaters fell. [Most of the skaters fell.]

All of the skaters **nearly** fell. [All of the skaters came close to falling but did not fall.]

Today Randall said he would help me build a birdhouse. [Randall made the statement today.]

Randall said he would help me build a birdhouse **today.** [Randall will help with the birdhouse today.]

Prepositional Phrases

Reference Note

For more information about **prepositions** and **prepositional phrases,** see pages 62 and 63.

A ***prepositional phrase*** includes a preposition, the object of the preposition, and any modifiers of that object.

A prepositional phrase used as an adjective generally should be placed directly after the word it modifies.

MISPLACED Ms. Ruiz got a sweater for her dog with a snowflake pattern.

CLEAR Ms. Ruiz got a sweater **with a snowflake pattern** for her dog.

MISPLACED This book describes Nat Turner's struggle for freedom by Judith Berry Griffin.

CLEAR This book **by Judith Berry Griffin** describes Nat Turner's struggle for freedom.

A prepositional phrase used as an adverb should be placed near the word it modifies.

MISPLACED Roberto read that some turtles can swim quite fast in a magazine.

CLEAR Roberto read **in a magazine** that some turtles can swim quite fast.

MISPLACED I watched a movie that George Lucas produced on Friday.

CLEAR **On Friday,** I watched a movie that George Lucas produced.

Avoid placing a prepositional phrase where it can modify either of two words. Place the phrase so that it clearly modifies the word you intend it to modify.

MISPLACED Cynthia Ann said after her ballet class she would take out the trash. [Does the phrase *after her ballet class* modify *said* or *would take*?]

CLEAR Cynthia Ann said she would take out the trash **after her ballet class.** [The phrase modifies *would take.*]

CLEAR **After her ballet class** Cynthia Ann said she would take out the trash. [The phrase modifies *said.*]

USAGE

Exercise 7 Correcting Misplaced Prepositional Phrases

Find any misplaced prepositional phrases in each of the following sentences. Then, revise the sentence, placing the phrase near the word it modifies. If a sentence is already correct, write *C.*

EXAMPLE 1. I read about the car thieves who were caught in this morning's paper.

1. I read in this morning's paper about the car thieves who were caught.

or

In this morning's paper, I read about the car thieves who were caught.

1. Michael went outside to trim the hedges with Bruce.
2. I saw the ants marching through my magnifying glass.

HELP

Some sentences in Exercise 7 may be corrected in more than one way. You need to give just one revision for each.

3. Angelo borrowed a radio from Kim with a weather band.
4. That man bought the rare photograph of Geronimo with the cellular telephone.
5. The robin sat carefully on the eggs in its nest.
6. The frog seemed to be staring at the moon in the pond.
7. We could see the wheat growing from our back windows.
8. The sound designer told us about recording a herd of gnus in class today.
9. Many people watched the televised ballgame in Fred's living room.
10. I found the collection of records your father bought in the attic.

USAGE

Reference Note

For more about **adjective clauses,** see page 91.

Adjective Clauses

An ***adjective clause*** modifies a noun or a pronoun. Most adjective clauses begin with a relative pronoun—*that, which, who, whom,* or *whose.*

Like adjective phrases, adjective clauses should generally be placed directly after the words they modify.

MISPLACED Mrs. Chu gives the sculptures to her friends that she carves. [Does Mrs. Chu carve her friends?]

CLEAR Mrs. Chu gives the sculptures **that she carves** to her friends.

MISPLACED The students met with a tutor who needed help in math. [Did the tutor need help in math?]

CLEAR The students **who needed help in math** met with a tutor.

COMPUTER TIP

A word-processing program can help you correct misplaced modifiers. First, examine all the modifying words, phrases, and clauses in your writing to make sure they are placed correctly. If you find a misplaced modifier, you can use the cut-and-paste function to place the modifier closer to the word it modifies.

HELP

Some sentences in Exercise 8 may be revised in more than one way. You need to give just one revision for each.

Exercise 8 Correcting Misplaced Adjective Clauses

Find any misplaced adjective clauses in each of the following sentences. Then, revise the sentence, placing the clause near the word it modifies. If a sentence is already correct, write *C.*

EXAMPLE 1. The students wanted to work on a project at the school that they had designed themselves.

1. The students at the school wanted to work on a project that they had designed themselves.

1. The girl is from my class that won the spelling bee.
2. The blue jay moved carefully through the snow with small hops, which had begun to melt.
3. I hardly recognized my uncle Ken when he came for a visit, whose beard had turned white.
4. Kwanzaa, which was first celebrated in 1966, is an African American holiday developed by Maulana Karenga.
5. The expression "that's the ticket," which means "that's the correct thing," comes from a mispronunciation of the French word *etiquette.*
6. My oldest brother just graduated from college, who lives in Rhode Island.
7. Jason's favorite shirt already has another stain on it, which was just washed.
8. That team played in front of a sellout crowd, which was having its best season ever.
9. "The Rum Tum Tugger" is a poem about a cat, which we studied in class.
10. We like to watch the many butterflies in the fields on the weekends that are behind our house.

USAGE

Review D Proofreading a Paragraph for Correct Placement of Modifiers

Most of the following sentences have misplaced modifying words, phrases, or clauses. If the sentence contains an error, revise the sentence by placing the modifier in the correct place. If the sentence is already correct, write *C.*

EXAMPLE **[1]** Sometimes the person can be a hero who seems least likely.

1. Sometimes the person who seems least likely can be a hero.

HELP Some sentences in Review D may be correctly revised in more than one way. You need to give just one revision for each.

[1] J.R.R. Tolkien's *The Hobbit* is a wonderful story that has a very complicated adventure about a simple person. **[2]** Hobbits are very small, quiet people, and most of the world had never heard of them until a few of them began to have adventures. **[3]** The hero of the story, Bilbo Baggins, is not a typical hero, who likes nothing more than chatting with his neighbors, sleeping, and eating. **[4]** Bilbo's quiet life is interrupted when the wizard Gandalf chooses him to help a band of dwarves from a dragon recover their treasure. [**5**] Bilbo saves the dwarves several times on their way to their old home under the Lonely Mountain, despite being small and shy. [**6**] Bilbo also finds a magical ring along the way that can make him invisible. [**7**] Bilbo gets the dwarves out of trouble with the ring and the wizard Gandalf. [**8**] When they finally reach the mountain, Bilbo tricks the dragon Smaug into revealing a spot in his armor that is weak. [**9**] The dragon is very angry and attacks a nearby town, but an archer kills Smaug, who has been told about the weak spot. [**10**] Bilbo goes back to his quiet life, but in *The Lord of the Rings* his nephew Frodo inherits the ring and saves the world.

Chapter Review

A. Identifying the Correct Forms of Modifiers

Choose the correct form of the modifier in parentheses in each of the following sentences.

1. Cool water tastes (*good, well*) on a hot day.
2. The wind howled (*fierce, fiercely*) last night.
3. Which twin is (*taller, tallest*), Marcus or Jim?
4. *Forever Friends* is the (*best, bestest*) book I've read this year.
5. Sergio has always played (*good, well*) during an important match.
6. The roses in the vase smelled (*sweet, sweetly*).
7. They could view the eclipse (*more clear, more clearly*) than we could.
8. Which of these two winter coats is the (*best, better*) value?
9. Of all the days in the week, Friday goes by (*more, most*) slowly for me.
10. Ernesto felt (*good, well*) about volunteering to help collect money for the homeless.
11. Is this the (*darkest, darker*) copy of the three?
12. The (*faster, fastest*) runner is the captain of the track team.
13. Mr. Chen told them to be (*better, more better*) prepared tomorrow.
14. Joni's way of solving the math puzzle was much (*more easier, easier*) than Ken's.
15. We felt (*sleepy, sleepily*) after lunch.

HELP

In some cases, a double negative can be corrected in more than one way. However, you need to give only one revision for each sentence in Part B.

B. Correcting Double Negatives

Most of the following sentences contain errors in the use of negative words. If the sentence is incorrect, write it correctly. If the sentence is already correct, write *C*.

16. None of us knows nothing about astronomy.
17. Wendell can hardly wait to see Serge Laîné in concert.
18. Kathy hasn't never heard of the Romanovs.

USAGE

19. Last night we couldn't see no stars through the telescope.
20. Whenever I want fresh strawberries, there are never none in the house.

C. Writing Comparative and Superlative Forms

Write the comparative and superlative forms for each of the following modifiers.

Remember to include forms showing decreasing comparison in your answers to Part C.

21. difficult	**26.** good
22. new	**27.** light
23. quickly	**28.** short
24. cold	**29.** clearly
25. fantastic	**30.** noisy

USAGE

D. Correcting Misplaced Phrases and Clauses

Find any misplaced phrases and clauses in each of the following sentences. Then, revise each incorrect sentence, placing the phrase or clause near the word it modifies.

31. I heard about the bad weather on the radio.
32. The man drove the sports car with the beard.
33. Arthur borrowed a mountain bike from his friend with eighteen speeds.
34. Uncle Mark and Aunt Jennifer were watching the meteor shower in the backyard.
35. We saw the fog rising from our car.
36. I gave a bracelet to my friend that was made of silver.
37. Mom saw a museum exhibit of ancient pottery made in the American Southwest on Tuesday.
38. Una read about the latest political developments in the newspaper.
39. The mayor said she would lead the St. Patrick's Day parade at her press conference.
40. The woman won the CD player who had on the red hat.

Writing Application

Using Negative Words in Description

Negative Words Everyone has a bad day now and then. Yesterday, it was your turn. You were late for school because your alarm clock did not go off. From then on, things just got worse. Write a letter to a friend giving a funny description of your unlucky day. Make sure that you use negative words correctly.

Prewriting Write down some notes about a real or imaginary bad day in your life. List at least five things that went wrong during the day. The events can be big or small. Tell how you felt when one thing after another went wrong.

Writing In your letter, explain the events of your day in the order they happened. Describe each event in detail. Also describe your reactions to the events. You may want to exaggerate some details for a humorous effect.

Revising Ask a friend to read your letter. Have you described the events clearly? Do your descriptions give a vivid, humorous picture of your day? If not, add or revise details.

Publishing Be sure that your letter follows the correct form for a personal letter. Proofread your letter carefully for errors in grammar, spelling and punctuation. Read through each sentence one more time to check that negative words are used correctly. With your teacher's permission, you and your classmates may wish to present your descriptions in class and vote on who survived the worst day.

CHAPTER

A Glossary of Usage

Common Usage Problems

1.0 Written and Oral English Language Conventions
Students write and speak with a command of standard English conventions appropriate to this grade level.
1.5 Spell frequently misspelled words correctly (e.g., *their, they're, there*).

Diagnostic Preview

Correcting Errors in Usage

Each of the following sentences contains an error in the use of formal, standard English. Rewrite each sentence correctly.

EXAMPLE **1.** I knew all the answers accept the last one.
1. I knew all the answers except the last one.

1. If you're going to the library, would you please bring these books there for me?
2. The water tasted kind of salty.
3. Has Jamila finished the assignment all ready?
4. Leon went to the doctor because he didn't feel good.
5. They should of asked for directions.
6. We found nothing but a old shoe.
7. Bao will try and fix her bike today.
8. The tuna looked all right but smelled badly.
9. Albert can't hardly wait to read that biography of the Olympic star Jesse Owens.
10. Why is this mitt more expensive then that one?
11. He knocked a bowl of plantains off of the table.
12. In rural Vietnam, children often take care of there family's water buffalo.

13. After school we use to have band practice.
14. Tanya made less mistakes after she had started practicing.
15. Do you know who's pencil this is?
16. Mr. Abeyto assigned me to this here seat.
17. A glitch is when a mistake is made by a computer.
18. Did Ann say how come she won't attend the meeting?
19. The food was shared between the families of the village.
20. At one time, Bessie Coleman was the only black woman pilot anywheres in the world.

USAGE

About the Glossary

This chapter contains an alphabetical list, or ***glossary,*** of common problems in English usage. You will notice that some examples in this glossary are labeled *nonstandard, standard, formal,* or *informal.*

The label ***nonstandard*** identifies usage that is acceptable only in the most casual speaking situations and in writing that attempts to re-create casual speech. ***Standard*** English is language that is grammatically correct and appropriate in formal and informal situations. ***Formal*** identifies standard usage that is appropriate in serious speaking and writing situations (such as in speeches and in writing for school). The label ***informal*** indicates standard usage common in conversation and in everyday writing such as personal letters. When doing the exercises in this chapter, be sure to use only standard English.

Reference Note

For a list of **words often confused,** see page 329. Use the **index** at the back of the book to find discussions of other usage problems.

The following are examples of formal and informal English.

Formal	Informal
angry	steamed
unpleasant	yucky
agreeable	cool
very impressive	totally awesome
accelerate	step on it

USAGE

a, an Use *a* before words beginning with a consonant sound; use *an* before words beginning with a vowel sound. Keep in mind that the sound, not the actual letter, that a word begins with tells you whether *a* or *an* should be used.

EXAMPLES The airplane was parked in **a** hangar.

She lives on **a** one-way street. [*A* is used because *one* begins with a consonant sound.]

My father works in **an** office.

They arrived **an** hour early. [*An* is used because *hour* begins with a vowel sound.]

accept, except *Accept* is a verb; it means "to receive." *Except* may be used as either a verb or a preposition. When it is used as a verb, *except* means "to leave out." As a preposition, *except* means "excluding" or "but."

EXAMPLES The winners of the spelling bee proudly **accepted** their awards. [verb]

Because Josh had a sprained ankle, he was **excepted** from gym class. [verb]

All the food **except** the won-ton soup was ready. [preposition]

ain't Avoid using this word in speaking and writing; it is nonstandard English.

all right *All right* can be used as an adjective that means "satisfactory" or "unhurt." As an adverb, *all right* means "well enough." *All right* should be written as two words.

EXAMPLES This tie looks **all right** with that blue shirt. [adjective]

The baby squirrel had fallen out of its nest, but it was **all right.** [adjective]

Lorenzo and I did **all right** on the pop quiz. [adverb]

"Beats me why I ain't gettin' no better marks in English."

a lot *A lot* should be written as two words.

EXAMPLE I can make **a lot** of my mom's recipes.

already, all ready *Already* means "previously." *All ready* means "completely prepared" or "in readiness."

EXAMPLES We looked for Jay, but he had **already** left.

I had studied for two hours on Sunday night and was **all ready** for the test on Monday.

among See **between, among.**

anyways, anywheres, everywheres, nowheres, somewheres These words should have no final *s.*

EXAMPLE They looked **everywhere** [not *everywheres*] for the missing puzzle piece.

at Do not use *at* after *where.*

NONSTANDARD Where is the Chinese kite exhibit at?

STANDARD Where is the Chinese kite exhibit?

bad, badly *Bad* is an adjective. It modifies nouns and pronouns. *Badly* is an adverb. It modifies verbs, adjectives, and adverbs.

EXAMPLES The milk smelled **bad.** [The predicate adjective *bad* modifies *milk.*]

Before I took lessons, I played the piano **badly.** [The adverb *badly* modifies the verb *played.*]

between, among Use *between* when you are referring to two things at a time even when they are part of a group consisting of more than two.

EXAMPLES Kim got in line **between** Lee and Rene.

Be sure to weed **between** all ten rows of carrots. [Although there are ten rows of carrots, the weeding is done *between* any two of them.]

Use *among* when you are referring to a group rather than to separate individuals.

EXAMPLE The four winners divided the prize **among** themselves.

STYLE TIP

A lot sounds vague and boring when it is used too often. When you revise your own writing, try to replace *a lot* with a more exact word or phrase whenever possible.

ORIGINAL
Ernie drinks a lot of water every day.

REVISED
Ernie drinks **at least six large glasses** of water every day.

USAGE

STYLE TIP

The expression *feel badly* is common in informal English. However, in formal English you should use *feel bad.*

INFORMAL
Beth felt badly about hurting José's feelings.

FORMAL
Beth felt **bad** about hurting José's feelings.

Exercise 1 Identifying Correct Usage

For each of the following sentences, choose the word or word group in parentheses that is correct according to the rules of formal, standard usage.

EXAMPLE 1. The picture on this page is titled *After Supper, West Chester,* but the scene could be almost (*anywhere, anywheres*).

1. *anywhere*

1. This colorful work was painted by (*a, an*) artist named Horace Pippin, who lived from 1888 to 1946.
2. By the time Pippin was in elementary school, he was (*already, all ready*) a talented artist.
3. In fact, he had won a drawing contest and had eagerly (*accepted, excepted*) the prize, a box of crayons and a set of watercolor paints.
4. In World War I, Pippin was once caught (*among, between*) U.S. troops and the enemy.
5. During this battle (*somewheres, somewhere*) in France, Pippin's right arm—the arm he used when painting—was seriously wounded.
6. For a long time, Pippin felt quite (*bad, badly*) about his disability, but he was determined to paint again.
7. After Pippin recovered, he tried (*alot, a lot*) of new ways to paint; the most successful was to hold up his right hand with his left arm.

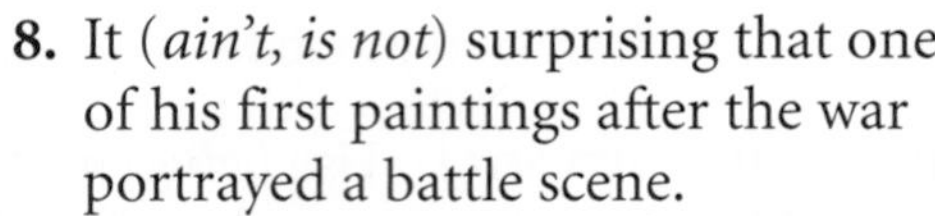

8. It (*ain't, is not*) surprising that one of his first paintings after the war portrayed a battle scene.
9. When Pippin painted *After Supper, West Chester,* in 1935, he was remembering the small town in Pennsylvania (*where he was born, where he was born at*).
10. I think that the painter of this peaceful scene must have felt (*all right, alright*) about his work and about himself.

Horace Pippin, *After Supper, West Chester* (1935). Collection Leon Hecht and Robert Pincus-Witten, New York. © 1991 Gridley/Graves.

bring, take *Bring* means "to come carrying something." *Take* means "to go carrying something." Think of *bring* as related to *come* (*to*) and *take* as related to *go* (*from*).

EXAMPLES Make sure that you **bring** your book when you come to my house.

Always remember to **take** your coat when you go outside during the winter.

could of Do not write *of* with the helping verb *could*. Write *could have*. Also avoid *ought to of, should of, would of, might of,* and *must of.*

EXAMPLES Yvetta wished she **could have** [not *could of*] gone to the movie Saturday night.

We **should have** [not *should of*] asked your mom for permission to go to the park.

don't, doesn't See page 135.

everywheres See **anyways,** etc.

except, accept See **accept, except.**

fewer, less *Fewer* is used with plural words. *Less* is used with singular words. *Fewer* tells "how many"; *less* tells "how much."

EXAMPLES This road has **fewer** stoplights than any of the other roads in the county.

This road has **less** traffic than any of the other roads in the county.

good, well *Good* is an adjective. Do not use *good* to modify a verb; use *well,* which can be used as an adverb.

NONSTANDARD Heather sings good.

STANDARD Heather sings **well.**

Although it is usually an adverb, *well* is also used as an adjective to mean "healthy."

EXAMPLE Keiko went home from school today because she didn't feel **well.**

TIPS & TRICKS

Could of, should of, etc., are common errors because they are mistaken for the contractions of *could have, should have,* etc. When spoken, *could've* sounds like *could of.* The difference is hardly noticeable in speech, but it is very noticeable in writing.

HELP

Use *fewer* with things that can be counted. Use *less* with things that cannot be counted.

EXAMPLE
Yolanda has (*fewer, less*) pets than Kristi does.

ASK
Can you count pets? [yes]

ANSWER
Yolanda has **fewer** pets than Kristi does.

EXAMPLE
This car has (*fewer, less*) trunk space than that car.

ASK
Can you count space? [no]

ANSWER
This car has **less** trunk space than that car.

NOTE *Feel good* and *feel well* mean different things. *Feel good* means "to feel happy or pleased." *Feel well* means "to feel healthy."

EXAMPLES I feel **good** when I'm with my friends.

Rashid had a cold, and he still doesn't feel **well.**

had of See **of.**

had ought, hadn't ought The verb *ought* should not be used with *had.*

NONSTANDARD They had ought to be more careful.
STANDARD They **ought** to be more careful.

NONSTANDARD You hadn't ought to have said that.
STANDARD You **oughtn't** to have said that.

or

You **shouldn't** have said that.

hardly, scarcely *Hardly* and *scarcely* are negative words. They should not be used with other negative words to express a single negative idea.

EXAMPLES Pedro **can** [not *can't*] **hardly** wait for the fiesta.

The sun **has** [not *hasn't*] **scarcely** shone today.

hisself, theirself, theirselves These words are nonstandard English. Use *himself* and *themselves.*

EXAMPLES Mr. Ogata said he would do the work **himself** [not *hisself*], I believe.

They congratulated **themselves** [not *theirselves*] on their victory.

how come In informal English, *how come* is often used instead of *why.* In formal English, *why* is preferred.

INFORMAL How come she can leave early?
FORMAL **Why** can she leave early?

USAGE

Exercise 2 Identifying Correct Usage

For each of the following sentences, choose the word or word group in parentheses that is correct according to the rules of formal, standard usage.

EXAMPLE 1. There might be (*fewer, less*) accidents if people were more alert around small children.

1. *fewer*

1. Everyone knows that children are not always as careful as they (*ought, had ought*) to be.
2. However, young children (*can hardly, can't hardly*) be blamed for being curious and adventurous.
3. Just a few days ago, I was involved in a scary situation that (*could of, could have*) led to a serious accident.
4. After I (*brought, took*) my little brother Gerald home from a walk, I called my friend Susan.
5. Gerald quickly wandered off by (*hisself, himself*).
6. I don't know (*how come, why*) he always disappears when I'm on the phone.
7. I found Gerald climbing onto the stove, and in (*fewer, less*) than a second, I lifted him down.
8. I told him that he (*could have, could of*) been burned.
9. He said he would be (*good, well*) from then on.
10. Although the experience was frightening, it turned out (*good, well*).

Oral Practice Proofreading a Paragraph for Correct Usage

Each of the following sentences has at least one error in the use of standard, formal English. Read each sentence aloud, and identify each error. Then, say the sentences again, correcting each error.

EXAMPLE [1] The game of soccer has proved to be more popular than the king of England hisself.

1. *hisself—himself*

[1] Derby, England, may have been the town where soccer was first played at. [2] Sometime around the third century A.D., an early version of the game was played among two towns.

USAGE

USAGE

[3] Anywheres from fifty to several hundred people played in a match. [4] Back then, soccer had less rules than it does today and the participants probably didn't behave very good. [5] By the fifteenth century, the government had all ready outlawed the sport. [6] The king said that young people had ought to be training theirselves in archery instead of playing soccer. [7] According to the king, archery practice was alright because bows and arrows could be used against a enemy. [8] However, many people didn't hardly obey the king's rule, and soccer continued to grow in popularity. [9] Perhaps later kings felt badly about outlawing soccer. [10] Eventually the government had to except that soccer had become the most popular sport in England.

its, it's *Its* is the possessive form of the personal pronoun *it*. *Its* is used to show ownership. *It's* is a contraction of *it is* or *it has*.

EXAMPLES The raccoon washed **its** face in the shallows of the stream. [possessive pronoun]

My grandparents have a dog; **it's** a collie. [contraction of *it is*]

It's been sunny and warm all day. [contraction of *It has*]

kind of, sort of In informal English, *kind of* and *sort of* are often used to mean "somewhat" or "rather." In formal English, however, it is better to use *somewhat* or *rather*.

INFORMAL That story is kind of funny.

FORMAL That story is **rather** funny.

learn, teach *Learn* means "to gain knowledge." *Teach* means "to instruct" or "to show how."

EXAMPLES The students from Vietnam are **learning** English.

Ms. Sanita is **teaching** them.

less See **fewer, less.**

lie, lay See page 168.

might of, must of See **could of.**

nowheres See **anyways,** etc.

of Do not use *of* with prepositions such as *inside, off,* and *outside.*

EXAMPLES Mrs. Cardona stood **outside** [not *outside of*] the office.

The child stepped **off** [not *off of*] the porch.

We heard a noise **inside** [not *inside of*] the engine.

Of is also unnecessary with *had.*

EXAMPLE If we **had** [not *had of*] known you were hungry, we would have brought some food.

Reference Note

For information on **using *of* with helping verbs,** see **could of,** page 225.

ought to of See **could of.**

rise, raise See page 166.

should of See **could of.**

sit, set See page 165.

somewheres See **anyways,** etc.

sort of See **kind of, sort of.**

suppose to, supposed to Do not leave the *d* off *supposed* when you write *supposed to.*

EXAMPLE They were **supposed to** [not *suppose to*] join us at the gate.

take, bring See **bring, take.**

than, then *Than* is a conjunction used in making comparisons. *Then* is an adverb meaning "next" or "after that."

EXAMPLES This cheese is tastier **than** that one.

First the phone rang, and **then** someone knocked on the door.

that there See **this here, that there.**

their, there, they're *Their* is the possessive form of *they.* It is used to show ownership. *There* is used to mean "at that place" or to begin a sentence. *They're* is a contraction of *they are.*

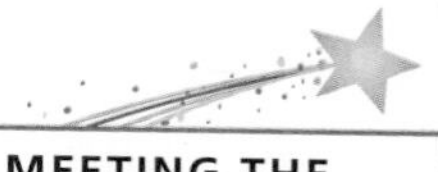

MEETING THE CHALLENGE

Mnemonics are things that aid the memory. They can be short poems, sentences that each start with a certain letter related to what you want to remember, or visual aids, to name just a few. Create a mnemonic to help you remember when to use *between* and *among*. Then, create another mnemonic for a usage problem of your choice.

EXAMPLES The children played happily with **their** toys. [*Their* tells whose toys.]

We are going over **there** very soon. [*There* tells where we are going.]

There are twelve members in our club. [*There* begins the sentence but does not add to the sentence's meaning.]

They're going to have a Juneteenth picnic. [*They're* is a contraction of *They are.*]

theirself, theirselves See **hisself,** etc.

them *Them* should not be used as an adjective. Use *the, these,* or *those.*

EXAMPLE How much are **those** [not *them*] baseball cards?

USAGE

Exercise 3 Identifying Correct Usage

For each of the following sentences, choose the word or word group in parentheses that is correct according to the rules of formal, standard English.

EXAMPLE 1. For years, scientists have studied Mayan writing on temples and (*inside of, inside*) caves.

1. inside

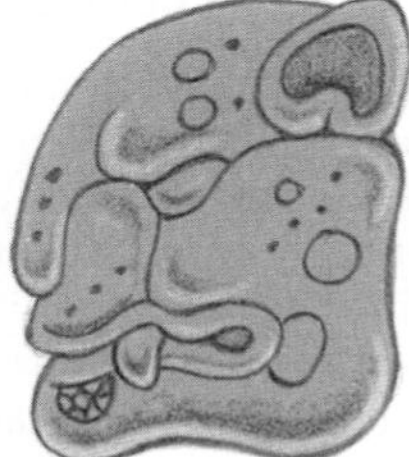

Jaguar

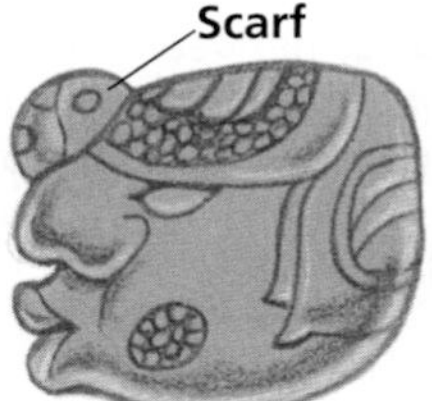

Lord

Man

1. Some scientists are (*learning, teaching*) themselves how to understand this writing.
2. The Ancient Mayas didn't use an alphabet to write (*there, their, they're*) language.
3. Instead, they drew symbols like (*them, these*) small pictures shown at left.
4. As you can see, the sign for jaguar looked (*somewhat, sort of*) like a jaguar.
5. At times, it could be difficult to tell what a picture was (*suppose, supposed*) to represent.
6. (*Its, It's*) meaning was made clear by the use of another small symbol.
7. (*There, Their, They're*) is an example of this technique in the illustration in the middle.

8. When a scarf symbol was added to the symbol for man, (*then, than*) the picture meant "lord."
9. Mayan writing contained other symbols that stood for syllables rather (*then, than*) entire words.
10. (*Its, It's*) clear we still have a great deal to learn about this beautiful, ancient language.

Review A **Identifying Correct Usage**

Choose the correct word or words in parentheses in each of the following sentences.

EXAMPLE 1. Our club will (*accept, except*) anyone interested in computers.
1. *accept*

1. Well, I (*should of, should have*) seen that coming.
2. Few chiefs were more powerful (*than, then*) Sitting Bull.
3. Maybe this dog can't find (*its, it's*) way home.
4. You didn't do too (*bad, badly*) in that last race.
5. David sings pretty (*good, well*), doesn't he?
6. Thanks, you've been (*a lot, alot*) of help!
7. We (*had ought, ought*) to plant our garden next week.
8. That book has (*all ready, already*) been checked out.
9. The lenses were dirty, but (*their, there, they're*) clean now.
10. Would you (*learn, teach*) us how to use those castanets?

this here, that there Do not use *here* and *there* after *this* and *that.*

EXAMPLE Do you want **this** [not *this here*] book or **that** [not *that there*] one?

try and In informal English, *try and* is often used for *try to.* In formal English, the correct form is *try to.*

INFORMAL Pat will try and explain the problem.
FORMAL Pat will **try to** explain the problem.

use to, used to Do not leave the *d* off *used* when you write *used to.*

EXAMPLE Dr. Chang **used to** [not *use to*] live next door to us.

USAGE

way, ways Use *way,* not *ways,* when referring to a distance.

EXAMPLE We traveled a long **way** [not *ways*] today.

well See **good, well.**

when, where Do not use *when* or *where* incorrectly to begin a definition.

NONSTANDARD A phrase is when a group of words is used as a part of speech.

STANDARD A phrase is a group of words that is used as a part of speech.

Do not use *where* for *that.*

EXAMPLE I read **that** [not *where*] the concert has been canceled.

whose, who's *Whose* is the possessive form of *who.* It shows ownership. *Who's* is a contraction of *who is* or *who has.*

EXAMPLES **Whose** dog is that? [possessive pronoun]

Who's [*Who is*] the bravest person you know?

He's the only one **who's** [*who has*] turned in a report.

would of See **could of.**

your, you're *Your* is the possessive form of *you. You're* is the contraction of *you are.*

EXAMPLES Do you have **your** watch with you? [possessive pronoun]

You're late today. [contraction of *you are*]

COMPUTER TIP

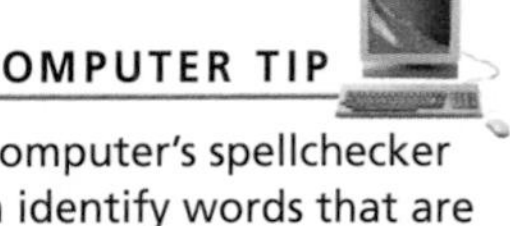

A computer's spellchecker can identify words that are nonstandard, such as *ain't, hisself,* and *everywheres.* However, the spellchecker cannot tell you when you have used a correctly spelled word in the wrong way. For example, if you use *whose* where you should use *who's,* the computer probably will not find the error. Always proofread your writing carefully to correct such errors in usage.

Exercise 4 Identifying Correct Usage

For each of the following sentences, choose the word or word group in parentheses that is correct according to the rules of formal, standard English.

EXAMPLE **1.** Take a map on (*your, you're*) next camping trip.
1. your

1. A trail map is (*when a map shows, a map that shows*) trails, campsites, and geographical features for a given area.

2. For a safe camping trip, a map like (*this here, this*) one can be very important.
3. Hikers who are not (*used to, use to*) an area often easily lose their way.
4. Every year, rangers report (*where, that*) some campers were lost for a day or more.
5. If you don't want to get lost, (*try and, try to*) get a good trail map.
6. In fact, every hiker in your group (*who's, whose*) able to read a map should have one.
7. With the map, you can choose a (*good, well*) location for your campsite.

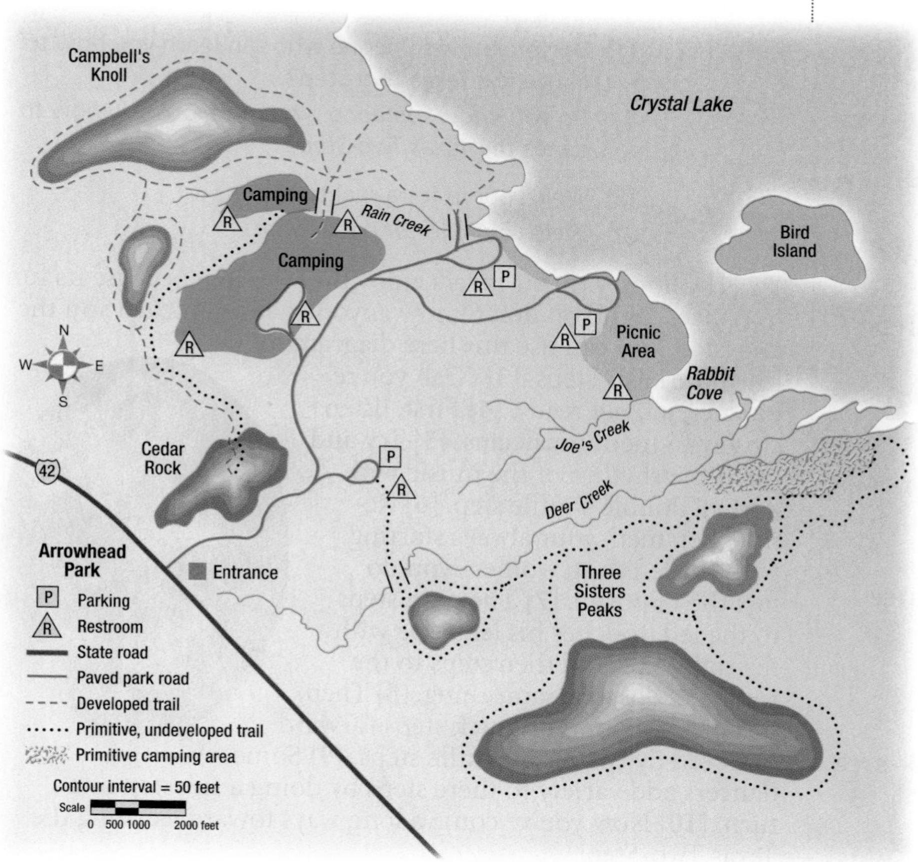

USAGE

8. When you begin your hike, mark where (*your, you're*) campsite is on the map.
9. If you go quite a (*way, ways*) from your campsite, note your path on the map, too.
10. As (*your, you're*) walking, your trail map can help you figure out exactly where you are.

Review B Proofreading a Paragraph for Correct Usage

Most of the sentences in the following paragraph contain errors in the use of formal, standard English. If a sentence is incorrect, rewrite it correctly. If a sentence is already correct, write *C.*

EXAMPLES **[1]** Do you know someone who can learn you how to dance the Texas Two-Step?

1. *Do you know someone who can teach you how to dance the Texas Two-Step?*

[2] Well, your in for a real treat!

2. *Well, you're in for a real treat!*

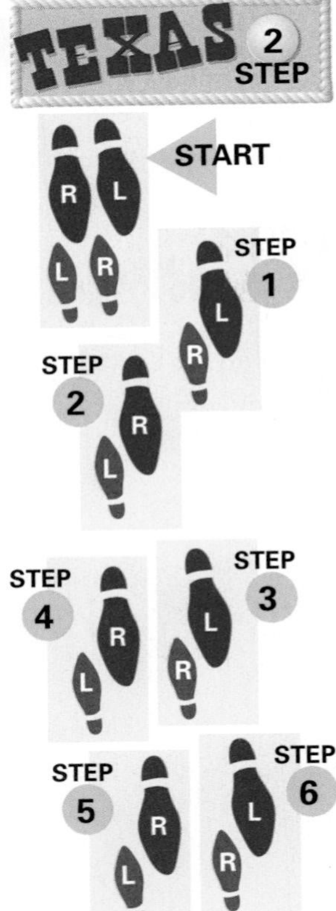

[**1**] Country music lovers enjoy the two-step because its fun to dance. [**2**] If you don't know anyone who can teach you the two-step, you can use this here diagram to learn the basic steps. [**3**] Grab you're partner and get ready. [**4**] First, listen closely to them musicians. [**5**] Try and catch the rhythm of the music with a small double shuffle step. [**6**] Remember, men, your always starting with the left foot; women, you do just the opposite. [**7**] The man steps to the left, touches his left shoe with his right one, and then steps to the right and does the same thing. [**8**] Then, he takes two kind of quick steps forward followed by two slow shuffle steps. [**9**] Some dancers add variety to there steps by doing a sidestep or a turn. [**10**] Now you've come a long ways toward learning the Texas Two-Step!

Chapter Review

A. Revising Sentences by Correcting Errors in Usage

In each of the following sets of sentences, choose the letter of the sentence that contains an error. Then, write the sentence correctly, using formal, standard English.

1. a. Everyone was at the meeting except Diego.
b. Does you're dog bite?
c. Andy waited outside the dentist's office.

2. a. The landfill smelled badly.
b. No one knew whose knapsack that was.
c. We could hardly wait for the rain to stop.

3. a. Mr. Catalano says that spiders ain't insects.
b. I feel rather tired today.
c. Do you accept personal checks?

4. a. Nina can run faster than he can.
b. Anna would have finished, but she was interrupted.
c. Be sure to bring a extra pencil with you.

5. a. The cow and its calf stood in the meadow.
b. Less students signed up for tutoring this month.
c. What is the difference between these brands of basketball shoes?

6. a. We did as we were told.
b. Everyone was already to go.
c. I used to enjoy playing tennis.

7. a. Penny, bring this book when you go home.
b. Ms. Michaelson told us that our plan was all right.
c. Julie said that it's already time to go.

8. a. The team had fewer fouls in the last game.
b. They looked everywhere for him.
c. Do you know where he is at?

9. a. Water-skiing is more fun than I thought.
   b. We hiked a long way before we pitched camp.
   c. Try and get to the meeting on time, please.

10. a. Their team has never beaten your team.
   b. A pop fly is when a ball is batted high into the infield.
   c. I finished my homework; then I called Duane.

B. Revising Sentences by Correcting Errors in Usage

Each of the following sentences contains an error in the use of formal, standard English. Rewrite each sentence correctly.

11. They could have come if the plane had of been on time.
12. My mom said that it is alright for you to have lunch with us.
13. We talked quietly between the three of us.
14. That parade created alot of work for the street cleaners.
15. This here beach is beautiful!
16. When the semi-trailer drove past the house, the picture fell off of Aunt Edna's wall.
17. Jim was suppose to rake the leaves yesterday.
18. Its one of the nicest beaches near Port Aransas.
19. I want to buy some of them crisp, green apples.
20. You hadn't ought to miss the national park.
21. After spending most of the weekend in the library, I was already for the exam.
22. Earlier in the race, I could of caught up with her.
23. "I'm doing good. How are you doing?"
24. Every major country in Western Europe accept Switzerland and Norway belongs to the European Union.
25. Mom and Dad treated theirselves to dinner at a fine restaurant on their anniversary.
26. It hasn't hardly rained all month in west Texas.
27. The birds flew toward there nests.
28. Boston is a long ways from San Francisco.
29. When I was a baby, I use to eat teething biscuits.
30. "Your late today," said Ms. Jimenez. "Be on time tomorrow."

Writing Application

Using Formal English in a Letter

Formal, Standard Usage You are an after-school helper at a day-care center. The teachers at the center plan to take the children on a field trip. One of the teachers has asked you to write a letter to send to the children's parents. The letter should tell where the children will visit and describe some of the things they will do there. The letter should also list any special items the children need to take with them.

Prewriting First, decide where the children will go on their field trip. They might go to a library, a park, a museum, or a fire station. Then, list the kinds of activities in which the children might participate. Note how the children will travel—for example, by bus or car. Also, note any special clothing or other things they might need for the field trip. List all the details you can imagine.

Writing Begin your draft with a polite greeting to the parents. Then, clearly explain why the children are going on the field trip. Invite the parents to call the day-care center with any questions they might have. In your letter, avoid using any informal or nonstandard expressions.

Revising Read over your work carefully, and then ask a friend to read your letter. Does your reader understand the information in the letter? Does the letter follow the guidelines for a proper business letter? Revise any information that is unclear.

Publishing Check your letter for correct spelling, punctuation, and grammar. With your teacher's permission, you may want to discuss the planned field trip with the rest of the class. Post your letter on a class bulletin board or Web page.

HELP

Use the Glossary of Usage to help you write the letter in formal, standard English.

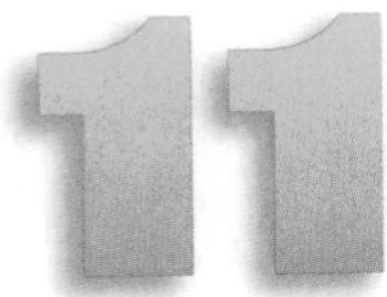

Capital Letters

Rules for Capitalization

1.0 Written and Oral English Language Conventions
Students write and speak with a command of standard English conventions appropriate to this grade level.
1.4 Use correct capitalization.

Diagnostic Preview

Correcting Sentences by Capitalizing Words

For each of the following sentences, correctly write each word that should be capitalized but is not. If a sentence is already correct, write *C*.

EXAMPLE **1.** our guest speaker will be mayor Masella.
1. Our, Mayor

1. Today i learned the song "simple gifts" from my friend.
2. "Hansel and Gretel" is a well-known fairy tale.
3. The kane county fall carnival will be held on saturday, october 19.
4. I believe that the recent trip to japan was organized by dr. alexander.
5. Let's ask the club treasurer, ms. lee.
6. Have you met professor martínez, rondelle?
7. Luis valdez filmed *the shepherd's tale*, a traditional mexican play, for television.
8. The greek god of war was ares.
9. My mother wrote to senator smith about the base closing.
10. members of congress often debate issues.
11. The letter began, "dear Ms. Joy."

12. Have you seen any of Mary cassatt's paintings?
13. I didn't know that there are mummies in the american museum of natural history.
14. A venezuelan exchange student will be living with our family for eight months.
15. The graduation ceremony was held at Newberry college.
16. When is the jewish holiday yom kippur this year?
17. Grandma asked me what i want for my birthday.
18. Monique said, "that movie is about World war II."
19. Next spring uncle William is going to take me on a hiking trip to mount Elbert.
20. Darnell took a rafting trip on the Colorado River.

Using Capital Letters

11a. Capitalize the first word in every sentence.

EXAMPLE **M**y sister has soccer practice after school. **T**hen she has to do her homework.

The first word of a directly quoted sentence should begin with a capital letter, whether or not the quotation comes at the beginning of your sentence.

EXAMPLE Reiko asked, "**H**ave you finished your report?"

Traditionally, the first word of every line of poetry begins with a capital letter.

EXAMPLE
Let the rain kiss you.
Let the rain beat upon your head with silver liquid drops.
Let the rain sing you a lullaby.
The rain makes still pools on the sidewalk.
The rain makes running pools in the gutter.
The rain plays a little sleep-song on our roof at night—
And I love the rain.

Langston Hughes, "April Rain Song"

NOTE Some poets do not follow this style. When you quote from a poem, use capital letters exactly as the poet uses them.

HELP—
Capitalize the first word of a sentence fragment used in dialogue.

EXAMPLE
Helena asked, "Have you read Terry Brooks' new novel?"
Jenny answered, "**N**o, not yet."

Reference Note

For more about **direct quotations,** see page 292.

Reference Note

For information on using **colons in letters,** see page 281. For information on using **commas in letters,** see page 276.

11b. Capitalize the first word in both the salutation and the closing of a letter.

SALUTATIONS **D**ear Service Manager:

Dear Adam,

My dear Brenda,

CLOSINGS **S**incerely,

Yours truly,

Very truly yours,

11c. Capitalize the pronoun *I.*

EXAMPLE When **I** returned home, **I** walked the dog.

Exercise 1 **Proofreading Sentences for Correct Capitalization**

If a sentence has one or more errors in capitalization, correctly write each word that should be capitalized. If a sentence is already correct, write *C.*

EXAMPLE **1.** What time should i call?

1. I

1. my library report on Edwin Arlington Robinson is due at the end of next month.
2. My sister memorized the limerick that begins, "a tutor who tooted a flute."
3. Aren't you glad that tomorrow is a holiday?
4. Elizabeth said, "we need to buy some more shampoo."
5. My grandparents let me watch television only after i have finished all my chores.
6. I used "yours truly" to close my letter.
7. How many yen did you spend during your vacation in Japan, Alexander?
8. "Everything i need to make the spaghetti sauce is right here," Nanna said.
9. two groups that i like will perform in concert next month in the park.
10. Greg said, "tomorrow is a holiday, so there will be no mail delivery."

MECHANICS

11d. Capitalize proper nouns.

A ***proper noun*** names a particular person, place, thing, or idea. Proper nouns are capitalized. A ***common noun*** names a kind or type of person, place, thing, or idea. A common noun generally is not capitalized unless it begins a sentence or is part of a title.

Reference Note

For more about **proper nouns** and **common nouns,** see page 26.

Proper Nouns	Common Nouns
Fairview **S**chool	middle school
November	month
Toni **M**orrison	writer
Red **S**ox	team
Kenya	country
Queen **E**lizabeth	queen
Motorola	company

NOTE As you may already have noticed, some proper nouns consist of more than one word. In these names, short words such as prepositions (those of fewer than five letters) and articles (*a, an,* and *the*) are not capitalized.

EXAMPLES **I**sle **o**f **W**ight **A**ttila **t**he **H**un

(1) Capitalize the names of persons and animals.

Capitalize initials that come before or in the middle of names.

Persons	
Kazue **S**awai	**H**arriet **T**ubman
Ulysses **S. G**rant	**J**ohn **H. C**ole, **J**r.
Heitor **V**illa-**L**obos	**W. C. H**andy

Animals	
Lassie	**R**over
Shamu	**S**ocks

STYLE  TIP

Some names consist of more than one part. The different parts may begin with capital letters only or with a combination of capital and lowercase letters. If you are not sure about the spelling of a name, ask the person with that name, or check a reference source.

EXAMPLES
du **M**aurier, **D**u**P**ont, **v**an **G**ogh, **V**an **B**uren, **L**a **V**erne, **d**e **l**a **T**our

(2) Capitalize geographical names.

Type of Name	Examples	
Continents	**A**sia **A**ustralia	**N**orth **A**merica **E**urope
Countries	**D**enmark **B**urkina **F**aso	**T**hailand **C**osta **R**ica
Cities, Towns	**M**inneapolis **H**avana	**N**ew **D**elhi **S**an **D**iego
States	**M**aryland **W**est **V**irginia	**M**ississippi **O**regon
Islands	**H**awaiian **I**slands **L**eyte	**I**sle of **W**ight **K**ey **W**est
Bodies of Water	**Y**angtze **R**iver **H**udson **B**ay	**L**ake **O**keechobee **C**aribbean **S**ea
Streets, Highways	**F**ront **S**treet **F**ifth **A**venue	**S**unset **B**oulevard **I**nterstate 55

NOTE In a hyphenated street number, the second part of the number is not capitalized.

EXAMPLE Forty-**n**inth Street

Type of Name	Examples	
Parks	**S**an **A**ntonio **M**issions	**Y**ellowstone **N**ational **P**ark
Mountains	**A**dirondacks **P**ine **M**ountain	**M**ount **K**ilimanjaro **A**ndes
Forests	**S**herwood **F**orest **B**lack **F**orest	**S**ierra **N**ational **F**orest
Sections of the Country	the **S**outh **C**orn **B**elt	the **N**orthwest **N**ew **E**ngland

MECHANICS

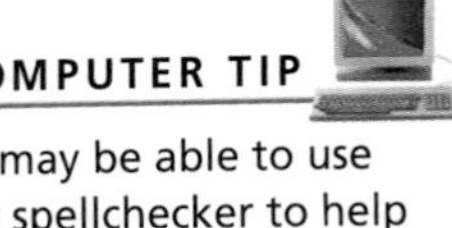

COMPUTER TIP

You may be able to use your spellchecker to help you correctly capitalize people's names, geographical names, and other proper nouns. Each time you use a proper noun in your writing, make sure you have spelled and capitalized it correctly. Then, add the name to your computer's dictionary or spellchecker.

NOTE Words such as *east, west, northeast,* or *southwest* are not capitalized when the words indicate a direction.

EXAMPLES Turn **e**ast when you reach the river. [direction]

Mae goes to college in the **E**ast. [section of the country]

Exercise 2 Writing Proper Nouns

For each common noun given below, write two proper nouns that name the same kind of person or thing. Be sure to use capital letters correctly.

EXAMPLE **1.** lake

1. Lake Louise, Lake Ontario

1. river
2. street
3. actor
4. park
5. friend
6. singer
7. island
8. state
9. country
10. ocean
11. dog
12. politician
13. city
14. pet
15. painter
16. explorer
17. mountain
18. lake
19. continent
20. athlete

HELP
A dictionary and an atlas can help you correctly complete Exercise 2.

Exercise 3 Proofreading for the Correct Use of Capital Letters

If a sentence has an error in capitalization, correctly write the word that should be capitalized. If the sentence is already correct, write *C.*

EXAMPLE **1.** Huge rigs pump oil from beneath the North sea.

1. Sea

1. María Ayala and eileen Barnes are going to Chicago.
2. Our neighbor Ken Oshige recently moved to canada.
3. Midway island is in the Pacific Ocean.
4. We could see mount Hood from the airplane window.
5. After you turn off the highway, head north for three miles.
6. During the sixteenth century, explorers from Spain brought horses to the west.
7. Several of us went camping near the guadalupe River.
8. My closest friend just moved to Ohio with shadow, her cat.
9. Hawaii Volcanoes National park is in Hawaii.
10. The bookstore is located on Maple street in New Orleans.

(3) Capitalize the names of organizations, teams, institutions, and government bodies.

Type of Name	Examples
Organizations	**M**ath **C**lub **O**akdale **C**hamber of **C**ommerce **B**oy **S**couts
Teams	**N**ew **Y**ork **M**ets **L**os **A**ngeles **L**akers **R**iverside **R**aiders
Institutions	**U**niversity of **O**klahoma **K**ennedy **M**iddle **S**chool **M**ount **S**inai **H**ospital
Government Bodies	**L**eague of **A**rab **S**tates **D**epartment of **E**ducation **F**ederal **B**ureau of **I**nvestigation

STYLE TIP

The names of government bodies are generally abbreviated.

EXAMPLES
FBI IRS

Reference Note

For more information on **abbreviations,** see pages 250 and 265.

NOTE Do not capitalize words such as *hotel, theater,* and *high school* unless they are part of a proper name.

EXAMPLES		
	Fremont **H**otel	the **h**otel
	Apollo **T**heater	a **t**heater
	Ames **H**igh **S**chool	that **h**igh **s**chool

(4) Capitalize the names of special events, holidays, and calendar items.

Type of Name	Examples	
Special Events	**W**orld **S**eries **N**ew **Y**ork **M**arathon	**P**arade of **R**oses **T**ulip **F**estival
Holidays	**T**hanksgiving **L**abor **D**ay	**M**artin **L**uther **K**ing, **J**r., **D**ay
Calendar Items	**S**unday **F**ather's **D**ay	**D**ecember **A**pril **F**ools' **D**ay

MECHANICS

NOTE Do not capitalize the name of a season unless it is part of a proper name.

EXAMPLES a **w**inter storm the **W**inter **F**estival

(5) Capitalize the names of historical events and periods.

Type of Name	Examples	
Historical Events	**B**oston **T**ea **P**arty **B**attle of **H**astings **W**ar of 1812	**N**ew **D**eal **M**arch on **W**ashington
Historical Periods	**B**ronze **A**ge **R**eformation	**G**reat **D**epression **R**enaissance

Exercise 4 Correcting Errors in the Use of Capital Letters

For the following sentences, identify each word that should be capitalized but is not. Then, write the word or words correctly.

EXAMPLE **1.** Hart middle school is having a book fair.
1. Middle School

1. Would you like to go to the movies this friday?
2. I think that the special Olympics will be held in our town this year.
3. What plans have you made for easter?
4. My sister and I were born at memorial Hospital.
5. The Rotary club donated equipment for our school's gym.
6. Did dinosaurs live during the stone Age?
7. My favorite baseball team is the Atlanta braves.
8. I always look forward to the first day of springfest.
9. The united states Congress is made up of the senate and the house of representatives.
10. Did you see any fireworks on the fourth of July?
11. Donna's youngest sister is going to join the girl scouts next Wednesday.
12. Our family has a wonderful time at the Alaska renaissance festival each year.

MECHANICS

13. The Grand hotel used to have Roman and Egyptian statues in its lobby.
14. Dave teaches at either the university of Florida or the university of Miami.
15. Why would you like to have lived during the middle ages?
16. If you like baseball games, you will enjoy watching the Texas rangers play.
17. Mrs. Nelson's class prepared the library display about civil rights day.
18. For fifteen years, spring carnival has been our school's main fund-raiser.
19. During the French revolution, people demanded their freedom and rights.
20. We'll be visiting my cousin's high school in may.

STYLE TIP

The words *black* and *white* may or may not be capitalized when they refer to people. Either way is correct.

EXAMPLE
During the Civil War, many **B**lack [or **b**lack] people joined the Union forces.

(6) Capitalize the names of nationalities, races, and peoples.

Type of Name	Examples	
Nationalities, Races, and Peoples	**M**exican	**S**wiss
	Micronesian	**C**aucasian
	Cherokee	**B**antu

(7) Capitalize the names of businesses and the brand names of business products.

Type of Name	Examples
Businesses	**J.** and **J.** **C**onstruction, **I**nc.
	Uptown **S**hoe **S**tore
	Grommet **M**anufacturing **C**ompany
Business Products	**G**oodyear **A**quatred
	Nikon **P**ronea
	Ford **R**anger

NOTE Names of types of products are not capitalized.

EXAMPLES Goodyear **t**ires, Nikon **c**amera, Ford **t**ruck

MECHANICS

(8) **Capitalize the names of ships, trains, aircraft, and spacecraft.**

Type of Name	Examples	
Ships	***S**anta **M**aria*	***M**onitor*
Trains	***C**oast **S**tarlight*	***C**ity of **M**iami*
Aircraft	***M**emphis **B**elle*	***S**pirit of **S**t. **L**ouis*
Spacecraft	***C**olumbia*	***L**unar **P**rospector*

(9) **Capitalize the names of buildings and other structures.**

Type of Name	Examples	
Buildings	**F**latiron **B**uilding **G**allier **H**all	**E**mpire **S**tate **B**uilding
Other Structures	**H**oover **D**am **A**lamodome	**G**olden **G**ate **B**ridge

(10) **Capitalize the names of monuments, memorials, and awards.**

Statue of **L**iberty	**L**incoln **M**emorial	**P**ulitzer **P**rize

(11) **Capitalize the names of religions and their followers, holy days and celebrations, sacred writings, and specific deities.**

Type of Name	Examples	
Religions and Followers	**B**uddhism **T**aoism	**C**hristian **J**ew
Holy Days and Celebrations	**P**urim **C**hristmas	**R**amadan **A**sh **W**ednesday
Sacred Writings	**D**ead **S**ea **S**crolls **B**ible	**K**oran **T**almud
Specific Deities	**A**llah **G**od	**V**ishnu **J**ehovah

Reference Note

For information on using **italics (underlining) for the names of vehicles,** see page 291.

COMPUTER TIP

A computer's spellchecker or style checker might spot some capitalization errors for you.

However, you cannot rely on these programs to find all your mistakes. Since many words are capitalized in some situations but not in others, the computer cannot find every error. Also, the computer might mistakenly highlight a word that is already correct.

Always proofread your writing carefully to make sure you have used capital letters correctly.

NOTE The words *god* and *goddess* are not capitalized when they refer to deities of ancient mythology. However, the names of specific mythological gods and goddesses are capitalized.

EXAMPLE The Roman **g**od of the sea was **N**eptune.

(12) Capitalize the names of planets, stars, constellations, and other heavenly bodies.

Mars	**P**luto	**N**orth **S**tar	**B**etelgeuse
Milky **W**ay	**B**ig **D**ipper	**U**rsa **M**inor	**S**irius

NOTE The word *earth* is not capitalized unless it is used along with the names of other heavenly bodies that are capitalized. The words *sun* and *moon* generally are not capitalized.

EXAMPLES China is home to one fourth of the people on **e**arth.

How far is Saturn from **E**arth?

The **s**un rose at 7:09 this morning.

Oral Practice **Identifying Words That Should Be Capitalized**

Read each of the following sentences aloud, and identify words that should be capitalized.

EXAMPLE **1.** We went to the leesburg library to learn more about african american history.

1. Leesburg Library, African American

1. The methodist quoted a verse from the bible.
2. Bob has a chevrolet truck.
3. On a clear night you can see venus from earth.
4. My teacher took a cruise on the *song of norway*.
5. Meet me in front of the woolworth building.
6. Pilar received the junior achievement award.
7. Otis made a detailed scale model of the spacecraft *nozomi*.
8. Elena wrote a poem about the greek god zeus.
9. Some navajo make beautiful silver jewelry.
10. Who were the first europeans to settle in mexico?

Review A Correcting Sentences by Capitalizing Proper Nouns

For each of the following sentences, correctly write the word or words that should be capitalized.

EXAMPLE 1. In the late nineteenth century, henry morton stanley explored an area of africa occupied by ancestors of the bambuti.

1. Henry Morton Stanley, Africa, Bambuti

1. The bambuti people live in the ituri forest, which is located in the northeast area of the Democratic republic of the congo.
2. This forest is located almost exactly in the middle of the continent of africa.
3. It lies north of mungbere, as shown in the boxed area on the map to the right.
4. The bambuti people, also known as twides, aka, or efe, have lived there for many thousands of years.
5. The earliest record of people like the Bambuti is found in the notes of explorers from egypt about 2500 B.C.
6. Other early reports of these people are found on colorful tiles in italy and in the records of explorers from portugal.

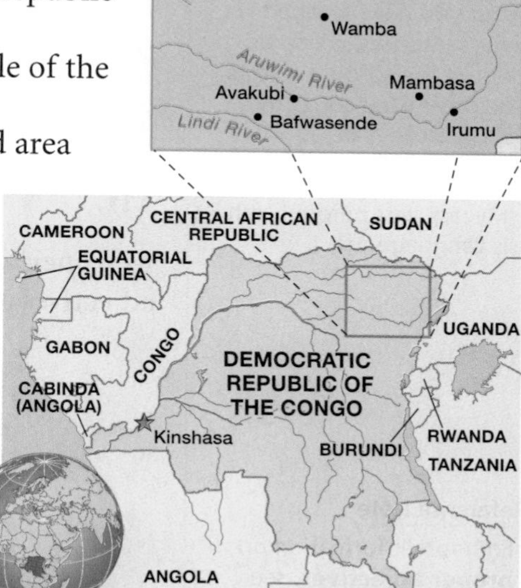

MECHANICS

7. Stanley met some of the bambuti people, but he didn't write much about them.
8. In the 1920s, paul schebesta went to africa to learn more about the Bambuti people.
9. He learned that the bambuti are very different from the bantu and from other neighbors.
10. In fact, the bambuti were probably the first people in the rain forest that stretches across central africa from the atlantic ocean on the western coast to the eastern grasslands.

MEETING THE CHALLENGE

Make a list of the school subjects you are taking this year. Then, choose four of the subjects and write a sentence for each. The sentences can be descriptive or can explain why a subject is fun, easy, or difficult. After you have finished your sentences, check to be sure the school subjects you have used correctly follow **Rule 11e**.

EXAMPLE
My last class before lunch is Language Arts I.

11e. Do not capitalize the names of school subjects, except course names followed by a numeral and the names of language classes.

EXAMPLES **s**ocial **s**tudies, **s**cience, **h**ealth, **a**rt, **W**oodworking II, **C**onsumer **E**ducation I, **S**panish, **E**nglish

11f. Capitalize proper adjectives.

A ***proper adjective*** is formed from a proper noun. Proper adjectives are usually capitalized.

Proper Noun	Proper Adjective
Mexico	**M**exican carvings
King **A**rthur	**A**rthurian legend
Judaism	**J**udaic laws
Mars	**M**artian landscape

Reference Note

For more information on **proper adjectives,** see page 40.

11g. Most abbreviations are capitalized.

Capitalize abbreviations that come before and after personal names.

EXAMPLES **M**r., **M**s., **M**rs., **D**r., **G**en., **M.D., RN, J**r., **S**r.

Capitalize abbreviations of the names of organizations, businesses, and government bodies.

EXAMPLES **I**nc., **C**o., **C**orp., **FBI, UN, NAACP, FDA**

In addresses, capitalize abbreviations such as those for roads, rooms, and post office boxes.

EXAMPLES **A**ve., **D**r., **R**d., **S**t., **A**pt., **R**m., **P.O. B**ox

Reference Note

For information on using **abbreviations,** see page 265.

Abbreviations of geographical names are capitalized.

EXAMPLES **N.Y.C.** **S**t. Louis **N.** America **O**kla.

NOTE A two-letter state abbreviation without periods is used when the abbreviation is followed by a ZIP Code. Each letter of the abbreviation is capitalized.

EXAMPLES Austin, **TX** 78704-6364

New Orleans, **LA** 70131-5140

Some abbreviations, especially those for measurements, are not capitalized.

EXAMPLES **e**tc., **e.g.**, **v**ol., **c**hap., **i**n., **y**d, **l**b, **cc**, **m**l, **m**m

Exercise 5 Correcting Errors in Capitalization

For each of the following sentences, correctly write each word or abbreviation that should be capitalized.

EXAMPLE **1.** I went with mrs. McCain to visit mr. Brennan in the retirement home.

1. Mrs., Mr.

1. The address was p.o. box 32, Green Bay, Wi 54305.
2. The new student had just moved to our town from st. Petersburg, Florida.
3. Will gen. Scott Quinn be speaking tonight?
4. Mr. Lloyd Mitchell, jr., has been appointed president of Sprockets and Widgets, inc.
5. The next speaker for Career Day will be Chet Patterson, rn, who works at the local hospital.
6. Blair O'Brien, cpa, has a top-floor office in the Hanley corp. building.
7. The Fbi, the Fda, and the Un have decided to cooperate on the investigation.
8. Are you taking art II or spanish?
9. Many scottish people have celtic, scandinavian, and irish ancestors.
10. The Chisholm Trail, which stretched over one thousand miles from San Antonio, tex., to Abilene, kans., was used by cowboys to drive cattle north.

MECHANICS

Review B Proofreading a Letter for Correct Capitalization

Read the following letter. For each numbered word group, identify any words or abbreviations that are not capitalized correctly. Rewrite the words or abbreviations with correct capitalization. If a sentence is already correct, write *C.*

EXAMPLE **[1]** 1066 south Norman st.

1. South, St.

March 14, 2009

Mr. Leonard Thornton
1234 Windswept Dr.
[1] Lancaster, Pa 17601

[2] dear Mr. Thornton:

[3] I think that the easiest thing you could do to help make lancaster better is to make it safer to ride bicycles here. **[4]** My friend James almost got hit by a car on his way to Memorial middle school. **[5]** As a member of our city's Transportation advisory Board, you can do a lot to encourage cyclists to wear helmets.

[6] Also, in Earth Science I class, we have learned that if more people used bicycles instead of cars, the air would be cleaner. **[7]** One company that I know of, Universal Solutions, inc., rewards people who ride bicycles to work. **[8]** Many cities, such as Boulder, colorado, are building bicycle lanes. **[9]** maybe you could help with programs like these. Thank you for your attention to this matter.

[10] yours truly,

Tate Washington

Tate Washington

MECHANICS

11h. Capitalize titles.

(1) Capitalize a person's title when the title comes before the person's name.

EXAMPLES **J**udge O'Connor **P**rincipal Walsh

Mrs. Santos **D**octor Ellis

Senator Topping **P**resident Truman

(2) Titles used alone or following a person's name generally are not capitalized.

EXAMPLES Judy Klein, our club **p**resident, led the meeting.

The **s**ecretary gave a speech to Congress.

However, a title used alone in direct address usually is capitalized.

EXAMPLES Can the cast come off today, **D**octor?

Good morning, **M**a'am [or **m**a'am].

(3) Capitalize a word showing a family relationship when the word is used before or in place of a person's name.

EXAMPLES Are **U**ncle Carlos and **A**unt Rosa here yet?

Either **M**om or **D**ad will drive us to the show.

Do not capitalize a word showing a family relationship when the word follows a possessive noun or pronoun.

EXAMPLE My **c**ousin Dena and her **n**iece Leotie made stew.

HELP

You may capitalize a title used alone or following a person's name if you want to emphasize the person's high office.

EXAMPLE

Please come and meet Texas' native daughter and our country's **S**ecretary of **S**tate.

Exercise 6 Correcting Sentences by Capitalizing Words

For each of the following sentences, correctly write the word or words that should be capitalized. If a sentence is already correct, write *C*.

EXAMPLE **1.** Thank you, aunt Shirley, for the pretty sweater.
1. Aunt

1. He says that judge Johnson is very strict.
2. Reuben's mother, mrs. Santos, owns the new restaurant.

3. Will your uncle be at the party?
4. Well, doctor Sakamoto, do I need braces?
5. Did the secretary of state attend the meeting?
6. Is cousin Josie going to Israel?
7. Please accept my apologies, senator.
8. On Saturday, aunt Latisha will arrive from Savannah.
9. Does professor Jones teach American history?
10. I learned to swim at grandpa Brown's cottage on the lake last summer.

Review C Using Capital Letters Correctly in Sentences

For each of the following sentences, correctly write the word or words that should be capitalized.

EXAMPLE **1.** The Civil war is sometimes called the war between the states.
1. War, War Between the States

1. There is a fountain in the middle of lake Eola.
2. dr. jones teaches at York high school.
3. Some of these folk songs are mexican.
4. the atlantic borders the states from maine to florida.
5. Someday i would like to bicycle through europe.
6. all of my friends came to the party.
7. Have you visited the Washington monument?
8. Our history class wrote letters to the secretary-general of the united nations.
9. There's a long detour on highway 50 just east of brooksville, dad.
10. Our first fall camping trip will be in october.

(4) Capitalize the first and last words and all important words in titles and subtitles.

Unimportant words in a title include:

- articles (*a, an, the*)
- coordinating conjunctions (*and, but, for, nor, or, so, yet*)
- prepositions of fewer than five letters (such as *by, for, into, on, with*)

Reference Note

For a list of **prepositions,** see page 63.

MECHANICS

Type of Name	Examples	
Books	*The **H**orse and **H**is **B**oy*	***D**ust **T**racks on a **R**oad*
Magazines	***S**ports **I**llustrated for **K**ids*	***E**ssence* ***R**eader's **D**igest*
Newspapers	***D**etroit **F**ree **P**ress* ***T**he **F**resno **B**ee*	***T**ulsa **T**ribune* ***T**he **D**enver **P**ost*
Poems	"**T**he **C**ity **I**s **S**o **B**ig" "**T**he **S**neetches"	"**F**or a **P**oet" "**S**team **S**hovel"
Short Stories	"**T**he **D**ay the **S**un **C**ame **O**ut"	"**T**he **S**ix **R**ows of **P**ompons"
Plays	***O**nce on **T**his **I**sland*	***A C**horus **L**ine*
Comic Strips	***P**eanuts*	***R**ose **I**s **R**ose*
Movies	***B**abe: **P**ig in the **C**ity*	***A B**ug's **L**ife* ***T**he **K**ing and **I***
Television Programs	***T**ouched by an **A**ngel* ***S**ister, **S**ister*	***S**tar **T**rek: **D**eep **S**pace **N**ine*
Videos	***T**he **L**ion **K**ing II: **S**imba's **P**ride*	***B**asic **S**ign **L**anguage*
Video Games	***M**ario **K**art 64*	***E**scape **V**elocity*
Albums and CDs	***B**ringing **D**own the **H**orse* ***T**iger **W**oods: **T**he **M**akings of a **C**hampion*	***M**i **T**ierra* ***R**ay of **L**ight* ***M**y **F**amily **T**ree: **A R**ecorded **H**istory*
Works of Art	***D**elfina and **D**imas*	***F**orever **F**ree*
Musical Works	"**O**h, **W**hat a **B**eautiful **M**orning"	***P**eter and the **W**olf* "**A**ngel of **M**ine"

Reference Note

For guidelines on using **italics (underlining)** and **quotation marks with titles,** see pages 290 and 297.

MECHANICS

HELP

To find out how to correctly word and capitalize the official title of a book, look on the title page of that book. For the official title of a newspaper or periodical, look on the masthead (the section that lists the title, publisher, editors, and other information), which usually appears on the editorial page or in the table of contents. Check to see if the word *the* is included as the first word in the official title. If *the* is not included, do not capitalize the word if you use it in front of the title.

EXAMPLES

My uncle reads ***The** New York Times.*

Do you have a copy of **the** *Detroit Free Press?*

MECHANICS

NOTE An article (*a, an,* or *the*) before a title is not capitalized unless it is the first word of the official title.

EXAMPLES Do you read **t**he *Sacramento Bee*?

Grandmother showed Nehal and me an article in ***T**he Workbasket.*

My mother reads ***T**he Wall Street Journal.*

Coordinating conjunctions and prepositions that begin a title or subtitle are capitalized.

EXAMPLES I have read ***T**hrough the Looking Glass* three times.

Marcia said that ***B**ut I'll Be Back Again* was very interesting.

Exercise 7 Writing Titles for Imaginary Works

Create a title for each item described below. Be sure each title is capitalized correctly.

EXAMPLE **1.** a video about training pet birds

1. How to Be Your Bird's Best Friend

1. a movie about an American Indian detective who solves a murder mystery
2. a magazine for people interested in video games about fly-fishing in Montana
3. a book about choosing the best breed of dog as a pet for your family
4. a song about saving the rain forests
5. a painting about life in a modern suburb somewhere in the United States
6. a poem about a new baby brother or sister coming home for the first time
7. a play about a student's first day at a new school in a South American country
8. a television show about the humorous people who visit the local library
9. a short story about students who go on a field trip to an animal park and get stuck there overnight
10. a newspaper published by the athletics department

Exercise 8 Correctly Capitalizing Titles

Correct any incorrect capital or lowercase letters in titles in the following sentences. If a sentence is already correct, write *C.*

EXAMPLE 1. Mom gave me an article called "the importance Of fitness."

1. *"The Importance of Fitness"*

1. "Heart And Soul" is the only piano duet we can play.
2. Do you read *National geographic World*?
3. My little sister loves *the Cat in the Hat.*
4. I saw *Around the World in Eighty Days* on television.
5. We enjoy watching reruns of *The Cosby show.*
6. My mother likes to work the crossword puzzle in *the New York times.*
7. The children look forward to receiving their copies of *Ranger rick* each month.
8. Tony's short story "a few words about Aunt Frederica's dog Smitty and all his friends" certainly has the longest title of any story written by a member of the class.
9. "A Poem About A Poem" is the title of Mary Elizabeth's funny poem.
10. Julie Andrews' singing is a special feature of the movie *the sound of music.*

Review D Proofreading a Paragraph to Correct Errors in Capitalization

Proofread the following paragraph, correcting any errors in the use of capital and lowercase letters.

EXAMPLE [1] what a huge Ship the *titanic* was!

1. *What, ship, Titanic*

[1] This magnificent ocean liner sank on april 15, 1912. [2] For more than seventy years, the *Titanic* lay untouched in the icy waters of the atlantic ocean. [3] Then, on September 1, 1985, Dr. Robert Ballard of the woods hole oceanographic institution and his crew found the ship. [4] To view the Ocean floor, the scientists used the remote-controlled vehicle *Argo,* shown on the next page. [5] once they discovered the ship, they attached a special underwater sled to *Argo.* [6] The sled,

MECHANICS

with its lights and camera, provided dr. Ballard with more than twenty thousand photographs of the *Titanic.* [7] In 1986, Dr. Ballard and his Team returned to explore the wreck of the british ocean liner once more. [**8**] using a minisubmarine, the team was able to explore the sunken ship. [**9**] after years of wondering about the *Titanic,* underwater explorers finally found the Wreck and uncovered the truth about its fate. [**10**] In his book *The discovery of the Titanic,* Dr. Ballard tells about his underwater adventures.

MECHANICS

Chapter Review

A. Proofreading Sentences for Correct Capitalization

For each of the following sentences, correctly write the word or words that contain an error in capitalization.

1. Sean's dog, Ransom, is a german shepherd.
2. Our Spring vacation begins on march 26.
3. Write to me at 439 Walnut street.
4. Mira asked, "do you know why the *Titanic* sank?"
5. In 1998, David Trimble and John Hume of Northern Ireland jointly won the Nobel peace prize.
6. As soon as i finish my English homework, i'll call you.
7. She would like to go to College someday.
8. We watched a scene from *Romeo And Juliet.*
9. Eric's orthodontist is dr. McCambridge.
10. On Saturday my aunt is taking us to jones beach.
11. Dad used the general Electric waffle iron to make breakfast.
12. have you seen my copy of *newsweek*?
13. The Peace corps volunteers helped build a bridge.
14. The capital of Peru is lima.
15. The French revolution changed european society.
16. The spacecraft *sputnik 2* carried a dog named Laika.
17. Tom's brother is a roman catholic priest.
18. Although I live in Biloxi now, I'm from the north.
19. I answered, "the gulf of Mexico, I think."
20. Are you taking spanish or art this year?

B. Correcting Sentences by Using Capital Letters Correctly

For the following sentences, correctly write each word that contains an incorrect capital or lowercase letter.

21. Malaysia is in the Southeastern part of Asia.

22. Its largest ethnic groups are malay, chinese, and indian.
23. The capital and largest city is kuala lumpur.
24. Much of the world's Rubber comes from Malaysia.
25. Other Major products are Tin and Palm Oil.
26. Most inhabitants of malaysia are muslims.
27. Malaysia is a constitutional monarchy headed by a King.
28. The Prime Minister is the Leader of the Government.
29. Many Malays wear the Sarong, a kind of skirt.
30. The Encyclopedia called *World book* can give you more information about Malaysia.

C. Correcting Errors in Capitalization

For the following sentences and word groups, correctly write each word and each abbreviation that should be capitalized.

31. Todd's new address is 1240 mud road, Setauket, Ny 11733-2851.
32. The exchange student is from San remo, Italy.
33. My parents' favorite television movie is *Lonesome dove.*
34. We went with mrs. Rigatti to see the floats in the San gennaro Festival.
35. It was a surprise to learn that uncle Elwood had been in the Cia all those years.
36. isn't your aunt Etta here?
37. Mont blanc, the highest peak in the alps, was first climbed in 1786.
38. We sent a petition to mayor Moore.
39. Millie enjoyed reading *Anne of Green gables* so much that she rented the movie.
40. yours sincerely, Beth Tewes

MECHANICS

Writing Application

Using Capital Letters in an Essay

Proper Nouns Your social studies teacher has asked you to write about a vacation you would like to take to a historical place. Write an essay telling where you would like to go and why you would like to go there. In your essay, use at least five proper nouns.

Prewriting First, brainstorm a list of historical places that interest you. Which of these places would you most like to visit? Write down notes about what you would do during your visit.

Writing Begin your rough draft by stating where you would like to go and why. Explain what historical event or events happened at that place. Then, tell what particular areas or landmarks you would visit. Be sure to use at least five proper nouns naming places, events, and people.

Revising Ask a friend to read your draft and tell you if any parts seem unclear or uninteresting. Then, revise anything that is confusing or boring.

Publishing Use an encyclopedia or other reference source to check the spelling of any proper nouns you have included. Proofread your essay carefully for any other errors in grammar, spelling, capitalization, and punctuation. Put your essay on poster board, along with pictures or drawings of the place you wrote about in your essay. With your teacher's permission, display your poster in the classroom.

HELP

An encyclopedia can help you learn more about historical places.

Punctuation

End Marks, Commas, Semicolons, Colons

1.0 Written and Oral English Language Conventions

Students write and speak with a command of standard English conventions appropriate to this grade level.

1.3 Use colons after the salutation in business letters, semicolons to connect independent clauses, and commas when linking two clauses with a conjunction in compound sentences.

Diagnostic Preview

Using Periods, Question Marks, Exclamation Points, Commas, Semicolons, and Colons Correctly

The following sentences lack necessary periods, question marks, exclamation points, commas, semicolons, and colons. Write the letter, word, or words that should be followed by a punctuation mark. Then, add the correct punctuation mark after each word. For numerals, write the entire numeral and insert the correct punctuation mark.

EXAMPLE **1.** Mr. Cotton my next-door neighbor asked me to pick up his mail while he is away

1. Cotton, neighbor, away.

1. The mangos and papayas and avocados will make a good fruit salad
2. Before the slide presentation began Ms Jee gave a short clear history of Korea
3. Ray Charles a popular singer and musician became blind at the age of seven
4. I've taken classes in photography ceramics and weaving
5. When will dinner be ready
6. Here comes a tornado
7. Cheryl will take gymnastics Eddie will take piano lessons

8. Ted mowed the lawn cleaned the garage and painted the shed
9. Would 6 30 P.M be too early
10. This Zuni ring was made in Santa Fe N Mex
11. I finished the letter but I haven't proofread it yet
12. Dear Senator Hutchison
13. We will learn about the federal court system then we will visit the county courthouse.
14. Sara Eric and Manuel can speak both Spanish and English
15. Hurry, get me some ice
16. Yes I did clean my room
17. When you go cross-country skiing, bring the following items skis boots poles and ski wax
18. Shall we leave at 9 00 A.M.
19. Mr Pak when is the Chinese New Year
20. The Scouts' annual dinner will be held February 19 2003.

End Marks

An ***end mark*** is a punctuation mark placed at the end of a sentence. *Periods, question marks,* and *exclamation points* are end marks. Periods are also used after some abbreviations.

12a. **Use a period at the end of a statement.**

EXAMPLES French is the official language of Haiti, but many people there speak Haitian Creole**.**

I will write to you soon**.**

I will let you know when I can visit**.**

12b. **Use a question mark at the end of a question.**

EXAMPLES Have you seen the new science fiction movie**?**

Where should I meet you**?**

12c. **Use an exclamation point at the end of an exclamation.**

EXAMPLES What a cute puppy that is**!**

Wow**!** This egg drop soup is hot**!**

Reference Note

For more information about **classifying sentences by purpose,** see page 18.

HELP

Periods (decimal points) are also used to separate dollars from cents and whole numbers from fractions.

EXAMPLES
$6**.**57 [six dollars and fifty-seven cents]
2**.**7 [two and seven tenths]

In some countries a comma is used instead of a period in such cases.

MECHANICS

STYLE TIP

In your own writing, make sure to use exclamation points only when you want to emphasize a strong feeling. Do not overuse exclamation points, or they will lose their effectiveness.

ORIGINAL
The little gray cat looked up at Judy! With one look, Judy knew this was the kitty for her! How lucky that she had visited the animal shelter today!

REVISED
The little gray cat looked up at Judy. With one look, Judy knew this was the kitty for her. How lucky that she had visited the animal shelter today!

MECHANICS

12d. Use either a period or an exclamation point at the end of a request or a command (an imperative sentence).

Use a period after an imperative sentence that makes a request or a mild command. Use an exclamation point after a strong command.

EXAMPLES Please sit down**.** [a request]

Sit down**.** [a mild command]

Sit down right now**!** [a strong command]

Oral Practice Adding End Marks to Sentences

Read each of the following sentences aloud. Then, say which end mark—a period, a question mark, or an exclamation point—should be added.

EXAMPLE **1.** What time is it
1. question mark

1. When does the bus come
2. What a great game that was
3. Did you bring your lunch today
4. Hyo was born in Korea
5. I don't understand the assignment
6. Who can identify the subject of this sentence
7. Pardon me, sir
8. Imagine me at the White House
9. Get the iguana back into your room right now
10. The legend for this map is in the lower right-hand corner

HELP
When you finish Exercise 1, you should have ten complete sentences.

Exercise 1 Correcting a Paragraph by Adding Capital Letters and End Marks

Decide where the sentences in the following paragraph begin and end. Rewrite each sentence, providing the needed capital letters and end marks.

EXAMPLE what an ancient art weaving is
What an ancient art weaving is!

have you ever been to Hawaii the first Europeans who landed there found chiefs dressed in beautiful feather cloaks feathers for cloaks like the one shown here came from thousands of birds different-colored feathers were arranged in royal designs the feathers were then attached to a base of woven fibers cloaks were worn in battle and for ceremonies most of the islanders did not wear such fine garments colorful prints are worn by all kinds of people on the islands every Friday is Aloha Friday on that day many people wear Hawaiian prints and live flowers

Robert Dampier, *Kamehameha III* (1825). Oil on canvas ($24\frac{1}{8}$" × $20\frac{1}{16}$"). Honolulu Academy of Arts, gift of Mrs. C. Montague Cooke, Jr., Charles M. Cooke III, and Mrs. Heston Wren, in memory of Dr. C. Montague Cooke, Jr., 1951.

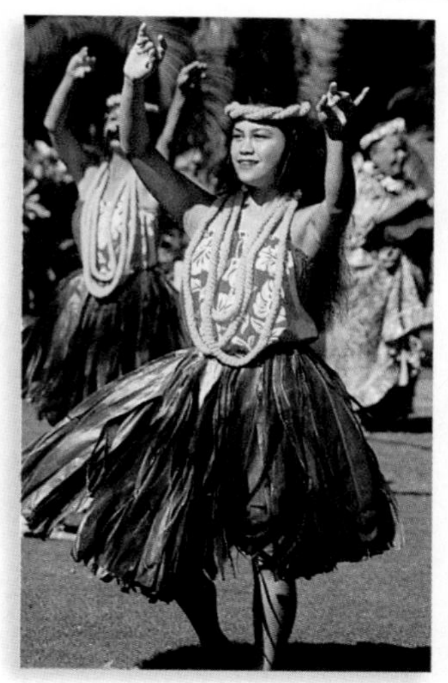

12e. Many abbreviations are followed by periods.

Types of Abbreviations	Examples			
Personal Names	I. M. Pei		J. C. Watts	
	Vicki L. Ruíz		M.F.K. Fisher	
Titles Used with Names	Mr.	Mrs.	Ms.	Jr.
	Dr.	Sr.	Ph.D.	D.D.S.
Organizations	Assn.	Co.	Corp.	Inc.

NOTE Abbreviations for government agencies and some widely used abbreviations are written without periods. Each letter of such abbreviations (which are called ***acronyms***) is capitalized.

EXAMPLES CIA (**C**entral **I**ntelligence **A**gency)

NOS (**N**ational **O**cean **S**ervice)

PC (**p**ersonal **c**omputer)

RFD (**R**ural **F**ree **D**elivery)

TV (**t**ele**v**ision)

STYLE TIP

When writing the initials of someone's name, place a space between two initials (as in *I. M. Pei*). Do not place a space between three initials (as in *M.F.K. Fisher*).

MECHANICS

Reference Note

For more on **using capital letters for abbreviations,** see page 250.

STYLE TIP

The abbreviations *A.D.* and *B.C.* need special attention. Place *A.D.* before the year and *B.C.* after the year.

EXAMPLES
231 **B.C.**
A.D. 590

There is one exception to this rule. For centuries expressed in words, place both *A.D.* and *B.C.* after the century.

EXAMPLES
fifth century **B.C.**
second century **A.D.**

HELP

If you are not sure whether to use periods with an abbreviation, look up the abbreviation in a dictionary, an encyclopedia, or another reliable reference source.

MECHANICS

Types of Abbreviations	Examples		
Times	A.M.	B.C.	Aug.
	P.M.	A.D.	Sat.
Addresses	Ave.	Blvd.	Ct.
	P.O. Box	Rd.	St.
Geographical Names	Ark.	Colo.	D.C.
	St. Paul	P.R.	U.S.

NOTE A two-letter state abbreviation without periods is used only when it is followed by a ZIP Code. Both letters of the abbreviation are capitalized. No mark of punctuation is used between the abbreviation and the ZIP Code.

EXAMPLES Washington, **DC** 20013

San Juan, **PR** 00904

Abbreviations for units of measure are usually written without periods and are not capitalized.

EXAMPLES cc, kg, ml, m, ft, lb, qt

However, you should use a period with the abbreviation *in.* (for *inch*) to prevent confusing it with the word *in.*

When an abbreviation that has a period ends a sentence, another period is not needed. However, a question mark or an exclamation point is used in such situations if it is needed.

EXAMPLES The game lasted until 8:30 P.M.

Did it start at 5:00 P.M.?

HELP

Some sentences in Review A need more than one punctuation mark.

Review A Correcting Sentences by Adding Punctuation

Write the following sentences, adding periods, question marks, and exclamation points where they are needed.

EXAMPLE
1. Some caterpillars become butterflies
1. *Some caterpillars become butterflies.*

1. Will Mr Highwater be teaching the science course

2. Just after 3:00 PM., the sun came out
3. The letter from Ms E J Hunter was dated Fri, Nov 12
4. How heavy the traffic was on First Avenue
5. Do your measuring cups say *ml* or *oz*
6. Address comments to 7890 E Kyle Dr, Oswego, New York.
7. By 300 B.C., Chinese cooks already had a philosophy of five tastes
8. The city of St Petersburg is situated on a peninsula
9. Apply at the loading dock at H J Movers, Inc
10. On TV tonight, Dr Melba West will explain nutrition.

Review B **Using Punctuation Correctly**

For each of the following sentences, write the word or words that should be followed by a period, question mark, or exclamation point. Add the proper punctuation after each word.

EXAMPLE 1. My neighbor Mr Nhuong showed me this picture of people celebrating the Vietnamese holiday Tet
1. *Mr., Tet.*

1. Unlike New Year's Day, which is always on Jan 1, Tet can fall on any day in late January or early February
2. Moreover, Tet isn't just one single day; the celebration lasts a whole week
3. Wouldn't you like a week-long holiday
4. Even here at 8420 Beaconcrest Ave, the Nhuong family still enjoy their traditions
5. According to Mr. Nhuong, the name of the first person to visit a house can bring good or bad luck to the family
6. Since my nickname is Lucky, the Nhuongs asked me to be their first visitor and to arrive by 7:00 AM
7. I tried hard not to be late
8. One of the Nhuongs' relatives flew in from Santa Barbara, Calif, later that morning
9. Mrs Nhuong prepared a huge breakfast, and we all sat down to enjoy it
10. What a great meal that was

Commas

End marks are used to separate complete thoughts. ***Commas,*** however, are generally used to separate words or groups of words within a complete thought. If you fail to use necessary commas, you may confuse your reader.

CONFUSING The members of the team are Jo Ann Jerry Lee Darrin Marcia and Jeanne. [How many members?]

CLEAR The members of the team are Jo Ann, Jerry Lee, Darrin, Marcia, and Jeanne. [five members]

Items in a Series

HELP — Some writers do not use a comma before the conjunction *and, or,* or *nor* when it joins the last two items in a series. However, sometimes such a comma is needed to make the meaning clear. Notice how using a comma before *and* changes the meaning in these examples.

EXAMPLES

Grandma, Mom, and Dad came to the game. [Three people were at the game.]

Grandma, Mom and Dad came to the game. [Grandma is being told who came to the game.]

Including the comma before the conjunction in such a series is not incorrect, so it is best always to use this comma.

MECHANICS

12f. Use commas to separate items in a series.

A ***series*** is three or more items written one after the other. The items may be single words or word groups.

Words in a Series
Sugar cane, bananas, and citrus fruits are grown in Jamaica. [nouns]
Yesterday I dusted, vacuumed, and mopped. [verbs]
The day was wet, cold, and windy. [adjectives]
Word Groups in a Series
At the beach we swam, built sand castles, and played volleyball. [predicates]
I searched for the lost contact lens in the sink, on the counter, and on the floor. [prepositional phrases]
Please punch the time card when you arrive, when you take lunch, and when you leave. [clauses]

When all the items in a series are joined by *and, or,* or *nor,* do not use commas to separate them.

EXAMPLES I've seen snakes **and** lizards **and** toads in our yard.

Shall we go bowling **or** rent a movie **or** listen to CD's?

Exercise 2 Proofreading Sentences for the Correct Use of Commas

Most of the following sentences need commas. If a sentence needs commas, write the word before each missing comma; then, add the comma. If a sentence is already correct, write *C.*

EXAMPLE 1. Mr. Schwan Mrs. Glover and Mr. Hu were nominated for Teacher of the Year.

1. *Schwan, Glover,*

1. I finished my dinner brushed my teeth combed my hair and ran out the door.
2. The nurse checked the patient's pulse took his temperature and gave him a glass of water.
3. For lunch we had milk tuna sandwiches and pears.
4. Cora Jack and Tomás entered the contest.
5. Marcus plays golf and football and volleyball.
6. The U.S. Marine Corps is prepared for battle on land on the sea and in the air.
7. For her birthday on September 27, my sister wants a dog and a cat and a hamster and a bird.
8. Jan told Raul where she had been, where she was, and where she was going.
9. This project is fun easy fast and inexpensive.
10. Balloons were floating in the living room the kitchen the bedrooms and the dining room.

12g. **Use commas to separate two or more adjectives that come before a noun.**

EXAMPLES Pita is a round**,** flat bread of the Middle East.

James Earl Jones certainly has a deep**,** strong**,** commanding voice.

Do not place a comma between an adjective and the noun immediately following it.

INCORRECT Alexandra and I found an old, rusty, bicycle in the vacant lot down the street.

CORRECT Alexandra and I found an old, rusty bicycle in the vacant lot down the street.

HELP

Use a semicolon rather than a comma between phrases in a series when the phrases contain commas.

EXAMPLE

The three sections of this project will be due on Tuesday, March 3**;** on Thursday, March 19**;** and on Friday, April 3.

Reference Note

For more information about **semicolons,** see page 279.

MECHANICS

TIPS & TRICKS

To see whether a comma is needed between two adjectives, insert *and* between the adjectives (*tall and pine,* for example). If *and* sounds awkward there, do not use a comma.

Another test you can use is to switch the order of the adjectives. If the sentence still makes sense when you switch them, use a comma.

STYLE TIP

In your reading, you may see very short compound sentences that do not use commas.

EXAMPLE
I'm tired and I'm hungry.

However, a comma before a conjunction in a compound sentence is always correct.

MECHANICS

Sometimes the last adjective in a series is thought of as part of the noun. In that case, do not use a comma before the last adjective.

EXAMPLES The tall pine tree [not *tall, pine tree*] swayed.

Kimchi is a spicy Korean dish [not *spicy, Korean dish*] made with pickled cabbage.

Exercise 3 Proofreading Sentences for the Correct Use of Commas

For each of the following sentences, write the word that should be followed by a comma; then, add the comma. If a sentence is already correct, write *C.*

EXAMPLE **1.** Mrs. Hirata taught us several beautiful old Japanese folk songs.

1. beautiful,

1. His calm wrinkled face told a story.
2. François Toussaint L'Ouverture was a brilliant patriotic Haitian leader.
3. The huge lively wriggling kingfish dropped from the hook.
4. There's a sleek shiny bicycle in the store window.
5. The sound of the soft steady rain put me to sleep.
6. We read Chief Black Hawk's moving farewell speech.
7. I washed my hands in the cold clear spring water.
8. May I please have some of that spicy delicious soup?
9. The old diary had ragged yellowed pages.
10. The crowded dining room is filled with people celebrating my parents' anniversary.

Compound Sentences

12h. **Use a comma before *and, but, for, nor, or, so,* or *yet* when it joins independent clauses in a compound sentence.**

EXAMPLES Theo will bring the potato salad, and Sarah will bring the apple juice.

Congress passed the bill, but I believe the president vetoed it.

I went to bed early, for I had a big day ahead of me.

NOTE Do not confuse a compound sentence with a simple sentence containing a compound verb. Usually, no comma is needed between the parts of a compound verb.

COMPOUND SENTENCE We ran relay races first, and then we ate lunch.

SIMPLE SENTENCE We ran the relay races first and then ate lunch. [The sentence contains a compound verb.]

However, a compound verb made up of three or more verbs generally does require commas.

EXAMPLE We **ran** the relay races**,** **ate** lunch**,** and then **prepared** for the individual races.

Reference Note

For more information on **compound sentences,** see pages 97 and 403. For more information on **compound verbs,** see page 14.

Exercise 4 Correcting Compound Sentences by Adding Commas

Some of the following sentences are compound and need to have commas added. If a sentence needs a comma, write the word or numeral before the missing comma; then, add the comma. If a sentence is already correct, write *C.*

EXAMPLE **1.** The storm brought heavy rain but a tornado did the most damage.

1. rain,

1. At the Native American Heritage Festival, Mary Johns wove baskets from sweet grass and Alice Billie made rings from beads.
2. The sailboat was almost hidden by the fog yet we could see part of the mast.
3. German Silva of Mexico was the fastest male runner in the 1994 and 1995 New York City Marathons and Tegla Loroupe of Kenya was the female winner in both races.
4. Would you like to play checkers or shall we go to the lake instead?
5. I called my friends and told them the news.
6. Jim practiced the piano piece all month for he wanted to do well at the recital.

7. Many people are used to celebrating New Year's Day on January 1 but the Chinese New Year begins between January 21 and February 19.
8. The lake contains fish and is home to several alligators.
9. The old oak tree shaded the house but the shade kept the grass from growing.
10. I wanted to buy a camera so I mowed yards in the neighborhood to earn extra money.

Interrupters

12i. **Use commas to set off an expression that interrupts a sentence.**

Two commas are used to set off an interrupting expression—one before and one after the expression.

EXAMPLES My favorite gospel singers**,** BeBe and CeCe Winans**,** were on TV last night.

As you leave**,** Jesse**,** please close the door quietly.

Sometimes an "interrupter" comes at the beginning or the end of the sentence. In such cases, only one comma is needed.

EXAMPLES Yes**,** I'll call back later.

How did you do in karate class today**,** Kami?

(1) **Use commas to set off appositives and appositive phrases that are not necessary to the meaning of a sentence.**

An ***appositive*** is a noun or a pronoun that identifies or describes another noun or pronoun beside it. An ***appositive phrase*** is an appositive with its modifiers.

EXAMPLES A gymnast**, Mrs. Shaw,** will coach us. [The appositive *Mrs. Shaw* identifies the gymnast.]

This book is about geology**, the science of the earth and its rocks.** [*The science of the earth and its rocks* is an appositive phrase that identifies *geology*.]

Do not use commas when an appositive is necessary to the meaning of a sentence.

MECHANICS

EXAMPLES My cousin Roberto lives in Puerto Rico. [I have more than one cousin and am using his name to identify which cousin I mean.]

The character Alice is based on Alice Liddell. [Alice is one of several characters; the appositive tells which character is meant.]

Exercise 5 Punctuating Appositives

Most of the following sentences contain at least one error in the punctuation of appositives and appositive phrases. Write each word that should be followed by a comma, and add the comma. If a sentence is already correct, write *C*.

EXAMPLE 1. Two cold drinks lemonade and punch were available to the guests.

1. *drinks, punch,*

1. The park a beautiful place for a party was lit by streetlights and had a bandstand.
2. Our hosts Mr. and Mrs. Worthington greeted us at the entrance.
3. Some of the men were wearing boaters straw hats popular at the time.
4. My friend Eliza Wolcott sat in the shade at our table.
5. Do you see an empty table a quiet place for conversation?
6. Somehow a puppy the pet of one of the guests got onto the dance floor.

Pierre Auguste Renoir, *Ball at the Moulin de la Galette* (1876). Paris, Musée d'Orsay, Paris, Giraudon/Art Resource, New York.

7. Edward Finch, the best dancer has his choice of partners.
8. Music mostly waltzes filled the air.
9. A young woman in a striped dress a new bride, is remembering her wedding.
10. Listen to laughter and lively conversation, the sounds of happy people.

(2) Use commas to set off words used in direct address.

EXAMPLES Ms. Jacobs, please explain the assignment.

Do you know who Santa Anna was, Beth?

You're right, Inés, to say he was a Mexican general.

In the sentences above, the words *Ms. Jacobs, Beth,* and *Inés* are ***nouns of direct address.*** They identify the person or persons spoken to or addressed.

HELP Some sentences in Exercise 6 need more than one comma.

Exercise 6 Correcting Sentences by Adding Commas

For each of the following sentences, write each word that should be followed by a comma; then, add the comma.

EXAMPLE **1.** Are you sure you left your book in the room James?

1. room,

1. Michi will you read the haiku you wrote?
2. Carla please bring me the newspaper when you finish with it.
3. Did you bring the tickets Jorge?
4. After all the work we've done Ann it would be a shame to turn it in late.
5. If you mow the lawn Kelly I'll rake the clippings.
6. Please Mom can you drive me to rehearsal?
7. Mr. Ferguson you have a telephone call.
8. You are dismissed class.
9. How long have you worked here David?
10. The problem my friends is simply lack of effort.

Introductory Words, Phrases, and Clauses

12j. Use a comma after certain introductory elements.

(1) Use a comma after *yes, no,* or any mild exclamation such as *well* or *why* at the beginning of a sentence.

EXAMPLES **Yes,** you may use my pencil.

Why, it's Arthur!

Well, I think you should apologize.

(2) Use a comma after two or more introductory prepositional phrases.

EXAMPLE **In the valley at the base of the hill,** a herd of buffalo grazes.

Also, use a comma after a single long introductory prepositional phrase.

EXAMPLE **On the winter morning when Kenan discovered the strange visitor,** the rosebush burst into bloom.

If the introductory prepositional phrase is short, a comma may or may not be used.

EXAMPLES **In the morning,** we'll tour the Caddo burial mounds.

In the morning we'll tour the Caddo burial mounds.

On that page, you will see a map of the park.

On that page you will see a map of the park.

(3) Use a comma after an introductory adverb clause.

EXAMPLE **After the show is over,** we will go out to eat.

NOTE An adverb clause that comes at the end of a sentence usually is not preceded by a comma.

EXAMPLE We will go out to eat **after the show is over.**

Exercise 7 Using Commas with Introductory Elements

If a comma is needed in a sentence, write the word before the missing comma and add the comma. If a sentence is already punctuated correctly, write *C*.

EXAMPLE 1. After he left we noticed that his hat was on the table.

1. left,

1. Before eating the birds were singing noisily.
2. On the table in the kitchen dinner was getting cold.
3. Although he trained hard for a month, Juan could not break his own record.
4. Yes that is a cardinal.
5. On her way to school in the morning Roseanne was thinking about her project.

Reference Note

For more about **prepositional phrases,** see page 63. For more about **adverb clauses,** see page 93.

HELP

Use a comma after a single short introductory prepositional phrase when the comma is necessary to make the sentence clear.

CONFUSING
In the evening sunlight faded in the western sky.

CLEAR
In the evening, sunlight faded in the western sky. [The comma is needed so that the reader does not read "evening sunlight."]

MEETING THE CHALLENGE

You have seen several examples of sentences that require commas to prevent misreading. Create five sentences in which a comma is necessary to prevent humorous misreading.

6. When I have time on the weekends I like to hook rugs.
7. Well you had better make up your mind soon.
8. With the decorations in the living room in place Julie was ready for her mother's birthday party.
9. In the corner of the room a night light showed the way to the door.
10. Because the snow cover was so thin the deer had no trouble finding food.

Conventional Uses

12k. **Use commas in certain conventional situations.**

(1) Use commas to separate items in dates and addresses.

EXAMPLES Bill Cosby was born on July 12**,** 1937**,** in Philadelphia**,** Pennsylvania.

Saturday**,** May 10**,** will be the day of the soccer playoff.

My aunt has lived at 41 Jefferson Street**,** Northfield**,** Minnesota**,** since 1998.

Notice that a comma separates the last item in a date or in an address from the words that follow it. However, a comma does not separate a month from a day (*July 12*) or a house number from a street name (*41 Jefferson Street*).

NOTE No punctuation is used between the state abbreviation and the ZIP Code.

EXAMPLE Cerritos, **CA 90701**

STYLE TIP

Business letters use a colon, not a comma, after the salutation.

EXAMPLE
Dear Ms. Hinojosa**:**

(2) Use a comma after the salutation of a personal letter and after the closing of any letter.

EXAMPLES Dear Grandma and Grandpa**,** Love**,**

Dear Tyrone**,** Sincerely**,**

Exercise 8 Using Commas Correctly in Conventional Situations

Write the following items and sentences, inserting or deleting commas as needed.

MECHANICS

EXAMPLE 1. Friday February 11 is the first day of the fair.
1. Friday, February 11, is the first day of the fair.

1. Yours truly
2. Shirley Chisholm was born on November 30 1924, in New York City.
3. The first female principal chief of the Cherokee Nation is Wilma Mankiller; she was born near Rocky Mountain Oklahoma.
4. Write to me at 327, Adams Way Darrouzett TX 79024.
5. The Harvest Carnival is on Friday October 23 2009.
6. Dear Uncle Sig
7. Address orders to Pretty Good Camping Supplies P.O. Box 528 Southborough, MA, 01772.
8. He made his stage debut on May, 25, 1928 in London England.
9. Friday July 9 2004 was my grandparents' golden wedding anniversary.
10. The main office in Santa Barbara California has a new fax number.

HELP

Commas are also used in numbers greater than and including one thousand. Use a comma before every third digit to the left of the decimal point.

EXAMPLE
7,386,149.00 [seven million three hundred eighty-six thousand one hundred forty-nine]

Unnecessary Commas

12l. Do not use unnecessary commas.

Too much punctuation can be just as confusing as not enough punctuation, especially where the use of commas is concerned.

CONFUSING My friend, Jessica, said she would feed my cat and my dog while I'm away, but now, she tells me, she will be too busy.

CLEAR My friend Jessica said she would feed my cat and my dog while I'm away, but now she tells me she will be too busy.

Have a reason for every comma or other mark of punctuation that you use. When there is no rule requiring punctuation and when the meaning of the sentence is clear without one, do not insert any punctuation mark.

MECHANICS

Review C Proofreading a Letter for the Correct Use of Commas

The sentences in the following letter each contain an error in the use of commas. Rewrite the letter, adding or deleting commas as needed.

EXAMPLES **[1]** July, 6, 2009

1. July 6, 2009

[2] Dear Tom

2. Dear Tom,

Dear Tom,

[1] Well on July 4, 2009, Aunt Lil kept her promise and took me up in her airplane. **[2]** Wow! What a view of the canyons valleys, and plateaus we had! **[3]** We flew over a hill, and saw a small herd of mustangs. **[4]** Aunt Lil circled above the horses and the plane's shadow frightened the stallion. **[5]** The whole herd stampeded with tails, and manes and hooves flying in a storm of dust all the way down into the valley. **[6]** One black colt trailed behind but his mother quickly nudged him onward. **[7]** In a moment the swift sturdy mustangs, descendants of the fiery steeds of the Spanish conquistadors, were galloping into the woods. **[8]** I wish you could have seen them Tom! **[9]** At least I remembered my camera so here is a picture of those beautiful horses.

[10] Yours truly

Sal

Semicolons

A semicolon is part period and part comma. Like a period, it can separate complete thoughts. Like a comma, it can separate items within a sentence.

12m. **Use a semicolon between parts of a compound sentence if they are not joined by *and, but, for, nor, or, so,* or *yet.***

EXAMPLES Todd's report is about Arizona; mine is about Utah.

The rain clouds are moving in quickly; let's head home.

NOTE Use a semicolon to join independent clauses only if the ideas in the independent clauses are closely related. Otherwise, use a period to make two separate sentences.

EXAMPLES Do not touch that tree frog; it may be poisonous. [The two ideas are closely related.]

Do not touch that tree frog. Everyone stay together. [The two ideas are not closely related.]

HELP

Use a semicolon rather than a comma between phrases in a series when the phrases contain commas.

EXAMPLE

The acrobats are traveling from Albuquerque, New Mexico; through Phoenix, Arizona; and finally to San Diego, California.

Exercise 9 Proofreading Sentences for the Correct Use of Semicolons

Most of the following sentences have commas where there should be semicolons. If a sentence needs a semicolon, write the words before and after the missing semicolon; then, insert the semicolon. If a sentence is already correct, write *C.*

EXAMPLE 1. Mary Vaux Walcott treasured her box of watercolor paints, she took it with her everywhere she went.

1. paints; she

1. As a young girl, she visited the Canadian Rockies each year, there she began to paint wildflowers.
2. She loved mountain climbing, she often crossed rugged areas to find new wildflowers.
3. She painted her flowers from life, for she did not like to rely on pencil sketches.
4. You can see five of her paintings on the next page, aren't they beautiful?

MECHANICS

5. Painting A shows a western red lily, such lilies wither quickly when picked.
6. Painting B is of a bottle gentian, a fall flower, it grows in bogs and swamps.
7. American wisteria is a climbing plant, and you can see in Painting C that it has many showy flowers.
8. Painting D shows blossoms of the American waterlily opening in early morning, their aroma draws insects.
9. Painting E is of Carolina jessamine, it spreads its fragrant flowers through treetops.
10. Mary Vaux Walcott is known as "the Audubon of North American wildflowers," for she painted more than seven hundred species.

A

B

C

D

E

Mary Vaux Walcott/ National Museum of American Art, Washington, D.C./ Art Resource, New York.

MECHANICS

Colons

A colon usually signals that more information follows.

12n. **Use a colon before a list of items, especially after expressions such as *the following* and *as follows*.**

EXAMPLES These are the winners of the poetry contest**:** Carmen Santiago, Justin Douglass, and Steven Yellowfeather.

Pack the following items for your overnight trip**:** a toothbrush, toothpaste, and your hairbrush.

The order of the colors seen through a prism is as follows**:** red, orange, yellow, green, blue, indigo, and violet.

NOTE Do not use a colon between a preposition and its object or between a verb and its object. Either omit the colon or reword the sentence.

INCORRECT My report includes: a table of contents, three chapters, illustrations, and a list of sources.

CORRECT My report includes a table of contents, three chapters, illustrations, and a list of sources.

CORRECT My report includes **the following parts:** a table of contents, three chapters, illustrations, and a list of sources.

Colons may also be used to introduce long, formal statements and quotations.

EXAMPLE Mark Twain had a very definite opinion on happiness**:** "The best way to cheer yourself up is to try to cheer somebody else up."

12o. **Use a colon between the hour and the minute when you write the time.**

EXAMPLES 8**:**55 A.M. 9**:**15 P.M. 6**:**22 this morning

12p. **Use a colon after the salutation of a business letter.**

EXAMPLES Dear Sir or Madam**:** Dear Mrs. Jordan**:**

Dear Sales Manager**:** To Whom It May Concern**:**

STYLE  TIP

Personal letters use a comma, not a colon, after the salutation.

EXAMPLE
Dear John**,**

MECHANICS

Exercise 10 Using Colons Correctly

Most of the following items contain an error in the use of colons. Rewrite each incorrect sentence to correct the error. If a sentence is already correct, write *C.*

EXAMPLE **1.** Bring the following items to class your notebook, a pencil, and your textbook.

1. Bring the following items to class: your notebook, a pencil, and your textbook.

1. We visited the following cities Bayamón, Ponce, and San Juan.

2. A good baby sitter should have the following qualities promptness, reliability, an interest in children, and common sense.

3. To stay healthy, you should not smoke or chew tobacco.

4. Add these items to your shopping list tissues, toothpaste, and shampoo.

5. A good friend should be: loving, loyal, and honest.

6. The first bell rings at 8 10 A.M., and the second bell rings twenty minutes later.

7. Your homework includes: your spelling worksheet, one chapter of reading, and a rough draft of your English composition for Monday.

8. The recipe for Brunswick stew called for these ingredients lamb, carrots, potatoes, and onions.

9. Every time we see her, Grandmother likes to remind us of her favorite Ben Franklin saying "Whatever is begun in anger ends in shame."

10. Dear Sir or Madam

HELP—
Some of the sentences in Review D contain more than one punctuation error.

Review D Proofreading a Letter for the Correct Use of Punctuation

Proofread the following letter for errors in punctuation. Then, rewrite the letter, adding the necessary periods, question marks, commas, semicolons, and colons.

EXAMPLE **[1]** 1200 E Halifax Avenue

1. 1200 E. Halifax Avenue

MECHANICS

[1]January 11 2009

Superintendent of Schools
Baltimore City Board of Education
200 E. North Avenue
Baltimore, MD 21202

[2]Dear Superintendent

[3]Would your students be interested in visiting an African American wax museum [4]The only one of its kind is right here in Baltimore [5]The Great Blacks in Wax Museum features life-size wax models of famous African Americans [6]These wax images include leaders in education, civil rights and science [7]The museum displays statues of the following people Rosa Parks, Phillis Wheatley, Crispus Attucks, Carter G Woodson, Dred Scott, Harriet Tubman, Booker T. Washington, Frederick Douglass, and many others.

[8]Our company offers students and teachers discount tours of the museum during Black History Month discount tours of other historic attractions are also available then [9]For more information, please call me between 8 30 A.M. and 5 30 P.M.

[10] Yours truly,

Jane Lee Harper

Jane Lee Harper
President
Uhuru Guided Tours

MECHANICS

Review E Using End Marks, Commas, Semicolons, and Colons Correctly

HELP — Some of the sentences in Review E contain more than one punctuation error.

Each of the following items contains at least one error in the use of end marks, commas, semicolons, or colons. Rewrite the items, adding or changing punctuation to correct each error.

EXAMPLE 1. Mrs. Hunter how long will the leaves remain that color.

1. Mrs. Hunter, how long will the leaves remain that color?

1. Liechtenstein a country not quite as large as Washington, D.C. is one of the smallest countries in Europe
2. The students gathered signatures on a petition and a spokesperson presented their argument for better sidewalks.
3. That must be the biggest fish in the whole lake?
4. Did you find out which president created the Peace Corps in 1961.
5. Dear Sir
6. No I haven't seen that new movie but I've heard it's absolutely terrific.
7. Fort Sumter; the site of the first shots fired in the Civil War; is located in Charleston South Carolina.
8. After the sparrows finished in the birdbath they flew up to the feeder!
9. A long white shiny limousine pulled into the parking lot, after that came a bus and a police officer on a motorcycle.
10. Before you may read your mystery novel you must finish your homework clean your room and walk the dog.

MECHANICS

Chapter Review

A. Using Punctuation Correctly

Periods, question marks, exclamation points, commas, semicolons, and colons are missing in the following items. Write the word or numeral before each missing punctuation mark, and add the correct mark.

1. Flora please pass the pepper
2. Did Fred once work for Interactive Corp
3. We are learning about meteorology the study of weather
4. The shirts come in the following four colors blue green brown and red
5. Yasunari Kawabata won the 1968 Nobel Prize in literature he was the first Japanese writer to win the prize
6. Watch out
7. I wish I could go to camp this summer but I have to stay home because I caught chickenpox.
8. Dear Mom and Dad
9. I taught Zachary how to swim
10. While Dr Sanchez is on jury duty Dr Kelley is seeing his patients
11. My youngest sister was born on April 12 1997
12. She is a bright lively child
13. His address is 2330 River Rd Sterling VA 22170-2322
14. The Mandan and Hidatsa peoples in North Dakota harvested wild rice and they traded it for buffalo hides and dried meat
15. Have you ever been to Austin Texas
16. Well Eric my favorite state in the Northwest is Washington
17. Tom a freshman plays violin in the local orchestra
18. I get up at 6 00 A M. on school days
19. Yes a taco is a fried filled tortilla
20. The meeting will be held Sunday February 23 at 2 00 P M

B. Using Punctuation Correctly

Periods, question marks, exclamation points, commas, semicolons, and colons are missing in the following items. Write the word or numeral before each missing punctuation mark, and add the correct mark.

21. Thanks for the new bike Grandpa.

22. What a friendly obedient dog you have

23. Dawn finished her report read the paper cooked dinner and set the table.

24. Can you tell me his address or should I ask someone else

25. Write to 637 West Elk Ave, Washington DC 20015-2602.

26. Our mechanic could not find anything wrong with the water pump the problem must be somewhere else.

27. Answer the following questions

(1) Was Lincoln a successful leader

(2) Could the Civil War have ended sooner

(3) How important was the naval blockade

28. One of our troop leaders Ms. Wells is teaching us photography.

29. We'll need some minnows worms aren't good bait in salt water.

30. Ned the oldest in my family has many responsibilities.

31. Aren't you going to Glasgow Scotland this summer

32. She hid the lantern the keys two maps and the gold.

33. Before June 1 1998 I had never heard of Christine then she was on the front page of every paper.

34. Get those filthy muddy cowboy boots of yours out of this house now

35. Chiles rellenos are very spicy you'll like them.

36. Go to the cave build a fire and wait for Sabrina.

37. No Teresa there was no TV in those days.

38. Color this one yellow Mr Papastratos won't mind.

39. Let's finish this we'll see about starting something new tomorrow.

40. Dear Mr President

Writing Application

Using End Marks in a Screenplay

Kinds of Sentences You are a scriptwriter for a popular TV show. You are writing a scene in which one of the characters wins one million dollars in a sweepstakes. Write down the character's response to the good news. Use a variety of end marks to help express the character's feelings.

Prewriting First, you will need to make up a character or use one from a TV show you have seen. How would that person feel if he or she won a million dollars? Write down some notes on how you think your character would react.

Writing Using your prewriting notes, write a draft of what your character will say. Make your draft at least one paragraph long. Use end punctuation to help express the character's emotions.

Revising Read your character's response aloud. Does it sound realistic? Check to make sure you have used a variety of end marks to express your character's feelings.

Publishing Check your writing for any errors in grammar, spelling, and punctuation. In small groups, exchange papers with another student. Take turns reading the papers to the group as if you each were one of the characters. Use the punctuation as a guide to what the character is feeling and to how you should read the response.

CHAPTER

Punctuation

Underlining (Italics), Quotation Marks, Apostrophes, Hyphens, Parentheses

1.0 Written and Oral English Language Conventions
Students write and speak with a command of standard English conventions appropriate to this grade level.

Diagnostic Preview

A. Proofreading Sentences for the Correct Use of Underlining (Italics) and Quotation Marks

Each of the following sentences contains at least one error in the use of underlining (italics) or quotation marks. Rewrite each sentence correctly.

EXAMPLE **1.** The recent movie of Shakespeare's "Hamlet" is true to the original play.

1. The recent movie of Shakespeare's Hamlet is true to the original play.

1. "The next short story we will be reading is called *All Summer in a Day,*" Mr. Willis told us.
2. My younger brother learned how to play the song Yesterday on the piano.
3. Isn't your favorite poem The Unicorn?
4. "Wasn't that a song? asked Carrie."
5. I think a folk singer wrote it, answered Tony.
6. Juanita said that "she would hum a bit of it."

7. Brad commented, “I think my parents have a copy of it”.
8. “Can you bring it to class”? Elena asked.
9. “Who said, Time is money”? Gerald asked.
10. “Benjamin Franklin wrote it,” answered Karen, “in a book called Advice to a Young Tradesman.”
11. “I think, said Theo, that you’re right.”
12. “Into the Woods” is a musical comedy in which characters from several different fairy tales meet in the same forest.
13. Kelly’s favorite episode of *Star Trek: Voyager* is titled Message in a Bottle.
14. Sean often wonders what makes van Gogh’s painting “Twelve Sunflowers in a Vase” so interesting.
15. Melba built a model of the Merrimack for extra credit in social studies.

B. Proofreading Sentences for the Correct Use of Apostrophes, Hyphens, and Parentheses

Each of the following sentences contains at least one error in the use of apostrophes, hyphens, or parentheses. Rewrite each sentence correctly.

EXAMPLE 1. We havent finished dinner yet.
1. We haven’t finished dinner yet.

16. John F. Kennedy 1917–1963 was the youngest person to be elected President of the United States.
17. Each classroom has thirty one desks.
18. This recipe I’m trying calls for fresh greens, potatoes, car rots, and onions. It’s a vegetarian dish.
19. The assembly featured a speech by the president elect of the student council.
20. Whos going to sample this dish?
21. Dont forget the soy sauce.
22. The two chefs dishes all were original recipes were delicious.
23. Jiro’s last name has two *l*s.
24. It is not healthy to eat high fat foods every day.
25. In the quiet early evening, we could hear the flapping of the geeses wings.

MECHANICS

Underlining (Italics)

COMPUTER TIP

If you use a computer, you may be able to set words in italics yourself. Most word processors can set fonts in italics.

MEETING THE CHALLENGE

Write the following categories in a column: book, play, newspaper/magazine, movie, television series, painting, long musical work. Next to each category, write the title of your favorite work. Then, make up a sentence using each of your favorite titles. After you have finished, check your work against the examples given in **Rule 13a.**

MECHANICS

Italics are printed letters that lean to the right—*like this.* When you handwrite or type, you show that a word should be italicized by underlining it. If your writing were printed, the typesetter would set the underlined words in italics. For example, if you wrote

Zora Neale Hurston wrote <u>Mules and Men.</u>

the sentence would be printed like this:

Zora Neale Hurston wrote *Mules and Men.*

13a. **Use underlining (italics) for titles and subtitles of books, plays, periodicals, films, television series, works of art, and long musical works.**

Type of Name	Examples
Books	*Number the Stars* *To Kill a Mockingbird* *Tibet: Through the Red Box*
Plays	*Song of Sheba* *Romeo and Juliet* *Life with Father*
Periodicals	*Sioux City Journal* *The Dallas Morning News* *Highlights for Children*
Films	*Babe: Pig in the City* *The Wizard of Oz* *Oliver & Company*
Television Series	*Under the Umbrella Tree* *Fun with Watercolors* *Reading Rainbow*

Reference Note

For examples of **titles that require quotation marks** instead of italics, see page 297.

Type of Name	Examples
Works of Art	*The Old Guitarist* *Mona Lisa* *Confucius and Disciples*
Long Musical Works	*The Pirates of Penzance* *The Nutcracker Suite* *A Little Night Music*

Generally, use italics for titles of works that stand alone, such as books, CDs, and television series. Use quotation marks for titles of works that are usually part of a larger work, such as short stories, songs, and episodes of a television series.

NOTE An article (*a, an,* or *the*) before the title of a magazine or a newspaper is not italicized or capitalized when it is part of a sentence rather than part of the title.

EXAMPLES I deliver **the** *Evening Independent.* [*The* is part of the sentence, not part of the title.]

Is that the latest issue of ***The*** *New Yorker*? [*The* is part of the magazine's title.]

13b. **Use underlining (italics) for names of trains, ships, aircraft, and spacecraft.**

Type of Name	Examples
Trains	*Stourbridge Lion* *Best Friend of Charleston*
Ships	*Lusitania* USS *Lexington*
Aircraft	*Solar Challenger* *Hindenburg*
Spacecraft	*Landsat-7* *Discovery*

HELP If you are not sure whether an article is part of a title, check the periodical's masthead (the section that lists the publisher, owners, editors, etc.) or the table of contents to find out the official title.

STYLE TIP

Now and then, writers will use italics (underlining) for emphasis, especially in written dialogue. Read the following sentences aloud. Notice that by italicizing different words, the writer can change the meaning of the sentence.

EXAMPLES

"Are you going to wear the *red* shoes?" asked Ellen. [Will you wear the red shoes, not the blue ones?]

"Are *you* going to wear the red shoes?" asked Ellen. [Will you, not your sister, wear them?]

"Are you going to *wear* the red shoes?" asked Ellen. [Will you wear them, or are you just trying them on?]

Italicizing (underlining) words for emphasis is a handy technique that should not be overused. It can quickly lose its impact.

MECHANICS

Exercise 1 **Using Underlining (Italics) Correctly**

For each of the following sentences, write each word or item that should be printed in italics and underline it.

EXAMPLE **1.** We saw Rodin's famous statue The Thinker.

1. The Thinker

1. The magazine Popular Science reports news about science.
2. Have you ever seen the movie The Shaggy Dog?
3. My favorite painting is Morning of Red Bird by Romare Bearden.
4. The Wright brothers built their first airplane, the Flyer, in 1903.
5. We read the play You're a Good Man, Charlie Brown.
6. On his famous voyage in 1492, Christopher Columbus acted as captain of the ship named the Santa Maria.
7. Which newspaper do you read, the Chicago Sun-Times or the Chicago Tribune?
8. My sister watches Sesame Street every day.
9. Aboard Vostok 1, Yuri A. Gagarin orbited Earth.
10. The book Stuart Little is by E. B. White.

Quotation Marks

13c. Use quotation marks to enclose a *direct quotation*—a person's exact words.

Be sure to place quotation marks both before and after a person's exact words.

EXAMPLES Our team leader says, "I try to practice every day."

"Let's go home," Jeanne suggested.

Do not use quotation marks for an ***indirect quotation***—a rewording of a direct quotation.

DIRECT QUOTATION Juan said, "The bus is late." [Juan's exact words]

INDIRECT QUOTATION Juan said that the bus was late. [not Juan's exact words]

DIRECT QUOTATION Juan asked, "Is the bus late?" [Juan's exact words]

INDIRECT QUOTATION Juan asked whether the bus was late. [not Juan's exact words]

13d. A directly quoted sentence begins with a capital letter.

EXAMPLES Mrs. Talbott said, "**P**lease get a pencil."

Kristina asked, "**I**s it my turn?"

13e. When an expression identifying the speaker interrupts a quoted sentence, the second part of the quotation begins with a lowercase letter.

EXAMPLE "Will you take care of my lawn and my pets," asked Mr. Franklin, "**w**hile I'm on vacation next month?"

When the second part of a divided quotation is a new sentence, it begins with a capital letter.

EXAMPLE "Yes, we will," I said. "**W**e can use the extra money."

13f. A direct quotation can be set off from the rest of the sentence by a comma, a question mark, or an exclamation point, but not by a period.

HELP—*To set off* means "to separate."

(1) If a quotation comes at the beginning of a sentence, a comma, question mark, or exclamation point usually follows it.

EXAMPLES "Dogs make better pets than cats do**,**" said Frank.

"Have you ever had a cat**?**" Donna asked.

"No, and I never will**!**" he replied.

(2) If a quotation comes at the end of a sentence, a comma usually comes before it.

EXAMPLE Maria asked**,** "What makes you say that?"

(3) If a quoted sentence is divided, a comma usually follows the first part and comes before the second part.

EXAMPLE "Oh**,**" Donna commented**,** "he's probably just saying that because he's never had a cat."

13g. **A period or a comma should be placed inside the closing quotation marks.**

EXAMPLE "I can't wait to see Shirley Caesar's new video**,**" James said. "It's supposed to come out next week**.**"

13h. **A question mark or an exclamation point should be placed inside closing quotation marks when the quotation itself is a question or an exclamation. Otherwise, it should be placed outside.**

EXAMPLES "What time will you be home from work, Mom**?**" asked Michael. [The quotation is a question.]

Who said, "All the world's a stage"**?** [The sentence, not the quotation, is a question.]

"Stop**!**" yelled the crossing guard. [The quotation is an exclamation.]

What a surprise to hear Susana say, "We're moving back to Puerto Rico in June"**!** [The sentence, not the quotation, is an exclamation.]

Exercise 2 **Punctuating and Capitalizing Quotations**

Rewrite the following sentences, using commas, end marks, quotation marks, and capital letters where they are needed. If a sentence is already correct, write *C.*

EXAMPLE **1.** We're going tubing next Saturday said Carlos.
1. "We're going tubing next Saturday," said Carlos.

1. May I go with you I asked.
2. We'd like to go, too added Barbara and Tranh.
3. Barbara asked who will bring tubes for everyone
4. Jim said I'll bring them
5. I offered to bring sandwiches and lemonade.
6. My dad will drive said Carlos he has a van.
7. Tranh told us that the river is fed by a glacier.
8. That means said Barbara that the water will be cold.
9. It should feel good I pointed out if Saturday is as hot as today is.
10. Carlos told all of us to meet him at his house at 8:30 A.M.

MECHANICS

Exercise 3 Punctuating and Capitalizing Quotations

Rewrite each of the following sentences correctly, using punctuation and capitalization as needed.

EXAMPLE 1. Clementine Hunter was born in 1887 said María and she died in 1988.

1. *"Clementine Hunter was born in 1887," said María, "and she died in 1988."*

Clementine Hunter (c.1945). Photo from the Mildred Bailey Collection, Natchitoches, Louisiana.

1. Staci said here is a photograph of this self-taught American artist.
2. Clementine Hunter was born in Natchitoches, Louisiana Staci remarked.
3. She started working on a plantation when she was only fourteen María added.
4. When she was fifty-three years old said Staci Hunter decided to do what she loved most—paint.
5. Staci continued she began painting on almost any surface that would hold the paint!
6. Her early pieces were painted on brown paper bags and cardboard boxes María remarked and then on canvas, wood, and paper.
7. Hunter used bright colors Mike explained to paint everyday scenes like this one, called *Wash Day.*
8. It may surprise you to learn added Mike that her paintings sold for as little as twenty-five cents fifty years ago!
9. María asked Mike didn't you say that her paintings are now worth thousands of dollars?
10. Moreover Staci concluded Clementine Hunter's paintings have been exhibited throughout the United States.

Clementine Hunter, *Wash Day.* The collection of Thomas N. Whitehead, courtesy of the Association for the Preservation of Historical Natchitoches, Louisiana, Melrose Plantation.

Exercise 4 Revising Indirect Quotations to Create Direct Quotations

Revise each of the following sentences to change the indirect quotation to a direct quotation. Be sure to use capital letters and punctuation marks where they are needed.

EXAMPLE 1. I asked the cashier for change for a dollar.
1. *"May I please have change for a dollar?" I asked the cashier.*

HELP You will need to change some pronouns and verb forms in Exercise 4.

1. The cashier replied that she was not allowed to make change unless a purchase was made.
2. I said that I needed a new pen.
3. The cashier told me that it cost seventy-nine cents.
4. I said that I would give her $1.79.
5. She told me she could give me change for a dollar.
6. The cashier asked how I wanted the change.
7. I said that three quarters, two dimes, and a nickel would be good.
8. She replied that she did not have any more dimes in her cash register.
9. Then I said that I would gladly take four quarters.
10. She said that was okay but asked why I wanted change.

13i. **When you write dialogue (conversation), begin a new paragraph every time the speaker changes.**

EXAMPLE

In Khanabad, Mulla Nasrudin was sitting in a tea house when a stranger walked in and sat down beside him.

The newcomer said:

"Why is that man over there sobbing his heart out?"

"Because I have just arrived from his hometown and told him that all his winter camel fodder was lost in a fire."

"It is terrible to be a bearer of such tidings," said the stranger.

"It is also interesting to be the man who will shortly tell him the good news," said Nasrudin. "You see, his camels have died of a plague, so he will not need the fodder after all."

Idries Shah, "Camel Fodder"

MECHANICS

13j. **When a quotation consists of several sentences, put quotation marks only at the beginning and the end of the whole quotation.**

EXAMPLE "Will Bao help with the play? Zachary has offered to make costumes," Aaron said.

13k. **Use single quotation marks to enclose a quotation within a quotation.**

EXAMPLE "Mrs. Engle distinctly said, 'Your book reports are due Thursday,'" Krista told me.

13l. **Use quotation marks to enclose the titles of short works such as short stories, poems, newspaper or magazine articles, songs, episodes of television series, and chapters and other parts of books.**

Type Of Name	Examples
Short Stories	"The Stone" "All Summer in a Day"
Poems	"Jetliner" "Song of the Sky Loom"
Articles	"Celebrating Our Heritage" "The Giants of Easter Island"
Songs	"Georgia on My Mind" "America the Beautiful"
Episodes of Television Series	"Kali the Lion" "The Trouble with Tribbles"
Chapters and Other Parts of Books	"Energy from the Stars" "I Go to Sea"

NOTE Titles that appear in quotation marks are set in single quotation marks when they appear within a quotation.

EXAMPLE Kris said, "Our class learned 'America the Beautiful' today."

TIPS & TRICKS

In general, the title of a work that can stand alone (for instance, a novel, a TV series, a collection of poems) is in italics. The title of a work that is usually part of a collection or series (for instance, a chapter of a book, an episode of a television series, a poem) is in quotation marks.

Reference Note

For examples of **titles that require italics** instead of quotation marks, see page 290.

Exercise 5 Punctuating Quotations and Titles

Rewrite the following sentences, adding single and double quotation marks where they are needed.

EXAMPLE **1.** I just finished the chapter The Circulatory System in our health book, Dell told me.

1. "I just finished the chapter 'The Circulatory System' in our health book," Dell told me.

1. Diane is learning the song This Little Rose for her recital.
2. Angelo, can we meet after school tomorrow? We need to practice our presentation, Sam said.
3. I'm sure I heard the announcer say, Schools are closed because of the storm, I said.
4. I can pronounce all the words in Lewis Carroll's poem Jabberwocky, Nina told Lou.
5. Ted said, My dad will pick us up on Saturday at 7:30 A.M. After the race, he is taking us to Lucy Chang's for lunch. Do you like Chinese food?
6. The weather should be nice tomorrow. Let's plan on hiking in the woods, Eric said.
7. Mrs. Banister said, The Fun They Had is a good short story, don't you think?
8. Have you read The Toaster? Sue May asked. It's the funniest poem I know.
9. One article in the newspaper this morning is titled Black Scientists Make History.
10. Strong's new song is Be True, Not Blue, and it's great! Marcie said.

Review A Punctuating Paragraphs in a Dialogue

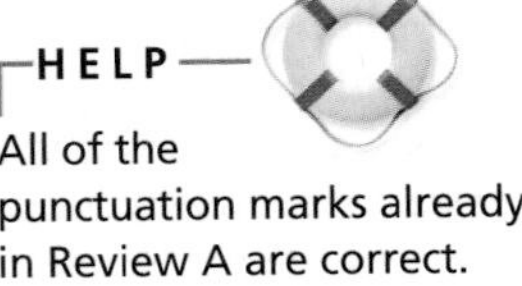

HELP — All of the punctuation marks already in Review A are correct.

Rewrite the following paragraphs, using capital letters as well as quotation marks and other marks of punctuation where they are needed.

EXAMPLE **[1]** What are you writing my grandfather asked.

1. "What are you writing?" my grandfather asked.

[1] Grandpa I said I'm writing a report about your hero, Octaviano Larrazolo. Can you tell me how he helped Mexican Americans?

[2] Grandpa got out his scrapbook. Octaviano did many things for our people he began. In 1912, New Mexico became a state. Octaviano and other Hispanic leaders wanted to be sure that Mexican Americans could hold political office. They wanted to make certain that they would always be allowed to vote. When New Mexico's new constitution was written, Octaviano and the other leaders fought for these rights.

[3] How did Mr. Larrazolo know how to protect the rights of people? I said.

[4] Grandpa replied he had studied law. His knowledge of the law helped him understand the constitution. It also helped him later when he became interested in politics.

[5] When did Mr. Larrazolo become involved in politics I asked.

[6] In 1916, he campaigned for Ezequiel Cabeza de Baca for governor said Grandpa. De Baca was elected, but he died a month later. Another election was held, and Larrazolo became New Mexico's governor.

[7] I asked what are some things that Mr. Larrazolo felt strongly about?

[8] He answered Octaviano believed that public schools should teach children about Mexican American culture. He also was in favor of both English and Spanish being spoken in schools. Here is a picture of him with his daughters.

[9] What else should I know about Octaviano Larrazolo I asked Grandpa.

[10] Octaviano was elected to the United States Senate in 1928 Grandpa said. He continued to work hard for the rights of Hispanic Americans until he died. If you want to read more about him, I have a copy of an article, Octaviano Larrazolo: New Mexico's Greatest Governor, here in my scrapbook.

Photo: Wesley Bradfield. Courtesy Museum of New Mexico, #47660.

MECHANICS

Apostrophes

Possessive Case

The ***possessive case*** of a noun or a pronoun shows ownership or possession.

EXAMPLES	**Heidi's** comb	no **one's** fault
	his jacket	**two weeks'** vacation
	our dog	**my** stepbrother

13m. To form the possessive case of a singular noun, add an apostrophe and an *s*.

EXAMPLES	a student**'s** grant	Tanaka**'s** store
	the child**'s** toy	Tess**'s** painting

NOTE A proper noun ending in *–s* may take only an apostrophe to form the possessive case if adding *–'s* would make the name awkward to say.

EXAMPLES the Netherlands' climate

Ms. Andrews' class

Exercise 6 Using Apostrophes for Singular Possessives

For each of the following sentences, identify the word that needs an apostrophe. Then, correctly write the word.

EXAMPLE **1.** Kenyans celebrate 1963 as the year of their countrys independence.

1. country's

1. Soon that young nations athletes were setting records in international sports.
2. Leading Kenyas world-class distance runners was Kipchoge Keino, shown on the next page.
3. Keino increased his endurance by running many miles in his homelands mountains.
4. In 1965, he burst into his sports top ranks by setting world records for both the 3,000-meter and the 5,000-meter races.

MECHANICS

5. Training in the mountains helped Keino win a gold medal at Mexico Citys 1968 Olympics.
6. His record in that years 1,500-meter race stood until 1984.
7. In fact, the Kenyan teams runners took home a total of eight medals in 1968.
8. In the 1972 Olympics, Keinos performance won him a second gold medal, this time for the 3,000-meter steeplechase.
9. A silver medal in the 1,500-meter race marked his careers remarkable completion.
10. His victories won Keino the worlds praise and set new standards for all runners.

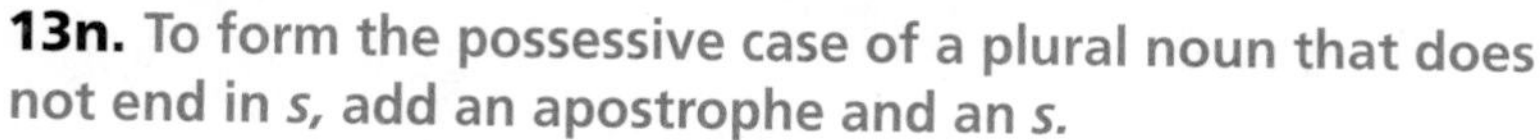

13n. **To form the possessive case of a plural noun that does not end in *s*, add an apostrophe and an *s*.**

EXAMPLES geese'**s** feathers men'**s** clothing

children'**s** books feet'**s** bones

13o. **To form the possessive case of a plural noun ending in *s*, add only the apostrophe.**

EXAMPLES boxes' lids ten minutes' time

beetles' shells the Ozawas' address

NOTE In general, you should not use an apostrophe to form the plural of a noun.

INCORRECT Two boy's left their books here.

CORRECT Two **boys** left their books here.

Reference Note

For information about **using apostrophes to form the plurals of letters, numerals, symbols, and words used as words,** see page 307.

Exercise 7 Writing Plural Possessives

For each of the following sentences, identify the word that needs an apostrophe. Then, correctly write the word.

EXAMPLE 1. Wild creatures survival depends on their ability to adapt.

1. creatures'

1. Animals ways of dealing with cold are fascinating.

2. At night, chickadees feathers are fluffed over the soft down next to their skin.
3. In addition, the birds breathing rates and heartbeats slow, and their body temperatures fall, saving energy.
4. Deers winter coats, made of hollow hairs filled with air, keep body heat from escaping.
5. Soft undercoats of fine hair are many animals thermal underwear.
6. In the picture on the left, you can see how squirrels tails, flattened against their backs and necks, keep them warm when they leave their nests.

7. The picture on the right shows how red foxes tails are used as muffs curled around their heads while they sleep.
8. Even though their fur is white, polar bears skin is black for absorbing heat from the sun.
9. In cold weather, fur grows on the bottom of snowshoe hares feet for protection.
10. Some wild creatures survival during freezing temperatures and snow depends on traits like these.

Review B Writing Possessives

Rewrite each of the following expressions by using the possessive case. Be sure to add apostrophes where they are needed.

EXAMPLE **1.** the speeches of the politicians
1. the politicians' speeches

1. the books of the children

2. the prize of the winner
3. the bed of the kittens
4. the home of my friend
5. the streets of the city
6. the fish of the teacher
7. the cars of the women
8. the dens of the foxes
9. the fables of Aesop
10. the medal of Rowan
11. the hiding place of the mice
12. the idea of the boss
13. the plans of the builders
14. the diet of moose
15. the climate of the Cook Islands
16. the lawnmower of the Barkers
17. the shoes of the girls
18. the elephants of the zoo
19. the roads of the cities
20. the computer of the company
21. the desks of the students
22. the driveway of the neighbor
23. the tail of the dog
24. the stories of Mark Twain
25. the history of Texas

13p. Do not use an apostrophe with possessive personal pronouns.

EXAMPLES Is this pencil **yours** or **mine**?

Our apartment is smaller than **theirs.**

Her enchiladas are spicier than **his.**

13q. To form the possessive case of many indefinite pronouns, add an apostrophe and an *s*.

EXAMPLES either**'s** topic

everyone**'s** favorite

somebody**'s** notebook

Reference Note

For more information about **possessive personal pronouns,** see page 177. For more information about **indefinite pronouns,** see page 34.

Oral Practice: The Possessive Case of Personal Pronouns and Indefinite Pronouns

Read each of the following expressions aloud. Then, change each expression so that it uses the possessive case, and say the new version aloud. Finally, say which expressions need an apostrophe when they are written.

EXAMPLE **1.** the speeches of everybody
1. everybody's speeches

1. the wishes of everyone
2. the fault of him
3. the answer of no one
4. the album of someone
5. the guess of me
6. the job of neither
7. the color of something
8. the deal of anyone
9. the sweaters of them
10. the notebook of you

STYLE TIP 

Some people consider contractions informal. Therefore, it is generally best not to use them in formal writing and speech.

Contractions

13r. Use an apostrophe to show where letters, numerals, or words have been left out in a contraction.

A ***contraction*** is a shortened form of a word, a numeral, or a group of words. The apostrophe in a contraction shows where letters, numerals, or words have been left out.

Common Contractions			
I am	I**'m**	they have	they**'ve**
1999	**'99**	here is	here**'s**
let us	let**'s**	you are	you**'re**
of the clock	**o'**clock	she is	she**'s**
movie is	movie**'s**	Bill has	Bill**'s**
he would	he**'d**	you will	you**'ll**

The word *not* can be shortened to *n't* and added to a verb. The spelling of the verb usually does not change.

EXAMPLES	is not . . . . is**n'**t	has not . . . . has**n'**t
	are not . . . . aren**'**t	have not . . . . haven**'**t
	does not. . . . . doesn**'**t	had not. . . . . hadn**'**t
	do not . . . . don**'**t	should not . . . . shouldn**'**t
	was not . . . . . . wasn**'**t	would not . . . . wouldn**'**t
	were not . . . . weren**'**t	could not . . . . . . couldn**'**t
EXCEPTIONS	will not . . . . . . **won't**	cannot. . . . . **can't**

Do not confuse contractions with possessive pronouns.

Contractions	Possessive Pronouns
It's [*It is*] raining. **It's** [*It has*] been a long day.	**Its** tires are flat.
Who's [*Who is*] your coach? **Who's** [*Who has*] been in my room?	**Whose** watch is this?
You're [*You are*] welcome.	**Your** sister won.
They're [*They are*] late.	**Their** house is next door.
There's [*There is*] the bell.	That car is **theirs.**

HELP

To avoid the common error of confusing *it's* for *its*, proofread your work carefully. When you come to the contraction *it's*, substitute *it is* or *it has.* If the sentence sounds right with the substitution, the contraction is probably correct. If it doesn't sound right, the possessive pronoun *its* is probably correct.

EXAMPLES

It's your turn. [*It is your turn* makes sense. The contraction for *It is* is correct.]

I like our new car, but it's trunk is very small. [. . . *but it is trunk is very small* does not make sense; the possessive pronoun *its* is needed in this sentence.]

Exercise 8 Using Apostrophes in Contractions

For the following sentences, write the word or numeral that requires an apostrophe and insert the apostrophe. If a sentence is already correct, write *C.*

EXAMPLE **1.** Well be leaving soon.
1. We'll

1. Youve been a big help.
2. Youd better hurry up.
3. Whose umbrella is this?
4. Were having a fund-raiser for the homeless.
5. I cant find my skateboard.
6. He promised hed wear his seat belt.
7. Lets get tickets to see the concert.

8. Its time to leave for the party.
9. Its wings are painted blue.
10. Ill wash the car tomorrow morning.
11. Daniel asked the decoration committee whos going to be in charge.
12. Isnt this the book we need?
13. Remember to give your dog fresh water.
14. Stephanie said shell bring a cardboard box from home.
15. This is a picture of my parents in 99, the year before my half-brother was born.
16. If that hummingbird returns to the feeder, Im going to take a picture.
17. Theirs will be the last band to perform.
18. The cold weather doesnt bother Jeremy much.
19. We should be back to school by three o clock.
20. Have you found out yet if youre on the team?

Exercise 9 Writing Contractions

For each of the following sentences, write the contraction of the italicized word or words.

EXAMPLE 1. *We will* see a performance of the puppet theater when we visit the Japan America Theatre in Los Angeles.
1. *We'll*

1. *Have not* you always wondered what goes on backstage at a puppet show?

2. *Here is* an illustration that takes you behind the scenes at a seventeenth-century puppet theater in Japan.
3. The audience *cannot* see all the backstage action because of the curtain.
4. The men *who are* handling the puppets in the picture are very highly trained.
5. They *do not* speak the characters' lines, though.
6. *It is* the man sitting on the right on the platform who narrates the play.
7. As you can see, *he is* accompanied by a musician.
8. On the right are more puppets; *they have* been hung there for future use.
9. In the box at the top, *that is* the Japanese word that means "puppet."
10. As *you will* notice, the Japanese system of writing is very different from ours.

Plurals

13s. **Use an apostrophe and an *s* to form the plurals of letters, numerals, and symbols, and of words referred to as words.**

EXAMPLES I think the word *Mississippi* has four *i*'**s**, four *s* '**s**, and two *p*'**s**.

Your *1*'**s** and *7*' **s** look alike.

You wrote +'**s** instead of *x*'**s** in these math problems.

Try not to use so many *you know* '**s** when you talk.

Exercise 10 **Forming Plurals by Using Apostrophes**

Correctly form the plural of each of the following items.

EXAMPLE **1.** *9*

1. 9's

1. *I*	**6.** *#*	**11.** *14*	**16.** *B*	**21.** *$*
2. *t*	**7.** *A*	**12.** *%*	**17.** *3*	**22.** *
3. *@*	**8.** *.com*	**13.** *at*	**18.** *+*	**23.** *uh oh*
4. *it*	**9.** *too*	**14.** *?*	**19.** *!*	**24.** *=*
5. *6*	**10.** *thou*	**15.** *and*	**20.** *of*	**25.** */*

MECHANICS

Hyphens

13t. Use a hyphen to divide a word at the end of a line.

When you divide a word at the end of a line, remember the following rules:

(1) Divide a word only between syllables.

INCORRECT Uncle Payat, Aunt Nina, and Ayita will jou-rney eighty miles to join us.

CORRECT Uncle Payat, Aunt Nina, and Ayita will jour-ney eighty miles to join us.

(2) Do not divide a one-syllable word.

INCORRECT They are bringing a salad, ham, and rye bre-ad.

CORRECT They are bringing a salad, ham, and rye bread.

(3) Do not divide a word so that one letter stands alone.

INCORRECT Is that your family's brand-new car parked a-cross the street?

CORRECT Is that your family's brand-new car parked across the street?

13u. Use a hyphen with compound numbers from *twenty-one* to *ninety-nine*.

EXAMPLE Until 1959, the United States had only forty-eight stars in its flag.

13v. Hyphenate a compound adjective when it comes before the noun it modifies.

EXAMPLES an activity that is well planned

a **well-planned** activity

a flavor that is long lasting

a **long-lasting** flavor

Some compound adjectives are always hyphenated, whether they come before or after the nouns they modify.

HELP — You may need to look up words in a dictionary to be sure of how to divide them into syllables.

STYLE TIP

Hyphens are often used in compound names. In such cases, the hyphen is thought of as part of the spelling of the name.

EXAMPLES
- Margaret Bourke-White
- Kung-sun Lung
- Terry-Jo
- Edward Levy-Lawson

If you are not sure whether a compound name is hyphenated, ask the person with that name, or look up the name in a reference source.

MECHANICS

EXAMPLES a **brand-new** bicycle
a bicycle that is **brand-new**

an **up-to-date** encyclopedia
an encyclopedia that is **up-to-date**

13w. Use a hyphen with the prefixes *all–, ex–, great–, self–,* and with the suffixes *–elect* and *–free.*

EXAMPLES

all-purpose	self-confidence
ex-students	governor-elect
great-grandfather	sugar-free

Exercise 11 Using Hyphens Correctly

Write each of the following words. Add hyphens to show where the word may be divided at the end of a line or where they are needed in a compound word. If a word should not be hyphenated, write *do not hyphenate.*

EXAMPLES
1. tomorrow
1. to-mor-row
2. self aware
2. self-aware
3. theme
3. do not hyphenate

1. loose
2. all star
3. temporary
4. ex wife
5. children
6. elect
7. principal
8. decorate
9. self help
10. through
11. immediately
12. fat free
13. seize
14. broomstick
15. great aunt
16. piano
17. preferred
18. grammar
19. lint free
20. among

HELP
If you are not sure whether a compound adjective is always hyphenated, look up the word in a dictionary.

HELP
The prefix *half–* often requires a hyphen, as in *half-life, half-moon,* and *half-truth.* However, sometimes *half* is used without a hyphen, either as a part of a single word (*halftone, halfway, halfback*) or as a separate word (*half shell, half pint, half note*). If you are not sure how to spell a word containing *half,* look up the word in a current dictionary.

COMPUTER TIP

Some word-processing programs will automatically divide a word at the end of a line and insert a hyphen. Sometimes the program will divide a word at the wrong place. Always check a printout of your writing to see how the computer has hyphenated words at the ends of lines. If a hyphen is used incorrectly, move the word to the next line or divide the word yourself by correctly inserting a "hard" hyphen (one that the computer will not move).

MECHANICS

Exercise 12 Using Hyphens in Numbers and in Compound Words

In the following sentences, identify each word or word group that needs a hyphen. Then, write the words or word groups correctly, using the required hyphens. If all words in a sentence are correct, write *C.*

EXAMPLE 1. My brother will be twenty one next week.
1. twenty-one

1. The ex mayor is now running for governor.
2. Are your information sources up to date?
3. The movie was well produced and well acted.
4. My sister, who is twenty seven, is getting married in March.
5. Gretchen's great grandmother came to the United States from the Netherlands.
6. Tree ripened peaches taste much better than peaches that are picked green.
7. To keep your photographs in good condition, put them in scrapbooks that are made with acid free paper.
8. When John was named an all American, his parents were very pleased.
9. That kind of flower is self pollinating, isn't it?
10. Six of the twenty six students in my class have hyphenated names.

Review C Using Apostrophes and Hyphens Correctly

Correctly write the word or letter that needs an apostrophe or a hyphen in each of the following sentences.

EXAMPLE 1. Wheres my history book?
1. Where's

1. Do you know where the atlases and the two diction aries are?
2. There are two *rs* in *tomorrow.*
3. The last speaker was the ex president of the Town Council.
4. The tiger cubs arent on view yet.
5. Is that one of Bessie Smiths songs?

6. Someone's gold bracelet is on the counter in the bath room.
7. Forty nine students signed the get-well card.
8. Is that salad dressing fat free?
9. Whos going to the fair this weekend?
10. Its almost time to leave.

Parentheses

13x. **Use parentheses to enclose material that is added to a sentence but is not considered of major importance.**

EXAMPLES The Civil War **(**1861–1865**)** is also known as the War Between the States.

My sister bought a beautiful lace mantilla **(**often pronounced man til´ə**)** when she was in Mexico.

Text enclosed in parentheses may be as short as a single word or as long as a short sentence. A short sentence in parentheses may stand alone or be contained within another sentence. Notice that a parenthetical sentence within a sentence is not capitalized and has no end mark.

EXAMPLES Please be quiet and respectful during the ceremony. **(**Turn off your cell phones.**)**

The first metal-framed skyscraper **(**it was ten stories tall**)** was built in Chicago in 1885.

Parenthetical expressions are usually set off by commas or parentheses. Some parenthetical elements, however, need stronger emphasis. In such cases, a **dash** is used.

EXAMPLES

Central Park**,** by the way**,** has a wonderful bird sanctuary.

Central Park **(**it's two and a half miles long**)** is a New York City attraction.

We went to Central Park for a picnic**—**it was such fun**—**on Sunday afternoon.

MECHANICS

Exercise 13 Correcting Sentences by Adding Parentheses

Insert parentheses where they are needed in the following sentences.

EXAMPLE **1.** My new computer my old one needed a new disk drive is amazingly fast.

1. My new computer (my old one needed a new disk drive) is amazingly fast.

1. Thomas Alva Edison 1847–1931 invented the phonograph and the electric light bulb.

2. Edison did not have a formal education his mother taught him at home, but he became a millionaire before he was fifty.
3. Some of the first incandescent pronounced in•kən•des´ənt bulbs used bamboo filaments.
4. Until most homes and businesses had electricity, the light bulb was only a novelty. Few places had electricity in 1880.
5. Edison built the first electric power plant it was known as the Pearl Street Station in 1882 in New York City.
6. Electricity became widespread during the industrialization of the United States 1870–1916.
7. Edison's work his inventions and his business practices helped the United States to become an industrial power.
8. Edison invested in companies that manufactured other electrical equipment lighting fixtures, generators, and power cables.
9. These companies the electrical equipment manufacturers joined with other companies to form General Electric in 1892.
10. Edison was friends with several other industrial leaders, including Henry Ford automobiles and Harvey Firestone tires.

NOTE Use brackets to enclose an explanation added to quoted or parenthetical material.

EXAMPLES In his speech, the ambassador to Australia said, "I wish to thank you and the wonderful, friendly people of your great country for this **[**the award**]**." [The words are enclosed in brackets to show that they have been inserted into the quotation and are not the words of the speaker.]

The Mississippi River and its tributaries drain most of the land that lies between the Rocky and the Appalachian Mountains. (See p. 647 for a map **[**Diagram A**]** of the drainage area.)

MECHANICS

Chapter Review

A. Using Underlining (Italics), Quotation Marks, Apostrophes, Hyphens, and Parentheses

Each of the following sentences contains at least one error in the use of underlining (italics), quotation marks, apostrophes, hyphens, or parentheses. Write each sentence correctly.

1. The childrens bikes were in the driveway.
2. Chapter Two is called *The Siamese Cat.*
3. “I remember making a barometer in the fourth grade. “I had to start over twice before it would work,” I said.
4. John read Robert Louis Stevenson’s novel Treasure Island.
5. While in the shower, I sometimes only when my family isn’t around to complain sing very loudly.
6. Washingtons largest city is named for Chief Seattle.
7. “Will you please show me how to make a weather vane”? begged Todd.
8. “It took me only forty five minutes to make a sundial,” Carlos remarked.
9. We built a model airplane, but it crashed on it’s test flight.
10. All student’s projects (both science and art) are due Friday.
11. Ray read an interesting article called *The Standing Stones of Wales and Brittany.*
12. Be sure to visit the USS “Lexington” in Corpus Christi.
13. Which newspaper do you prefer, The New York Times or Newsday?
14. Next time, please be prompt, Al, said Ms. Li as I walked in late.
15. Everyone’s report the two page book report is due Friday.
16. “Bill’s exact words,” said Sean, “were ‘I’ll be back at noon.”
17. In her English class, Janice is reading the Dylan Thomas poem Fern Hill.
18. Have you seen the magazine “Highlights for Children”?
19. Please don’t use so many *like*s when you speak.
20. Isn’t twenty questions the average length for an exe-rcise of this kind? (It’s the last exercise in the chapter.)

B. Revising Indirect Quotations to Create Direct Quotations

Revise each of the following sentences by changing the indirect quotation to a direct quotation. Be sure to use capital letters and punctuation marks where they are needed.

HELP You will need to change some pronouns and verb forms in Part B.

21. Our teacher warned us that we could not take any breaks during the exam.
22. Lisa said that she would call me at eight o'clock.
23. Mom told us not to be late.
24. The police officer asked us to wait behind the fence.
25. I asked the museum guard where the *Mona Lisa* was.
26. Taylor said that two hours should be long enough.
27. Stephanie replied that she would be in the city for five days.
28. Dr. Grizzard reminded us to take our vitamins every day.
29. Wendy asked her father if he would drive her to the library.
30. Giulio exclaimed happily that he had never been so surprised in his life.

C. Punctuating a Dialogue

Rewrite the following dialogue, using quotation marks and other marks of punctuation where they are needed. Remember to begin a new paragraph every time the speaker changes.

[**31**] Oh, Travis, said Lucy, when are you leaving? [**32**] I told you, Lucy, replied Travis. I'm planning to leave soon. At around ten o'clock. [**33**] Oh, said Lucy. Listen, Trav, I'm afraid I won't be able to come with you after all. Something has come up. [**34**] Well, Grandma will certainly be disappointed, remarked Travis. She's been looking forward to seeing her two grandkids on her birthday. [**35**] Yes, but that's just it, said Lucy. I haven't bought anything for her birthday yet. I just haven't had the time. [**36**] Well, guess what, Sis. I took care of that yesterday. Travis went over to the desk and took something out of the drawer. [**37**] Your present to Grandma is this framed photograph of me. [**38**] You're kidding, said Lucy. [**39**] And continued Travis, my present to her is this framed photograph of you. What do you think? [**40**] I think you're crazy, but we can discuss that on the way there. Let's go!

MECHANICS

Writing Application

Using Apostrophes in a Letter

Contractions and Possessives You have been so busy at summer camp that you have not had time to write to your best friend. Write your friend a letter telling about your first week at camp. Be sure to use apostrophes correctly to make your meaning clear.

Prewriting If you have never been to a summer camp, ask a friend or relative who has been to one to tell you about it. Write down some notes on your activities at summer camp. Use your experience or your imagination to describe activities such as sports, crafts, and hiking trips. Also, make some notes about the camp itself.

Writing Include specific details about the natural setting and special or daily activities at the camp. Tell your friend what you have enjoyed most. Try to give your friend a clear, vivid picture of your first week.

Revising Ask a friend or a family member to read your letter. Can he or she imagine the activities you have described? If not, revise your letter to make it clearer and more descriptive.

Publishing Be sure you have used the correct form for personal letters. As you proofread your letter, take extra care with apostrophes. Check your use of contractions and pronouns like *its, it's, your, you're, their,* and *they're.* Also, look for any other errors in grammar, spelling, and punctuation. Exchange letters with a classmate, and see how your camp experiences, real or imagined, are similar and how they are different.

Spelling

Improving Your Spelling

1.0 Written and Oral English Language Conventions

Students write and speak with a command of standard English conventions appropriate to this grade level.

1.5 Spell frequently misspelled words correctly (e.g., *their, they're, there*).

Diagnostic Preview

A. Proofreading Sentences for Correct Spelling

Correctly write the word that is misspelled in each of the following sentences.

EXAMPLE **1.** The dog is diging in the flower garden again.
1. digging

1. The children are happyest when swimming in the pool on a hot afternoon.
2. The porch chaires look newer than the tables.
3. Our nieghbor was born in Texas, I believe.
4. The Tolbys bought blueberrys for the party.
5. Uncle Steven is driveing through seven foreign countries on his trip.
6. Is the weather in Arizona ever changable?
7. Five womans auditioned for the leading role in the Broadway production.
8. I think the Peter, Paul, and Mary folk songs of the sixties are truely delightful.
9. Matthew and Kim bravly rescued the baby raccoon from the muddy ditch.
10. Would you kindly dig up the potatos and let them dry in the cellar?

B. Proofreading Sentences to Correct Spelling Errors

Choose the correct word or words from the choices in parentheses in each of the following sentences.

EXAMPLE 1. Please give (*you're, your*) book orders to me today.
1. your

11. Angela is taking five (*courses, coarses*) this semester.
12. Nora said she was (*already, all ready*) for the banquet.
13. "Please pass me a (*peace, piece*) of bread," Gary said.
14. The (*altar, alter*) at the Spanish mission is marble.
15. The (*plain, plane*) to Ontario is ahead of schedule.
16. People often (*loose, lose*) pennies in stores and on streets.
17. We saw the (*principal, principle*) pass by twice.
18. Whose (*stationery, stationary*) has initials at the top?
19. (*There, Their*) shop sells shirts, dresses, and scarves.
20. "You'd better get these (*breaks, brakes*) fixed right away," the mechanic said.

Good Spelling Habits

The following techniques can help you spell words correctly.

1. **To learn the spelling of a word, pronounce it, study it, and write it.** Pronounce words carefully. Mistakes in speaking can cause mistakes in spelling. For instance, if you say *ad•je•tive* instead of *ad•jec•tive,* you will be more likely to spell the word incorrectly.
   - First, make sure that you know how to pronounce the word correctly, and then practice saying it.
   - Second, study the word. Notice any parts that might be hard to remember.
   - Third, write the word from memory. Check your spelling.
   - If you misspelled the word, repeat the three steps of this process until you can spell the word correctly.
2. **Use a dictionary.** If you are not absolutely sure about the spelling of a word, look it up in a dictionary. Do not guess about the correct spelling.

HELP

If you are not sure how to pronounce a word, look it up in a dictionary. In a dictionary, you will usually find the pronunciation given in parentheses after the word. The information in parentheses will show you the sounds used, the syllable breaks, and any accented syllables or word breaks. A guide to the pronunciation symbols is usually found at the front of a dictionary.

STYLE TIP

In some names, marks that show how to pronounce a word are considered part of the spelling.

PEOPLE
Muñoz Søren Fauré

PLACES
Neuchâtel Košice
Cap-Haïtien

If you are not sure about the spelling of a name, ask the person with that name or look it up in a dictionary or other reference source.

MECHANICS

3. **Spell by syllables.** A ***syllable*** is a word part that can be pronounced as one uninterrupted sound.

EXAMPLES ear•ly [two syllables]

av•er•age [three syllables]

Instead of trying to learn how to pronounce and spell a whole word, break it into its syllables whenever possible. It is easier to learn a few letters at a time than to learn all of them at once.

4. **Keep a spelling notebook.** Divide each page into four columns:

COLUMN 1 Correctly spell any word you have misspelled. (Never enter a misspelled word.)

COLUMN 2 Write the word again, dividing it into syllables and indicating which syllables are accented or stressed. (You will probably need to use a dictionary.)

COLUMN 3 Write the word once more, circling the spot that gives you trouble.

COLUMN 4 Write down any comments that might help you remember the correct spelling.

Here is an example of how you might make entries for two words that are often misspelled.

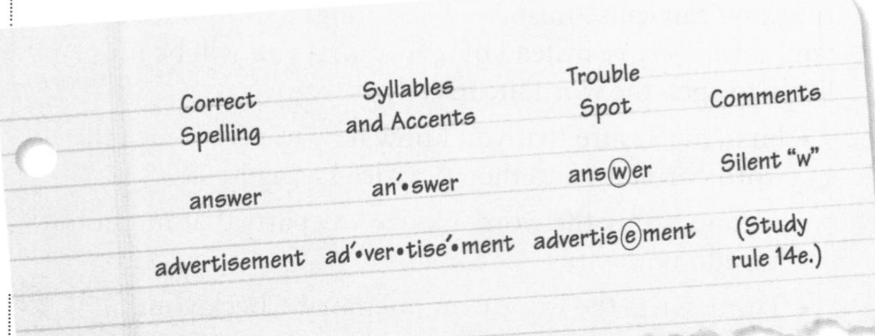

Correct Spelling	Syllables and Accents	Trouble Spot	Comments
answer	an′•swer	ans(w)er	Silent "w"
advertisement	ad′•ver•tise′•ment	advertis(e)ment	(Study rule 14e.)

5. **Proofread for careless spelling errors.** Re-read your writing carefully, and correct any mistakes and unclear letters. For example, make sure that your *i*'s are dotted, your *t*'s are crossed, and your *g*'s do not look like *q*'s.

Spelling Rules

ie and *ei*

14a. **Write *ie* when the sound is long *e,* except after *c.***

EXAMPLES chi**ie**f, bel**ie**ve, br**ie**f, rec**ei**ve, c**ei**ling

EXCEPTIONS **ei**ther, n**ei**ther, prot**ei**n, s**ei**ze

Write *ei* when the sound is not long *e,* especially when the sound is long *a.*

EXAMPLES n**ei**ghbor, w**ei**gh, r**ei**ndeer, h**ei**ght, for**ei**gn

EXCEPTIONS fr**ie**nd, f**ie**rce, anc**ie**nt, misch**ie**f

HELP

This verse may help you remember the *ie* rule:

I before *e*
Except after *c,*
Or when sounded like *a,*
As in *neighbor* and *weigh.*

If you use this rhyme, remember that "*i* before *e*" refers only to words in which these two letters are in the same syllable and stand for the sound of long *e,* as in the examples under Rule 14a.

Exercise 1 Writing Words with *ie* and *ei*

Complete the following letter by adding *ie* or *ei* to each numbered word.

EXAMPLE I wrote Aunt Hannah a **[1]** br____f thank-you note.
1. brief

December 12, 2009

Dear Aunt Hannah,

Thank you very much for the **[1]** sl____gh you recently sent me. I **[2]** rec____ved it on the **[3]** ____ghth of this month, just in time for our first big snowstorm. My new **[4]** fr____nds and I have great fun pulling each other across the **[5]** f____lds in it. The **[6]** n____ghbor's dog races alongside us, barking **[7]** f____rcely all the way.

So far, I like living here in Vermont, but I can't quite **[8]** bel____ve how different everything is from life in California. Thank you again for your gift.

Your loving **[9]** n____ce,

Mai

P.S. If only we had some **[10]** r____ndeer to pull us!

MECHANICS

Prefixes and Suffixes

Prefixes

A ***prefix*** is a letter or a group of letters added to the beginning of a word to create a new word that has a different meaning.

14b. When adding a prefix to a word, do not change the spelling of the word itself.

EXAMPLES dis + satisfy = dis**satisfy**

mis + lead = mis**lead**

un + done = un**done**

pre + view = pre**view**

a + typical = a**typical**

Exercise 2 Spelling Words with Prefixes

Combine each of the following prefixes and words to create a new word.

EXAMPLE **1.** mis + place

1. misplace

1. fore + word
2. un + natural
3. in + dependent
4. mis + use
5. un + common
6. im + patient
7. pre + historic
8. mis + spell
9. dis + satisfied
10. re + assert

Exercise 3 Spelling Words with Prefixes

Create ten different words by combining the prefixes given below with the words listed beside them. (You may use a prefix or word more than once.) Check each of your new words in a dictionary. Then, use each word in a sentence.

Prefixes			Words			
un–	mis–	dis–	able	do	judge	place
pre–	over–	re–	cover	trust	pay	informed

EXAMPLE *1. repay—I'll repay you when I get my allowance.*

MEETING THE CHALLENGE

Base words *(part, take)* can stand alone or combine with other word parts to make new words *(partly, mistake).* A root is the main part of the word. It carries the word's meaning. Word roots *(–dict–, –vis–),* like prefixes and suffixes, cannot stand alone and are combined with other word parts to form words *(dictionary, visible).*

Form new words by adding a prefix, a suffix, or both to the following base words and word roots.

BASE WORDS
cycle, graph, gram, verse

WORD ROOTS
–crit–, –fer–, –gest–, –loc–

Suffixes

A ***suffix*** is a letter or a group of letters added at the end of a word to create a new word that has a different meaning.

14c. **When adding the suffix *–ness* or *–ly* to a word, do not change the spelling of the word itself.**

EXAMPLES kind + ness = **kind**ness

tough + ness = **tough**ness

sincere + ly = **sincere**ly

slow + ly = **slow**ly

EXCEPTIONS For most words that end in *y,* change the *y* to *i* before adding *–ly* or *–ness.*

happy + ly = happ**ily**

friendly + ness = friendl**iness**

14d. **Drop the final silent e before adding a suffix that begins with a vowel.**

Vowels are the letters *a, e, i, o, u,* and sometimes *y.* All other letters of the alphabet are ***consonants.***

EXAMPLES cause + ing = **caus**ing

reverse + ible = **revers**ible

strange + er = **strang**er

adore + able = **ador**able

EXCEPTIONS Keep the silent *e* in words ending in *ce* and *ge* before adding a suffix beginning with *a* or *o*.

manage + able = manag**eable**

courage + ous = courag**eous**

notice + able = notic**eable**

HELP

Some words that end with a silent *e* can either keep the *e* or drop it when a suffix is added.

EXAMPLES

judge + ment = judg**ment** *or* judg**ement**

acknowledge + ment = acknowledg**ment** *or* acknowledg**ement**

love + able = lov**able** *or* lov**eable**

14e. **Keep the final silent *e* before adding a suffix that begins with a consonant.**

EXAMPLES hope + less = hop**eless**

place + ment = plac**ement**

EXCEPTIONS argue + ment = argu**ment**

true + ly = tru**ly**

MECHANICS

Exercise 4 Spelling Words with Suffixes

Combine each of the following words and suffixes to create a new word.

EXAMPLE **1.** sudden + ness

1. suddenness

1. active + ity
2. sure + ly
3. state + ment
4. locate + ion
5. courage + ous
6. silly + ness
7. suspense + ful
8. little + est
9. decorate + ed
10. trace + able

TIPS & TRICKS

When you proofread your own writing, you will find more spelling errors by looking at each word separately. To focus on each word, try using a piece of paper to hide some of the nearby words or lines. You can even cut a slit in a sheet of paper and move it over your writing to show just a few words at a time.

14f. **For words that end in a consonant plus *y*, change the *y* to *i* before adding a suffix.**

EXAMPLES cry + ed = cr**ied** lonely + est = lonel**iest**

pretty + er = prett**ier** lazy + ness = laz**iness**

EXCEPTION Keep the *y* if the suffix begins with an *i*.

carry + ing = carr**ying**

NOTE Keep the *y* if the word ends in a vowel plus *y*.

EXAMPLES stay + ed = sta**yed** key + ed = ke**yed**

EXCEPTIONS day + **ly** = daily pay + **ed** = paid

14g. **Double the final consonant before adding *–ing, –ed, –er,* or *–est* to a one-syllable word that ends in a single vowel followed by a single consonant.**

EXAMPLES beg + ing = be**gging** sad + er = sa**dder**

chat + ed = cha**tted** big + est = bi**ggest**

When a one-syllable word ends in two vowels followed by a single consonant, do not double the consonant before adding *–ing, –ed, –er,* or *–est.*

EXAMPLES sleep + ing = slee**ping** cool + er = coo**ler**

treat + ed = trea**ted** fair + est = fai**rest**

Exercise 5 Spelling Words with Suffixes

Combine each of the following words and suffixes to create a new word.

EXAMPLE **1.** creep + er

1. creeper

1. say + ing
2. slim + er
3. squeak + ing
4. rainy + est
5. steady + ness
6. beat + ing
7. rely + ing
8. easy + ly
9. chop + ed
10. play + ed

Review A Proofreading Sentences for Correct Spelling

Most of the following sentences contain a misspelled word. Write each misspelled word correctly. If a sentence is already correct, write *C.*

EXAMPLE **1.** My grandma often says, "Let sleepping dogs lie."

1. sleeping

1. It's unnusual weather for this time of year.
2. In 1991, Lithuania regained its independence from the Soviet Union.
3. With Sacagawea's help, the explorers Lewis and Clark maped out the Northwest.
4. Now that Bao Duc is on the team, our hiting has improved.

HELP In Review A, none of the proper nouns are misspelled.

MECHANICS

5. Serita and I can easyly make enough rice for the class.
6. We visited my grandmother in the Dominican Republic during the rainyest month of the year.
7. Please resstate the question.
8. My sister has the loveliest voice I've ever heard.
9. Former astronaut Sally Ride earned recognition for her courage and steadyness.
10. The temperature has droped at least ten degrees.

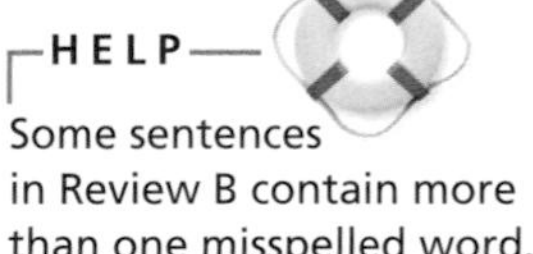

HELP — Some sentences in Review B contain more than one misspelled word.

MECHANICS

Review B Proofreading a Paragraph for Correct Spelling

For each sentence in the following paragraph, correctly write the word or words that are misspelled. If a sentence is already correct, write *C*.

EXAMPLE **[1]** My cousin Chris was very couragous after she was baddly hurt in a car accident.
1. *courageous; badly*

[**1**] After the accident, Chris found that she truely needed other people. [**2**] Her friends, family, and nieghbors gladly helped her. [**3**] However, Chris liked the idea of geting along on her own as much as she could, so she was disatisfied. [**4**] Fortunatly, she was able to join an exciting program called Helping Hands. [**5**] This program provides monkeys like this one as friends and helpers for people with disabilities. [**6**] Chris said that the baby monkeys are raised in loveing foster homes for four years and then they go to Boston to recieve special training. [**7**] There, they learn how to do tasks on command, such as opening and closeing doors, turning lights on and off, and puting discs into a DVD or CD player. [**8**] Chris has been happyly working with her own monkey, Aldo, for six months now. [**9**] Aldo retreives anything that Chris has droped, works the TV remote control, and even scratches Chris's back when it itches! [**10**] Chris is always jokeing, "Pretty soon Aldo will be writting my book reports for me!"

Forming the Plurals of Nouns

14h. Follow these rules for spelling the plurals of nouns:

(1) To form the plurals of most nouns, add *s.*

SINGULAR	snack	oven	Juliet	breeze	umbrella
PLURAL	snack**s**	oven**s**	Juliet**s**	breeze**s**	umbrella**s**

NOTE Make sure that you do not confuse the plural form of a noun with its possessive form. In general, you should not use an apostrophe to form the plural of a word.

INCORRECT The boy's stayed after school for choir practice.

CORRECT The **boys** stayed after school for choir practice. [plural]

CORRECT The **boys' choir** has practice today. [possessive]

Reference Note

For a discussion of **possessive forms of nouns,** see page 300. For information on using an apostrophe and an *s* to form **plurals of letters, numerals, symbols, and words used as words,** see page 307.

(2) Form the plurals of nouns ending in *s, x, z, ch,* or *sh* by adding *es.*

SINGULAR	glass	fox	buzz	itch	bush	Jones
PLURAL	glass**es**	fox**es**	buzz**es**	itch**es**	bush**es**	Jones**es**

HELP

Some one-syllable words ending in *z* double the final consonant when forming plurals.

EXAMPLES
quiz fez
qui**zz**es fe**zz**es

Oral Practice Giving the Plurals of Nouns

Read each of the following nouns aloud. Then, say and spell the plural form of each noun.

EXAMPLES
1. scratch
1. scratches
2. ax
2. axes

1. night
2. dish
3. address
4. lens
5. box
6. branch
7. loss
8. peach
9. waltz
10. Smith
11. complex
12. faucet
13. cobra
14. doctor
15. ditch
16. Sanchez
17. tax
18. glue
19. occurrence
20. radish

(3) Form the plurals of nouns that end in a consonant plus *y* by changing the *y* to *i* and adding *es*.

SINGULAR	country	mummy	berry
PLURAL	countr**ies**	mumm**ies**	berr**ies**
EXCEPTION	With proper nouns, just add *s*.		
	the Shelby**s**	the Mabry**s**	the O'Grady**s**

(4) Form the plurals of nouns that end in a vowel plus *y* by adding *s*.

SINGULAR	boy	turkey	holiday	Riley
PLURAL	boy**s**	turkey**s**	holiday**s**	Riley**s**

(5) Form the plurals of nouns that end in a vowel plus *o* by adding *s*.

SINGULAR	rodeo	patio	kangaroo	Romeo
PLURAL	rodeo**s**	patio**s**	kangaroo**s**	Romeo**s**

(6) Form the plurals of nouns that end in a consonant plus *o* by adding *es*.

SINGULAR	tomato	echo	veto	torpedo
PLURAL	tomato**es**	echo**es**	veto**es**	torpedo**es**
EXCEPTIONS	auto—auto**s**	Latino—Latino**s**	Soto—Soto**s**	

HELP

Form the plurals of most musical terms ending in *o* by adding *s*.

SINGULAR
piano trio
soprano cello

PLURAL
piano**s** trio**s**
soprano**s** cello**s**

MECHANICS

Exercise 6 Spelling the Plurals of Nouns

Spell the plural form of each of the following nouns.

EXAMPLE **1.** story
1. stories

1. toy
2. apology
3. valley
4. try
5. piano
6. potato
7. emergency
8. chimney
9. radio
10. video
11. journey
12. stereo
13. county
14. hero
15. delay
16. scenario
17. agony
18. solo
19. O'Malley
20. zoo

(7) The plurals of a few nouns are formed in irregular ways.

SINGULAR	woman	mouse	foot	man	child
PLURAL	wom**en**	m**ice**	f**ee**t	m**en**	child**ren**

(8) Some nouns are the same in the singular and the plural.

SINGULAR AND PLURAL fowl sheep spacecraft Sioux

(9) Form the plurals of numerals, letters, symbols, and words referred to as words by adding an apostrophe and *s*.

SINGULAR	1990	*A*	+	*and*
PLURAL	1990**'s**	*A*'**s**	+**'s**	*and*'**s**

STYLE TIP

When it refers to the computer device, the word *mouse* can form a plural in two ways: *mouses* or *mice.* Someday one form may be the preferred style. For now, either is correct.

STYLE TIP

In your reading, you may notice that some writers do not use apostrophes to form the plurals of numerals, letters, symbols, and words referred to as words.

EXAMPLE
Her great-grandparents moved here from Italy sometime in the **1940s.**

However, using an apostrophe in such cases is not wrong and is sometimes necessary for clarity. Therefore, it is usually best to use the apostrophe.

Exercise 7 Spelling the Singular and Plural Forms of Nouns

Spell the singular form and the plural form of each italicized word in the following sentences.

EXAMPLES
1. We use strong line to fish for *salmon.*
   1. *salmon—singular; salmon—plural*
2. Field *mice* invaded the food supplies in the tent.
   2. *mouse—singular; mice—plural*

1. Our guide, Robert Tallchief, a *Sioux,* knows all about the animals called llamas.
2. Robert and his father use llamas like the ones shown below to carry equipment people need for hiking and for catching *fish.*
3. The trips are very popular with both men and *women.*

HELP

If you do not know the plural form of a word, look up the word in a dictionary. Some dictionaries list more than one plural form of a noun, such as *deer* and *deers.* While both forms are acceptable, you should use the preferred form, which is listed first in the dictionary, to complete the exercises in this textbook.

MECHANICS

4. *Children* especially are fascinated and amused by the sure-footed llamas.
5. However, the llama has one very disagreeable habit—if upset, it bares its *teeth* and spits.
6. The Tallchiefs' llama trips have attracted tourists from all over the world, including many *Japanese*.
7. One highlight of these trips is viewing *moose* in their natural habitat.
8. *Deer* thrive in this area of the Northwest.
9. In addition, families of mountain *sheep* clamber up the steep cliffs.
10. Most people who go on the llama trips take many pictures of the wild *geese*.

Review C **Proofreading Sentences for Correct Spelling**

For each of the following sentences, correctly write the word or words that are misspelled. If a sentence is already correct, write *C*.

HELP—Some sentences in Review C have more than one misspelled word.

MECHANICS

EXAMPLE 1. Aunt Dorothy's old-time sayings are echos of her childhood.
1. echoes

1. Aunt Dorothy Kelly talks mostly in expressions from the 1930's and earlyer.
2. If we get into mischeif, she exclaims, "You little monkies!"
3. When my brother's run through the house, she shakes her head and mutters, "Boys will be boys."
4. Every time she can't find her eyeglasses, Aunt Dorothy says, "I've beaten the bushes, looking for them."
5. Aunt Dorothy believes that there are only two things in life that are certain: death and taxs.
6. We've heard her say "There's no use crying over spilled milk" and "Wishs won't wash dishs" about a thousand times apiece.
7. When we want something because our friends have it, Aunt Dorothy says we're trying to keep up with the Jones'.
8. Sometimes we get tired of hearing these little bits of folk wisdom, especially when Aunt Dorothy and all the little Kellies come over to visit for the holidays.

9. However, Aunt Dorothy is so sweet that we just smile and listen to her proverbs and storys.
10. Sometimes she says something really worthwhile, like "There are only two things that money can't buy—true love and home-grown tomatos."

Words Often Confused

People often confuse the words in each of the following groups. Some of these words are ***homonyms.*** They are pronounced the same, but they have different meanings and spellings. Other words in this section have the same or similar spellings, but have different meanings.

Word	Meaning and example
already	[adverb] *at an earlier time* The show has *already* begun.
all ready	[adjective] *all prepared; completely prepared* The floats are *all ready* for the fiesta.
altar	[noun] *a table or stand used for religious ceremonies* My uncle Chee wove the cloth for the *altar.*
alter	[verb] *to change* A flood can *alter* a riverbed.
altogether	[adverb] *entirely* I'm *altogether* lost.
all together	[adjective] *in the same place;* [adverb] *at the same time or place* Is everyone *all together*? Let's sit *all together* at the movie.
brake	[noun] *a device to stop a machine* The front *brake* on my bike squeaks.
break	[verb] *to fracture; to shatter;* [noun] *a fracture; an interruption; a rest* Try not to *break* your promises. Let's take a five-minute *break.*

Reference Note

In the Glossary of Usage in Chapter 10, you can find many other words that are often confused or misused. You can also look them up in a dictionary.

MECHANICS

Exercise 8 Choosing Between Words Often Confused

For each of the following sentences, choose the correct word or words from the pair in parentheses.

EXAMPLE **1.** Can the artist (*altar, alter*) the design?
1. alter

1. Did you help (*brake, break*) the piñata, Felipe?
2. Who arranged the flowers on the (*altar, alter*)?
3. I've (*all ready, already*) seen that movie.
4. My mom was (*all together, altogether*) pleased with my report card.
5. Don't forget to set the emergency (*brake, break*) when you park on a hill.
6. Our family will be (*all together, altogether*) at Thanksgiving this year.
7. "Will you (*altar, alter*) this sundress for me, Mom?" Angie asked.
8. You were (*all together, altogether*) right about the show times for the movie.
9. The Great Circus Parade is (*already, all ready*) to begin.
10. Unfortunately, handblown glass figurines (*break, brake*) very easily.

MECHANICS

TIPS & TRICKS

Here's a way to remember the difference between *capital* and *capitol*. There's a d**o**me on the capit**o**l.

capital	[noun] *a city; the location of a government* Havana is the *capital* of Cuba.
capitol	[noun] *a building; statehouse* Our state *capitol* is made of granite.
choose	[verb, rhymes with *shoes*] *to select* Did you *choose* the movie for today?
chose	[verb, past tense of *choose*, rhymes with *shows*] Who *chose* the movie yesterday?
cloths	[noun] *pieces of cloth* My aunt brought these kente *cloths* home from Ghana.
clothes	[noun] *wearing apparel* Bob irons his own *clothes.*

coarse	[adjective] *rough; crude; not fine* Some cities still use *coarse* salt to melt snow on streets and roads.
course	[noun] *a path of action; a series of studies;* [also used in the expression *of course*] What *course* should we follow to accomplish our goal? The counselor suggested several *courses* for us to take. I can't, *of course,* tell you what to do.
desert	[noun, pronounced des'•ert] *a dry, sandy region; a wilderness* Plants and animals of the *desert* can survive on little water.
desert	[verb, pronounced de•sert'] *to abandon; to leave* Don't *desert* your friends when they need you.
dessert	[noun, pronounced de•sert'] *the final, sweet course of a meal* What's for *dessert* tonight?

Exercise 9 **Choosing Between Words Often Confused**

For each of the following sentences, choose the correct word from the pair of words in parentheses.

EXAMPLE **1.** The sand on the beach is (*coarse, course*).
1. coarse

1. The Mojave (*Desert, Dessert*) is located in California.
2. Juan packed lightweight (*clothes, cloths*) to wear on his trip.
3. The sailor set a (*coarse, course*) for the port of Pago Pago.
4. When was the (*capital, capitol*) built, and how long has the state legislature been meeting there?
5. For (*desert, dessert*) we had pears and cheese.
6. Each team must (*choose, chose*) a captain.
7. The polishing (*cloths, clothes*) are by the wax on the shelf.
8. "Of (*coarse, course*) you may go!" Mr. Vance said.
9. The (*capital, capitol*) is the second-largest city in the state.
10. The cooking (*coarse, course*) lasted six weeks last summer.

Review D Proofreading Sentences for Words Often Confused

For each of the following sentences, correctly write the word that is misused.

EXAMPLE **1.** The students are already for the Fall Festival.
1. all ready

1. Throughout history, most societies and cultures, from the hot dessert regions to the cold northern regions, have celebrated the harvest.
2. The Jewish celebration of Sukkot marks the time when the harvest was gathered and the people were already for winter.
3. The most important tradition of Sukkot called for the family to live altogether in a temporary shelter called a sukkah.
4. Today, of coarse, many Jews still celebrate Sukkot but simply eat a meal outdoors under a shelter like the one pictured below.
5. Native Americans believed that without the help of the gods, there would be a brake in their good fortune.
6. During their planting ceremonies, most Native Americans, like the ones at left, dressed in special cloths.
7. To thank their harvest gods, the Chinese and Japanese placed wheat on alters.
8. Today, the Japanese do not altar this tradition much.
9. In most Japanese cities, including the capitol, the people hold parades to thank the ocean for the food it provides.
10. Many families in the United States celebrate Thanksgiving by sharing a meal, often with pumpkin pie for desert.

MECHANICS

hear	[verb] *to receive sounds through the ears* When did you *hear* the news?
here	[adverb] *in this place* The mail is *here.*
its	[possessive form of *it*] *belonging to it* You should not judge a book by *its* cover.
it's	[contraction of *it is* or *it has*] *It's* your turn, Theresa. *It's* been a long day.
lead	[verb, rhymes with *need*] *to go first; to be a leader* Will you *lead* the singing, Rachel?
led	[verb, past tense of *lead*, rhymes with *red*] *went first; guided* The dog *led* its master to safety.
lead	[noun, rhymes with *red*] *a heavy metal; graphite used in pencils* *Lead* is no longer used in household paints. Use a pencil with a softer *lead* if you want to draw dark, heavy lines.
loose	[adjective, rhymes with *goose*] *not tight* A *loose* wheel on a bike is dangerous.
lose	[verb, rhymes with *shoes*] *to suffer loss* That sudden, loud noise made me *lose* my place.

MECHANICS

Exercise 10 Choosing Between Words Often Confused

For each of the following sentences, choose the correct word from the pair of words in parentheses.

EXAMPLE 1. Rabbi Epstein (*lead, led*) our group during our tour of Israel.

1. led

1. We could (*hear, here*) the patter of the rain on the (*lead, led*) roof from a block away.
2. A kimono is a (*loose, lose*) Japanese garment with short, wide sleeves and a sash.
3. Mom said that (*its, it's*) your turn to wash the dishes.

4. (*Hear, Here*) is a good article about Black History Month.
5. I hope the team doesn't (*loose, lose*) its opening game.
6. Who will (*lead, led*) the team to victory tomorrow?
7. "Wait (*hear, here*) while I open the door," Peter ordered.
8. The weights were as heavy as (*led, lead*).
9. (*Its, It's*) taken too long to respond to your letter.
10. The (*lead, led*) in this mechanical pencil is almost gone.

passed	[verb, past tense of *pass*] *went by* We *passed* you on the way to school.
past	[noun] *time that has gone by;* [preposition] *beyond;* [adjective] *ended* You can learn much from the *past.* The band marched *past* the school. The *past* week was a busy one.
peace	[noun] *quiet, order, and security* People all over the world long for *peace.*
piece	[noun] *a part of something* I had a delicious *piece* of spinach pie at the Greek festival.
plain	[adjective] *simple; common;* [noun] *a flat area of land* Raul's directions were *plain* and clear. The coastal *plain* was flat and barren.
plane	[noun] *a flat surface; a tool; an airplane* A rectangle is a four-sided *plane* with four right angles. Wood shavings curled from the *plane* to the workshop floor. The *plane* flew nonstop to Atlanta.
principal	[noun] *the head of a school;* [adjective] *chief, main* The vice *principal* is at the high school. The committee's *principal* task is preserving the park.
principle	[noun] *a rule of conduct; a basic truth* Freedom of speech is one of the *principles* of democracy.

TIPS & TRICKS

Here's a way to remember the difference between *peace* and *piece*. You eat a pi**e**ce of **pie.**

TIPS & TRICKS

To remember the spelling of *principal,* use this sentence: The princi**pal** is your **pal.**

MECHANICS

Exercise 11 Choosing Between Words Often Confused

For each of the following sentences, choose the correct word from the pair of words in parentheses.

EXAMPLE 1. The (*passed, past*) president served two terms, not three.

1. past

1. The Old Order Amish wear (*plain, plane*) clothes.
2. Many Americans believe that the golden rule is a good (*principal, principle*) by which to live.
3. Mark likes the (*piece, peace*) and quiet of the country.
4. One (*piece, peace*) of the puzzle was missing.
5. Komako used a (*plain, plane*) to smooth the rough edge of the door.
6. We flew in an enormous Singapore Airlines (*plain, plane*) to Frankfurt, Germany.
7. By studying the (*passed, past*), we understand the present.
8. She was (*principal, principle*) of the school for years.
9. Gail Devers quickly (*passed, past*) the other runners.
10. The trees are just (*passed, past*) their lovely fall colors.

Review E Proofreading a Paragraph to Correct Errors in Words Often Confused

For the sentences in the following paragraph, correctly write each incorrect word.

EXAMPLE [1] Often, people don't know how precious something is until they loose it.

1. lose

[**1**] Several months ago, my aunt had what we all thought was a plane old cold. [**2**] In the passed, her doctor had told her there was no cure for a cold, so my aunt didn't even seek treatment. [**3**] No one knew that she had an ear infection that would led to a hearing loss in one ear. [**4**] Very soon, my aunt realized that she was hearing only peaces of conversations and could no longer hear out of her left ear. [**5**] When she went to the doctor, he explained that an infection had caused her to loose hearing in that ear. [**6**] The doctor gave her a chart showing the principle types of hearing aids. [**7**] He suggested

MECHANICS

the in-the-canal hearing aid because its barely noticeable when in place. [**8**] It's small size really surprised me. [**9**] The doctor told my aunt that, of coarse, new advances in hearing technology are being made every day now. [**10**] Some people who could not here at all before can now be helped.

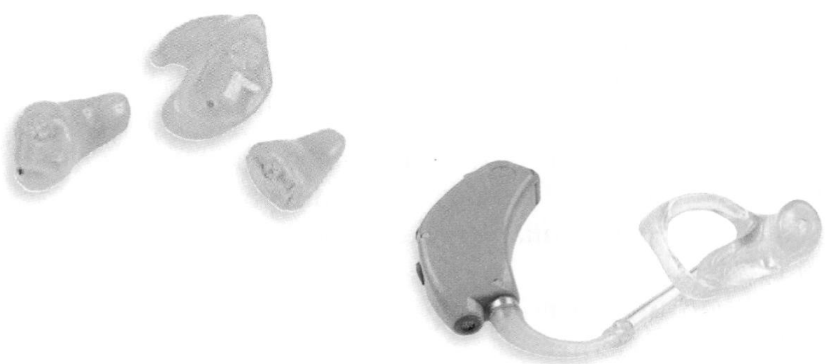

MECHANICS

TIPS & TRICKS

Here is an easy way to remember the difference between *stationary* and *stationery.* You write a lett**er** on station**er**y.

stationary	[adjective] *in a fixed position* The desks are *stationary,* but the chairs can be moved.
stationery	[noun] *writing paper* Sarah designs her own *stationery.*
their	[possessive form of *they*] *belonging to them* *Their* pitcher struck out six players.
there	[adverb] *at or to that place;* [also used to begin a sentence] I'll see you *there.* *There* are more than two million books in the Harold Washington Library in Chicago.
they're	[contraction of *they are*] *They're* right behind you.
threw	[verb, past tense of *throw*] *tossed* Zack *threw* the ball to me.
through	[preposition] *in one side and out the other* Let's walk *through* the park.

Exercise 12 Choosing Between Words Often Confused

For each of the following sentences, choose the correct word from the choices in parentheses.

EXAMPLE 1. (*Their, They're, There*) goes the space shuttle!
1. *There*

1. The 100-yard dash will begin over (*their, there, they're*) by the fence.
2. In a flash, the girls (*threw, through*) everything into (*their, there, they're*) lockers and ran onto the field.
3. The planet earth was once thought to be (*stationary, stationery*) in space.
4. (*Threw, Through*) the door bounded a large dog.
5. Are you sure (*their, there, they're*) not coming?
6. "Who (*through, threw*) the pass that led to the touch-down?" Jill asked.
7. I think that the red envelopes do not go with the pink (*stationery, stationary*) at all.
8. (*They're, Their*) planning to see a new science fiction movie sometime this weekend.
9. We drove (*threw, through*) Kansas and Oklahoma on the way to Texas.
10. (*Their, There*) is a Cajun band playing in the park this afternoon until 4:00.

to	[preposition] *in the direction of; toward* We drove *to* Carson City.
too	[adverb] *also; more than enough* Am I invited, *too*? Your poem has *too* many syllables to be a haiku.
two	[adjective or noun] *one plus one* Ms. Red Cloud's last name is *two* separate words. *Two* of the pandas woke up then.
weak	[adjective] *feeble; not strong* People with *weak* ankles have difficulty ice-skating.
week	[noun] *seven days* The club meets once a *week*.

(continued)

MECHANICS

COMPUTER TIP

A computer can help you catch spelling mistakes. Remember, though, that a computer's spellchecker cannot point out homonyms that are used incorrectly. Learn how to proofread your own writ-ing. Never rely entirely on a spellchecker.

(continued)

who's	[contraction of *who is* or *who has*] *Who's* wearing a watch? *Who's* seen Frida Kahlo's paintings?
whose	[possessive form of *who*] *belonging to whom* I wonder *whose* backpack this is.
your	[possessive form of *you*] *belonging to you* Rest *your* eyes now and then when you read.
you're	[contraction of *you are*] *You're* next in line.

Exercise 13 Choosing Between Words Often Confused

For each of the following sentences, choose the correct word from the choices in parentheses.

EXAMPLE **1.** I wonder (*who's, whose*) won the election.
1. who's

1. (*Who's, Whose*) story did you like best?
2. Walking (*to, too*) the grocery store, he began to feel (*weak, week*).
3. Does (*your, you're*) dad work for the newspaper, (*to, too, two*)?
4. It took me a (*weak, week*) to complete my project for history class.
5. If (*your, you're*) not making that noise, (*who's, whose*) making it?
6. "Is there (*too, two*) much flour in the tortilla dough?" Alinda asked.
7. Always fasten (*you're, your*) seat belt when (*you're, your*) riding in a vehicle.
8. They asked (*who's, whose*) painting was chosen (*to, too*) be entered in the contest.
9. (*Too, Two*) of the foreign exchange students are from southern India.
10. "See you next (*weak, week*)!" the ballet teacher said to the students cheerfully.

Review F Choosing Between Words Often Confused

For each of the following sentences, choose the correct word or words from the choices in parentheses.

EXAMPLE **1.** Don't (*loose, lose*) your house key.
1. lose

1. Oh, Rebecca, which of these (*to, too, two*) boxes of (*stationary, stationery*) do you like better?
2. The Israelis and the Palestinians met in Madrid, the (*capital, capitol*) of Spain, for the (*peace, piece*) talks.
3. (*Principal, Principle*) Wong raised his hand for silence, and the students waited to (*hear, here*) what he would say.
4. These curtains will likely be hard to (*altar, alter*) because the fabric is so (*coarse, course*).
5. (*Its, It's*) (*all together, altogether*) too easy to confuse similar words.
6. Ruth vowed to (*lead, led*) the life of an exile rather than to (*desert, dessert*) Naomi.
7. Can that (*plain, plane*) (*brake, break*) the sound barrier?
8. We're (*all ready, already*) for the big game against our rivals this (*weak, week*).
9. (*Your, You're*) next chore is to dust; the dust (*clothes, cloths*) are on the counter.
10. The two friends (*passed, past*) the time pleasantly reading (*there, their, they're*) books.

Review G Proofreading a Paragraph to Correct Spelling Errors and Errors in Words Often Confused

For each sentence in the following paragraph, correctly write each misspelled or misused word. If a sentence is already correct, write *C.*

EXAMPLE **[1]** Its time to test you're knowledge of South American history.
1. It's; your

[1] Starting about A.D. 1200, people known as the Incas began too take over the western portion of South America. [2] Look at the map on the next page, and you'll see that thier

MECHANICS

territory included mountains, seacoasts, river valleys, and desserts. [**3**] The capitol of the Incan empire was Cuzco. [**4**] The Incas created an impressive road system that connected Cuzco with the rest of there empire. [**5**] These hardworking people also built storehouses and developped large irrigation projects. [**6**] To help them manage their huge empire, they used a device called a quipu as their principle method of keeping records. [**7**] The quipu (shown below) is a series of knotted, colored cords. [**8**] With it, the Incas recorded such information as the number of people liveing in an area, the movements of the planets, and the amount of goods in storage. [**9**] The Incan civilization lasted until the Spanish arrived in the mid-1500s'. [**10**] In only a short time, Spanish conquistadors were able to defeat the Incas and brake up their empire.

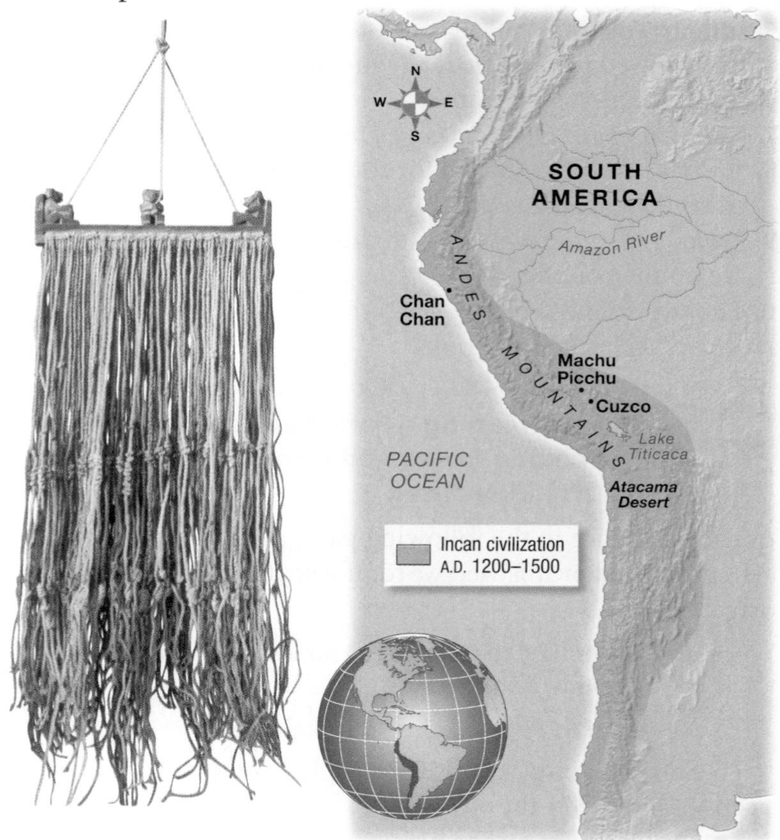

MECHANICS

Chapter Review

A. Proofreading Sentences for Correct Spelling

For each of the following sentences, correctly write the word that is misspelled.

HELP No proper nouns in the Chapter Review are misspelled.

1. The company's cheif accountant wrote the schedule.
2. Mr. Santander gave a breif speech before the ceremony.
3. Breatheing hard, we finally reached the summit.
4. Chickens and gooses are common fowl.
5. We changed the subject to avoid having an arguement.
6. How many *I*s did you use in your letter to Irene?
7. Mom and Dad have no tolerance for lazyness.
8. Spain and Portugal are two countrys I have always wanted to visit.
9. The new store on the corner will sell computer disks, computers, and stereoes.
10. My grandmother's recipe calls for half a clove of garlic and two garden tomatos.
11. Three small, active childs came running out of the house.
12. We cut several large branchs off the pine tree.
13. After she ran through the patch of stinging nettles, Alice had itchs up and down her legs.
14. We were surprised to see two pianoes on the stage instead of only one.
15. I am very interested in the history of anceint Egypt.
16. "The last thing we want," said the new sales manager, "is a disatisfied customer."
17. The first thing you notice in San Miguel is the friendlyness of the people.
18. That dinosaur skeleton must have been the bigest thing in the whole museum.
19. Aunt Rina has lost weight; she looks much slimer than she has in a long time.
20. Strawberrys are my favorite fruit.

B. Choosing Between Words Often Confused

For each of the following sentences, choose from each pair in parentheses the word that will make the sentence correct.

21. Nothing would persuade him to (*altar, alter*) his plans.
22. Berlin is the (*capitol, capital*) of Germany.
23. Sometimes the wisest (*course, coarse*) of action is to do nothing.
24. Samantha tried on the new (*cloths, clothes*) she received on her birthday.
25. For (*desert, dessert*) we had red grapes, strawberries, frozen yogurt, and melon.
26. The vast (*planes, plains*) of Patagonia stretch from the mountains to the ocean.
27. "Your cousins are over (*their, there*)," said Mr. Octavius. "I think this is (*there, their*) luggage."
28. In all the confusion, it was difficult to tell (*whose, who's*) things belonged to whom.
29. We were somewhat surprised when an overloaded pickup truck (*past, passed*) us going uphill.
30. On their way (*too, to*) the train station, they were held up in the (*stationary, stationery*) traffic.

C. Proofreading a Paragraph to Correct Spelling Errors

For each sentence in the following paragraph, correctly write the word or words that are misspelled. If a sentence is already correct, write *C.*

[**31**] Dublin, the capitol of Ireland, has a beautiful locateion between the sea and the mountains. [**32**] The city has a rich and interesting passed. [**33**] The Viking's established Dublin in the mid-800's, though a small settlement had existed previously on the site. [**34**] Norman soldiers from England captured Dublin in 1170 and built St. Patrick's Cathedral and Dublin Castle their. [**35**] The castle remained the center of British rule in Ireland throughout the next 700 years. [**36**] War and piece came and went. [**37**] By the 1700's, Dublin was growing fast. [**38**] It's cultural life flourished, and manufacturing and trade increased.

MECHANICS

[39] Unfortunatly, between 1916 and 1922, much property was destroyed during the war of independence and a civil war. [40] Today, Dublin is growing and prosperous and is faceing the challenges common to most modern big citys.

Writing Application

Using Correct Spelling in a Personal Letter

Following Spelling Rules You are writing a letter to congratulate your cousin Mary, who has been awarded first prize in a spelling bee. Write a paragraph expressing your congratulations and saying how important you think it is to use correct spelling. In your paragraph, use at least five words often confused.

Prewriting Jot down a list of reasons correct spelling is important. You might mention making a good impression and making communication easier. Also, compose sentences about how difficult it must be to remember correct spelling in front of an audience and how impressed you are that Mary managed to do so.

Writing Begin your rough draft by stating how hard it is to spell correctly in English and how important it is to continue developing that skill. Then, congratulate Mary on her award and say that her success will inspire you to continue working hard at learning correct spelling.

Revising Have a friend or classmate read your draft. Have you clearly stated the importance of correct spelling? Is your pleasure at your cousin's success clearly described?

Publishing Make sure you have not used any homonyms incorrectly. Then, proofread your letter for any errors in grammar, punctuation, and spelling. You and your classmates may wish to post your letters on a class bulletin board or Web page.

Spelling Words

- contact
contract
advance
depth
comment
summit
sketch
nonsense
splendid
ethnic
liquid
impulse

- globe
grove
slope
slice
roast
spike
choke
praise
squeeze
breathe
gross
thigh

- shout
youth
amount
pounds
mountain
thousands
proof
crawled
account
launched
rumors
saucer

- turtle
nightmare
burnt
curb
purse
declare
scarce
inserts
sparkling
source
nervous
warrant

- enough
though
straight
rough
courage
eighth
system
although
sleigh
boulder
biscuit
dough

- freight
foreign
receive
receiver
belief
relief
weighed
reins
fierce
heights
thieves
achieve

- grandfather
fairy tales
bedtime
cupboard
upright
teenager
thunderstorm
barefoot
middle-class
middle-aged
bodyguard
so-called

- grown
groan
guest
guessed
creek
creak
weather
whether
sore
soar
stake
steak

- angle
angel
costume
custom
affect
effect
adopt
adapt
device
devise
decent
descent

- varied
centuries
colonies
applies
occupied
identified
enemies
activities
denied
allied
industries
qualified

- beaten
musical
rotten
German
Indian
Roman
explorer
stretcher
critical
criminal
political
original

- escape
gotten
velvet
engine
insist
admire
index
intense
further
frantic
convince
instinct

- agent
evil
local
eager
famous
fiber
razor
vital
rival
basis
cheetah
scenic

- speaking
spelling
wondered
bragged
healed
scrubbed
answered
threatened
admitted
committed
referring
preferred

- insurance
conference
ambulance
absence
instance
audience
allowance
intelligence
assurance
appearance
obedience
presence

- activity
ability
argument
personality
electricity
championship
community
majority
responsibility
curiosity
necessity
authority

- approach
accuse
applause
affection
accompany
assign
appreciate
accurate
association
apparent
accustomed
assistance

- continued
commander
commit
constitution
confusing
commence
commotion
commercial
communicate
communities
communication
committee

- elephant
confident
instant
element
servant
excellent
opponent
permanent
assistant
innocent
significant
sufficient

- talent
novel
treason
comic
profit
token
weapon
gopher
pleasant
siren
frigid
spiral

- habit
display
clever
gather
empty
chaos
suspense
Saturn
oval
orphan
fatal
crystal

- media
fungi
bacteria
stimulus
stimuli
larvae
radius
nucleus
nuclei
species
salmon
hippopotamus

- curious
tremendous
enormous
obvious
delicious
mysterious
executive
creative
fabulous
legislative
negative
sensitive

- unpredictable
disagreement
renewal
unemployment
unexpectedly
unfortunately
unusually
reproduction
reconstruction
disagreeable
unsuccessful
uncomfortable

- wonderfully
thoughtfully
relationship
respectively
naturally
nervously
gracefully
actively
joyfully
beautifully
successfully
accidentally

- illegal
impolite
impossible
invisible
irregular
inexpensive
impure
inability
impatient
indigestion
indefinite
incredible

- descriptive
description
prescribed
inspector
spectacle
spectacular
scribbled
inscription
subscription
spectrum
spectators
transcripts

- erupt
abrupt
bankrupt
inject
disrupting
disruption
eject
reject
rejected
rupture
corrupt
interrupt

Correcting Common Errors

1.0 Written and Oral English Language Conventions
Students write and speak with a command of standard English conventions appropriate to this grade level.

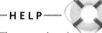

HELP
The exercises in this chapter test your knowledge of the rules of **standard, formal English.** These are the rules you should follow in your schoolwork.

Reference Note
For more information about **standard** and **nonstandard English** and **formal** and **informal English,** see page 221.

Key Language Skills Review

This chapter reviews key skills and concepts that pose special problems for writers.

- **Sentence Fragments and Run-on Sentences**
- **Subject-Verb Agreement**
- **Pronoun-Antecedent Agreement**
- **Verb Forms**
- **Pronoun Forms**
- **Comparison and Placement of Modifiers**
- **Double Negatives**
- **Standard Usage**
- **Capitalization**
- **Punctuation—Commas, End Marks, Semicolons, Colons, Quotation Marks, and Apostrophes**
- **Spelling**

Most of the exercises in this chapter follow the same format as the exercises found throughout the grammar, usage, and mechanics sections of this book. You will notice, however, that two sets of review exercises are presented in standardized test formats. These exercises are designed to provide you with practice not only in solving usage and mechanics problems but also in dealing with these kinds of problems on standardized tests.

Exercise 1 Identifying Sentences and Sentence Fragments

Identify each of the following word groups as a *sentence* or a *sentence fragment.* If a word group is a sentence, rewrite it correctly, using a capital letter at the beginning and adding an end mark.

Reference Note

For information on **sentences** and **sentence fragments,** see pages 4 and 386.

EXAMPLES
1. the squirrel hopped across the branch
   1. *sentence—The squirrel hopped across the branch.*
2. Jeremy's collection of comic books
   2. *sentence fragment*

1. near the door of the classroom
2. all members of the safety patrol
3. sumo wrestling is popular in Japan
4. please pass me the fruit salad
5. will become a member of Junior Achievement
6. after school Sonya repaired her backpack
7. what an active puppy that is
8. lived in British Columbia for many years
9. do you like the sound of ocean waves
10. on the top shelf of the refrigerator
11. ate goat cheese every day in Norway
12. that's a fantastic idea
13. because rap music is still popular
14. not everyone wants to play the game
15. a tree was placed on top of the completed building
16. when the armadillos enter another state
17. stopped traffic for half an hour
18. John the plumber around noon
19. please return the books by tomorrow afternoon
20. plugged in the computer and nothing happened

Reference Note

For information on **sentence fragments,** see pages 4 and 386.

Exercise 2 Revising Sentence Fragments

Some of the following word groups are sentence fragments. First, identify the fragments. Then, make each fragment a complete sentence by adding (1) a subject, (2) a verb, or (3) both. You may need to change the punctuation and capitalization, too. If the word group is already a complete sentence, write *S.*

EXAMPLE 1. Finished reading an exciting book by Jean Craighead George.

1. *I finished reading an exciting book by Jean Craighead George.*

1. Titled *The Case of the Missing Cutthroats.*
2. A book for young detectives who love nature.
3. In the book, a girl named Spinner goes fishing.
4. During the trip, she catches a giant cutthroat trout.
5. Thought cutthroat trout had died out where she was fishing in the Snake River.
6. Both she and her family are surprised by her catch.
7. Puzzled by the presence of a cutthroat trout.
8. What has happened to the cutthroat trout?
9. Spinner and her cousin Al on an adventure.
10. Hope to find clues that will help them solve the mystery.

HELP

Most of the sentences in Exercise 3 can be correctly revised in more than one way. You need to give only one revision for each sentence.

COMMON ERRORS

Exercise 3 Identifying and Revising Run-on Sentences

Decide which of the following word groups are run-on sentences. Then, revise each run-on sentence by (1) making two separate sentences or (2) using a comma and a coordinating conjunction. You may have to change the punctuation and capitalization, too. If the word group is already a complete sentence, write *S.*

EXAMPLE 1. Both girls enjoy playing soccer one is usually the goalie.

1. *Both girls enjoy playing soccer, and one is usually the goalie.*

or

Both girls enjoy playing soccer. One is usually the goalie.

Reference Note

For information on **run-on sentences,** see page 388.

1. Puffins are shorebirds, they have brightly colored beaks and ducklike bodies.
2. Cement is a fine powder it is mixed with sand, water, and small rocks to make concrete.
3. Alicia collects birth dates, she has recorded the birthdays of all her friends and of her favorite movie stars.
4. We may go to the Zuni arts and crafts fair on Saturday we may wait until next weekend.
5. The band placed first in regional competitions, it did not win at the state contests.
6. I plan to go to the Florida Keys someday, I want to skin-dive for seashells.
7. Kerry is having a party tomorrow night, we are planning to go.
8. The school board could vote to remodel the old cafeteria, or they may decide to build a new one.
9. My brother would like to live on a space station someday I would, too.
10. These rocks are too heavy for me to lift, I asked Christy to help me move them.

Exercise 4 Identifying and Revising Run-on Sentences

Identify which of the following word groups are run-on sentences. Then, revise each run-on sentence by (1) making two separate sentences or (2) using a comma and a coordinating conjunction. You may have to change the punctuation and capitalization, too. If the word group is already a complete sentence, write *S.*

EXAMPLE 1. The Navajo woman allowed the children to try on jewelry, it was made out of silver and beautiful turquoise.

1. The Navajo woman allowed the children to try on jewelry. It was made out of silver and beautiful turquoise.

1. Sheila liked a ring with one stone in the middle it didn't fit her finger.
2. She found another ring with three small stones, it was a perfect fit for her.

HELP

Most of the sentences in Exercise 4 can be correctly revised in more than one way. You need to give only one revision for each sentence.

Reference Note

For information on **run-on sentences,** see page 388.

COMMON ERRORS

3. Aaron picked out a turquoise watchband, and he also found a ring with blue stones and fire agates.
4. The watchband had little pieces of turquoise in the shape of a star he really wanted to buy it.
5. Both Maria and Francine spied a necklace a rough chunk of turquoise was hung from a silver chain.
6. Thad may spend his allowance on a turquoise ring he may save up his money for a watchband.
7. Several children had never seen turquoise before, they wanted to know if the stones were real.
8. The saleswoman's arms were covered with bracelets everyone noticed her.
9. Ruben put six bracelets on his arms, and then he couldn't get all of them off.
10. The group wanted to see more turquoise jewelry the woman had sold many pieces earlier in the day.

HELP — Most of the sentences in Exercise 5 can be correctly revised in more than one way. You need to give only one revision for each sentence.

Reference Note

For information on **sentence fragments,** see pages 4 and 386. For information on **run-on sentences,** see page 388.

COMMON ERRORS

Exercise 5 Correcting Run-on Sentences and Sentence Fragments

Decide which of the following word groups are run-on sentences and which are sentence fragments. Then, revise each word group to make one or more complete sentences. Remember to use correct capitalization and punctuation. If a word group is already a complete sentence, write *S.*

EXAMPLES
1. Do you like brightly colored art you should see Faith Ringgold's paintings.
   1. *Do you like brightly colored art? You should see Faith Ringgold's paintings.*
2. Uses color boldly and imaginatively.
   2. *Ringgold uses color boldly and imaginatively.*

1. Ringgold was born in Harlem in 1930 at a young age, she knew she wanted to be an artist.
2. Today her artwork in museums around the world.
3. Paints on fabric and sometimes uses fabric to frame her paintings.
4. Her creativity led her to invent a whole new art form she decided to call it the "story quilt."
5. Story quilts blend storytelling with painting.

6. One of Ringgold's series of story quilts about an African American woman in Paris.
7. Much of her work represents her African American roots.
8. Ringgold's painting *Tar Beach* is based on her childhood experiences she completed the work in 1988.
9. Shows a playground on the roof of an apartment building.
10. Behind the rooftop lies the George Washington Bridge, a bridge with a string of lights that reminded Ringgold of a diamond necklace.

Exercise 6 Choosing Verbs That Agree in Number with Their Subjects

For each of the following sentences, choose the form of the verb in parentheses that agrees with the subject.

EXAMPLE 1. Everyone except my twin sisters (*want, wants*) to go to the powwow.
1. wants

1. Here (*come, comes*) the marching bands in the parade!
2. Several of my friends (*has, have*) trail bikes.
3. I (*don't, doesn't*) like to swim when the water is cold.
4. Neither the guinea pigs nor the hamster (*is, are*) awake yet.
5. (*Has, Have*) Mr. Baldwin and Sherry been talking long?
6. One of the scientists (*was, were*) Isaac Newton.
7. Thunderstorms usually (*don't, doesn't*) bother me.
8. (*Is, Are*) the Chinese cookbooks still on sale?
9. All of the movie (*was, were*) filmed in Vietnam.
10. The boy in the red shoes (*run, runs*) fast.

Reference Note

For information on **verb forms,** see page 147. For information on **subject-verb agreement,** see page 124.

Exercise 7 Proofreading Sentences for Correct Subject-Verb Agreement

Most of the following sentences contain a verb that does not agree in number with its subject. If a verb form is incorrect, write the correct form. If a sentence is already correct, write *C*.

EXAMPLE 1. A carved slice of potato make a good stamp.
1. makes

1. Images from this type of stamp are called potato prints.

Reference Note

For information on **subject-verb agreement,** see page 124.

2. Both my cousins and my younger brother Michael creates potato prints.
3. It don't cost much to make these prints.
4. A firm potato, a knife, paint, a paintbrush, and paper is the necessary supplies.
5. My friend James find unique shapes and patterns in his mother's old magazines.
6. He then carves these designs on the flat surfaces of cut potatoes.
7. Next, each carved design on the potato slices are coated with paint.
8. Pieces of fabric or a sheet of paper offer a good surface for stamping.
9. Each of my cousins like to make greeting cards with stamped designs.
10. Other uses for a potato stamp includes making writing paper and wrapping paper.

Exercise 8 Choosing Pronouns That Agree with Their Antecedents

For each of the following sentences, choose the pronoun in parentheses that agrees with its antecedent.

Reference Note

For information on **pronoun-antecedent agreement,** see page 137.

EXAMPLE 1. The engineers showed (*his, their*) plans for the new bridge.

1. their

1. J. W. and I hope to have (*our, their*) skits ready in time for the talent show.
2. Two boys and one girl have received honors, and all of (*her, their*) parents are very proud.
3. During the last serve, with the crowd watching, Danny's tennis racket flew out of (*his, our*) hand.
4. We treated (*ourselves, themselves*) to Chinese noodles and stir-fried vegetables for supper.
5. The table is made of oak and is quite solid, but one of (*his, its*) legs is broken.
6. The members of the Asian Students Club asked to have (*its, their*) picture taken with the school mascot.

7. Neither Jack nor Charles wants to have (*his, their*) hair cut by Lisa.
8. Arlene asked Samuel to go on the picnic, but (*he, she*) hasn't given an answer yet.
9. The squirrels and the rabbits play in the yard; (*they, it*) seem to have a lot of fun.
10. Each of the girls will receive (*their, her*) own directions.

Exercise 9 Proofreading for Pronoun-Antecedent Agreement

Most of the following sentences contain a pronoun that does not agree with its antecedent. Write each incorrect pronoun and then the correct form. If a sentence is already correct, write *C*.

Reference Note

For information on **pronoun-antecedent agreement,** see page 137.

EXAMPLES
1. The asteroids will not hit Earth, but it will come close.
   1. it—they
2. Each of the boys thought that their independent project was the best one.
   2. their—his

1. Dad wrote out the check to the painters although he had not finished the painting job for him.
2. Tom Sawyer tricked his friends into doing his work, but they enjoyed it.
3. Jesse Owens, Willie Mays, and Joe Louis were sports stars in their day, and many people still remember him.
4. Have you ever noticed how the bears at the zoo really enjoy sunning itself?
5. Several of the men in our town plan to donate his time to Habitat for Humanity.
6. Each of the girls wanted to read their report first.
7. Did Randy or Tomás finish cleaning their desk first?
8. Our grandparents gave us a surprise party when we came home from camp.
9. Either José or Andrew will arrive early so that they can help us finish the posters.
10. Each of the cats was chasing their toys.

HELP—

Some sentences in Exercise 10 may have more than one correct answer. You need to give only one answer for each sentence.

Reference Note

For information on **regular verb forms,** see page 148.

COMMON ERRORS

Exercise 10 Using the Principal Parts of Regular Verbs

Give the form of the italicized verb that will correctly complete each of the following sentences.

EXAMPLE **1.** *roll* The dog ____ on its back for us to pet it.

1. rolled
or
rolls

1. *climb* Yesterday the cat ____ the tree.
2. *joke* I can never tell when Bob is ____.
3. *shop* My friend and I once ____ all day at a mall in Bloomington, Minnesota.
4. *fill* Have the fans ____ the auditorium yet?
5. *enter* Too many cars are ____ the parking lot.
6. *watch* The class is ____ a video about the ancient Incan culture in Peru.
7. *call* Who ____ my name a few seconds ago?
8. *measure* My mother has ____ the space for the new bookcase.
9. *load* Two men ____ our furniture into the truck.
10. *jump* A deer has ____ over the fence.
11. *laugh* We ____ for a long time over Ira's joke.
12. *fix* Steven is ____ the computer.
13. *wash* Cora's brother has ____ his new car at least a dozen times.
14. *play* Have you ____ the soundtrack from that movie for Isaac yet?
15. *walk* Mother and I ____ three miles on the county road yesterday morning.
16. *talk* The young boys are ____ about starting their own soccer team.
17. *hammer* The carpenter ____ the nails into the crossbeam in almost no time at all.
18. *observe* Benjamin's family is ____ Yom Kippur in the traditional way.
19. *help* Regular exercise has ____ many people to stay physically fit.
20. *dress* Are you ____ up for the banquet tonight?

Exercise 11 Using Irregular Verbs

For each italicized verb, give the past or the past participle form that will correctly complete the sentence.

EXAMPLE 1. *drink* The guests ____ all of the raspberry tea.
1. *drank*

1. *blow* The wind has ____ the kite out of the tree!
2. *shrink* The boy in the movie had ____ to the size of a squirrel.
3. *steal* "I've never ____ anything in my life," Abe declared in his defense.
4. *drive* Pat and Justin ____ go-carts at the park.
5. *freeze* The water in the birdbath has ____.
6. *sink* The toy boat has ____ in the sudsy bath water.
7. *throw* Each athlete has ____ the javelin twice.
8. *sing* The choir ____ at the celebration last night.
9. *swim* Have you ever ____ in warm mineral water?
10. *burst* The balloon ____ when the cat clawed it.
11. *teach* Mrs. Randall has ____ at Rosenwald Middle School for years.
12. *give* Last year I ____ part of my allowance to the United Way.
13. *run* Our car is old and unattractive, but it has ____ well for many years.
14. *eat* Sharon baked two small potatoes and ____ both of them.
15. *fly* "That hawk has ____ over the yard twice," Justin said.
16. *write* Many people have ____ about the Mexican myth of Quetzalcoatl.
17. *begin* It has ____ to snow, but the flakes are very small and dry.
18. *come* "Who ____ to Dad's surprise birthday party?" Miriam asked.
19. *speak* Lin and Jeff have ____ about their tickets to everyone in class.
20. *do* It's a good feeling to know that you have ____ your best.

Reference Note

For information on **irregular verb forms,** see page 150.

Reference Note

For information on **irregular verb forms,** see page 150.

Exercise 12 Proofreading for Errors in Irregular Verbs

Most of the following sentences contain incorrect verb forms. Identify each error, and write the correct form of the verb. If the sentence is already correct, write *C.*

EXAMPLE 1. We have went to the African art exhibit two weekends in a row.

1. *went—gone*

1. Sarah done well at yesterday's track meet.
2. My stepfather brung me a stuffed animal when I was in the hospital.
3. Nickelodeon movie theaters begun to be quite popular in the United States around 1905.
4. Manuel's grandfather come to the United States forty years ago.
5. We seen the Rio Grande when we drove through the state of New Mexico.
6. Chris knew that a basement was a good place to take shelter during a tornado.
7. Judy taked a few minutes to decide what to say.
8. Maria's team choosed the oak tree in her front yard as home base.
9. The poison ivy in the woods gived me a rash.
10. Dr. Seuss wrote the poem "The Sneetches."
11. The blue pitcher that my godparents buyed for me in Denmark is on the table in the living room.
12. Do you remember what running records Carl Lewis breaked?
13. The girls on the front porch have drank their lemonade too quickly.
14. My shirt and pants tore on the barbed wire as I climbed through the fence.
15. Jina's mother and stepfather have went to the same church for thirty-five years.
16. A raccoon felled from the roof of our house, but it was not injured.
17. In a very generous mood, Marsha lended her favorite scarf to Natalie.

18. The family made the giant scarecrow to scare away the grackles from their backyard garden.
19. The young artist drawed a lovely picture of the waves and rocks on the Oregon coast.
20. Gwen catched the ball even though Craig threw it fast and high.

Exercise 13 Using the Past and Past Participle Forms of Verbs

For the italicized verb in each of the following sentences, give the past or past participle form that will correctly complete the sentence.

Reference Note

For information on **verb forms,** see page 147.

EXAMPLE 1. *establish* Robert D. Ballard, a marine geologist, ____ the JASON Foundation for Education.

1. *established*

1. *create* JASON, an underwater robot, was ____ for scientific research.
2. *build* JASON was ____ to dive much deeper than humans can dive.
3. *sink* More than 1,600 years ago, the Roman ship *Isis* ____ in the Mediterranean Sea.
4. *know* Ballard ____ that students would want to share in the exploration of the wrecked ship.
5. *make* A network of satellites ____ it possible for many students to see JASON explore the wreck.
6. *see* Some 250,000 schoolchildren ____ JASON on giant video screens.
7. *ask* While JASON searched the ship, students ____ questions of Ballard and his team.
8. *take* Ballard has ____ students on some amazing electronic field trips by televising himself working with JASON.
9. *give* He has ____ much of his time and energy to involving students in scientific discoveries.
10. *write* Ballard has ____ about finding the *Isis* and about the 1985 discovery of the *Titanic,* which sank in 1912.

Exercise 14 Choosing Correct Pronoun Forms

Reference Note

For information on **pronoun forms,** see page 177.

Choose the correct form of the pronoun in parentheses in each of the following sentences.

EXAMPLE **1.** The catcher gave (*she, her*) the signal.
1. her

1. The winners may be you and (*her, she*).
2. Gregory asked (*her, she*) to the dance.
3. The ending of the movie really amazed Andrew and (*us, we*)!
4. Should Emily and (*they, them*) make the spaghetti?
5. The bus driver gave (*he, him*) a warning.
6. The competition is really between Mario and (*I, me*).
7. Who bought (*her, she*) that opal necklace?
8. The best player on our team is (*him, he*).
9. The next step for Michael and (*them, they*) is to check with the principal.
10. My cousin and (*me, I*) are learning to do origami in our class at the community center.
11. You and (*I, me*) can work together on a report about American Indians of the Southwest.
12. The physical education teacher designed a special exercise program for (*her, she*).
13. The ones who asked to see our pictures from the Miami zoo are (*they, them*).
14. (*Us, We*) always enjoy the plays at the children's theater, especially when they are performed outdoors.
15. (*He, Him*) plays the guitar quite well and has performed in a band.
16. Ms. Ruel asked Kei and (*I, me*) to recite the French nursery rhyme.
17. "I'd like to go to the movies with (*they, them*)," Thi said after meeting Carmela and Tony.
18. Aunt Edna is buying new backpacks for Carl and (*I, me*).
19. Last week (*them, they*) began taking tennis lessons after school.
20. Will you or (*I, me*) be the first one with the correct answer?

Exercise 15 Proofreading for Correct Pronoun Forms

Most of the following sentences contain a pronoun that has been used incorrectly. Identify each incorrect pronoun. Then, write the correct form. If a sentence is already correct, write *C.*

EXAMPLE **1.** Cassie sat between Melissa and I at the concert.
1. I—me

1. Who did you meet at the skating rink last night?
2. You and them are the only ones who are going on the hike.
3. My pen pal in Vietnam will soon receive another letter from me.
4. Just between you and I, the other book was much easier to understand.
5. One of the actors in that play was her.
6. The pencils, paints, and colored paper belong to Kimiko and he.
7. Matthew has invited you and I to his party next weekend.
8. Either her or I will make a poster for Black History Month.
9. Who is the fastest runner on the baseball team?
10. They and us went swimming in Lake Travis.

Reference Note

For information on **pronoun forms,** see page 177.

Exercise 16 Choosing Correct Regular and Irregular Modifiers

Choose the correct form of the adjective or adverb in parentheses in each of the following sentences.

EXAMPLE **1.** The stars tonight look (*more bright, brighter*) than usual.
1. brighter

1. This puzzle book is (*difficulter, more difficult*) than the other one.
2. Kevin is the (*taller, tallest*) of the four Sutherland brothers.
3. The (*most exciting, excitingest*) day of our trip to Indonesia was still to come.
4. I like drawing, but I like painting (*best, better*).
5. If you blend strawberries, bananas, and yogurt really (*good, well*), you'll have a great drink.
6. Felicia had the (*worst, worse*) case of chickenpox of anyone in the sixth grade.

Reference Note

For information on **using modifiers correctly,** see Chapter 9.

7. My brothers and I were taught how to wash, iron, and mend clothes, and we are (*gladder, glad*) that we were.
8. Rachel can't decide which of the two wallpaper patterns would look (*prettier, prettiest*) in her room.
9. Our schoolyard has been (*cleanest, cleaner*) since the Ecology Club asked people not to litter.
10. I am going to practice American Sign Language until I sign (*good, well*) enough to communicate easily.

Exercise 17 Correcting Errors in the Use of Modifiers

Reference Note

For information on **using modifiers correctly,** see Chapter 9.

Rewrite each of the following sentences, correcting any errors in the use or placement of modifiers.

EXAMPLE **1.** Do you like Western boots or hiking boots most?
1. most—more

1. Ernest runs very good, but William can run even better.
2. Katherine is the more curious of the four Matsuo children.
3. Which flavor of frozen yogurt do you think would be worser, cheddar or carrot?
4. Tell me, did you do gooder on this week's spelling test than on last week's?
5. Annie brings homegrown tomatoes to her friends that she picks from her garden.
6. The astronaut met with children who had commanded a mission aboard the space shuttle.
7. Gloria became more worriedly as the storm grew worse.
8. Of the Amazon, Nile, and Mississippi rivers, the Nile is the longer.
9. We rented that scary movie at the video store from which the filmmakers spun off a television series.
10. Have you ever read *Fahrenheit 451,* the novel about book burning by Ray Bradbury?
11. After carefully rehearsing several times, Toni felt confidently about giving her speech.
12. Vincente made a cover for his textbook with his initials on it.
13. Janelle found a recipe for broiling catfish in a cookbook.

COMMON ERRORS

14. If you look close at the painting, you can see how tiny the brush strokes are.
15. We looked through the old photo album in the kitchen that we had just found in the attic.
16. It was a large crop, and it grew good, too.
17. Icarus foolish flew nearer to the sun than he should have.
18. In different parts of the world, we have read about unusual customs.
19. Aunt Dee and Uncle Mike enjoyed the CD of the symphony in their living room.
20. We found the sheet music for songs your mother used to sing in the piano bench.

Exercise 18 Correcting Double Comparisons and Double Negatives

Revise each of the following sentences to correct the double comparison or double negative.

EXAMPLE 1. Grandma thought learning to swim would be more harder than it was.

1. *Grandma thought learning to swim would be harder than it was.*

Reference Note

For information on **double comparisons** and **double negatives,** see pages 206 and 209.

1. My sister gave me her soccer ball because she never plays soccer no more.
2. You can get a more clearer idea of what the trail is like by looking at this map.
3. We couldn't hardly believe our eyes when we saw what was under the rock!
4. You shouldn't stand nowhere around a tall tree during a thunderstorm.
5. Keisha's uncle Anthony just adopted the most strangest pet I've ever seen.
6. My little sister can't scarcely reach the doorknob without standing on tiptoe.
7. I'm not going to put off practicing my bongo drums no more.
8. That was the most worst movie we've ever seen.

COMMON ERRORS

9. Didn't neither of the books have the information you needed?
10. I've read that potbellied pigs learn more faster than dogs do.

Exercise 19 Identifying Correct Usage

Reference Note

For information on **common usage errors,** see Chapter 10.

For each of the following sentences, choose the word or word group in parentheses that is correct according to the rules of formal, standard English.

EXAMPLE 1. My aunt Claire was working in Athens, Greece, (*then, than*).

1. then

1. Everyone from the volleyball team is here (*accept, except*) Roseanne.
2. Steve said he thought the new batting lineup looked (*alright, all right*).
3. The two friends felt (*bad, badly*) after arguing.
4. The children helped (*theirselves, themselves*) to the curry.
5. Do you know (*whose, who's*) sunglasses these are?
6. The boys will (*try to, try and*) finish painting today.
7. Be sure to (*bring, take*) your lunch when you go to the park.
8. The ten students in the art class divided all of the construction paper and markers (*between, among*) themselves.
9. (*Who's, Whose*) going to show them how to dance?
10. Heat lightning occurs too far from people for them to hear (*its, it's*) accompanying thunder.

Exercise 20 Correcting Errors in Usage

Reference Note

For information on **common usage errors,** see Chapter 10.

Each of the following sentences contains an error in the use of formal, standard English. Identify each error, and then write the correct usage.

EXAMPLE 1. Them fish are called sea horses.

1. Them—Those

1. Where are sea horses found at?
2. Sea horses are found in tropical and temperate waters—not anywheres that is very cold.

3. Baby sea horses often use they're curved tails to hold on to each other.
4. That there sea horse used its tail to grasp some seaweed.
5. Don't you think that it's head looks amazingly like a tiny horse's head?
6. The little fin on a sea horse's back moves so fast that you can't hardly see it.
7. Several students asked the teacher how come the eyes of a sea horse work independently of each other.
8. My stepsisters and I use to look for sea horses when we lived near the coast in California.
9. The teacher reminded us to bring home a parental approval form for the field trip to the city aquarium.
10. When your at the aquarium, remember to stop by the sea horse exhibit.

Exercise 21 Proofreading Sentences for Correct Usage

Each of the following sentences contains an error in English usage. Identify each error. Then, write the correct usage.

EXAMPLE **1.** Do you all ready know about the Pantanal?
1. all ready—already

Reference Note

For information on **common usage errors,** see Chapter 10.

1. The Pantanal is the largest wetland anywheres on earth.
2. To get an idea of it's size, imagine an area about the size of Arkansas.
3. Most of the Pantanal is located inside of Brazil.
4. The area contains a enormous wealth of wildlife.
5. Our science teacher is learning us about the jaguar, the giant anteater, and other animals that live there.
6. The Pantanal may be more important for wading birds such as storks then any other place in South America.
7. In addition, alot of other birds, such as toucans and macaws, live there.
8. The Pantanal has swamps that sometimes have absorbed heavy rains that otherwise might of flooded nearby areas.
9. However, the Pantanal ain't all swamps; it also contains forests.
10. Although the Pantanal is a long ways from where I live, I hope to have a chance to explore it someday.

Grammar and Usage Test: Section 1

DIRECTIONS In each of the following sentences, a word group is underlined. Using the rules of formal, standard English, choose the answer that most clearly expresses the meaning of the sentence. If there is no error, choose A. Indicate your response by shading in the appropriate oval on your answer sheet.

EXAMPLE 1. The fish smelled badly, so we didn't buy any.

(A) smelled badly
(B) smells badly
(C) smelled bad
(D) smelling bad

ANSWER 1.    

1. Roz and I catched fireflies in a jar.
   (A) I catched
   (B) me catched
   (C) I caught
   (D) me caught

2. Fun hiking in the wilderness preserve.
   (A) Fun hiking in the wilderness preserve.
   (B) While having fun hiking in the wilderness preserve.
   (C) Hiking in the wilderness preserve was fun.
   (D) Have had fun hiking in the wilderness preserve.

3. The election resulted in a runoff between he and I.
   (A) he and I
   (B) him and me
   (C) him and I
   (D) he and me

4. In bowling, a strike is when a bowler knocks down all ten pins on the first throw in a frame.
   (A) is when
   (B) occurs when
   (C) is where
   (D) is because

5. Have you heard of Lawrence and Lorne Blair, two brothers who traveled in Indonesia for ten years?
   - (A) Blair, two brothers who traveled in Indonesia for ten years?
   - (B) Blair? Two brothers who traveled in Indonesia for ten years.
   - (C) Blair, two brothers whom traveled in Indonesia for ten years?
   - (D) Blair and two brothers who traveled in Indonesia for ten years?

6. Is this here drill bit the right size?
   - (A) Is this here
   - (B) Is that there
   - (C) Is this here kind of
   - (D) Is this

7. Here your car keys.
   - (A) Here your car keys.
   - (B) Here are your car keys.
   - (C) Here's you're car keys.
   - (D) Here is your car keys.

8. The dog barked the baby awoke.
   - (A) The dog barked the baby awoke.
   - (B) The dog barked, the baby awoke.
   - (C) The dog barked, and the baby awoke.
   - (D) The dog barking and the baby awoke.

9. I shouldn't of waited to start my essay.
   - (A) shouldn't of
   - (B) shouldn't have
   - (C) ought not to of
   - (D) oughtn't not to have

10. Mrs. Levine asked how come Darnell and he aren't ready to leave yet.
    - (A) how come Darnell and he aren't
    - (B) how come Darnell and him aren't
    - (C) why Darnell and he isn't
    - (D) why Darnell and he aren't

Grammar and Usage Test: Section 2

DIRECTIONS Read the paragraph below. For each of the numbered blanks, select the word or word group that best completes the sentence. Indicate your response by shading in the appropriate oval on your answer sheet.

EXAMPLE Two species of elephant __(1)__ today: the African elephant and the Asian elephant.

1. (A) does exist
   (B) exists
   (C) have been existing
   (D) exist

ANSWER 1. 

Each of these species has __(1)__ own unique features; for example, the African elephant has __(2)__ ears and tusks than the Asian elephant does. Although different in some ways, both species of elephant __(3)__ strong, intelligent, and social. Both have poor sight and are colorblind but can smell and hear quite __(4)__. Elephants can detect the scent of __(5)__ human who is over a mile away. __(6)__ hearing is so good that they can communicate over distances of more than two miles, using sounds __(7)__ any that humans can hear. Unfortunately, human population growth, farming, industry, and illegal hunting __(8)__ a decline in the elephant population. For instance, poachers have killed thousands of African elephants for their ivory tusks; in fact, from 1979 to the early 1990s, the number of elephants in Africa __(9)__ from 1,300,000 to fewer than 600,000. __(10)__ protect elephants, the trade of ivory was outlawed worldwide in 1989.

1. (A) it
   (B) its'
   (C) it's
   (D) its

2. (A) larger
   (B) more larger
   (C) the more larger
   (D) the most largest

3. (A) they are
   (B) are
   (C) are being
   (D) is

4. (A) well
   (B) good
   (C) better
   (D) best

COMMON ERRORS

5. (A) a
(B) an
(C) the
(D) this

6. (A) They're
(B) There
(C) Their
(D) They

7. (A) more lower than
(B) lower than
(C) more low then
(D) lower then

8. (A) will have caused
(B) causes
(C) are causing
(D) is cause

9. (A) shrinks
(B) shrank
(C) shrinked
(D) is shrinking

10. (A) 2
(B) Too
(C) Two
(D) To

COMMON ERRORS

Exercise 22 Correcting Errors in Capitalization

Each of the following word groups contains at least one error in capitalization. Correct the errors either by changing capital letters to lowercase letters or by changing lowercase letters to capital letters.

Reference Note

For information on **capitalization rules,** see Chapter 11.

EXAMPLE 1. abilene, texas

1. Abilene, Texas

1. the smoky mountains
2. rutherford B. hayes
3. *Alice In Wonderland*
4. university of kansas
5. labor day
6. near lake Placid
7. it's already tuesday!
8. english or Art II
9. washington monument
10. marta Hinojosa, m.d.
11. neptune and other planets
12. second day of hanukkah
13. my Uncle Jack
14. an airplane called *spirit of st. louis*
15. a river running South
16. Bryce canyon national park
17. 912 valentine st.
18. president Cleveland
19. "i'm home!"
20. newbery medal

Exercise 23 Correcting Errors in Capitalization

Correct the capitalization errors in the following sentences either by changing capital letters to lowercase letters or by changing lowercase letters to capital letters.

Reference Note

For information on **capitalization rules,** see Chapter 11.

EXAMPLE 1. i went to see a play last saturday.

1. I went to see a play last Saturday.

1. Our drama teacher, ms. soto, took us to see it.
2. the new play was first performed by the south Texas performance company.

COMMON ERRORS

3. this theater group's founder and director is the translator, playwright, and theater scholar joe rosenberg.
4. He has established an exchange program for theater students from the united states, mexico, and south america.
5. In addition, mr. rosenberg has written a full-length play titled *saturday stranger,* which was published in germany.
6. Mr. Rosenberg has also edited a Book called *¡aplauso! hispanic Children's theater.*
7. the book includes plays by héctor santiago, roy conboy, and lisa loomer, among others.
8. the plays are printed in both english and spanish.
9. these plays draw on hispanic literary traditions native to such places as mexico, puerto rico, and cuba.
10. Next month the southwest middle school drama club plans to perform one of the plays from this book.

Exercise 24 Using Periods, Question Marks, and Exclamation Points Correctly

For each of the following sentences, write each letter or word that should be followed by a period, question mark, or exclamation point, and add the proper punctuation.

EXAMPLE 1. Senator Jackson, can you meet with our class at 8:15 A M

1. A.M.?

Reference Note

For information on **using end marks,** see page 263.

1. Please follow me
2. Will you please help me carry my books
3. Where in the downtown library is the new display of Peruvian pottery
4. Watch out for that car
5. Dr Williamson taught me to fly a model helicopter
6. Anthony asked Rose whether her favorite cartoonist was Charles M Schulz
7. One fossil recently discovered in these mountains dates back to three million B C
8. What a surprise that was
9. Have you ever brought your skateboard to school
10. The letter addressed to 4613 Sleepy Hollow Blvd, Kingston, NY 12401, must be for Mrs C R Smith

HELP

Some sentences in Exercise 24 need more than one punctuation mark.

Exercise 25 Proofreading Sentences for the Correct Use of Commas

Reference Note

For information on **using commas,** see page 268.

Each of the following sentences is missing at least one comma. Write the word or numeral that should be followed by a comma, and add the comma.

EXAMPLE **1.** Oh I hope we win the track meet when we go to Salina Kansas next week.

1. Oh, Salina, Kansas,

1. Sheila ran laps on Monday Tuesday and Wednesday.

2. On February 23 2008 my family had a reunion in San Juan Puerto Rico.

3. Yes that is the dog they adopted from the animal shelter.

4. Because my father is going to teach me to play the guitar soon he is showing me how to tune one now.

5. No I have never read *The Hobbit.*

6. Scissors pins tacks and other sharp items should be kept out of the reach of young children.

7. Athena the Greek goddess of crafts wisdom and war is often shown with an owl on her shoulder.

8. Douglas never leaves shopping carts in parking spaces set aside for people who have disabilities and neither should anyone else.

9. My aunt and I bought nails lumber and paint for the bird-houses we plan to build.

10. Professor Chang will you explain the differences between these two kinds of cells?

Exercise 26 Using Semicolons and Colons Correctly

Reference Note

For information on **using semicolons and colons,** see pages 279 and 281.

The following sentences lack necessary colons and semicolons. Write the words or numerals that come before and after the needed punctuation, and insert the proper punctuation.

EXAMPLE **1.** My grandmother is coming to visit we will meet her at the airport.

1. visit; we

1. We picked subjects for our reports I chose sea turtles.

2. Our school day used to start at 8 15 now it starts at 8 00.

COMMON ERRORS

3. The following items will be needed for the new playground swings, slides, and picnic tables.
4. The rain just ended maybe we will get a chance to see a double rainbow.
5. We can save water in these ways turning off the faucet while brushing our teeth, pouring only as much as we plan to drink, and taking showers instead of baths.
6. At the farmers' market, shoppers were discussing the recent election they were discussing the weather, too.
7. "Dear Sir or Madam" is one proper way to begin a business letter, but not the only way.
8. Plains Indians include the following peoples Comanche, Osage, Pawnee, Crow, and Blackfeet.
9. At 6 30 A.M. my alarm went off I couldn't believe it was time to get up.
10. My wish list is as follows a mountain bike, better grades, and a kitten.

Exercise 27 Punctuating and Capitalizing Quotations

Revise the following numbered items, using quotation marks, other marks of punctuation, and capital letters where needed. If a sentence is already correct, write *C.*

EXAMPLE 1. I admire Marian Wright Edelman said Paul she has worked hard for children's rights.

1. *"I admire Marian Wright Edelman," said Paul. "She has worked hard for children's rights."*

1. In 1973, Edelman founded the Children's Defense Fund, a nonprofit organization that has helped many people said Mr. Knepp.
2. Paul commented that just the other day he had read an article titled Edelman: The Children's Defender.
3. Justin said I'd like to work to protect children's rights, too, one day.
4. Edelman was born in 1939 Paul told us she grew up in Bennettsville, South Carolina.
5. Mr. Knepp said that Marian Wright Edelman is one of our country's greatest civic leaders.

Some sentences in Exercise 27 may be correctly revised in more than one way. You only need to give one revision for each sentence.

Reference Note

For information on **using quotation marks,** see page 292. For information on **using capital letters,** see Chapter 11.

6. Please tell me more about Edelman's career as a lawyer, Ashley said.
7. She graduated from Yale Law School in 1963 he said And soon became the first African American woman licensed to practice law in Mississippi.
8. Mr. Knepp added Edelman has handled many civil rights cases and has always made community service a priority.
9. did Edelman say that she had been taught as a child to make service a central part of her life? Justin asked.
10. Yes Ashley answered I remember reading that in her autobiography, *The Measure of Our Success: A Letter to My Children and Yours.*

Reference Note

For information on **punctuating dialogue,** see page 296.

Exercise 28 Punctuating Dialogue

Revise the following dialogue, adding quotation marks and other marks of punctuation and replacing lowercase letters with capital letters where necessary. Remember to begin a new paragraph each time the speaker changes.

EXAMPLE **[1]** The legend of Greyfriars Bobby is so moving, Jennifer exclaimed, that I'll never forget it!

1. "The legend of Greyfriars Bobby is so moving," Jennifer exclaimed, "that I'll never forget it!"

[**1**] Bobby was a special dog, Jennifer said, and extremely loyal to his master. [**2**] Tony asked, "can you believe that Bobby actually lived by his master's grave for fourteen years?" [**3**] Jennifer said, My cousin went to Edinburgh, Scotland, and saw Bobby's grave. [**4**] It is in Greyfriars churchyard, near his master's grave. [**5**] When did Bobby die? Tony asked. [**6**] He died in 1872, Jennifer replied. [**7**] "the people in the town fed Bobby and cared for him until his death."

[**8**] "Bobby slept during the day, Tony recalled because, before his master died, they had worked together at night."

[**9**] Jennifer said, "yes, his master, old Jock, guarded cattle that were sold at the market." [**10**] Tony said, In Edinburgh there is a statue of Greyfriars Bobby on top of a drinking fountain for dogs.

Exercise 29 Using Apostrophes Correctly

Rewrite the following word groups, inserting an apostrophe wherever one is needed.

EXAMPLE 1. the womens class
1. the women's class

1. if theyve gone
2. no ones fault
3. that statues condition
4. so lets try
5. since youre going home
6. that giants castle
7. theirs werent faded
8. the Rockies highest peak
9. when there isnt time
10. these books authors
11. Arkansas governor
12. if everybodys there
13. made all As in school
14. one pueblos history
15. the five camels saddles
16. born in 84
17. and theres the dog
18. the sheeps wool
19. when youll find out
20. two *o*s in the word *igloo*
21. arent able to
22. the one whos late
23. when Im tired
24. around 10 oclock
25. those two books pages

Reference Note

For information on **using apostrophes,** see page 300.

Exercise 30 Correcting Spelling Errors

Most of the following words are misspelled. If a word is not spelled correctly, write the correct spelling. If a word is already spelled correctly, write *C*.

EXAMPLE 1. mispeak
1. misspeak

1. percieve
2. disolve
3. gladest
4. charging
5. comedies
6. sillyness
7. taxs
8. tryed
9. potatos
10. traceing
11. classes
12. sleigh
13. matchs
14. videoes
15. funnyer
16. toyes
17. schoolling
18. wieght
19. loosness
20. Gomezs
21. managable
22. unatural
23. ladys
24. runing
25. finaly

Reference Note

For information on **spelling rules,** see page 319.

Exercise 31 Choosing Between Words Often Confused

Reference Note

For information on **words often confused,** see page 329.

For each of the following sentences, choose the word or word group in parentheses that will make the sentence correct.

EXAMPLE 1. Matthew suggested that I (*altar, alter*) the first paragraph of my story.

1. alter

1. Have you (*all ready, already*) finished your latest painting?
2. (*Your, You're*) pets need good food, clean water, warm shelter, and loving attention.
3. Be careful not to (*lose, loose*) any of those puzzle pieces, or we'll have to buy a new puzzle.
4. Chuckwallas are harmless lizards that may grow to be two feet long and live in rocky (*desserts, deserts*) in the United States and Mexico.
5. Manuel dreamed of finding a sunken ship and (*it's, its*) treasure chest.
6. The school (*threw, through*) away tons of paper and cardboard before the recycling program was started.
7. (*Whose, Who's*) planning to bring food and drinks to the fiesta tomorrow?
8. We drove (*passed, past*) the park, across the bridge, and around the lake to the dock.
9. Marcie's enthusiasm for playing in the marching band was (*plain, plane*) to see.
10. The guide (*lead, led*) the scouts through the museum.
11. Former President Jimmy Carter has been greatly involved in efforts to bring (*piece, peace*) to various countries all over the world.
12. In less than one (*weak, week*), Sandra's mother will begin her new job as editor-in-chief of the newspaper's new Washington bureau.
13. (*There, Their*) are many kinds of trees in our neighborhood, and they provide plenty of shade.
14. The gravel in the driveway is (*coarse, course*), but it still feels good on my bare feet.
15. The flagpole itself was (*stationary, stationery*), but the flag flapped in the breeze.

16. "The lamp may (*brake, break*) if you try to carry it on its side and with one hand," Dad cautioned.
17. What is the (*capital, capitol*) of Puerto Rico?
18. Mr. Edgars is a good man whose (*principles, principals*) include honesty and fairness.
19. When we sit outside on the porch, we can't (*hear, here*) the phone ring.
20. We read (*threw, through*) Gary Soto's book of poetry and picked out some poems to memorize.

Exercise 32 Proofreading Sentences for Errors in Spelling and Words Often Confused

For each of the following sentences, identify and correct any error in spelling or usage. If a sentence is already correct, write *C*.

EXAMPLE 1. The Iroquois people's name for themselfs means "we longhouse builders."

1. *themselfs—themselves*

1. In our American history coarse, we learned that the Iroquois constructed large dwellings called longhouses.
2. Years ago, nearly all Iroquois lived in forests and built they're longhouses out of logs and strips of bark.
3. Several individual familys lived in each of these longhouses.
4. When a couple marryed, the husband would move into the longhouse of his wife's extended family, called a clan.
5. Each family had it's own separate area with a sleeping platform that was raised about a foot above the ground.
6. They kept the longhouse neat by storing many of their belongings on shelfs above their sleeping platforms.
7. Fires were made in hearths in a central corridor, and smoke rose threw holes cut in the longhouse roof.
8. When it rained or snowed, slideing panels were used to close the holes.
9. The bigest longhouses measured more than two hundred feet in length.
10. Such large longhouses could shelter ten or more individual families at a time.

Reference Note

For information on **spelling rules,** see page 319. For information on **words often confused,** see page 329.

HELP — Many of the sentences in Exercise 33 contain more than one error.

Exercise 33 Proofreading a Paragraph for Errors in Mechanics

For the sentences in the following paragraph, correct each error in mechanics. If a sentence is already correct, write *C.*

EXAMPLES **1.** Have you ever seen the movie *the Wizard of Oz*?
1. The Wizard of Oz

2. You may not know that its based on a book.
2. it's

[**1**] The book was written by l. frank Baum. [**2**] He was born on May 15 1856 in the state of New York. [**3**] When he was a teenager he was interested in the theater his father a wealthy oilman gave him several theaters to manage. [**4**] In 1881 he wrote *The maid of Arran*, a successful play. [**5**] For many years he worked at several jobs, including storekeeper newspaper reporter and traveling salesman. [**6**] In 1900 he published a childrens book called *The Wonderful Wizard of Oz*, which was a bestseller for two years in a row. [**7**] Baum adapted the book into a successful play, and he even made several silent movies about Oz. [**8**] Baum died in Hollywood California in 1919 after twenty years the famous film starring Judy Garland as Dorothy was made in the same city. [**9**] During the making of the film, the actor who played the wizard discovered that L. Frank Baum's name was sewn into the lineing of the wizard's coat. [**10**] According to Baum's wife, it really was Baum's old coat the movie studio's wardrobe department had bought it at a secondhand clothing shop.

HELP — Most items in Exercise 34 contain more than one error.

Exercise 34 Proofreading a Business Letter for Correct Grammar, Usage, and Mechanics

Correct the errors in grammar, usage, and mechanics in the numbered items in the following letter.

EXAMPLE **[1]** 254 Thirty second street
1. 254 Thirty-second Street

254 Thirty-second Street
Syracuse, NY 13210
[1] November 5 2009

Ms. Susan Loroupe
[2] *Syracuse daily times*
598 Seventh Avenue
Syracuse, NY 13208

[3] Dear Ms Loroupe

[4] Thank you for taking time during you're busy workday to show the Van Buren Middle School Journalism Club around the Newspaper's offices.

[5] Us club members are glad to have had the chance to see how newspaper articles are wrote and printed. [6] Especially enjoyed seeing the presses—even more then talking with the design artists and editors! [7] We were surprised that the presses were so loud and we were impressed by how quick and efficient everyone worked. [8] Please thank the artists, to, for showing us how they use computer's to arrange the art and photos on the pages.

Sincerely,

Carlos Lopez

Carlos Lopez
[9] journalism club Secretary
[10] Van Buren middle school

COMMON ERRORS

Mechanics Test: Section 1

DIRECTIONS Each numbered item below contains an underlined word or word group. Choose the answer that shows the correct capitalization, punctuation, and spelling of the underlined part. If there is no error, choose answer D (Correct as is). Indicate your response by shading in the appropriate oval on your answer sheet.

EXAMPLE **[1]** Quincy, MA 02158

(A) Quincy, Mass. 02158
(B) Quincy MA, 02158
(C) Quincy, M.A. 02158
(D) Correct as is

ANSWER **1.** (A) (B) (C) 

147 Hickory Lane
Quincy, MA 02158
[1] May 11 2009

The Hobby Shop
[2] 2013 forty-First Street
Los Angeles, CA 90924

[3] Dear Mr. Shaw

While I was visiting **[4]** my aunt Laura, who's house is near your store, she bought a model airplane from you. **[5]** Two of my freinds have **[6]** already tryed to help me get the plane to fly, but we haven't been able to. **[7]** Putting the plane together was not difficult; the problem is that the engine will not start. Also, I found no stickers in the box when I opened **[8]** it and the box says that there should be stickers for the plane's wings. I have enclosed the engine and my **[9]** aunt's reciept. I hope that **[10]** youre able to send me stickers and a new engine soon.

Sincerely,
Timothy Martin

Timothy Martin

1. (A) May, 11 2009
   (B) May 11, 2009
   (C) May, 11, 2009
   (D) Correct as is

2. (A) 2013 Forty First Street
   (B) 2013 Forty-first street
   (C) 2013 Forty-first Street
   (D) Correct as is

3. (A) Dear Mr. Shaw,
   (B) Dear Mr. Shaw:
   (C) Dear mr. shaw:
   (D) Correct as is

4. (A) my aunt Laura, whose
   (B) my Aunt Laura, whose
   (C) my Aunt Laura, who's
   (D) Correct as is

5. (A) Two of my friends
   (B) To of my freinds
   (C) Too of my friends
   (D) Correct as is

6. (A) all ready tryed
   (B) already tried
   (C) all ready tried
   (D) Correct as is

7. (A) Puting the plane
   (B) Puting the plain
   (C) Putting the plain
   (D) Correct as is

8. (A) it and the box says that their
   (B) it, and the box says that their
   (C) it, and the box says that there
   (D) Correct as is

9. (A) aunt's receipt
   (B) Aunt's receipt
   (C) aunts' reciept
   (D) Correct as is

10. (A) your
    (B) you're
    (C) your'
    (D) Correct as is

Mechanics Test: Section 2

DIRECTIONS Each of the following sentences contains an underlined word or word group. Choose the answer that shows the correct capitalization, punctuation, and spelling of the underlined part. If there is no error, choose answer D (Correct as is). Indicate your response by shading in the appropriate oval on your answer sheet.

EXAMPLE 1. Today the school librarian Mr. Woods will show us a video.

(A) librarian, Mr. Woods
(B) librarian, Mr. Woods,
(C) librarian Mr. Woods,
(D) Correct as is

ANSWER   B 

1. I wonder what the capital of Spain is?
   (A) capital of Spain is.
   (B) capitol of Spain is.
   (C) capitol of Spain is?
   (D) Correct as is

2. The mouses' nest may be in the garage.
   (A) mouses
   (B) mices
   (C) mice's
   (D) Correct as is

3. "What did you see at the park?" asked my grandfather.
   (A) see at the park"? asked my grandfather.
   (B) see at the park," asked my grandfather?
   (C) see at the park? asked my grandfather."
   (D) Correct as is

4. Felix, you've been a naughty kitten this passed week!
   (A) passed weak
   (B) past weak
   (C) past week
   (D) Correct as is

5. Aisha exclaimed, "see how much these crystals have grown!"
   (A) exclaimed, "See
   (B) exclaimed! "See
   (C) exclaimed "see
   (D) Correct as is

6. The Olympic team waved at the crowd, the audience cheered.
   (A) crowd; the audeince
   (B) crowd: the audience
   (C) crowd, and the audience
   (D) Correct as is

7. The Kalahari Desert is in southern Africa.
   (A) Kalahari Dessert
   (B) kalahari desert
   (C) Kalahari desert
   (D) Correct as is

8. "Its snowing," observed Mrs. Daniels.
   (A) "It's snowwing,"
   (B) "It's snowing,"
   (C) Its snowing,
   (D) Correct as is

9. The Red Cross is asking for: blankets, sheets, and pillows.
   (A) for; blankets,
   (B) for, blankets,
   (C) for blankets,
   (D) Correct as is

10. Robert Frost's poem The Road Not Taken is famous.
   (A) poem *The Road Not Taken*
   (B) poem "The Road Not Taken"
   (C) poem "the Road not Taken"
   (D) Correct as is

PART 2 Sentences

16 Writing Effective Sentences

17 Sentence Diagramming

GO TO: go.hrw.com
KEYWORD: HLLA

Writing Effective Sentences

1.0 Written and Oral English Language Conventions
Students write and speak with a command of standard English conventions appropriate to this grade level.
1.1 Use simple, compound, and compound-complex sentences; use effective coordination and subordination of ideas to express complete thoughts.

Diagnostic Preview

A. Identifying Sentences, Sentence Fragments, and Run-on Sentences

Identify each of the following word groups as a *sentence,* a *sentence fragment,* or a *run-on sentence.* Rewrite fragments to make complete sentences. Rewrite run-ons to make one or more complete sentences. Use correct capitalization and punctuation.

EXAMPLE 1. We visited Arkansas, my aunt lives there now.
1. run-on—We visited Arkansas. My aunt lives there now.

1. Riding a beautiful, black Arabian horse.
2. If you don't mind, I'd like to rest a minute.
3. Dinner was great, Dad cooked my favorite dish.
4. Is Tony my first cousin?
5. When I wake up, I do a few exercises, then I shower.

B. Combining Sentences

Combine the two sentences in each of the following items to make a single sentence by adding connecting words, inserting words or phrases, or using compound or complex sentences.

EXAMPLE 1. We went to the state fair. We had a good time.
1. We had a good time when we went to the state fair.

6. I collect interesting rocks. My sister collects pressed flowers.
7. Robert read a book. Sara had already read it.

8. When you go, turn out the lights. Please also lock the door.
9. Snails are mollusks. Slugs are also mollusks.
10. The painting shows a waterfall. The waterfall is beautiful.

C. Revising Stringy Sentences and Sentences with Passive Voice

Revise each stringy or awkward sentence so that it is clear and so that each verb is in the active voice.

EXAMPLE **1.** Dinner was ready, so we all gathered around the table, and then dinner was eaten.

1. When dinner was ready, we all gathered around the table and ate.

11. I had asked my little sister to help me set the table, so that had been done already.
12. My brother likes potatoes, and the kind that he likes best is mashed potatoes.
13. I made the salad, and I made the side dish of carrots.
14. The main dish was made up of noodles with mushrooms and red sauce, and it was enjoyed by everyone.
15. That we eat together as many nights a week as we can is what is preferred by my parents.

D. Using Transitions

Rewrite the following paragraph, adding transitions that make the meaning clearer and make the paragraph easier to read.

EXAMPLE Ari had the idea that he was forgetting something. He didn't know what it could be.

Ari had the feeling that he was forgetting something; however, he didn't know what it could be.

Ari set out to walk to soccer practice. He knew that he would have to hurry. He had waited until later than usual to leave. Ari had gone a few blocks. He realized that he had forgotten his jersey. He would not be able to get it and still get to practice on time. He decided to go on without his jersey. Ari remembered that he needed his jersey. The coach had said there

SENTENCES

would be team pictures tonight. Ari stopped at a friend's house and called his sister to ask her to bring his jersey to the field.

Writing Clear Sentences

Your goal in writing should always be to communicate clearly with your reader. A clear sentence gives your reader just enough information. It does not leave out any important pieces, and it does not run together or string together too many ideas at once. Clear sentences make it easier for your reader to understand what you are saying. In this chapter you will learn about three enemies of clear writing: *sentence fragments, run-on sentences,* and *stringy sentences.*

Sentence Fragments

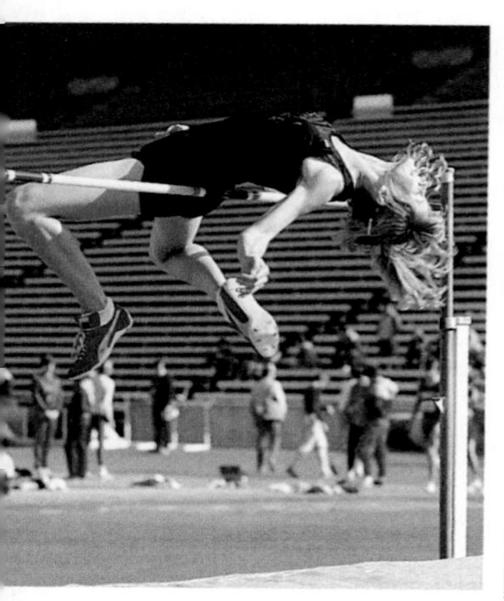

What kind of sentence could you write about this picture? You might write something like this:

The high jumper flips backwards over the bar.

or

How high the bar is!

or

How does she know where to jump?

These groups of words say different things, but they have something in common. Each is a *complete sentence.* A ***complete sentence*** is a group of words that expresses a complete thought and that has a subject and a verb.

A part of each thought is expressed by the verb: *flips, is, does know.* Another part is expressed by the subject: *high jumper, bar, she.*

A ***sentence fragment*** is a part of a sentence that is punctuated as if it were a complete sentence. A fragment is confusing because it does not express a complete thought. The following word groups are the example sentences—with some important words left out. Notice how unclear the word groups are when written as fragments.

Flips backwards over the bar. [The subject is missing. *Who* or *what* flips?]

How high the bar! [The verb is missing. *What about* how high the bar?]

Where to jump. [This word group does not express a complete thought. *What about* where to jump?]

Use this simple three-part test to help you decide whether a word group is a sentence fragment or a complete sentence.

1. Does the group of words have a *subject*?
2. Does the word group have a *verb*?
3. Does the word group express a *complete thought*?

You know the word group is a complete sentence if you answer "yes" to all three questions above. If you answer "no" to a question, the word group is a sentence fragment.

Oral Practice Recognizing Fragments

Read each of the following word groups aloud, and say whether it is a sentence fragment or a sentence. Remember that a complete sentence meets three requirements: It has a subject, it has a verb, and it expresses a complete thought.

EXAMPLE **1.** Wanted a hamster.
1. sentence fragment

1. We visited the pet shop in the mall.
2. A bright-eyed hamster chewing on pieces of carrot.
3. Named him Mustard.
4. Has pouches inside each fat cheek.
5. The pouches are for carrying food.
6. Newspaper in lots of little shreds.
7. Making his cage quite comfortable.
8. He is plump and has white and tan fur.
9. A diet of mostly fruit, vegetables, and grain.
10. If you decide to raise hamsters.

TIPS & TRICKS

Sometimes a fragment is really a part of a nearby sentence. You can correct the fragment by attaching it to the sentence that comes before or after it.

SENTENCE WITH FRAGMENT
Mark is practicing his hook shot. Because he wants to try out for the basketball team.

SENTENCE
Mark is practicing his hook shot **because he wants to try out for the basketball team.**

When you attach a fragment to a sentence, be sure to check your new sentence for correct punctuation and capitalization.

SENTENCES

Exercise 1 Revising Fragments

COMPUTER TIP

If you are using a computer, you can use a word-processing program to help eliminate sentence fragments. Using the cut and paste commands, you can easily try attaching a fragment to both the sentence before it and the sentence after it. Doing so will allow you to see which sentence makes more sense. Check your writing for correctness and completeness after making changes.

Some of the following word groups are sentence fragments. First, identify the fragments. Then, revise each fragment by (1) adding a subject, (2) adding a verb, or (3) attaching the fragment to a complete sentence. You may also need to change the punctuation and capitalization in your revised sentence. If a word group below is already a complete sentence, write *S* on your paper.

EXAMPLE **1.** It a stormy Wednesday night.
1. It was a stormy Wednesday night.

1. Was watching TV alone.
2. A movie about aliens invading from space.
3. Suddenly, the lights went out on the whole block.
4. Because the batteries in the flashlight were dead.
5. A strange noise in the backyard.
6. After our dog started to bark.
7. Crept slowly to the door and looked out.
8. Two small, glowing eyes in the dark.
9. When I saw it was just the cat from next door.
10. Maybe I should stop watching scary movies.

Run-on Sentences

A ***run-on sentence*** is actually two or more sentences run together with no punctuation between them or with only a comma between them. It is often hard to tell where one idea in a run-on ends and the next one begins.

Like sentence fragments, run-on sentences usually appear in your writing because you are in a hurry to get your thoughts down on paper. There is more than one way to revise a run-on sentence. You can break the run-on into two complete sentences, or you can link the two ideas with a comma and a coordinating conjunction such as *and, but,* or *or.*

RUN-ON In 1962 John Glenn became the first American to orbit Earth, he made his second space flight on the space shuttle *Discovery* in 1998, when he was 77 years old.

CORRECT In 1962 John Glenn became the first American to orbit Earth**. He** made his second space flight on the space shuttle *Discovery* in 1998, when he was 77 years old. [The sentence has been broken into two complete sentences.]

or

In 1962 John Glenn became the first American to orbit Earth**, and** he made his second space flight on the space shuttle *Discovery* in 1998, when he was 77 years old. [Two complete ideas have been linked by a comma and the word *and*.]

NOTE A comma alone is not enough to link two complete ideas in a sentence. If you use just a comma between two complete ideas, you create a run-on sentence.

RUN-ON Sally Ride was the first American woman in space, she was a member of a shuttle crew.

CORRECT Sally Ride was the first American woman in space**. S**he was a member of a shuttle crew.

Reference Note

For more information about using **commas with coordinating conjunctions,** see page 270.

HELP

You can also use semicolons to correct run-on sentences.

RUN-ON
I am interested in space exploration, in fact, I would like to be an astronaut.

CORRECTED
I am interested in space exploration**;** in fact, I would like to be an astronaut.

Reference Note

For more information on **using semicolons,** see page 279.

SENTENCES

Exercise 2 Identifying and Revising Run-on Sentences

Decide which of the following groups of words are run-ons. Revise each run-on by (1) making it into two separate sentences, or (2) using a comma and a coordinating conjunction. You may have to change the punctuation and capitalization, too. If the group of words is already correct, write *C.*

EXAMPLE **1.** People in business and in school use the Internet on a daily basis, they can use the Internet at home, too.

1. People in business and in school use the Internet on a daily basis. They can use the Internet at home, too.

1. People constantly search for faster ways to communicate, the Internet is one tool that helps people share information quickly.
2. The earliest form of the Internet was designed over thirty years ago, and it was created to be used by the military.
3. The Internet has changed a great deal since then now it can be used by almost anyone who uses a computer.
4. The first e-mail program was invented in 1972, e-mail is a way to send messages from one computer to another.
5. Twenty years later, scientists in Switzerland created the World Wide Web, and *Internet* quickly became a household word.
6. The scientists planned to use the Web to share research with scientists in other parts of the world the new invention soon interested businesses and government organizations.
7. The programs that make the Internet and the World Wide Web work are very complicated they are not hard to use.
8. Many schools and libraries have computers that are connected to the Internet and the World Wide Web.
9. The World Wide Web began with four newsgroups in 1991, but it soon included millions of sites.
10. Many sites on the World Wide Web focus on school subjects, news, and hobbies, these sites can be useful sources of information.

Review A Revising Sentence Fragments and Run-on Sentences

Decide which of the following word groups are fragments and run-ons. Then, revise each of these word groups to make it clear and complete. Remember to add correct capitalization and punctuation. If a word group is already correct, write *C*.

EXAMPLE
1. Most humans see very well, they often assume other life forms see as they do.
1. *run-on—Most humans see very well, and they often assume other life forms see as they do.*

1. Not all animals see the world in the same way humans see the world.
2. See only light and dark shapes.
3. Squids and octopuses have very advanced eyes they see almost as well as humans.

4. The jeweled squid lives deep underwater in the Indian Ocean, it has white, blue, and red lights around its eyes to help it see in the dark water.
5. Several other sea creatures have their own "headlights," these lights are sometimes produced by helpful bacteria, which the fish store in special skin pouches.
6. Some owls can catch mice in total darkness by hearing alone others can find a mouse by the light of one candle placed nearly a quarter of a mile away from the mouse.
7. Grazing animals must have a wide field of vision so that they will know when an enemy is coming.
8. Rabbits and deer eyes on the sides of their heads.
9. Mammals that hunt other animals for food must be able to judge distance well, therefore, their eyes are usually located toward the front of their faces.
10. Most apes do not hunt other animals for food, their eyes are in much the same position as human eyes, apes also see the same range of colors humans see.

SENTENCES

Stringy Sentences

For variety, you will sometimes want to join sentences and sentence parts with *and.* If you string many ideas together with *and,* though, you create a ***stringy sentence.*** Stringy sentences ramble on and on. They do not give the reader a chance to pause between ideas.

STRINGY The ostrich is the largest living bird, and it stands nearly eight feet tall, and it weighs over three hundred pounds when it is fully grown, and this speedy bird can run up to forty miles an hour!

SENTENCES

BETTER The ostrich is the largest living bird. It stands nearly eight feet tall, and it weighs over three hundred pounds when it is fully grown. This speedy bird can run up to forty miles an hour!

In the revised version, only two ideas are linked by *and*. These ideas can be combined into one sentence because they are closely related. Notice that a comma is used before the word *and*. The comma is also necessary to show a slight pause between the two complete ideas.

Exercise 3 Identifying and Revising Stringy Sentences

Revise each of the following stringy sentences by breaking it into two or more sentences.

EXAMPLE **1.** Raccoons look like cute, mischievous animals wearing a mask, and they are often seen in residential areas, and they frequently eat pet food left outside.

1. Raccoons look like cute, mischievous animals wearing a mask. They are often seen in residential areas, and they frequently eat pet food left outside.

Thomas and José were playing softball at school, and Thomas hit the ball very hard, and then he saw it roll under the steps of the library. Thomas peered under the dark steps to recover his ball, and when he reached for it, he saw a giant raccoon, and Thomas wasn't sure what to do next! José told Thomas that raccoons are fierce fighters, and then José warned him not to anger the raccoon, and by this time, other softball players had gathered to offer advice. Thomas finally rolled the ball out from under the steps with a baseball bat, and the raccoon stayed completely still, but it hissed and looked fiercely at the group, and then Thomas saw why the raccoon was behaving so strangely. Five baby raccoons were hiding behind the mother, and they were too small to protect themselves, and the mother raccoon was trying to frighten the softball players away!

Active and Passive Voice

A verb in the ***active voice*** expresses an action done *by* its subject. A verb in the ***passive voice*** expresses an action done *to* its subject.

ACTIVE VOICE The band teacher **instructed** us. [The subject, *teacher,* performs the action.]

PASSIVE VOICE We **were instructed** by the band teacher. [The subject, *We,* receives the action.]

ACTIVE VOICE **Did** we **play** the march well? [The subject, *we,* performs the action.]

PASSIVE VOICE **Was** the march **played** well by us? [The subject, *march,* receives the action.]

In a passive sentence, the verb phrase always includes a form of *be* and the past participle of the main verb. Other helping verbs may also be included.

ACTIVE The artist **had used** oils for the painting.

PASSIVE Oils **had been used** by the artist for the painting.

Reference Note

For more information on **past participles,** see page 147.

Exercise 4 Identifying Active and Passive Voice

For each of the following sentences, tell whether the verb is in the *active voice* or the *passive voice.*

EXAMPLE **1.** The truck was filled with dirt by the workers.

1. passive

1. The new play was reviewed favorably by the critics.
2. The firefighters finally have put out the forest fire.
3. The flight attendant described the safety features of the plane.
4. The unhappy baby was comforted by his mother.
5. Did Dan misplace his car keys again?
6. The campfire had not been extinguished by the campers.
7. Mary Beth was chosen as the team leader.
8. The free tickets will be raffled on Tuesday.
9. Did the strong wind blow the leaves off the trees?
10. Have the cabinet members been named by the new president?

Using the Passive Voice

The passive voice emphasizes the person or thing receiving the action. The passive voice is useful when you do not know who performed the action or when you do not want to reveal the performer of the action.

EXAMPLES The territory **was explored** in the early 1700's. [The person who explored the territory is unknown.]

"A bad choice **was made** for the location of the party," said Marie. [The speaker does not want to reveal who made the choice.]

Although you may want to use the passive voice in situations like those above, the active voice is stronger and more direct. The passive voice generally requires more words to express a thought than the active voice does, and too many passive sentences can cause your writing to sound weak or awkward. It is generally best to avoid using the passive voice except in the situations described above.

Exercise 5 Using Verbs in the Active Voice and the Passive Voice

For each of the following sentences, tell whether the verb is in the *active voice* or the *passive voice*. Then, revise each sentence that contains a verb in the passive voice so that the verb is in the active voice.

EXAMPLE 1. My book report was just completed.
1. *passive—I just completed my book report.*

1. Marta hung the wet laundry on the clothesline.
2. Have you read today's newspaper?
3. On Monday, our old newspapers, glass, and aluminum cans will be picked up by the recycling company.
4. Tod's braces were adjusted by the orthodontist.
5. For the last two days, the geese have been flying south.
6. The copier was repaired by the technician in just one hour.
7. Would Gail have left the party so soon?

8. We had been searching the stores for an antique oak table and chairs.
9. On Wednesday, art projects will be displayed by the sixth-graders.
10. Have the tall bushes in front of the post office been pruned by the gardeners?

SENTENCES

Review B Revising Stringy Sentences and Sentences Containing Passive Voice

Some of the following sentences are stringy sentences, and some sentences have verbs in the passive voice. First, identify which sentences are stringy and which have verbs in the passive voice. Then, rewrite each stringy sentence as two or more clear sentences. Rewrite each sentence with a verb in passive voice so the verb is in active voice.

EXAMPLE **1.** Jim's new bicycle was ridden by him on his very first try.
1. passive—Jim rode his new bicycle on his very first try.

1. Our family planned a picnic for Saturday, and the day started off sunny and bright, and suddenly it started to rain, and we ate in the car.
2. A fine nest of twigs and string was built in the apple tree by the pair of robins.
3. When we visited my grandmother, we took a taxi to the airport, and we flew to Chicago, and then we drove for four hours, and we arrived just in time for supper.
4. The printer for my computer made an odd noise, and the paper jammed, and we couldn't remove the jam, and we finally took the printer to the shop for repair.
5. According to this morning's newspaper, the election ballots had been counted before the deadline by the workers at the polls.
6. The fine, dry snow had been blown into drifts three feet high by the strong, north wind.
7. Rachel planned every detail of the party, and then she invited the guests, and she cleaned the house, and she prepared all of the food.
8. The fifty miles of county roads were cleaned and maintained by a crew of only two workers.

9. The eight-week-old kittens were weaned by the mother cat before they were adopted by Eileen.
10. Reid trained every day, and he was in excellent condition, and he competed in many track meets, and he won many medals.

SENTENCES

Combining Sentences

Good writers usually use some short sentences, but they don't use them all the time. An entire paragraph of short sentences makes writing sound choppy. For example, notice how dull and choppy the following paragraph sounds.

> Quicksand is really just sand. The sand is wet. The sand is loose. You can sink in quicksand. It will not actually suck you down. You might get caught in quicksand. You can lie on your back. You can float. Then you can roll or wriggle. Your movements must be slow. You can get to solid ground this way.

Now, see how the writer has revised the paragraph by combining some of the short sentences. Notice how sentence combining has helped to eliminate some repeated words and ideas. The result is a smoother paragraph that has much more variety.

> Quicksand is really just wet, loose sand. You can sink in quicksand, but it will not actually suck you down. If you are caught in quicksand, you can lie on your back and float. Then you can slowly roll or wriggle to solid ground.

You can combine sentences in several different ways. Sometimes you can insert a word or a group of words from one sentence into another sentence. Other times you can combine two related sentences by using a connecting word.

TIPS & TRICKS

To get ideas for a variety of ways to organize your ideas into sentences, look at sentences written by professional authors. Try imitating the style of a favorite author by using similar sentence structures in your own sentences or paragraphs.

Inserting Words

One way to combine two sentences is to pull a key word from one sentence and insert it into the other sentence. Sometimes you can just add the key word to the first sentence and drop the rest of the second sentence. Other times you will need to change the form of the key word before you can insert it.

ORIGINAL Dr. Martin Luther King, Jr., was a civil rights leader. He was an American.

COMBINED Dr. Martin Luther King, Jr., was an **American** civil rights leader. [The noun *American* was inserted as an adjective to modify *civil rights leader.*]

ORIGINAL He was famous for his brilliant speeches. His fame was international.

COMBINED He was **internationally** famous for his brilliant speeches. [The adjective *international* was changed to the adverb *internationally* and was inserted to modify *famous.*]

ORIGINAL Dr. King led the civil rights movement in the early 1960's. The movement was growing.

COMBINED Dr. King led the growing civil rights movement in the early 1960's. [The verb form *growing* was inserted as a participle to modify *civil rights movement.*]

TIPS & TRICKS

When you change the forms of key words, you often add endings such as *–ed, –ing, –ful,* and *–ly* to make adjectives and adverbs.

EXAMPLES
- skill → skill**ed**
- crash → crash**ing**
- use → use**ful**
- quiet → quiet**ly**

SENTENCES

Exercise 6 Combining Sentences by Inserting Words

Each of the following items contains two sentences. Combine the two sentences by taking the italicized key word from the second sentence and inserting it into the first sentence. The directions in parentheses will tell you how to change the form of the key word if you need to do so.

EXAMPLE

1. Chief Joseph was a Nez Perce Indian chief who fought for his people. He was a *brave* fighter. (Add *–ly.*)

1. Chief Joseph was a Nez Perce Indian chief who fought bravely for his people.

1. The name Joseph was given to his father by missionaries. The missionaries were *Christian.*
2. Chief Joseph's name, Hin-mah-too-yah-lat-ket, means "thunder rolling down the mountains." That is his *Nez Perce* name.
3. The United States government ordered the Nez Perce to move from their homeland. The homeland was *beloved* by the Nez Perce.
4. The government wanted to open the Wallowa Valley in Oregon to white settlers. The valley was *beautiful.*
5. Chief Joseph fought the United States Army to defend his people's homeland. The fighting was *fierce.* (Add *–ly.*)
6. When he realized he could not win, he led the Nez Perce band more than one thousand miles. The band was in *retreat.* (Add *–ing.*)
7. The Nez Perce thought that they had escaped. They were *weary.*
8. The soldiers quickly marched two hundred miles to catch the Nez Perce. The soldiers were *determined.*
9. The soldiers easily defeated the Nez Perce band. The Nez Perce band had been *weakened.*
10. Chief Joseph's surrender speech is famous. The speech is *moving.*

Inserting Groups of Words

Often, you can combine two related sentences by taking an entire group of words from one sentence and adding it to the other sentence. When the group of words is inserted, it adds detail to the information in the first sentence.

Reference Note

For more information on **prepositional phrases,** see page 63.

ORIGINAL The first known baseball game was played in 1846. It was played in Hoboken, New Jersey.

COMBINED The first known baseball game was played in 1846 **in Hoboken, New Jersey.** [The prepositional phrase *in Hoboken, New Jersey* was inserted to modify the verb phrase *was played.*]

ORIGINAL The game ended with a score of 23–1. It was played by the New York Baseball Club and the Knickerbockers.

COMBINED **Played by the New York Baseball Club and the Knickerbockers,** the game ended with a score of 23–1. [The participial phrase *Played by the New York Baseball Club and the Knickerbockers* was inserted to modify the noun *game.*]

ORIGINAL The players were all amateurs. They were in the first organized baseball league.

COMBINED The players **in the first organized baseball league** were all amateurs.

ORIGINAL The All-American Girls Professional Baseball League had ten teams at its 1948 peak. The league was the subject of a 1992 movie.

COMBINED The All-American Girls Professional Baseball League**, the subject of a 1992 movie,** had ten teams at its 1948 peak. [The appositive phrase *the subject of a 1992 movie* was inserted to identify or rename the subject, *The All-American Girls Professional Baseball League.*]

ORIGINAL Many people around the world play baseball. They play baseball so they can exercise and have fun.

COMBINED Many people around the world play baseball **to exercise and have fun.** [The infinitive phrase *to exercise and have fun* was inserted. It is used as an adverb, modifying *play.*]

After you combine two sentences, be sure to read your new sentence carefully. Then, ask yourself the following questions:

- Is my new sentence clear?
- Does it make sense?
- Does it sound better than the two shorter sentences?

If you answer "no" to any of the above questions, try to combine the sentences in a different way. Then, ask yourself the questions again.

TIPS & TRICKS

If you move a phrase from one sentence to the *beginning* of the other sentence, you may need to add a comma after the introductory phrase.

Reference Note

For information about and practice using **commas with appositive phrases,** see page 272.

Exercise 7 Combining Sentences by Inserting Word Groups

Combine each pair of sentences by taking the underlined word group from the second sentence and inserting it into the first sentence. Be sure to add commas if they are needed.

EXAMPLE 1. Jorge read *Storm Chaser: Into the Eye of a Hurricane* for his science report. Jorge is a boy in my class.

1. *Jorge, a boy in my class, read* Storm Chaser: Into the Eye of a Hurricane *for his science report.*

1. *Storm Chaser* is an exciting book. It is by Keith Elliot Greenberg.
2. The book is a true story about a pilot named Brian Taggart, who flies a P-3 aircraft. He flies the aircraft directly into dangerous storms.
3. Taggart works for the National Oceanic and Atmospheric Administration. He is trained in the study of weather.
4. He also trained to learn to fly the P-3 at low altitude through hurricanes. He trained for years to learn this skill.
5. The low altitude is very dangerous because there is little time to react to violent wind gusts. The pilots often fly at an altitude of only 1,500 feet.
6. Before the pilots reach the calm eye of the storm, they must fly through dangerous weather. This weather, which includes high winds, heavy rain, hail, and severe air currents, is very dangerous.
7. Scientists aboard this P-3 collect information about hurricanes. The scientists collect this information using computers and other machines.
8. The weather instruments record information about wind speed and barometric pressure changes. The instruments collect this information while the aircraft flies through the hurricane.
9. Pilots like Brian help weather forecasters predict where and when a storm will hit land. These pilots are called "hurricane hunters."
10. During the non-hurricane season, the P-3 pilots work on other weather-related projects. Other weather-related projects include interesting work such as predicting the amount of snowfall for the Winter Olympics.

Using Connecting Words

Another way you can combine sentences is by using connecting words called ***conjunctions.*** Conjunctions allow you to join closely related sentences and sentence parts.

Joining Subjects and Verbs

Sometimes two sentences are so closely related that they have the same subjects or verbs. If two sentences have the same subject, you can combine them by making a ***compound verb.*** If the sentences have the same verb, you can combine them by making a ***compound subject.***

The conjunction you use is important. It tells your reader how the two subjects or verbs are related to one another.

- Use *and* to join similar ideas.

ORIGINAL The Sun Dance is an American Indian tradition. The Spirit Dance is an American Indian tradition.

COMBINED **The Sun Dance and the Spirit Dance** are American Indian traditions. [compound subject]

- Use *but* to join contrasting ideas.

ORIGINAL Mike will cook the main course. Mike will buy the dessert.

COMBINED Mike **will cook** the main course **but will buy** the dessert. [compound verb]

- Use *or* to show a choice between ideas.

ORIGINAL Sara Tallchief may be elected president of the student council. Frances O'Connor may be elected president of the student council.

COMBINED **Sara Tallchief or Frances O'Connor** may be elected president of the student council. [compound subject]

Exercise 8 Combining Sentences by Joining Subjects and Verbs

Use *and, but,* or *or* to combine each of the following pairs of sentences. If the sentences have the same verb, make one sentence with a compound subject. If the sentences have the same

Reference Note

For information about and practice using **conjunctions,** see page 66.

HELP

Coordinating conjunctions such as *and, but,* and *or* are used to join words or word groups that are closely related. This joining of words or word groups is called ***coordination.***

HELP

When you use the conjunction *and* to link two subjects, your new compound subject will be plural. Remember to make the verb plural, too. A verb must agree with the subject in number.

EXAMPLE

Carlos and Hannah play on the same team. [The plural subject *Carlos and Hannah* takes the plural verb *play.*]

SENTENCES

subject, make one sentence with a compound verb. The hints in parentheses will help you.

EXAMPLE 1. The climbing perch is a fish that can walk. The mudskipper is a fish that can walk. (Join with *and.*)

1. The climbing perch and the mudskipper are fish that can walk.

1. Climbing fish have side fins that work much like feet. Mudskippers have side fins that work much like feet. (Join with *and.*)

2. Mudskippers walk on mud flats. Mudskippers even climb trees. (Join with *and.*)

3. Mudskippers use their pectoral fins to move themselves along the ground. They use their tails to launch themselves into the air. (Join with *but.*)

4. The mudskippers absorb oxygen from water filtered through their skin. They also absorb oxygen from the air. (Join with *and.*)

5. Adult mudskippers dig a hole in the mud in which to lay their eggs. They dig another hole in which to live. (Join with *and.*)

6. Mudskippers can hop more than a yard at a time. Mudskippers can catch insects as the insects fly. (Join with *and.*)

7. Walking catfish are native to the East Indies. They have been seen in Florida. (Join with *but.*)

8. Walking catfish might be found in warm, muddy water. Climbing perch might be found in warm, muddy water. (Join with *or.*)

9. Fish farm owners in areas that have walking catfish must protect their fish ponds. They can lose many fish to the walking fish with the big appetite. (Join with *or.*)

10. Walking catfish will live in a large aquarium. They will eat smaller fish in the same tank. (Join with *but.*)

SENTENCES

Joining Sentences

Sometimes you may want to combine two related sentences that express equally important ideas. You can connect the two sentences by using a comma and *and, but,* or *or.* The result is a ***compound sentence.***

ORIGINAL A group of frogs is called an *army*. A group of turtles is called a *bale*.

COMBINED A group of frogs is called an *army*, **and** a group of turtles is called a *bale*.

Other times you may want to combine two sentences that are related in a special way. One sentence helps explain the other sentence by telling *who, what, where, when, why,* or *how.* A good way to combine these sentences is to add a connecting word that shows the special relationship. In this kind of sentence combining, you create a ***complex sentence.***

Reference Note

For more about **complex sentences,** see page 99.

ORIGINAL The drawbridge was pulled up. The enemy knights could not get into the castle.

COMBINED **When** the drawbridge was pulled up, the enemy knights could not get into the castle.

ORIGINAL Their leader had not counted on the princess. The princess knew how to operate the drawbridge.

COMBINED Their leader had not counted on the princess, **who** knew how to operate the drawbridge.

Some connecting words that you can use to create complex sentences are given below. The word that you choose will depend on what you want your sentence to say.

after	before	so that	when	who
although	how	that	whether	whom
as	if	until	which	whose
because	since	what	while	why

HELP

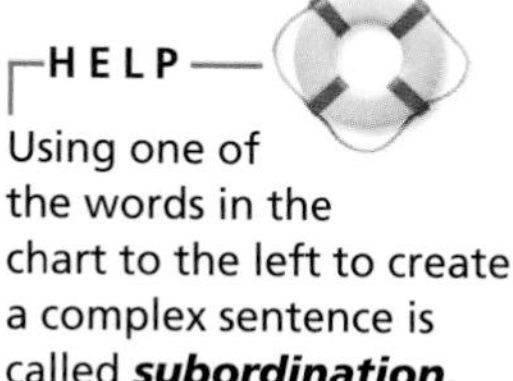

Using one of the words in the chart to the left to create a complex sentence is called ***subordination.***

SENTENCES

MEETING THE CHALLENGE

A compound-complex sentence can help you express complicated ideas and show how they fit together. A compound-complex sentence has two or more independent clauses and at least one subordinate clause. Try combining the short sentences in each item below into a compound-complex sentence.

1. The marching band began to play the first piece. The trumpets were featured in that piece. The trumpet players were at the front of the band's formation.
2. People go on vacation every summer. They pay me for my service. I mow lawns, water plants, and collect mail.

Exercise 9 **Combining Complete Sentences**

Following are ten pairs of short, choppy sentences that need improving. Make each pair into one sentence by using the connecting word given in parentheses. Be sure to change the capitalization and the punctuation where necessary.

EXAMPLE **1.** Planets move quickly. Stars move slowly. (*but*)
1. Planets move quickly, but stars move slowly.

1. I would like to learn more about stars. They are interesting and beautiful. (*because*)
2. Planets do not give off light of their own. Stars do. (*but*)
3. Some stars are fainter than our sun. Some are many times brighter. (*and*)
4. The sun is just a medium-sized star. It is close enough to the earth to look larger than all the other stars. (*but*)
5. Even the largest stars look like little points of light. They are millions of miles away. (*because*)
6. On a clear night, a person without a telescope can see about 3,000 stars. A person using a three-inch-diameter telescope can see about 600,000 stars. (*while*)
7. The sun changes hydrogen into helium and energy. This energy escapes from the sun in the form of light. (*after*)
8. The sun was formed about five billion years ago. It has enough hydrogen to last many more years. (*although*)
9. Our sun will change. The change will be slow. (*while*)
10. We must continue to study the stars and planets. We will understand how we fit into our vast universe. (*so that*)

Using Transitions

Carefully written sentences help make a reading passage clear and understandable. Sometimes, though, those sentences need some help to show how the ideas are related. If you are telling a story, the reader needs to know what comes first, next, and so on. If you are explaining an idea or how something works, the reader needs to know how the different parts relate to each other—how they connect.

The words that help show how ideas are related are called ***transitional words and phrases.*** They act as signposts to the reader, pointing out relationships between ideas, between sentences, and between paragraphs. They can show similarities and differences; they can show causes and effects; and they can show time, place, and importance. The following chart lists some common transitional words and phrases.

Transitional Words and Phrases		
Showing Similarities	also in addition and	another like too
Showing Differences	although but	however instead
Showing Causes and Effects	as a result because	since so
Showing Time	after before finally first	next second then when
Showing Place	above nearby	here there
Showing Importance	first last	mainly most important

SENTENCES

Exercise 10 Identifying Transitional Words and Phrases

Read the following passage and identify the type of transition that each underlined word or phrase expresses. Write *sim.* for similarity, *dif.* for difference, *C/E* for cause and effect, *time* for time, *place* for place, and *import.* for importance.

EXAMPLE 1. Preparation for a hike is more important than any other detail.

1. *import.*

SENTENCES

[1] Before you begin a hike, you must choose a route. [2] First, study the map, and then determine how far you want to hike. [3] In addition to getting a map if the route is new to you, be sure to talk to someone who has hiked the route before. Maps are very informative, [4] but the knowledge an experienced hiker can share is even more valuable. [5] Then, gather your supplies. [6] Although you may have hiked your chosen route in the spring, a summer hike requires more water and, probably, a hat. [7] Another requirement is additional sunscreen. You don't want to have an accident on the trail [8] since many trails are remote. You are not likely to find a doctor [9] nearby, so brush up on your safety training. Plan to rest occasionally, too, instead of hiking the route all at one try. [10] As a result of your preparation, you are sure to have a great time.

Review C Revising a Paragraph by Combining Sentences

The following paragraph sounds choppy because it has too many short sentences. Use the methods you have learned in this section to combine some of the sentences. After you have revised the paragraph, read the choppy version and the new version aloud. You will notice how much better the paragraph sounds after you have revised it.

EXAMPLE Ancient cities provide information. The information is about how people lived.

Ancient cities provide information about how people lived.

Some of the world's oldest cities have been found in Sumer. Sumer is the land between the Tigris and the Euphrates rivers. These early cities began as villages. The villages were made of farms. Sumerian merchants began to trade with their neighbors in the mountains. The Sumerians sold the mountain people grains. The mountain people sold the Sumerians lumber, stone, and copper. Over five thousand years ago, Sumerians invented a system of writing. They invented their writing system to keep track of their trading. We know much about how ancient Sumerians lived. They left us many written records.

Review D Writing Clear Sentences

The following paragraph is hard to read because it contains some sentence fragments and run-on sentences as well as choppy and stringy sentences. Identify **two** fragments by underlining them; identify **one** run-on sentence by double underlining it; and identify **two** stringy sentences by putting brackets around them. Then, revise those sentences using the methods you have learned. Also, combine sentences in at least **two** other places, and identify **three** transitional words or phrases by circling them.

EXAMPLE Have you ever seen a sumo wrestling match? A style of Japanese wrestling. A goal is to eject the opponent from the ring, another goal is to make the opponent touch the ground with some part of his body other than his feet.

Have you ever seen a sumo wrestling match? Sumo is a style of Japanese wrestling. The goal is to eject the opponent from the ring or to make the opponent touch the ground with some part of his body other than his feet.

Sumo wrestling is an unusual sport, not only because of the unique and impressive appearance of the athletes. On average weigh 330 pounds and dress in traditional loincloths. Sumo is based in myth. It is also based in ritual. There is a myth that the Japanese people gained control of Japan when a god won a sumo match with another leader. From a rival group. The earliest sumo matches, dating back over 1500 years, were rituals performed to ensure

SENTENCES

a good harvest, and sumo later became a way to entertain royalty, and Japan then entered a time of military rule, and sumo wrestlers were used in fighting. When peace returned, sumo became entertainment again, it came to be known as the national sport of Japan. The ritual elements of early sumo remain today. At tournaments, each day opens with a colorful and exciting ritual performed by the wrestlers. The ritual is called *dohyo-iri*. *Dohyo-iri* means "entering the ring." In this ceremony the wrestlers enter the ring, and then the highest ranked wrestler comes into the ring, and he claps and stomps on the ground in a very formal way, and when he is finished other highly ranked wrestlers repeat the clapping and stomping. The ceremony symbolically drives evil spirits away. The world got to see this ceremony when it was part of the 1998 Winter Olympics opening ceremony in Nagano, Japan.

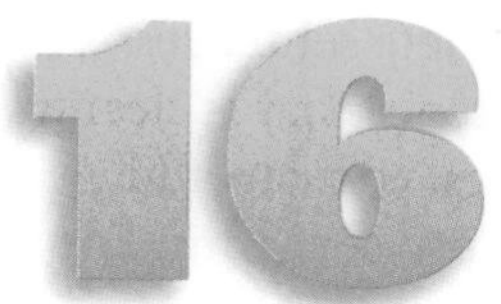

Chapter Review

A. Identifying Sentences, Sentence Fragments, and Run-on Sentences

Identify each of the following word groups as a *sentence,* a *sentence fragment,* or a *run-on sentence.* If a word group is a sentence fragment, rewrite it to make a complete sentence. If a word group is a run-on sentence, rewrite it to make it one or more complete sentences. Remember to use correct capitalization and punctuation.

EXAMPLES
1. Because you know the difference between those kinds of birds.

   1. frag.—Because you know the difference between those kinds of birds, you should make the captions for the photos.

2. Marion left.

   2. sent.

3. The temperature is dropping, I think it will freeze tonight.

   3. run-on—The temperature is dropping. I think it will freeze tonight.

1. The best movie of all the ones showing.
2. I know the person who painted the mural at the downtown library.
3. Stop.
4. Drive two miles, after the water tower, turn left.
5. Went with Georgia to the store for more eggs and flour.
6. That is my uncle, he is a member of the school board.
7. Because Lloyd and Joan have already sold their house.
8. I will go to the orthodontist tomorrow she is going to fit me for a new retainer.
9. The computer crashed again, so I restarted it.
10. Before I had saved enough money to buy a new bicycle.

B. Combining Sentences

Each of the following items contains two complete sentences. Combine these sentences to make a single sentence that is clearer and more interesting. To combine the sentences, you can add connecting words, insert words or phrases, or use compound or complex sentences.

EXAMPLE **1.** The ant carried a large leaf across the sidewalk. Then it carried the leaf up the tree trunk.

1. The ant carried a large leaf across the sidewalk and up the tree trunk.

11. I save money. I have a savings account at my mother's credit union.

12. Taylor will write Grandmother a thank-you note. Grandmother sent Taylor a new sweater.

13. Please remember to give your parents the permission slip. Return it tomorrow after they have signed it.

14. Will you paint your room light blue? Or will you paint it yellow?

15. Mr. Byrd asked Jonah to help arrange the desks. Mr. Byrd is the principal.

C. Revising a Passage to Improve Sentence Style

The passage below contains stringy sentences, sentences containing awkward uses of the passive voice, and sentences that need transitions between them. Rewrite the passage to make it clearer and to improve the sentences.

EXAMPLE What do you do during the summer? Vacation plans are made in some families by the entire family, and vacation plans are made in other families by just the parents, and the children wait excitedly to hear about those plans.

What do you do during the summer? In some families, the entire family makes vacation plans. In other families, just the parents make vacation plans while the children wait excitedly to hear about those plans.

We take a weeklong vacation in the summer, and we sometimes visit my mother's best friend, Barbara. She lives in a small house on an island just off the coast of Florida. She says she likes living there because the beach changes all the time, and it is always new and interesting to her. We were there, and we went for a walk on a very long fishing pier, and a huge sea turtle was seen by several of us. The water was very clear. We could see how big the turtle was. I think its shell was about four feet across. It came up for air, and its head looked almost the size of a human head. Barbara was asked several questions about the turtle. Barbara said that at that beach more turtles are seen now than in earlier years. She said that turtle eggs are sometimes laid in nests in the sand, and people mark where the nests are, and people try not to walk where the nests are, and the baby turtles hatch during a full moon and make their way to the water.

CHAPTER

Sentence Diagramming

1.0 Written and Oral English Language Conventions
Students write and speak with a command of standard English conventions appropriate to this grade level.
1.1 Use simple, compound, and compound-complex sentences.

The Sentence Diagram

A ***sentence diagram*** is a picture of how the parts of a sentence fit together. It shows how the words in the sentence are related.

Subjects and Verbs

Reference Note

For more about **subjects** and **verbs,** see page 7.

To diagram a sentence, first find the simple subject and the simple predicate, or verb, and write them on a horizontal line. Then, separate the subject and verb with a vertical line. Keep any capital letters, but leave out sentence punctuation.

EXAMPLES Dogs bark.

Dogs | bark

Children were singing.

Children | were singing

The preceding examples are easy because each sentence contains only a simple subject and a verb. Now, look at a longer sentence.

EXAMPLE My older brother is studying Arabic in school.

To diagram the simple subject and the verb of this sentence, follow these three steps:

Step 1: Separate the complete subject from the complete predicate.

complete subject	complete predicate
My older brother	is studying Arabic in school.

Step 2: Find the simple subject and the verb.

simple subject	verb
brother	is studying

Step 3: Draw the diagram.

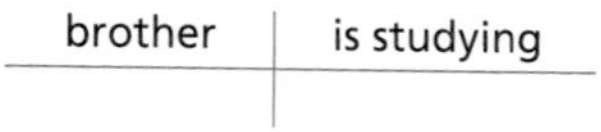

brother | is studying

Exercise 1 **Diagramming Simple Subjects and Verbs**

Diagram the simple subject and verb in each of the following sentences.

EXAMPLES **1.** Aunt Carmen is teaching me to cook.

1. Aunt Carmen | is teaching

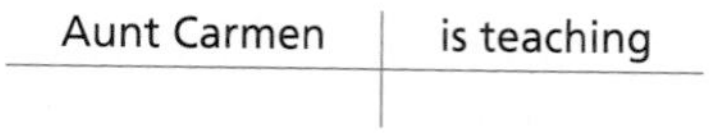

2. The dog sleeps in the garage.

2. dog | sleeps

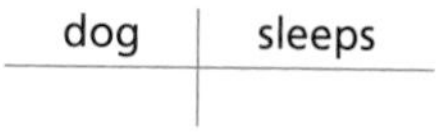

1. My family goes to the store together every Saturday.
2. We shop at the grocery store at the corner of our street.
3. I select the red beans, rice, meat, and cheese.
4. Grandma López must have written the shopping list.
5. Rosita is buying the chile peppers and cilantro.

HELP Remember that simple subjects and verbs may consist of more than one word.

SENTENCES

SENTENCES

Compound Subjects

Reference Note

For more about **compound subjects,** see page 13.

To diagram a compound subject, put the subjects on parallel lines. Then, put the connecting word (the conjunction, such as *and, but,* or *or*) on a dotted line between the subject lines.

EXAMPLE **Koalas** and **kangaroos** are found in Australia.

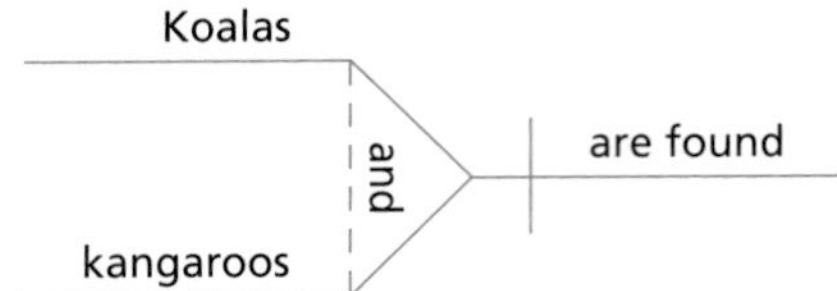

Compound Verbs

Reference Note

For more about **compound verbs,** see page 14.

To diagram a compound verb, put the two verbs on parallel lines. Then, put the conjunction on a dotted line between the verbs.

EXAMPLE Callie **washes** and **dries** the dishes after dinner.

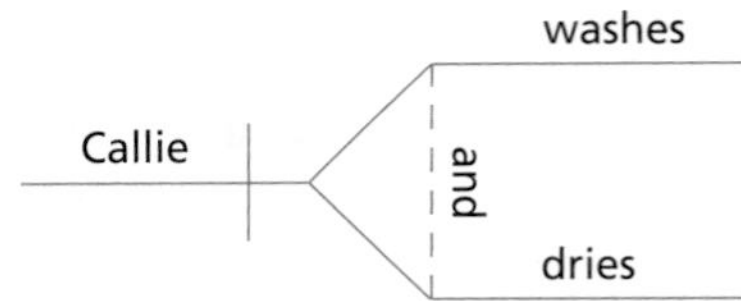

Compound Subjects and Compound Verbs

A sentence with both a compound subject and a compound verb combines the two patterns you just learned.

EXAMPLE The **cat** and her **kittens ate** and then **slept.**

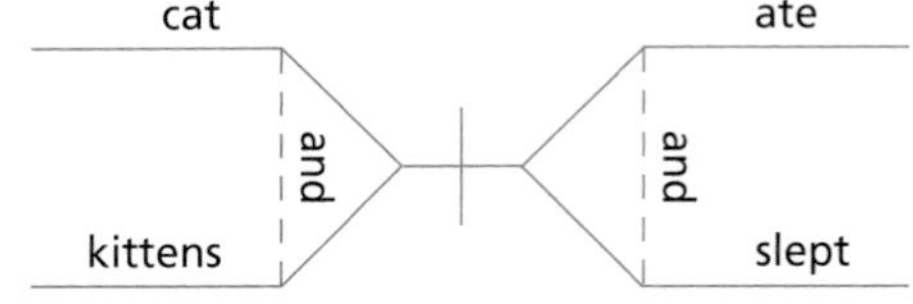

Exercise 2 Diagramming Compound Subjects and Compound Verbs

Diagram the simple subjects and verbs in the following sentences.

HELP

Sentences in Exercise 2 may contain compound subjects, compound verbs, or both.

EXAMPLE 1. Brittany and La Tonya skated and skied last winter.

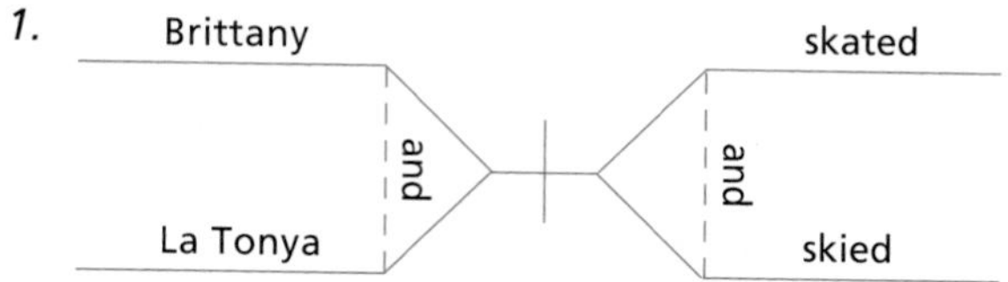

1. Ursula LeGuin and Nicholasa Mohr are my favorite authors.
2. Ms. Sanchez and Mr. Charles teach Spanish.
3. Bill Russell first played and later coached in the NBA.
4. My friends and I hurried home and told our parents the good news.
5. The students and the teacher visited the museum but did not have time for a complete tour.

Questions

To diagram a question, first make the question into a statement without changing or dropping any words. Then, diagram the sentence.

EXAMPLE Can all insects fly? [question]
All insects can fly. [statement]

insects | Can fly

Notice that the diagram uses the capitalization of the original sentence.

Understood Subjects

In an imperative sentence (a request or command) the subject is always understood to be *you.* Place the understood subject *you* in parentheses on the horizontal line.

EXAMPLE Look over there.

(you) | Look

Reference Note

For more information about **questions,** see page 18.

HELP

Remember that in a diagram, the subject always comes first, even if it does not come first in the sentence.

Reference Note

For information about **imperative sentences** and **understood subjects,** see page 18.

SENTENCES

Exercise 3 Diagramming Questions and Commands

Diagram the simple subjects and verbs in the following sentences.

EXAMPLE 1. Please wash the dishes.

1. (you) | wash

1. Eat the rest of your jambalaya.
2. Do you know much about the Jewish holidays?
3. Where is the driver going?
4. Please help me with these cartons.
5. Why are they standing in line?

Adjectives and Adverbs

Reference Note

For more information about **adjectives,** see page 38.

Adjectives and adverbs are written on slanted lines connected to the words they modify. Notice that possessive pronouns are diagrammed in the same way adjectives are. Also notice that the articles *a, an,* and *the* are included as adjectives.

Adjectives

EXAMPLES **yellow** bird **her best** blouse **a playful** puppy

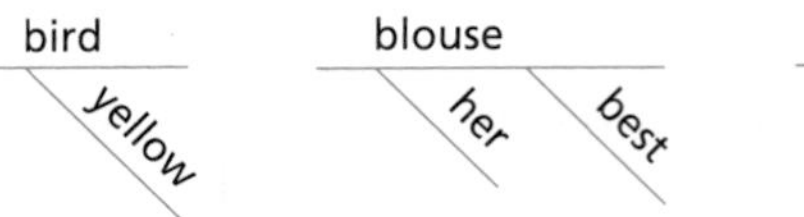

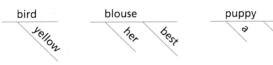

Exercise 4 Diagramming Sentences with Adjectives

Diagram the subjects, verbs, and adjectives in the following sentences.

EXAMPLE 1. A strong, cold wind blew all night.

1. My favorite singer is coming to town.
2. The long, grueling hike tired us.
3. Red, ripe tomatoes grow there.
4. The two brave astronauts stepped into space.
5. Is a funny movie playing downtown?

Adverbs

When an adverb modifies a verb, the adverb is placed on a slanted line below the verb.

EXAMPLES wrote **quickly** walked **there slowly**

When an adverb modifies an adjective or another adverb, it is placed on a slanted line connected to the word it modifies.

EXAMPLES **incredibly** large poster runs **very** fast

Reference Note
For more about **adverbs,** see page 59.

SENTENCES

Exercise 5 Diagramming Sentences with Adverbs

Diagram the subjects, verbs, adjectives, and adverbs in the following sentences.

EXAMPLE **1.** We almost always recycle newspapers.

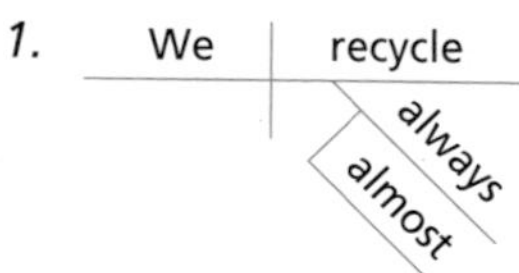

1. Our team recently won the championship.
2. That new band plays very loudly.
3. Her two brothers visited Chinatown yesterday.

4. The busy librarian almost never rests.
5. An extremely unusual program will be broadcast tonight.

SENTENCES

Prepositional Phrases

Reference Note

For more information about **prepositional phrases,** see page 63.

Prepositional phrases are diagrammed below the words they modify. Write the preposition on a slanting line. Then, write the object of the preposition on a horizontal line connected to the slanting line. Notice that the slanting line extends a little beyond the horizontal line.

Adjective Phrases

Reference Note

For more about **adjective phrases,** see page 79.

EXAMPLES time **of day** several **in a row**

time
of
day

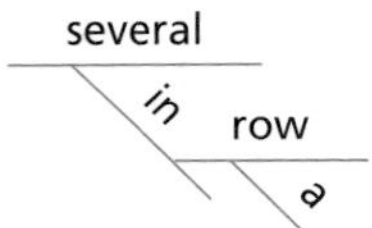

Adverb Phrases

Reference Note

For more about **adverb phrases,** see page 83.

EXAMPLES walked **on the moon** are ready **for the test**

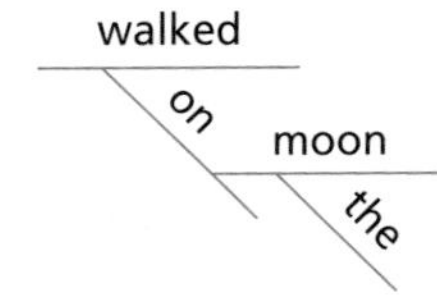

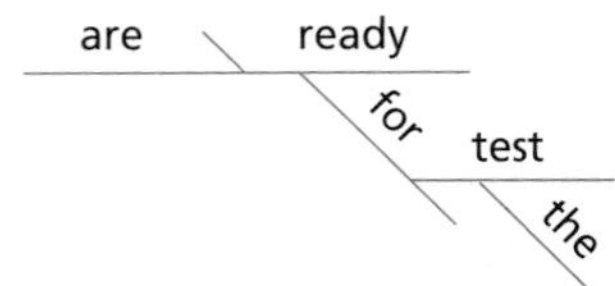

moves quickly **for an old dog**

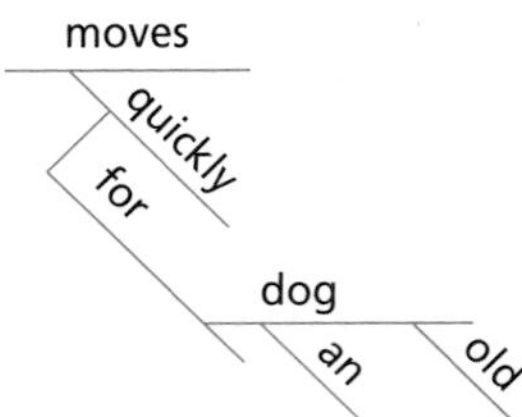

Exercise 6 Diagramming Sentences with Prepositional Phrases

Diagram the following sentences.

EXAMPLE **1.** The freighter slowed for the first lock.

1. freighter | slowed
The
for lock
the first

1. Tamales are wrapped in corn husks.
2. The soccer team from Brazil ran onto the field.
3. My friend from India skis very well.
4. The students in his class went to the library.
5. Catherine Zeta-Jones and Will Smith may star in that new movie.

SENTENCES

Direct and Indirect Objects

Direct Objects

A direct object is diagrammed on the horizontal line with the subject and verb. A short vertical line separates the direct object from the verb.

Reference Note

For more about **direct objects,** see page 107.

EXAMPLE We have been playing **CD's.**

We | have been playing | CD's

Compound Direct Objects

EXAMPLE Rachel enjoys **soccer** and **basketball.**

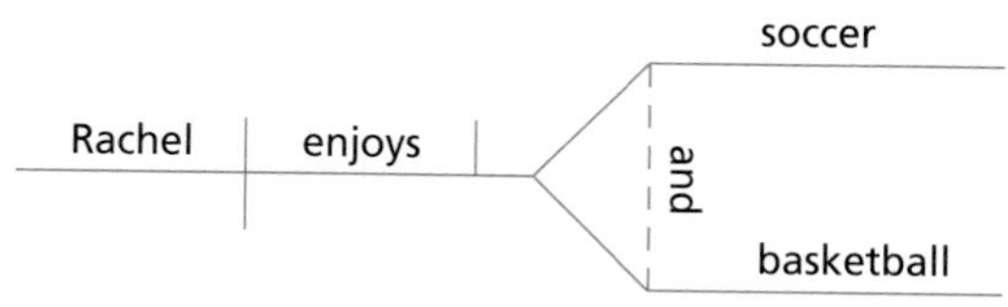

Reference Note

For more information about **compound direct objects,** see page 107.

SENTENCES

Indirect Objects

Reference Note
For more about **indirect objects,** see page 109.

The indirect object is diagrammed on a horizontal line beneath the verb. The verb and the indirect object are joined by a slanting line.

EXAMPLE Dad fixed **us** some spaghetti.

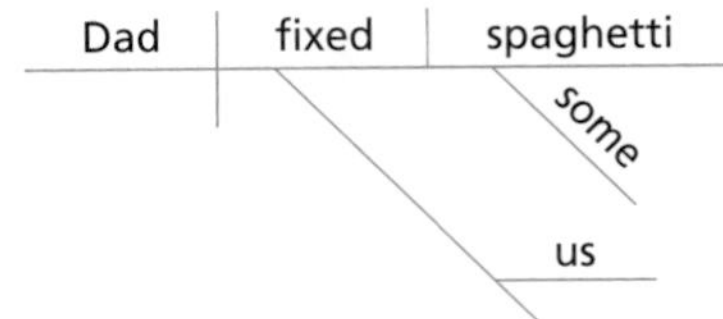

Compound Indirect Objects

Reference Note
For more information about **compound indirect objects,** see page 110.

EXAMPLE Marisa gave her **brother** and **me** some grapes.

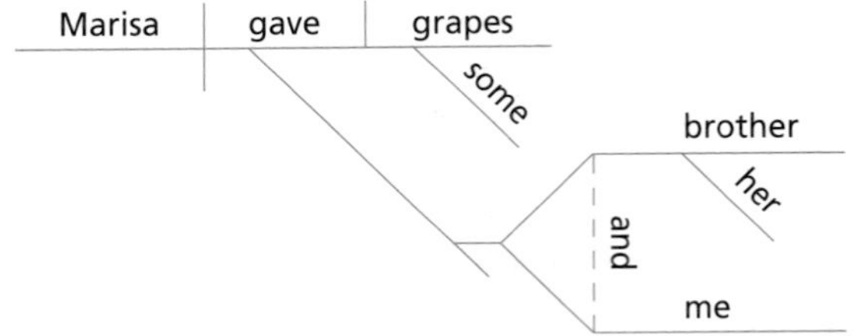

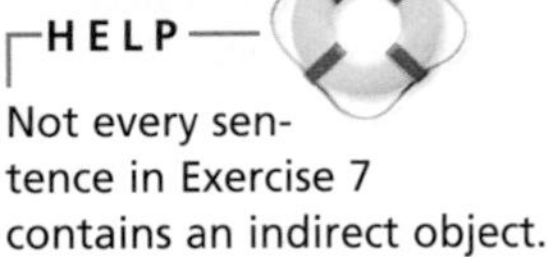

Not every sentence in Exercise 7 contains an indirect object.

Exercise 7 Diagramming Direct Objects and Indirect Objects

Diagram the following sentences.

EXAMPLE 1. He handed her the report.

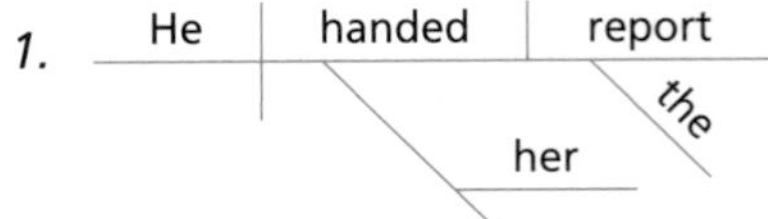

1. Amy Tan wrote that book.
2. Marcus made a touchdown.
3. My grandmother knitted me a sweater.
4. Marilyn won a bronze medal in the Special Olympics.
5. I bought Jolene and her sister a present.

Subject Complements

A subject complement is diagrammed on the horizontal line with the subject and the verb. The complement comes after the verb. A line slanting toward the subject separates the subject complement from the verb.

Predicate Nominatives

EXAMPLE Mickey Leland was a famous **congressman** from Texas.

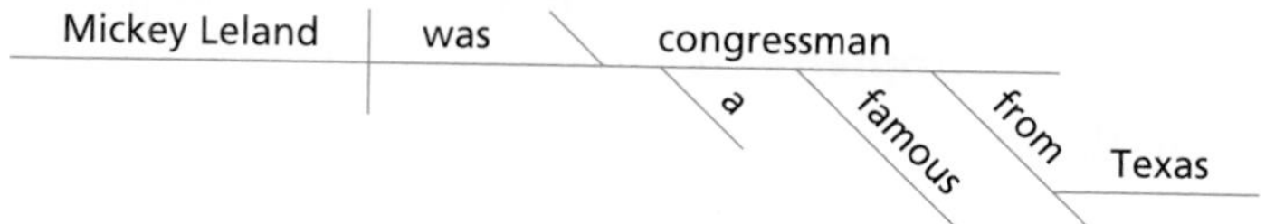

Reference Note

For more information about **predicate nominatives,** see page 112.

Compound Predicate Nominatives

EXAMPLE Suzanne is a **singer** and a **dancer**.

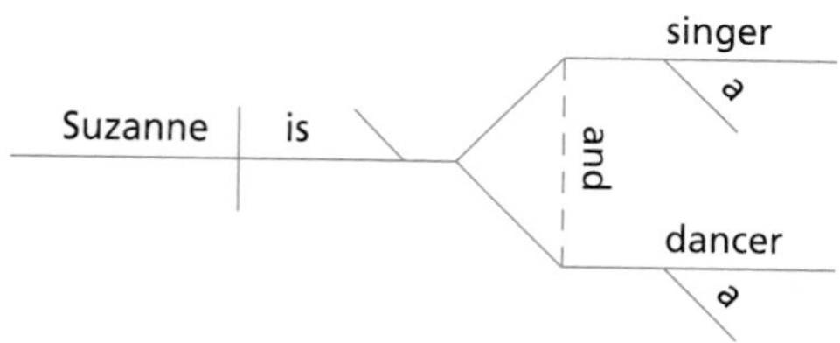

Reference Note

For more information on **compound predicate nominatives,** see page 113.

Predicate Adjectives

EXAMPLE The guitarist was very **skillful.**

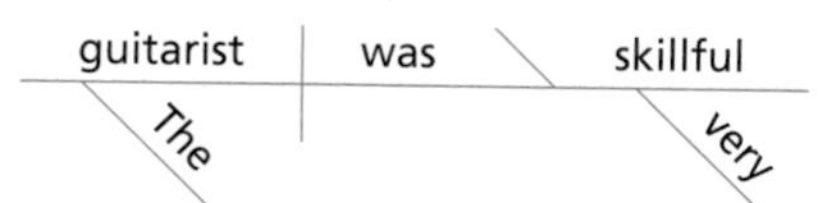

Reference Note

For more information on **predicate adjectives,** see page 114.

SENTENCES

Compound Predicate Adjectives

EXAMPLE They were **weary** but **patient**.

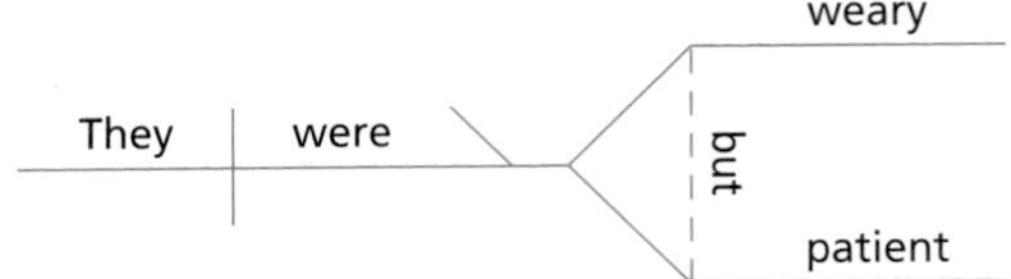

Reference Note

For more about **compound predicate adjectives,** see page 115.

Exercise 8 **Diagramming Sentences with Subject Complements**

Diagram the following sentences.

EXAMPLE 1. Ms. Chang is an excellent teacher and a fine lawyer.

1.

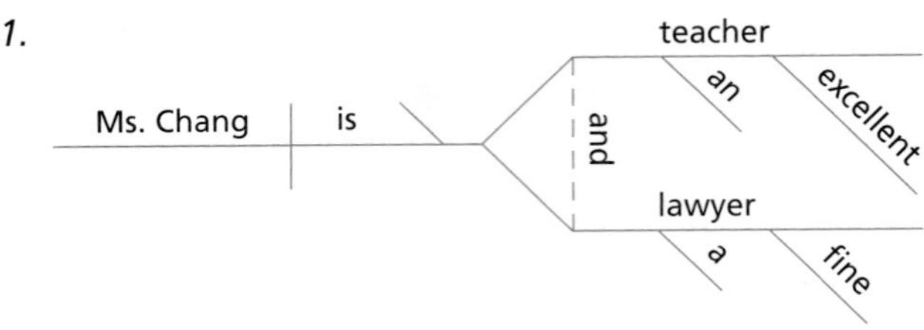

1. Your little brother looks quite sleepy.
2. Ossie Davis was an actor and a playwright.
3. These CD's are oldies but goodies.
4. Coyote is a trickster in American Indian mythology.
5. The library is full of interesting books.

Subordinate Clauses

Adjective Clauses

Diagram an adjective clause by connecting it with a broken line to the word it modifies. Draw the broken line between the relative pronoun and the word to which it relates. The adjective clause is diagrammed below the independent clause.

Reference Note

For more information about **independent clauses,** see page 89. For more about **adjective clauses,** see pages 91 and 214. For more about **relative pronouns,** see pages 37 and 214.

EXAMPLE Certain land crabs **that are found in Cuba** can run fast.

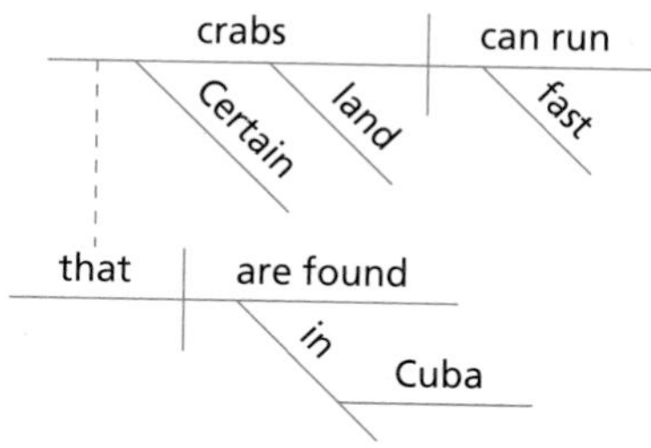

Adverb Clauses

Diagram an adverb clause by using a broken line to connect the adverb clause to the word it modifies. Place the subordinating conjunction that introduces the adverb clause on the broken line. The adverb clause is diagrammed below the independent clause.

EXAMPLE **When Halley's Comet returns,** I will be a very old man.

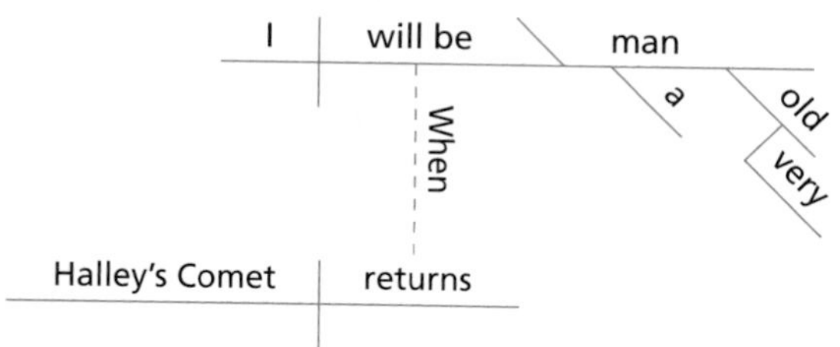

PEANUTS reprinted by permission of United Feature Syndicate, Inc.

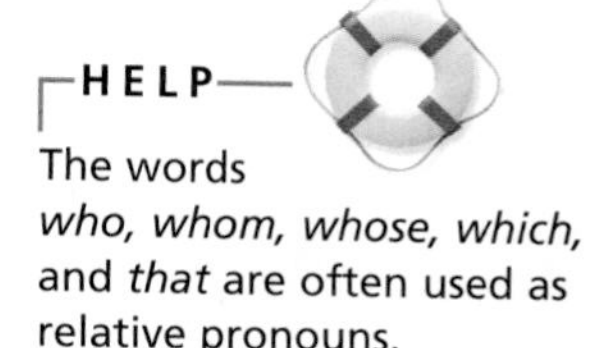

The words *who, whom, whose, which,* and *that* are often used as relative pronouns.

Reference Note

For more information about **adverb clauses,** see page 93. For a list of **subordinating conjunctions,** see page 90.

HELP

The words *after, because, if, since, unless, when,* and *while* are often used as subordinating conjunctions.

SENTENCES

Exercise 9 **Diagramming Sentences with Adjective Clauses and Adverb Clauses**

Diagram the following sentences.

EXAMPLE **1.** If you go to the library, will you return this book?

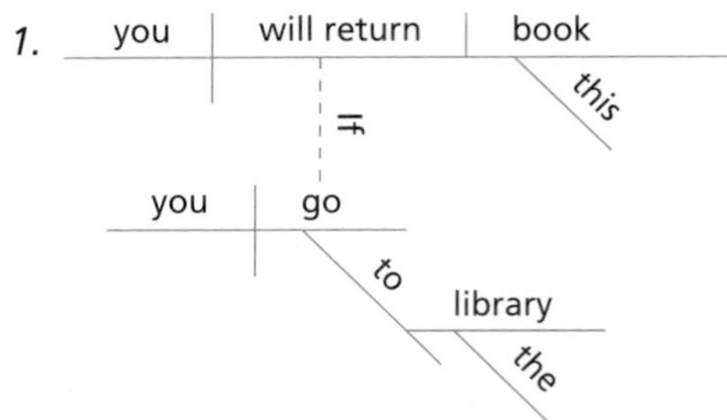

1. Mark Twain wrote books that are famous.
2. When you visit, the park will be open.
3. After Dawn saw the pandas, she wrote a report about them.
4. The people who were invited will see the performance.
5. Replace the scissors where you found them.

The Kinds of Sentence Structure

Simple Sentences

Reference Note

For more about **simple sentences,** see page 96.

A simple sentence contains one independent clause.

EXAMPLE The coach gave Alfonso a pat on the back. [one independent clause]

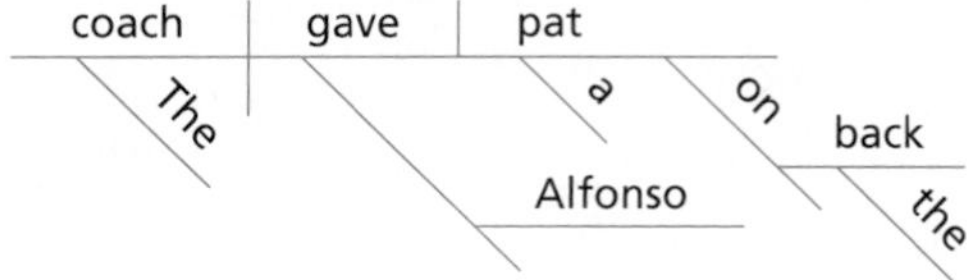

Compound Sentences

A compound sentence contains at least two independent clauses. The second independent clause in a compound sentence is diagrammed below the first and is joined to it by a coordinating conjunction.

EXAMPLE Ostriches walk in a funny way, but they can run fast. [two independent clauses]

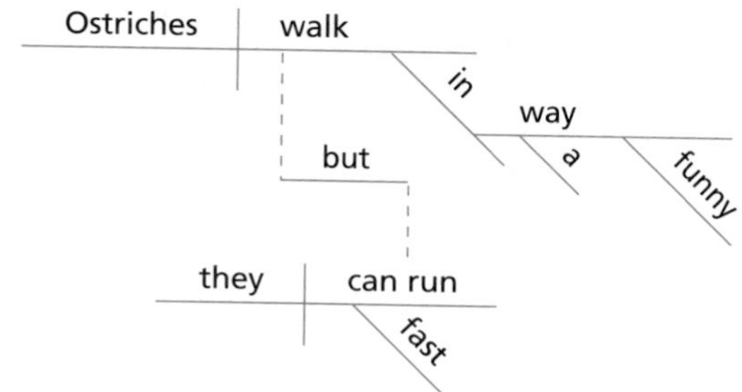

Reference Note

For more information about **compound sentences,** see page 97. For more about **coordinating conjunctions,** see page 66.

SENTENCES

NOTE The coordinating conjunctions are *and, but, for, nor, or, so,* and *yet*.

Exercise 10 Diagramming Compound Sentences

Diagram the following compound sentences.

EXAMPLE **1.** Genna went to the mall, but I stayed home.

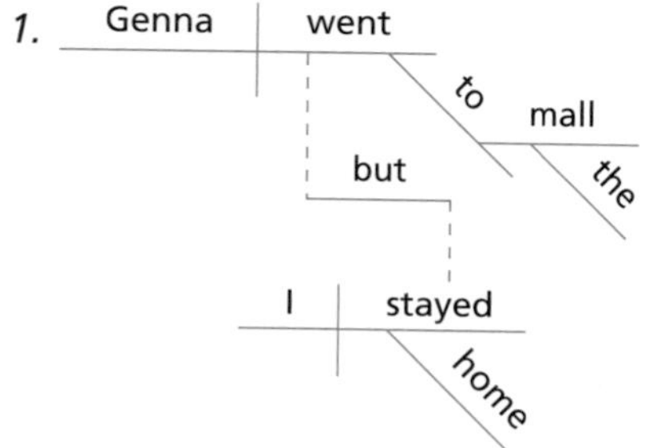

1. Lisa likes soccer, but I prefer basketball.
2. Gabriela Mistral is a poet, but she has also written essays.
3. Cactuses are desert plants, yet they can grow in milder climates.
4. I can give Jewel the news tonight, or you can call her now.
5. Chinese immigrants worked on the railroad in the West, but Irish immigrants built the railroad in the East.

SENTENCES

Complex Sentences

A complex sentence contains one independent clause and at least one subordinate clause.

Reference Note

For more about **complex sentences,** see page 99.

EXAMPLE Leon received a letter that was mailed from Germany. [one independent clause and one subordinate clause]

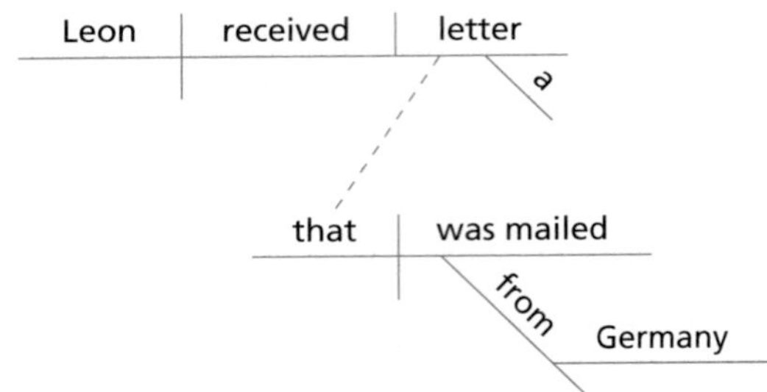

Compound-Complex Sentences

A compound-complex sentence contains two or more independent clauses and at least one subordinate clause.

Reference Note

For more about **compound-complex sentences,** see page 100.

EXAMPLE After we rehearse this scene, we will move to another room, and the stage crew will work on the set. [two independent clauses and one subordinate clause]

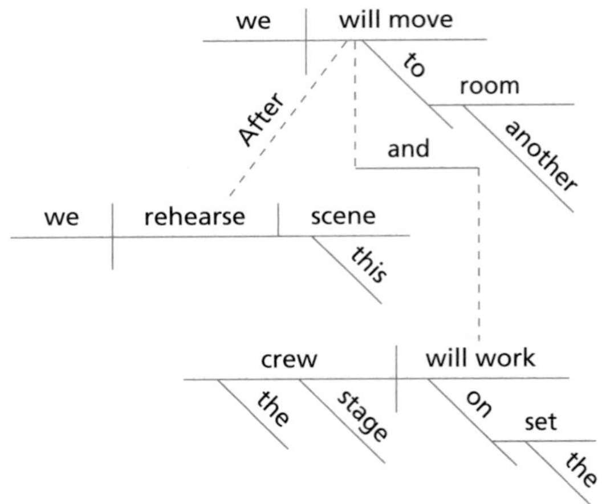

Exercise 11 Diagramming Complex and Compound-Complex Sentences

Diagram the following complex and compound-complex sentences.

EXAMPLE **1.** If the Bulldogs win their last two games, they will finish in first place.

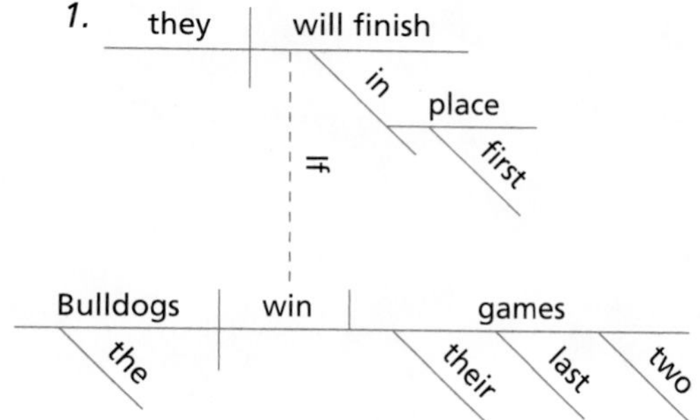

1. Hector walked to school because his bicycle had a flat tire.
2. Rosa was the contestant who knew the correct answer.
3. Unless the rain stops soon, the umpire will cancel the game.
4. As the lights dimmed, the audience grew quiet.
5. The student that designs the best cover receives a free yearbook, so many students will be entering designs.

SENTENCES

PART 3 Resources

GO TO: go.hrw.com
KEYWORD: HLLA

The History of English

Origins and Uses

A Changing Language

No one knows exactly when or how English got started. We do know that English and many other modern-day languages come from an early language that was spoken thousands of years ago. The related languages still resemble that parent language, just as you resemble your parents. For example, notice how similar the words for *mother* are in the following modern-day languages.

ENGLISH	mother	FRENCH	mère
SPANISH	madre	ITALIAN	madre
SWEDISH	moder		

Over 1,500 years ago, a few small tribes of people invaded the island that is now Britain. These tribes, called the Angles and Saxons, spoke the earliest known form of English, called ***Old English.*** Old English was very different from the English we speak.

English continued to evolve through a form known as ***Middle English.*** While our language has always changed and grown, some of our most basic words have been around since the very beginning.

EARLY WORD			
hand	dohtor	andswaru	hleapan
PRESENT-DAY WORD			
hand	daughter	answer	leap

Changes in Meaning It may be hard to believe that the word *bead* once meant "prayer." Many English words have changed meaning over time. Some of these changes have been slight. Others have been more obvious. Below are a few examples of words that have changed their meanings.

naughty—In the 1300s, *naughty* meant "poor or needy." In the 1600s, the meaning changed to "poorly behaved."

lunch—In the 1500s, a *lunch* was a large chunk of something, such as bread or meat.

caboose—*Caboose* entered the English language in the 1700s when it meant "the kitchen of a ship."

Even today the meanings of words may vary depending on where they are used. For example, in America a *boot* is a type of shoe, but in Great Britain, a *boot* may refer to the trunk of a car.

Changes in Pronunciation and Spelling

If you traveled back in time a few hundred years, you would probably have a hard time understanding spoken and written English.

- **Changes in pronunciation** English words used to be pronounced differently from the way they are pronounced today. For example, in the 1200s, people pronounced *bite* like *beet* and *feet* like *fate.* They also pronounced the vowel sound in the word *load* like our word *awe.*

  You may have wondered why English words are not always spelled as they sound. Changes in pronunciation help account for many strange spellings in English. For example, the *w* that starts the word *write* was not always silent. Even after the *w* sound that started the word *write* was dropped, the spelling stayed the same. The *g* in *gnat* and the *k* in *knee* were once part of the pronunciations of the words, too.

- **Changes in spelling** The spellings of many words have changed over time. Some changes in spelling have been accidental. For example, *apron* used to be spelled *napron.* People mistakenly attached the *n* to the article *a*, and *a napron* became *an apron.* Here are some more examples of present-day English words and their early spellings.

EARLY SPELLING			
jaile	locian	slæp	tima
PRESENT-DAY SPELLING			
jail	look	sleep	time

- **British vs. American spelling and pronunciation** Pronunciations and spellings still vary today. For instance, the English used in Great Britain differs from the English used in the United States. In Great Britain, people pronounce *bath* with the vowel sound of *father* instead of the vowel sound of *cat.* The British also tend to drop the *r* sound at the end of words like *copper.* In addition, the British spell some words differently from the way people in the United States do.

AMERICAN		
theater	pajamas	labor
BRITISH		
theatre	pyjamas	labour

Word Origins

English grows and changes along with the people who use it. New words must be created for new inventions, places, or ideas. Sometimes, people borrow words from other languages to create a new English word. Other times, people use the names of people or places as new words.

- **Borrowed words** As English-speaking people came into contact with people from other cultures and lands, they began to borrow words. English has borrowed hundreds of thousands of words from French, Hindi, Spanish, African languages, and many other

RESOURCES

languages spoken around the world. In many cases, the borrowed words have taken new forms.

FRENCH ange ENGLISH angel	HINDI champo ENGLISH shampoo
KIMBUNDU mbanza ENGLISH banjo	SPANISH patata ENGLISH potato

- **Words from names** Many things get their names from the names of people or places. For example, in the 1920s, someone in Bridgeport, Connecticut, discovered a new use for the pie plates from the Frisbie Bakery. He turned one upside down and sent it floating through the air. The new game sparked the idea for the flying plastic disk of today.

RESOURCES

Dialects of American English

You probably know some people who speak English differently from the way you do. Different groups of people use different varieties of English. The kind of English we speak sounds most normal to us even though it may sound unusual to someone else. The form of English a particular group of people speaks is called a ***dialect.*** Everyone uses a dialect, and no dialect is better or worse than another.

Ethnic Dialects Your cultural background can make a difference in the way you speak. A dialect shared by people from the same cultural group is called an ***ethnic dialect.*** Because Americans come from many cultures, American English includes many ethnic dialects. One of the largest ethnic dialects is the Black English spoken by many African Americans. Another is the Hispanic English of many people whose families come from places such as Mexico, Central America, or Cuba.

Regional Dialects Do you *make* the bed or *make up* the bed? Would you order a *sub* with the *woiks* or a *hero* with the *werks*? In the evening, do you eat *supper* or *dinner*? How you answer these questions is probably influenced by where you live. A dialect shared by people from the same area is called a ***regional dialect.*** Your regional dialect helps determine what words you use, how you pronounce words, and how you put words together.

Not everyone from a particular group speaks that group's dialect. Also, an ethnic or regional dialect may vary depending on the speaker's individual background and place of origin.

Standard American English

Every dialect is useful and helps keep the English language colorful and interesting. However, sometimes it is confusing to try to communicate using two different dialects. Therefore, it is important to be familiar with ***standard American English.*** Standard English is the most commonly understood variety of English. In this textbook you can find some of the rules for using standard English. Language that does not follow these rules and guidelines is called ***nonstandard English.*** Nonstandard English is considered inappropriate in many formal situations.

NONSTANDARD I don't want no more spinach.

STANDARD I don't want **any** more spinach.

NONSTANDARD Jimmy was fixing to go hiking with us.

STANDARD Jimmy was **about** to go hiking with us.

Formal and Informal Read the following sentences.

Many of my friends are excited about the game.

A bunch of my friends are psyched about the game.

Both sentences mean the same thing, but they have different effects. The first sentence is an example of ***formal English,*** and the second sentence is an example of ***informal English.***

Formal and informal English are each appropriate for different situations. For instance, you would probably use the formal example if you were talking to a teacher about the game. If you were talking to a friend, however, the second sentence might sound natural. Formal English is frequently used in news reports and in schools and businesses.

■ **Colloquialisms** Informal English includes many words and expressions that are not appropriate in more formal situations. The most widely used informal expressions are *colloquialisms.* ***Colloquialisms*** are colorful words and phrases of everyday conversation. Many colloquialisms have meanings that are different from the basic meanings of words.

EXAMPLES

I wish Gerald would *get off my case.*

Don't get *all bent out of shape* about it.

We were about to *bust* with laughter.

■ **Slang** ***Slang*** words are made-up words or old words used in new ways. Slang is highly informal language. It is usually created by a particular group of people, such as students or people who hold a particular job, like computer technicians or artists. Often, slang is familiar only to the groups that invent it.

Sometimes slang words become a lasting part of the English language. Usually, though, slang falls out of style quickly. The slang words in the sentences below will probably seem out of date to you.

That was a really *far-out flick.*

Those are some *groovy duds* you're wearing.

I don't have enough *dough* to buy a movie ticket.

Test Smarts

Taking Standardized Tests in Grammar, Usage, and Mechanics

Becoming "Test-Smart"

Standardized achievement tests, like other tests, measure your skills in specific areas. Standardized achievement tests also compare your performance to the performance of other students at your age or grade level. Some language arts standardized tests measure your skill in using correct capitalization, punctuation, sentence structure, and spelling. Such tests sometimes also measure your ability to evaluate sentence style.

The most important part of preparing for any test, including standardized tests, is learning the content on which you will be tested. To do this, you must

- listen in class
- complete homework assignments
- study to master the concepts and skills presented by your teacher

In addition, you also need to use effective strategies for taking a standardized test. The following pages will teach you how to become test-smart.

General Strategies for Taking Tests

1. **Understand how the test is scored.** If no points will be taken off for wrong answers, plan to answer every question. If wrong answers count against you, plan to answer only questions you know the answer to or questions you can answer with an educated guess.

2. **Stay focused.** Expect to be a little nervous, but focus your attention on doing the best job possible. Try not to be distracted with thoughts that aren't about the test questions.

3. **Get an overview.** Quickly skim the entire test to get an idea of how long the test is and what is on it.

4. **Pace yourself.** Based on your overview, figure out how much time to allow for each section of the test. If time limits are stated for each section, decide how much time to allow for each item. Pace yourself, and check every five to ten minutes to see if you need to work faster. Try to leave a few minutes at the end of the testing period to check your work.

5. **Read all instructions.** Read the instructions for each part of the test carefully. Also, answer the sample questions to be sure you understand how to answer the test questions.

6. **Read all answer choices.** Carefully read *all* of the possible answers before you choose an answer. Note how each possible answer differs from the others. You may want to make an *x* next to each answer choice that you rule out.

7. **Make educated guesses.** If you do not know the answer to a question, see if you can rule out one or more answers and make an educated guess. Don't spend too much time on any one item, though. If you want to think longer about a difficult item, make a light pencil mark next to the item number. You can go back to that question later.

8. **Mark your answers.** Mark the answer sheet carefully and completely. If you plan to go back to an item later, be sure to skip that number on the answer sheet.

9. **Check your work.** If you have time at the end of the test, go back to check your answers. This is also the time to try to answer any questions you skipped. Make sure your marks are complete, and erase any stray marks on the answer sheet.

Strategies for Answering Grammar, Usage, and Mechanics Questions

The questions in standardized tests can take different forms, but the most common form is the multiple-choice question. Here are some strategies for answering that kind of test question.

Correcting parts of sentences

One kind of question contains a sentence with an underlined part. The answer choices show several revised versions of that part. Your job is to decide which revised version makes the sentence correct or whether the underlined part is already correct. First, look at each answer carefully. Immediately rule out any answer in which you notice a grammatical error. If you are still unsure of the correct answer, try approaching the question in one of these two ways.

- **Think how you would rewrite the underlined part.** Look at the answer choices for one that matches your revision. Carefully read each possible answer before you make your final choice. Often, only tiny differences exist between the answers, and you want to choose the *best* answer.

- **Look carefully at the underlined part and at each answer choice, looking for one particular type of error, such as an error in capitalization or spelling.** The best way to look for a particular error is to compare the answer choices to see how they differ both from each other and from the underlined part of the question. For example, if there are differences in capitalization, look at each choice for capitalization errors.

After ruling out incorrect answers, choose the answer with no errors. If there are errors in each of the choices but no errors in the underlined part, your answer will be the "no error" or "correct as is" choice.

EXAMPLE

Directions: Choose the answer that is the **best** revision of the underlined words.

1. My neighbor is painting his <u>house and my brother helped him.</u>
   - **A.** house; and my brother is helping him.
   - **B.** house, and my brother had helped him.
   - **C.** house, and my brother is helping him.
   - **D.** Correct as is

Explanation: In the example above, the possible answers contain differences in punctuation and in verb tense. Therefore, you should check each possible answer for errors in punctuation and verb tense.

- **A.** You can rule out this choice because it has incorrect punctuation.
- **B.** This choice creates inconsistent verb tenses, so you can rule out this answer.
- **C.** This choice has correct punctuation and creates consistent verb tenses.
- **D.** You can rule out this choice because the original sentence lacks correct punctuation between the clauses.

Answer: Choice C is the only one that contains no errors, so the oval for that answer choice is darkened.

Correcting whole sentences This type of question is similar to the kind of question previously described. However, here you are looking for mistakes in the entire sentence instead of just an underlined part. The strategies for approaching this type of question are the same as for the other kind of sentence-correction questions. If you don't see the correct answer right away, compare the answer choices to see how they differ. When you find differences, check each choice for errors relating to that difference. Rule out choices with errors. Repeat the process until you find the correct answer.

EXAMPLE

Directions: Choose the answer that is the **best** revision of the following sentences.

1. After Brad mowed the lawn, he swept the sidewalk and driveway, then he took a shower. And washed his hair.
   - **A.** After Brad mowed the lawn, he swept the sidewalk and driveway. Then he took a shower and washed his hair.
   - **B.** After Brad mowed the lawn, he swept the sidewalk and driveway. Then he took a shower, and washed his hair.
   - **C.** After Brad mowed the lawn. He swept the sidewalk and driveway; then he took a shower and washed his hair.
   - **D.** Correct as is

   D

Explanation: The original word groups and answer choices have differences in sentence structure and punctuation, so you should check each answer choice for errors in sentence structure and punctuation.

- **A.** This choice contains two complete sentences and correct punctuation.
- **B.** This choice contains two complete sentences and incorrect punctuation.
- **C.** This choice begins with a sentence fragment, so you can rule it out.
- **D.** You can rule out this choice because the original version contains a sentence fragment.

Answer: Choice A is the only one that contains no errors, so the oval for that answer choice is darkened.

Identifying kinds of errors This type of question has at least one underlined part. Your job is to determine which part, if any, contains an error. Sometimes, you also may have to decide what type of error (capitalization, punctuation, or spelling) exists. The strategy is the same whether the question has one or several underlined parts. Try to identify an error, and check the answer choices for that type of error. If the original version is correct as written, choose "no error" or "correct as is."

EXAMPLE

Directions: Read the following sentences and decide which type of error, if any, is in the underlined part.

1. Marcia, Jim, and Leroy are participating in Saturday's charity marathon. they are hoping to raise one hundred dollars for the new children's museum.

- **A.** Spelling error
- **B.** Capitalization error
- **C.** Punctuation error
- **D.** Correct as is

  C 

Explanation: If you cannot tell right away what kind of error (if any) is in the original version, go through each answer choice in turn.

- **A.** All the words are spelled correctly.
- **B.** The sentences contain a capitalization error. The second sentence incorrectly begins with a lowercase letter.
- **C.** The sentences are punctuated correctly.
- **D.** The sentences contain a capitalization error, so you can rule out this choice.

Answer: Because the passage contains a capitalization error, the oval for answer choice B is darkened.

Revising sentence structure Errors covered by this kind of question include sentence fragments, run-on sentences, repetitive wording, misplaced modifiers, and awkward construction. If you don't immediately spot the error, examine the question and each answer choice for specific types of errors, one type at a time. If you cannot find an error in the original version and if all of the other answer choices have errors, then choose "no error" or "correct as is."

EXAMPLE

Directions: Read the following word groups. If there is an error in sentence structure, choose the answer that best revises the word groups.

RESOURCES

1. Mary Lou arranged the mozzarella cheese and fresh tomatoes. On a platter covered with lettuce leaves.
   A. Mary Lou arranged the mozzarella cheese and fresh tomatoes on a platter covered with lettuce leaves.
   B. Mary Lou arranged the mozzarella cheese and fresh tomatoes, on a platter covered with lettuce leaves.
   C. Mary Lou arranged the mozzarella cheese and fresh tomatoes; on a platter covered with lettuce leaves.
   D. Correct as is

Explanation: The original word groups and answer choices have differences in sentence structure and punctuation.

A. This choice is correctly punctuated and contains a correct, complete sentence.

B. This choice contains an incorrect comma, so you can rule it out.

C. This choice contains an incorrect semicolon, so you can rule it out.

D. The original word groups contain a sentence fragment, so D cannot be correct.

Answer: Choice A is the only one that contains no errors, so the oval for that answer choice is darkened.

Questions about sentence style

These questions are often not about grammar, usage, or mechanics but about content and organization. They may ask about tone, purpose, topic sentences, supporting sentences, audience, sentence combining, appropriateness of content, or transitions. The questions may ask you which is the *best* way to revise the passage, or they may ask you to identify the *main* purpose of the passage. When you see words such as *best*, *main*, and *most likely* or *least likely*, you are not being asked to correct errors; you are being asked to make a judgment about style or meaning.

If the question asks for a particular kind of revision (for example, "What *transition* is needed between sentence 4 and sentence 5?"), analyze each answer choice to see how well it makes that particular revision. Many questions ask for a general revision (for example, "Which is the *best* way to revise the last sentence?"). In such situations, check each answer choice and rule out any choices that have mistakes in grammar, usage, or mechanics. Then, read each choice and use what you have learned in class to judge whether the revision improves the original sentence. If you are combining sentences, be sure to choose the answer that includes all important information, that demonstrates good style, *and* that is grammatically correct.

EXAMPLE

Directions: Choose the answer that shows the **best** way to combine the following sentences.

1. Jacques Cousteau was a filmmaker and author. Jacques Cousteau explored the ocean as a diver and marine scientist.
   A. Jacques Cousteau was a filmmaker and author; Jacques Cousteau explored the ocean as a marine scientist.
   B. Jacques Cousteau was a filmmaker and author, he explored the ocean as a diver and marine scientist.
   C. Jacques Cousteau was a filmmaker

and author who explored the ocean as a diver and marine scientist.

D. Jacques Cousteau was a filmmaker, author, diver, and scientist.

Explanation:

A. Answer choice A is grammatically correct but unnecessarily repeats the subject *Jacques Cousteau* and leaves out some information.

B. Choice B is a run-on sentence, so it cannot be the correct answer.

C. Choice C is grammatically correct, and it demonstrates effective sentence combining.

D. Choice D is grammatically correct but leaves out some information.

Answer: Because answer choice C shows the best way to combine the sentences, the oval for choice C is darkened.

Fill-in-the-blanks This type of question tests your ability to fill in blanks in sentences, giving answers that are logical and grammatically correct. A question of this kind might ask you to choose a verb in the appropriate tense. A different question might require a combination of adverbs (*first, next*) to show how parts of the sentence relate. Another question might require a vocabulary word to complete the sentence.

To approach a sentence-completion question, first look for clue words in the sentence. *But, however,* and *though* indicate a contrast; *therefore* and *as a result* indicate cause and effect. Using sentence clues, rule out obviously incorrect answer choices. Then, try filling in the blanks with the remaining choices to determine which answer choice makes the most sense. Finally, check to be sure your choice is grammatically correct.

EXAMPLE

Directions: Choose the words that **best** complete the sentence.

1. When Jack _____ the dog, the dog _____ water everywhere.

A. washes, splashed

B. washed, will be splashing

C. will have washed, has splashed

D. washed, splashed

Explanation:

A. The verb tenses (present and past) are inconsistent.

B. The verb tenses (past and future) are inconsistent.

C. The verb tenses (future perfect and present perfect) are inconsistent.

D. The verb tenses (past and past) are consistent.

Answer: The oval for choice D is darkened.

Using Your Test Smarts

Remember: Success on standardized tests comes partly from knowing strategies for taking such tests—from being test-smart. Knowing these strategies can help you approach standardized achievement tests more confidently. Do your best to learn your classroom subjects, take practice tests if they are available, and use the strategies outlined in this section. Good luck!

Grammar at a Glance

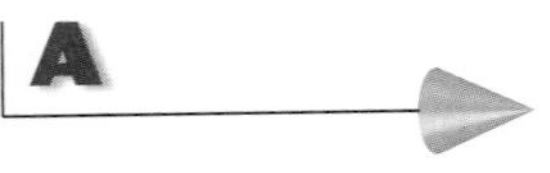

HELP

Grammar at a Glance is an alphabetical list of special terms and expressions with examples and references to further information. When you encounter a grammar or usage problem in the revising or proofreading stage of your writing, look for help in this section first. You may find all you need to know right here. If you need more information, **Grammar at a Glance** will show you where in the book to turn for a more complete explanation. If you do not find what you are looking for in **Grammar at a Glance,** turn to the index.

abbreviation An abbreviation is a shortened form of a word or a phrase.

- **capitalization of** (See page 250.)

TITLES USED WITH NAMES	**M**r.	**D**r.	**J**r.	**P**h.**D.**	
KINDS OF ORGANIZATIONS	**C**o.	**I**nc.	**D**ept.	**C**orp.	
PARTS OF ADDRESSES	**B**lvd.	**A**ve.	**S**t.	**P.O. B**ox	
NAMES OF STATES	[without ZIP Codes]			**K**y. **W**is.	**W**yo. **N.J.**
	[with ZIP Codes]			**KY** **WI**	**WY** **NJ**
TIMES	**A.M.**	**P.M.**	**B.C.**	**A.D.**	

- **punctuation of** (See page 265.)

WITH PERIODS	(See preceding examples.)
WITHOUT PERIODS	VCR UN PBS NASA
	DC (D**.**C**.** without ZIP Code)
	kg ft lb yd cm
	[Exception: in**.**]

action verb An action verb expresses physical or mental activity. (See page 52.)

EXAMPLES Stefan **rode** the bike over the bridge.

Teresa **trimmed** the hedge and **raked** the leaves.

I **thought** about the problem.

active voice Active voice is the voice a verb is in when it expresses an action done by its subject. (See page 393. See also **passive voice.**)

EXAMPLE He **ran** his first marathon last year.

adjective An adjective modifies a noun or a pronoun. (See page 38.)

EXAMPLE **The** Nobles live in **a beautiful, old** house.

adjective clause An adjective clause is a subordinate clause that modifies a noun or a pronoun. (See page 91.)

EXAMPLE The woman **who directs the City Ballet** is from Romania.

adjective phrase A prepositional phrase that modifies a noun or a pronoun is called an adjective phrase. (See page 79.)

EXAMPLE Fruit **from Mr. Park's market** always seems fresher than the produce **in the grocery store.**

adverb An adverb modifies a verb, an adjective, or another adverb. (See page 59.)

EXAMPLE **Occasionally,** when he's feeling **especially** energetic, Dino goes ice-skating.

adverb clause An adverb clause is a subordinate clause that modifies a verb, an adjective, or an adverb. (See page 93.)

EXAMPLE **Before I watch TV,** I have to do my homework.

adverb phrase A prepositional phrase that modifies a verb, an adjective, or an adverb is called an adverb phrase. (See page 83.)

EXAMPLE **At the shore,** Trish and Sandy played volleyball.

affix An affix is a word part that is added before or after a base word or root. (See **prefix** and **suffix.**)

EXAMPLES dis + like = **dis**like

un + wind = **un**wind

complete + ly = complete**ly**

say + ing = say**ing**

agreement Agreement is the correspondence, or match, between grammatical forms. Grammatical forms agree when they have the same number and gender.

- **of pronouns and antecedents** (See page 137.)

SINGULAR **Marcie** could not check out the book because **she** did not have **her** library card with **her.**

PLURAL **Readers** who do not have **their** library cards with **them** cannot check out books.

SINGULAR Every afternoon, **each** of the students is given time to write in **his or her** journal.

PLURAL Every afternoon, **all** of the students are given time to write in **their** journals.

- **of subjects and verbs** (See page 124.)

SINGULAR That **box** of blankets **is** for the homeless shelter.

PLURAL The **blankets** in that box **are** for the homeless shelter.

SINGULAR **Mixed vegetables, roasted potatoes, or rice pilaf comes** with any seafood entree.

PLURAL **Rice pilaf, mixed vegetables, or roasted potatoes come** with any seafood entree.

SINGULAR **Each** of these books **was written** by Amy Tan.

PLURAL **All** of these books **were written** by Amy Tan.

SINGULAR **Neither Eli nor Leo wants** to go skateboarding.

PLURAL **Both Eli and Leo want** to go skateboarding.

SINGULAR Here **is** my **collection** of baseball cards.

PLURAL Here **are** the most valuable baseball **cards** in my collection.

SINGULAR Where **is** my **wallet?**
PLURAL Where **are** the **tickets?**

SINGULAR **He doesn't** know how to play jai alai.
PLURAL **They don't** know how to play jai alai.

antecedent An antecedent is the word or word group that a pronoun stands for. (See page 30.)

EXAMPLE **Patricia** told **Aunt Sally** and **Uncle Ted** that **she** was thinking of **them.** [*Patricia* is the antecedent of *she. Aunt Sally* and *Uncle Ted* are the antecedents of *them.*]

apostrophe

- **to form contractions** (See page 304. See also **contraction.**)

  EXAMPLES hasn't you'll let's o'clock '01

- **to form plurals of letters, numerals, symbols, and words used as words** (See page 307.)

  EXAMPLES *a*'s, *e*'s, *i*'s, *o*'s, and *u*'s

  A's, *I*'s, and *U*'s

  v's and *w*'s

  1900's

  UFO's

  +'s and –'s

  using *and*'s instead of *&*'s

- **to show possession** (See page 300.)

  EXAMPLES the astronaut's spacesuit

  the astronauts' spacesuits

  someone's book bag

  Kim's and Mariah's math projects

  Kim and Mariah's math project

appositive An appositive is a noun or a pronoun placed beside another noun or pronoun to identify or describe it. (See page 272.)

RESOURCES

EXAMPLE	The manager, **Max,** always brought his lunch to work.

appositive phrase An appositive phrase consists of an appositive and its modifiers. (See page 272.)

EXAMPLE	Claude Baker, **the manager of our local branch,** has been in banking for ten years.

article The articles, *a, an,* and *the,* are the most frequently used adjectives. (See page 38.)

EXAMPLE	**The** jetliner, **a** new model, had **an** eventful voyage.

RESOURCES

B

bad, badly (See page 223.)

NONSTANDARD	This tuna salad smells badly.
STANDARD	This tuna salad smells **bad.**

base A base word can stand alone or combine with other word parts to make new words. Prefixes and suffixes can be added to a base to create many different words. (See page 320.)

EXAMPLES	light	trade	civil
	twi**light**	**trade**-off	un**civil**
	lighting	**trade**r	**civil**ly

base form The base form, or infinitive, is one of the four principal parts of a verb. (See page 147.)

EXAMPLE	Lee helped me **lift** the heavy box.

brackets (See page 312.)

EXAMPLES Joshua read from the newspaper, "On Saturday **[**December 1**]**, Mayor Johnston resigned due to poor health."

Refer to the chart (page 485 **[**Section D**]**) for other causes of pollution.

capitalization

- **of abbreviations** (See page 250. See also **abbreviation.**)
- **of first words** (See page 239.)

EXAMPLES **I**n Norse mythology, Thor is the god of thunder, war, and strength.

His sister asked him, "**H**ave you already fed our goldfish today?"

Dear Mrs. Yellowfeather:

Yours truly,

- **of proper nouns and proper adjectives** (See pages 26 and 40.)

Proper Noun	Common Noun
Col. **C**urtis **L.** **B**rown, **J**r.	astronaut
Charles the **W**ise	leader
North **A**merica	continent
Argentina	country
Elk **P**oint, **S**outh **D**akota	city and state
Kodiak **I**sland	island
Yukon **R**iver	body of water
Guadalupe **P**eak	mountain
Cheyenne **M**ountain **Z**oological **P**ark	park
Siuslaw **N**ational **F**orest	forest
Luray **C**averns	caves
the **S**outhwest	region
Twenty-**f**ourth **S**treet	street
World **H**ealth **O**rganization (**WHO**)	organization
Federal **A**viation **A**dministration (**FAA**)	government body
North **C**arolina **S**tate **U**niversity (**NCSU**)	institution
Klondike **G**old **R**ush	historical event
Ice **A**ge	historical period
Little **L**eague **W**orld **S**eries	special event
Hana **M**atsuri, or **F**lower **F**estival	holiday
February, **M**ay, **A**ugust, **N**ovember	calendar items
winter, **s**pring, **s**ummer, **f**all (**a**utumn)	seasons
Nez **P**erce	people
Islam	religion

(continued)

(continued)

Proper Noun	Common Noun
Protestant	religious follower
God (*but* the Greek **g**od **A**pollo)	deity
Rosh **H**ashanah	holy days
Koran	sacred writing
Joshua **T**ree **N**ational **M**onument	monument
Metropolitan **M**useum of **A**rt	building
Caldecott **M**edal	award
Uranus	planet
Canopus	star
Delphinus, or **D**olphin	constellation
HMS ***L**eopard*	ship
***L**unar **P**rospector*	spacecraft
Physical **S**cience **I** (*but* **p**hysical **s**cience)	school subject
Cherokee	people or language

■ **of titles** (See page 253.)

EXAMPLES **M**ayor Maria Sanchez [preceding a name]

Maria Sanchez, the city's **m**ayor [following a name]

Welcome, **M**ayor. [direct address]

Uncle Darnell [*but* our **u**ncle Darnell]

*The **C**all of the **W**ild* [book]

***S**aved by the **B**ell* [television series]

***A**mahl and the **N**ight **V**isitors* [musical composition]

"**O**ver the **R**ainbow" [song]

"**T**he **S**mallest **D**ragonboy" [short story]

"**I** **A**m of the **E**arth" [poem]

***R**eader's **D**igest* [magazine]

*The **W**ashington **P**ost* [newspaper]

***R**ose **I**s **R**ose* [comic strip]

case of pronouns Case is the form a pronoun takes to show how it is used in a sentence. (See page 177.)

NOMINATIVE Louis and **she** were the finalists in the spelling bee. [part of the compound subject of the verb *were*]

The only sixth-graders in the contest were Felicia and **he.** [part of the compound predicate nominative referring to the subject *sixth-graders*]

We volunteers spent Saturday afternoon making piñatas for the fiesta. [subject followed by the noun appositive *volunteers*]

Who painted *Cow's Skull: Red, White and Blue*? [subject of the verb *painted*]

Who is the author of *Yolanda's Genius*? [predicate nominative referring to the subject *author*]

OBJECTIVE On Friday, Ms. Yabuuchi took **them** on a field trip to the planetarium. [direct object of the verb *took*]

Gwen sent **me** an invitation to her family's Kwanzaa party. [indirect object of the verb *sent*]

I went with Carla and **her** to a Japanese tea ceremony. [part of the compound object of the preposition *with*]

The judge awarded each of **us** contestants a certificate of achievement. [object of the preposition *of,* followed by the noun appositive *contestants*]

Whom did the coach select as the captain of the team? [direct object of the verb *did select*]

In the last line of the poem, to **whom** is the speaker referring? [object of the preposition *to*]

POSSESSIVE **Your** birthday is the same day as **mine** is. [*Your* is used as an adjective before the subject *birthday; mine* is used as the subject of the verb *is.*]

clause A clause is a group of words that contains a subject and a verb and that is used as part of a sentence. (See page 89. See also **independent clause** and **subordinate clause.**)

INDEPENDENT CLAUSE she stripped the walls of the living room

SUBORDINATE CLAUSE before I painted them

colon (See page 281.)

before lists

EXAMPLES Amber's favorite fables by Aesop are as follows**:** "Belling the Cat," "The Fox and the Grapes," and "The Frogs Who Wished for a King."

I need to get a few items at the pet shop**:** a bag of colored gravel for the aquarium, a small mirror for the birdcage, and a new collar for my pet Chihuahua.

in conventional situations

EXAMPLES 9**:**15 A.M. Genesis 4**:**1–16

*State Names, Seals, Flags and Symbols***:** *A Historical Guide*

Dear Dr. Kawabata**:**

comma (See page 268.)

in a series

EXAMPLES Dad made chicken quesadillas and topped them with a relish of diced tomatoes**,** onions**,** and chilies.

The book is a collection of stories that tell about the daring exploits of Heracles**,** King Arthur**,** Gilgamesh**,** and fourteen other heroes of ancient times.

in compound sentences

EXAMPLES My neighbor Mr. Kim owns a hardware store**,** and occasionally he hires me to restock the shelves.

We should leave now**,** or we may not get home before curfew.

with introductory elements

EXAMPLES Well**,** were you able to get the pitcher's autograph after the ballgame?

Yes**,** here's the baseball that he autographed!

with interrupters

EXAMPLES The Jaw-Dropper**,** the world's fastest roller coaster**,** is at the amusement park near my house.

On Saturday afternoon, Tyrone, let's play miniature golf after we finish our chores.

■ **in conventional situations**

EXAMPLES San Antonio, Texas, is the home of the Alamo.

I was born on July 17, 1998, in Des Moines, Iowa.

Is 483 Cottonwood Way, Columbia, SC 29250-3840, your current address?

comparison of modifiers (See page 199.)

■ **comparison of adjectives and adverbs**

Positive	Comparative	Superlative
sharp	sharp**er**	sharp**est**
friendly	friendl**ier**	friendl**iest**
loyal	**more** loyal	**most** loyal
cheerfully	**less** cheerfully	**least** cheerfully
good/well	**better**	**best**

■ **comparing two**

EXAMPLES These red grapes are **sweeter** than those.

Jiro speaks the language **more fluently** than Anzu does.

■ **comparing more than two**

EXAMPLES Of the nine planets, Mercury is **nearest** the sun.

Of a gazelle, a cheetah, and an ostrich, which animal can run **most swiftly**?

Alaska is the **largest** of all the U.S. states.

complement A complement is a word or word group that completes the meaning of a verb. (See page 105. See also **direct object, indirect object, predicate nominative** and **predicate adjective.**)

EXAMPLES Ed gave **Martha** a **nod.**

Rei is the **leader** because he is so **organized.**

RESOURCES

complex sentence A complex sentence has one independent clause and at least one subordinate clause. (See page 99.)

EXAMPLES Two of my favorite writers are Katherine Paterson, who wrote *Bridge to Terabithia,* and Beverly Cleary, who wrote *Dear Mr. Henshaw.* [one independent clause and two subordinate clauses]

When Jason and I were stargazing last night, we clearly saw the planets Venus, Mars, Jupiter, and Saturn. [one subordinate clause and one independent clause]

compound-complex sentence A compound-complex sentence has two or more independent clauses and at least one subordinate clause. (See page 100.)

EXAMPLES Most people think of dolphins as gentle, playful creatures, but as the documentary film shows, they can become fiercely aggressive predators in the wild. [one subordinate clause between two independent clauses]

When we were in Boston last summer, we visited The Computer Museum; we were especially impressed by the exhibit called The Giant Walk-Through Computer. [one subordinate clause followed by two independent clauses]

compound sentence A compound sentence has two or more independent clauses and no subordinate clauses. (See page 97.)

EXAMPLE This Saturday, the Library Club at our school will hold a book fair; the price of each hardcover book will be one dollar, and the price of each paperback will be fifty cents. [three independent clauses]

compound subject A compound subject is made up of two or more subjects that are connected by a conjunction and have the same verb. (See page 13.)

EXAMPLES **Spaghetti** or **lasagna** will be served at the banquet.

Do **Alma, Kelsey,** and **Liz** want to join us for lunch?

compound verb A compound verb consists of two or more verbs that are joined by a conjunction and have the same subject. (See page 14.)

EXAMPLES My aunt Martha **grows** her own vegetables and **shares** them with her neighbors.

Lane **tumbled** and **slid** down the steep incline.

conjunction A conjunction joins words or groups of words. (See page 66.)

EXAMPLE **Both** Sy **and** Ben went to the Chinese restaurant, **but** they had to wait before being served, **for** the power was out.

contraction A contraction is a shortened form of a word, a numeral, or a group of words. Apostrophes in contractions indicate where letters or numerals have been omitted. (See page 304. See also **apostrophe.**)

EXAMPLES we'd [we had *or* we would] it's [it is *or* it has]

who's [who is *or* who has] won't [will not]

'98 [a year ending in *98*] o'clock [of the clock]

coordinating conjunction A coordinating conjunction joins words or word groups that are used in the same way. (See page 66.)

EXAMPLES You can have strawberries **or** peaches for dessert.

The squirrels chattered **and** barked at the blue jays.

coordination Coordination is the use of a conjunction to link ideas of approximately equal importance. (See page 401. See also **coordinating conjunction.**)

EXAMPLES **Apricots and raspberries** are my favorite fruits.

Dan likes **canoeing** on Inks Lake **and camping.**

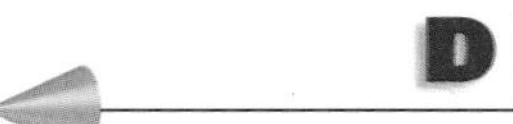

dashes (See page 311.)

EXAMPLES That CD—thanks for letting me borrow it—has become one of my favorites.

I thought I hung my coat on the—oh, there it is.

declarative sentence A declarative sentence makes a statement and is followed by a period. (See page 18.)

EXAMPLE Birmingham is the second-largest city in the United Kingdom**.**

dependent clause (See **subordinate clause.**)

direct object A direct object is a word or word group that receives the action of the verb or shows the result of the action. A direct object answers the question *Whom?* or *What?* after a transitive verb. (See page 107.)

EXAMPLE Ms. Echavarría saw **John** and **Peter.**

double comparison A double comparison is the nonstandard use of two comparative forms (usually *more* and *–er*) or two superlative forms (usually *most* and *–est*) to express comparison. In standard usage, the single comparative form is correct. (See page 206.)

NONSTANDARD King's Holly, a shrub growing in Tasmania, is considered the world's most oldest living plant.

STANDARD King's Holly, a shrub growing in Tasmania, is considered the world's **oldest** living plant.

double negative A double negative is the nonstandard use of two or more negative words to express a single negative idea. (See page 209.)

NONSTANDARD Without her eyeglasses, Ally couldn't hardly read the letters in the bottom line of the eye chart.

STANDARD Without her eyeglasses, Ally **could hardly** read the letters in the bottom line of the eye chart.

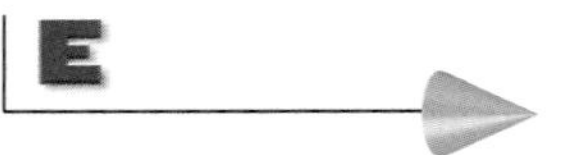

end marks (See page 263.)

- **with sentences**

EXAMPLES At the state fair, we rode in a hot-air balloon**.** [declarative sentence]

Have you ever ridden in a hot-air balloon**?** [interrogative sentence]

Wow! [interjection] What a thrilling adventure that was! [exclamatory sentence]

Don't be afraid to look down. [imperative sentence]

- **with abbreviations** (See **abbreviation.**)

EXAMPLES Your tae kwon do class begins at 7:00 P.M.

Doesn't your tae kwon do class begin at 7:00 P.M.?

exclamation point (See **end marks.**)

exclamatory sentence An exclamatory sentence expresses strong feeling and is followed by an exclamation point. (See page 19.)

EXAMPLE How kind you are!

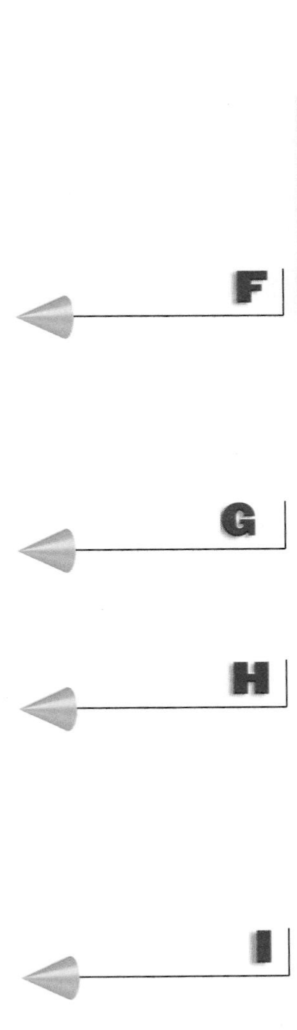

fragment (See **sentence fragment.**)

future perfect tense (See **tense of verbs.**)

future tense (See **tense of verbs.**)

good, well (See page 204.)

EXAMPLES Doreen is a **good** saxophone player.
Doreen plays the saxophone **well** [not *good*].

hyphen (See page 308.)

- **to divide words**

EXAMPLE The bright star Sirius is part of the constellation Canis Major.

- **in compound numbers**

EXAMPLE In a leap year, February has twenty-nine days.

imperative sentence An imperative sentence gives a command or makes a request and is followed by either a period or an exclamation point. (See page 18.)

EXAMPLES Please close the window. [request]
Close the window! [command]

indefinite pronoun An indefinite pronoun refers to a person, place, thing, or idea that may or may not be specifically named. (See page 34.)

EXAMPLES We ate **all** of the soup for lunch.

Everyone was ready to go to the museum.

independent clause An independent clause (also called a main clause) expresses a complete thought and can stand by itself as a sentence. (See page 89.)

EXAMPLE After you get home, **please water the plants.**

indirect object An indirect object is a word or word group that often comes between a transitive verb and its direct object and that tells to whom or to what or for whom or for what the action of the verb is done. (See page 109.)

EXAMPLE Give the **dog** a bath.

infinitive An infinitive is a verb form, usually preceded by *to*, that is used as a noun, an adjective, or an adverb. (See page 147.)

EXAMPLE Sharon and I agreed **to study** together.

interjection An interjection expresses emotion and has no grammatical relation to the rest of the sentence. (See page 68.)

EXAMPLE **Wow,** look at that sunset!

interrogative sentence An interrogative sentence asks a question and is followed by a question mark. (See page 18.)

EXAMPLE Is Clay Regazzoni still racing?

intransitive verb An intransitive verb is a verb that does not take an object. (See page 55.)

EXAMPLE The crowd **laughed,** but Bob only **smiled.**

irregular verb An irregular verb is a verb that forms its past and past participle in some way other than by adding *–d* or *–ed* to the base form. (See page 150. See also **regular verb.**)

Base Form	Present Participle	Past	Past Participle
be	[is] being	was, were	[have] been
begin	[is] beginning	began	[have] begun
bring	[is] bringing	brought	[have] brought
burst	[is] bursting	burst	[have] burst
fall	[is] falling	fell	[have] fallen
go	[is] going	went	[have] gone
make	[is] making	made	[have] made

italics (See **underlining.**)

its, it's (See page 228.)

EXAMPLES **Its** [the snow leopard's] scientific name is *Panthera uncia.*

It's [It is] considered an endangered species.

It's [It has] been overhunted for **its** fur.

lie, lay (See page 168.)

EXAMPLES Anxious about his first day at a new school, Harry **lay** awake most of the night. [past tense of *lie*]

Aunt Una **laid** the map on the table and showed us the route we would travel. [past tense of *lay*]

linking verb A linking verb connects the subject with a word that identifies or describes the subject. (See page 53.)

EXAMPLE Cousin Marty **became** a clarinetist.

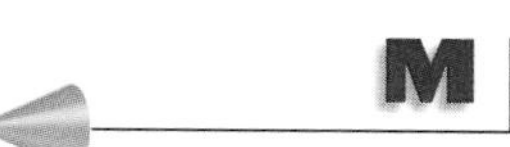

misplaced modifier A misplaced modifier is a word, phrase, or clause that seems to modify the wrong word or words. (See page 211.)

RESOURCES

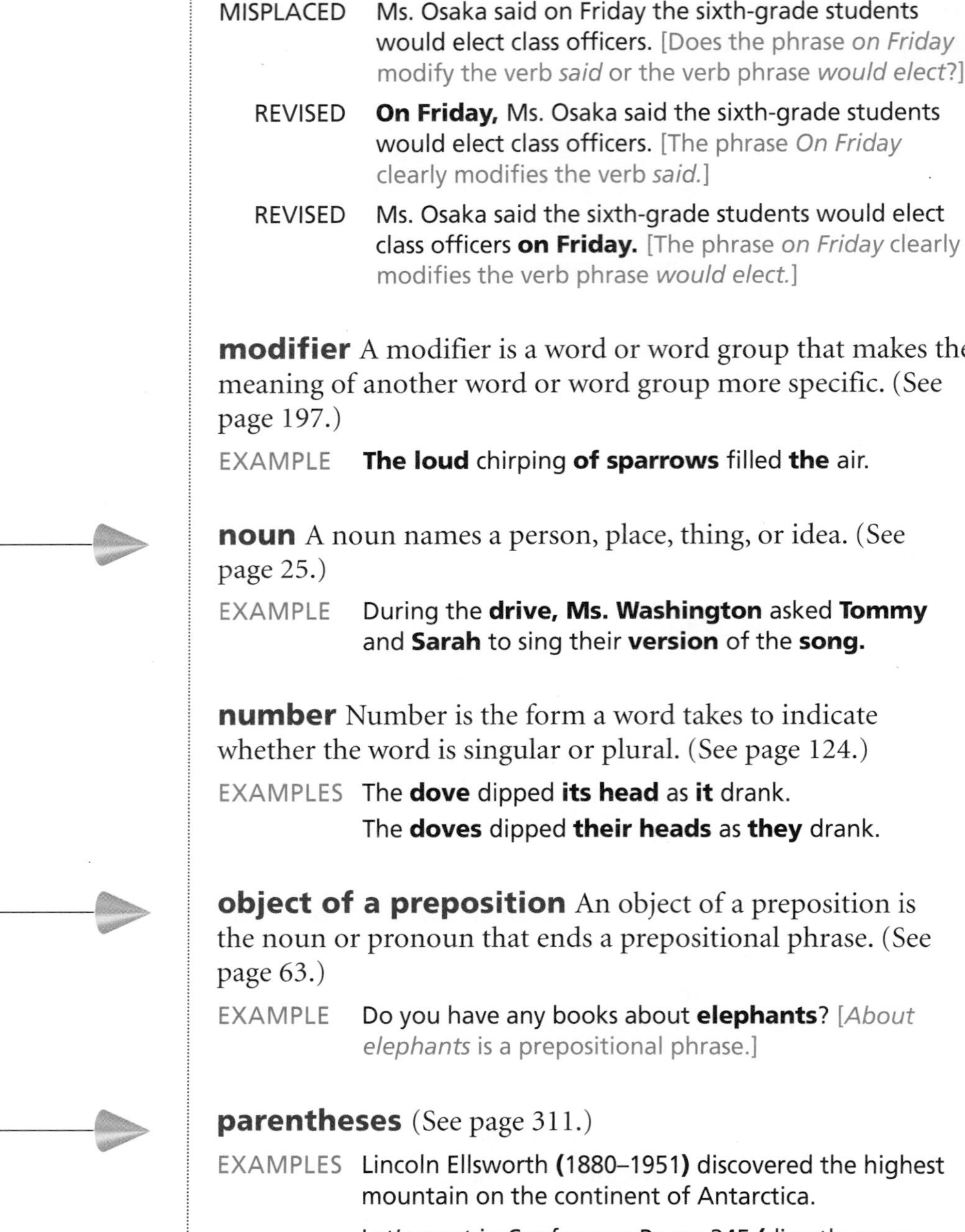

MISPLACED Ms. Osaka said on Friday the sixth-grade students would elect class officers. [Does the phrase *on Friday* modify the verb *said* or the verb phrase *would elect*?]

REVISED **On Friday,** Ms. Osaka said the sixth-grade students would elect class officers. [The phrase *On Friday* clearly modifies the verb *said.*]

REVISED Ms. Osaka said the sixth-grade students would elect class officers **on Friday.** [The phrase *on Friday* clearly modifies the verb phrase *would elect.*]

modifier A modifier is a word or word group that makes the meaning of another word or word group more specific. (See page 197.)

EXAMPLE **The loud** chirping **of sparrows** filled **the** air.

N

noun A noun names a person, place, thing, or idea. (See page 25.)

EXAMPLE During the **drive, Ms. Washington** asked **Tommy** and **Sarah** to sing their **version** of the **song.**

number Number is the form a word takes to indicate whether the word is singular or plural. (See page 124.)

EXAMPLES The **dove** dipped **its head** as **it** drank.

The **doves** dipped **their heads** as **they** drank.

O

object of a preposition An object of a preposition is the noun or pronoun that ends a prepositional phrase. (See page 63.)

EXAMPLE Do you have any books about **elephants**? [*About elephants* is a prepositional phrase.]

P

parentheses (See page 311.)

EXAMPLES Lincoln Ellsworth **(**1880–1951**)** discovered the highest mountain on the continent of Antarctica.

Let's meet in Conference Room 245 **(**directly across from the library**)**.

participial phrase A participial phrase consists of a participle and any complements and modifiers it has. (See page 399.)

EXAMPLE Marcy is the only sixth-grader **running this race.**

participle A participle is a verb form that can be used as an adjective. (See page 397.)

EXAMPLE Elena tickled the **smiling** baby.

passive voice The passive voice is the voice a verb is in when it expresses an action done to its subject. (See page 393. See also **active voice.**)

EXAMPLE The tire **was punctured** in three places.

past perfect tense (See **tense of verbs.**)

past tense (See **tense of verbs.**)

period (See **end marks.**)

phrase A phrase is a group of related words that does not contain both a verb and its subject and that is used as a single part of speech. (See page 76.)

EXAMPLE Marcia **is designing** a dress **for her cousin Francine's wedding.** [*Is designing* is a verb phrase. *For her cousin Francine's wedding* is a prepositional phrase.]

predicate The predicate is the part of a sentence that says something about the subject. (See page 9.)

EXAMPLES She **is waiting for the bus.**

Does Walter **know Rebecca?**

predicate adjective A predicate adjective is an adjective that completes the meaning of a linking verb and that modifies the subject of the verb. (See page 114.)

EXAMPLE At the farm, the cows looked **sleek** and **healthy.**

RESOURCES

predicate nominative A predicate nominative is a noun or pronoun that completes the meaning of a linking verb and identifies or refers to the subject of the verb. (See page 112.)

EXAMPLE The first passengers to exit were **Ron** and **Dee.**

prefix A prefix is a word part that is added before a base word or root. (See page 320.)

EXAMPLES un + solved = **un**solved

im + mature = **im**mature

dis + satisfied = **dis**satisfied

preposition A preposition shows the relationship of a noun or a pronoun to some other word in a sentence. (See page 62.)

EXAMPLE **At** the market, Tancredo bought green peppers, cheese, and tomatoes **for** the meal he was planning.

prepositional phrase A prepositional phrase is a group of words that includes a preposition, an object of the preposition, and any modifiers of that object. (See page 63.)

EXAMPLE A book **of swashbuckling adventure** is *Treasure Island,* **by Robert Louis Stevenson.**

present perfect tense (See **tense of verbs.**)

present tense (See **tense of verbs.**)

pronoun A pronoun is used in place of one or more nouns or pronouns. (See page 30.)

EXAMPLE Julie told Mom and Dad **she** would be happy to drive **them** to the airport.

question mark (See **end marks.**)

quotation marks (See page 292.)

- **for direct quotations**

EXAMPLE "On our vacation in Mexico," said Mrs. Tamayo, "we visited Chichén Itzá, where we saw the ruins of pyramids and temples that the Maya had built."

- **with other marks of punctuation** (See also preceding example.)

EXAMPLES "In what year was the first Earth Day celebration held?" asked Megan.

Who is the main character in Gary Soto's story "The No-Guitar Blues"?

The teacher asked, "What do you think Benjamin Franklin meant when he wrote the proverb 'Hunger is the best pickle'?"

- **for titles**

EXAMPLES "Amigo Brothers" [short story]

"Madam and the Rent Man" [short poem]

"Under the Sea" [song]

RESOURCES

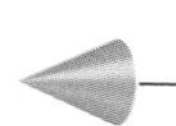

regular verb A regular verb is a verb that forms its past and past participle by adding *–d* or *–ed* to the base form. (See page 148. See also **irregular verb.**)

Base Form	Present Participle	Past	Past Participle
ask	[is] asking	asked	[have] asked
drown	[is] drowning	drowned	[have] drowned
move	[is] moving	moved	[have] moved
risk	[is] risking	risked	[have] risked
suppose	[is] supposing	supposed	[have] supposed
use	[is] using	used	[have] used

rise, raise (See page 166.)

EXAMPLES When the sun **rose,** the restless scouts were still awake. [past tense of *rise*]

The orchestra conductor **raised** the baton to begin the concert. [past tense of *raise*]

root A root is the main part of the word. It carries the word's meaning. Prefixes and suffixes can be added to a root to create new words. (See page 320. See also **base.**)

EXAMPLES	–act–	–log–	–ped–
	action	bio**log**y	**ped**icure
	re**act**	geo**log**ical	bi**ped**

run-on sentence A run-on sentence is two or more complete sentences run together as one. (See page 388.)

RUN-ON Nishi and I have been computer pen pals for two years she lives in Tokyo, Japan I live in Omaha, Nebraska.

REVISED Nishi and I have been computer pen pals for two years**;** she lives in Tokyo, Japan**, and** I live in Omaha, Nebraska.

REVISED Nishi and I have been computer pen pals for two years**.** **S**he lives in Tokyo, Japan**, and** I live in Omaha, Nebraska.

S

semicolon (See page 279.)

EXAMPLE In 1993, Ramon Blanco from Spain became the oldest person to scale Mount Everest**;** he was sixty years old at the time.

sentence A sentence is a group of words that contains a subject and a verb and that expresses a complete thought. (See page 4.)

EXAMPLE The fish (**S**) swam (**V**) lazily in the clear water.

sentence fragment A sentence fragment is a group of words that is punctuated as if it were a complete sentence but that does not contain both a subject and a verb or that does not express a complete thought. (See pages 4 and 386.)

FRAGMENTS Hera, the queen of the Greek gods, casting a spell on Hercules. Because she was jealous of him.

SENTENCE Hera, the queen of the Greek gods, cast a spell on Hercules because she was jealous of him.

simple sentence A simple sentence has one independent clause and no subordinate clauses. (See page 96.)

EXAMPLE On the Internet, Milo and I accessed a search engine and searched for information about King Tutankhamen. [one independent clause with a compound subject and a compound verb]

sit, set (See page 165.)

EXAMPLES Carmen **sat** on the bench, anxiously waiting for Coach Engle to send her back into the game. [past tense of *sit*]

Anthony **set** the box of dominoes on the table, hoping that someone in his family would play the game with him. [past tense of *set*]

stringy sentence A stringy sentence is a sentence that has too many independent clauses. Usually, the clauses are strung together with coordinating conjunctions like *and* or *but.* (See page 391.)

STRINGY One day, the gods Jupiter and Mercury decided to come down to the earth to test the people of Phrygia for their hospitality, so the gods disguised themselves as peasants who were in desperate need of food and shelter, and they stopped at hundreds of houses, and at each one the "peasants" were turned away, but finally, they came to the very small house of a poor, elderly couple named Baucis and Philemon.

REVISED One day, the gods Jupiter and Mercury decided to come down to the earth to test the people of Phrygia for their hospitality. The gods disguised themselves as peasants who were in desperate need of food and shelter. They stopped at hundreds of houses, and at each one the "peasants" were turned away. Finally, they came to the very small house of a poor, elderly couple named Baucis and Philemon.

subject The subject tells whom or what a sentence is about. (See page 7.)

EXAMPLE The **geraniums** bloomed early this year.

RESOURCES

subject complement A subject complement is a word or word group that completes the meaning of a linking verb and identifies or describes the subject. (See page 112. See also **predicate adjective** and **predicate nominative.**)

EXAMPLES My cousin Brian is a **software technician.**

The art room was **messy.**

subordinate clause A subordinate clause (also called a *dependent clause*) does not express a complete thought and cannot stand alone as a sentence. (See page 90. See also **adjective clause** and **adverb clause.**)

EXAMPLE **After I read that article,** I changed my opinion.

subordination Subordination is the use of dependent clauses to express ideas of less importance than those expressed in independent clauses. (See page 403. See also **subordinate clause.**)

EXAMPLES You can bring the book back **whenever it is convenient.**

The writer **who reviewed the new movie** was very positive.

If we leave by seven o'clock, we will be on time.

suffix A suffix is a word part that is added after a base word or root. (See page 321.)

EXAMPLES steady + ly = steadi**ly**

forgive + ness = forgive**ness**

obey + ing = obey**ing**

adore + able = ador**able**

shop + ing = shop**ping**

syllable A syllable is a word part that can be pronounced as one uninterrupted sound. (See page 318.)

EXAMPLES sleep [one syllable]

en • gine [two syllables]

di • a • gram [three syllables]

tense of verbs The tense of verbs indicates the time of the action or of the state of being that is expressed by the verb. (See page 160.)

Present Tense	
I do	we do
you do	you do
he, she, it does	they do
Past Tense	
I did	we did
you did	you did
he, she, it did	they did
Future Tense	
I will (shall) do	we will (shall) do
you will (shall) do	you will (shall) do
he, she, it will (shall) do	they will (shall) do
Present Perfect Tense	
I have done	we have done
you have done	you have done
he, she, it has done	they have done
Past Perfect Tense	
I had done	we had done
you had done	you had done
he, she, it had done	they had done
Future Perfect Tense	
I will (shall) have done	we will (shall) have done
you will (shall) have done	you will (shall) have done
he, she, it will (shall) have done	they will (shall) have done

their, there, they're (See pages 229 and 336.)

EXAMPLES Candace and Ruben moved **their** desks closer to the window. [*Their* tells whose desks.]

We stood **there** in the cold rain until the bus arrived. [*There* tells where we stood.]

There are five days left until the end of school. [*There* begins the sentence but does not add to the meaning of the sentence.]

They're planning a surprise birthday party for Emily. [*They're* is a contraction of *They are.*]

transitions Transitions are words or word groups that help show how ideas and details in words, phrases, sentences, and paragraphs are related. (See page 404.)

EXAMPLES **In addition** to tomatoes, we also grow lettuce. [*In addition* shows similarities.]

The sky is mostly gray; **however,** there are some small patches of blue. [*However* shows differences.]

I left the game at 5:00 P.M. **because** I was meeting a friend at 5:30. [*Because* shows cause and effect.]

transitive verb A transitive verb is an action verb that takes an object. (See page 55.)

EXAMPLE Their dog **chased** our cat.

U

underlining (italics) (See page 290.)

- **for titles**

EXAMPLES *The Way to Rainy Mountain* [book]

National Geographic World [magazine]

Sleeping Gypsy [work of art]

Duke Bluebeard's Castle [long musical composition]

- **for names of vehicles**

EXAMPLES *Orient Express* [train]

Air Force One [aircraft]

V

verb A verb expresses an action or a state of being. (See page 49.)

EXAMPLE Evelyn **wore** a blue blazer.

Is the desert nearby?

verb phrase A verb phrase consists of a main verb and at least one helping verb. (See page 50.)

EXAMPLES The helicopter **should have been** here by now.

I **have** never **heard** Michael sing.

voice (See page 393. See also **active voice** and **passive voice.**)

well (See ***good, well.***)

who, whom (See page 188.)

EXAMPLES **Who** was the first astronaut to walk in space? [nominative form used as the predicate nominative referring to the subject *astronaut*]

Whom have you invited to your bat mitzvah party? [objective form used as the direct object of the verb phrase *have invited*]

RESOURCES

INDEX

A

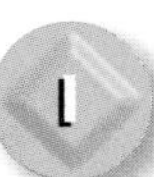

ACKNOWLEDGMENTS

For permission to reprint copyrighted material, grateful acknowledgment is made to the following sources:

"April Rain Song" from *The Collected Poems of Langston Hughes* by Langston Hughes. Copyright © 1994 by The Estate of Langston Hughes. Reproduced by permission of **Alfred A. Knopf, Inc., a division of Random House, Inc.,** and electronic format by permission by **Harold Ober Associates Incorporated.**

"Camel Fodder" from *The Subtleties of the Inimitable Mulla Nasrudin* by Idries Shah. Copyright © 1983 by **The Octagon Press, Ltd., London.** Reproduced by permission of the publisher.

PHOTO CREDITS

Abbreviations used: (t)top, (tl)top left, (tc)top center, (tr)top right, (l)left, (lc)left center, (c)center, (rc)right center, (r)right, (bl)bottom left, (bc)bottom center, (br)bottom right.

TABLE OF CONTENTS: Page v (lc), Rod Planck/Photo Researchers, Inc.; vii, Image Copyright ©2001 PhotoDisc, Inc.; viii, H. Knaus/SuperStock; ix, Photograph by Franko Khoury, National Museum of African Art, Eliot Elisofon Photographic Archives, Smithsonian Institution; x, Mike Okoniewski /The Image Works; xiii, Fred Bavendam/Peter Arnold, Inc.; xv, Carl Purcell/Photo Researchers, Inc.

CHAPTER 1: Page 5, SuperStock; 9, Russel Dian/HRW Photo; 10, Comstock; 15, David Allen/CORBIS; 20, Spencer Swager/Tom Stack & Associates.

CHAPTER 2: Page 27, Orion Press, Japan; 29, Image Copyright ©2001 PhotoDisc, Inc.; 30, Shawn Thew/epa/CORBIS; 36, Photograph by Franko Khoury, National Museum of African Art, Eliot Elisofon Photographic Archives, Smithsonian Institution; 39, China Tourism Press/The Image Bank/Getty Images; 42, Image Copyright ©2001 PhotoDisc, Inc.; 43, SuperStock.

CHAPTER 3: 52, Jerry Jacka Photography/Courtesy: The Heard Museum, Phoenix, Arizona; 55, Evan Agostini/Getty Images; 57, Banana Stock/Alamy; 58 (bc), Dr. Ronald H. Cohn/ The Gorilla Foundation/Koko.org; 58 (l), Sam Dudgeon/HRW; 61, Lionel Delvigne/Stock Boston; 69, Linda Kelen.

CHAPTER 4: Page 1931, True Fresco, 22'7" x 29'9", San Francisco Art Institute. Photo Credit: David Wakely; 85, Michael Newman/Photo Edit; 87 (br), Katherine Feng/Viesti Collection; 87 (c), Lowell Georgia/Photo Researchers, Inc.; 98, ©1994 J. Lotter Gurling/Tom Stack & Associates; 99, Michele Burgess/Stock Boston.

CHAPTER 5: Page 111, Image Copyright 2001 Photodisc, Inc.; 117, H. Knaus/SuperStock.

CHAPTER 6: Page 126, Bruce Davidson/Animals Animals; 128, CORBIS/W. Perry Conway; 134, Joe Viesti/Viesti Collection; 137, Bob Couey/Seaworld Inc. © 1998. All rights reserved. Reproduced by permission.; 142, Image Copyright ©2001 PhotoDisc, Inc.

CHAPTER 7: Page 150, Hampton University Museum, Hampton, Virginia; 157, Bettmann/CORBIS; 171, ©1997 Radlund & Associates for Artville.

CHAPTER 8: Page 179, National Museum of American Art, Washington DC/Art Resource, NY; 183 (b), Mike Okoniewski/ The Image Works; 183 (t), Joe Jaworski/HRW Photo; 190, Image Copyright ©2001 PhotoDisc, Inc.

CHAPTER 9: Page 208 (bl), Giraudon/Art Resource, NY.; 208 (br), Gianni Dagli Orti/CORBIS.

CHAPTER 10: Page 228, Image Copyright ©2001 PhotoDisc, Inc.; 234, Photo Image Technologies.

CHAPTER 11: Page 249, SuperStock; 258, Margaret Sulanowska/Woods Hole Oceanographic Institution.

CHAPTER 12: Page 265, Carl Purcell/Photo Researchers, Inc.; 267, Michael Newman/Photo Edit; 273, Giraudon/Art Resource, New York; 278, Eastcott/Momatiuk/Animals Animals.

CHAPTER 13: Page 295, Clementine Hunter, (c.1945). Photo from the Mildred Bailey Collection, Mildred H. Bailey, Natchitoches, Louisiana; 301, Keystone/Sygma; 302 (lc), Rod Planck/Photo Researchers, Inc.; 302 (rc), Gordon and Cathy Illg/Animals Animals/Earth Scenes; 319, Aaron Horowitz/CORBIS.

CHAPTER 14: Page 324, Chris Brown/SIPA Press; 327, A. Ramey/Photo Edit; 332, Photo Edit; 336 (tc), Aaron Haupt/ Photo Researchers, Inc.; 336 (tr), Aaron Haupt/Photo Researchers, Inc.; 340, Werner Forman Archive/Museum fur Volkerkunde, Berlin/Art Resource, NY; 350, Richard Weiss/ HRW Photo.

CHAPTER 15: Page 357, News Office, Woods Hole Oceanographic Institution; 363, Fred Bavendam/Peter Arnold, Inc.; 369, Courtesy of Joe Rosenberg; 372, Robert Trippett/ SIPA Press.

CHAPTER 16: Page 386, Jim Corwin/Stock Boston; 391 (bl), Patti Murray/Animals Animals/Earth Scenes; 391 (bc), SuperStock; 391 (br), Toni Angermayer/Photo Researchers, Inc.; 392, Image Copyright ©2001 PhotoDisc, Inc.; 397, Huntington Library/SuperStock; 399, Bettmann/CORBIS; 402, Zigmund Leszczynski/Animals Animals/Earth Scenes.